The Production-Comprehension Interface in Second Language Acquisition

Also available from Bloomsbury

The Interactional Feedback Dimension in Instructed Second Language Learning,
by Hossein Nassaji
Second Language Acquisition in Action, by Andrea Nava and Luciana Pedrazzini
Social Networks in Language Learning and Language Teaching,
edited by Avary Carhill-Poza and Naomi Kurata
Study Abroad and the Second Language Learner, edited by Martin Howard
Task Sequencing and Instructed Second Language Learning, by Melissa Baralt
Teaching Pragmatics and Instructed Second Language Learning, by Nicola Halenko

The Production-Comprehension Interface in Second Language Acquisition

An Integrated Encoding-Decoding Model

Anke Lenzing

BLOOMSBURY ACADEMIC
LONDON • NEW YORK • OXFORD • NEW DELHI • SYDNEY

BLOOMSBURY ACADEMIC
Bloomsbury Publishing Plc
50 Bedford Square, London, WC1B 3DP, UK
1385 Broadway, New York, NY 10018, USA
29 Earlsfort Terrace, Dublin 2, Ireland

BLOOMSBURY, BLOOMSBURY ACADEMIC and the Diana logo
are trademarks of Bloomsbury Publishing Plc

First published in Great Britain 2021
This paperback edition published in 2022

Copyright © Anke Lenzing, 2021

Anke Lenzing has asserted her right under the Copyright, Designs
and Patents Act, 1988, to be identified as Author of this work.

For legal purposes the Acknowledgements on p. xii constitute
an extension of this copyright page.

All rights reserved. No part of this publication may be reproduced or
transmitted in any form or by any means, electronic or mechanical,
including photocopying, recording, or any information storage or
retrieval system, without prior permission in writing from the publishers.

Bloomsbury Publishing Plc does not have any control over, or responsibility for,
any third-party websites referred to or in this book. All internet addresses given
in this book were correct at the time of going to press. The author and publisher
regret any inconvenience caused if addresses have changed or sites have ceased
to exist, but can accept no responsibility for any such changes.

A catalogue record for this book is available from the British Library.

A catalog record for this book is available from the Library of Congress.

ISBN: HB: 978-1-3501-4873-4
PB: 978-1-3502-0350-1
ePDF: 978-1-3501-4874-1
eBook: 978-1-3501-4875-8

Typeset by Integra Software Services Pvt. Ltd.

To find out more about our authors and books visit www.bloomsbury.com
and sign up for our newsletters.

Contents

List of figures	vi
List of tables	ix
Acknowledgements	xii
List of abbreviations	xiv
Introduction	1
1 The architecture of human language processing	7
2 The relation between production and comprehension in language processing	29
3 The view on second language acquisition: *Processability Theory* and the *Multiple Constraints Hypothesis*	47
4 The *Integrated Encoding-Decoding Model of SLA*	89
5 The English passive as a test case for the *Integrated Encoding-Decoding Model of SLA*	99
6 The study: Methodological considerations	117
7 Testing the *Integrated Encoding-Decoding Model of SLA*	135
Concluding remarks	221
Appendix	224
Notes	225
References	229
Index of subjects	250

Figures

1.1	A blueprint for the speaker (from Levelt 1989: 9, fig. 1.1). © 1989 Massachusetts Institute of Technology, by permission of The MIT Press	9
1.2	Grammatical encoding (from Bock & Levelt 1994: 946, fig. 1). © 1994 Academic Press	12
1.3	Fragment of a lexical network (from Levelt 1999: 97, fig. 4.4). © 1999 Oxford University Press. Reproduced with permission of the Licensor through PLSclear	14
1.4	Structure conceptual message (from Levelt 1989: 164, fig. 5.1). © 1989 Massachusetts Institute of Technology, by permission of The MIT Press	16
1.5	The model of language processing according to the *Online Cognitive Equilibrium Hypothesis* (from Karimi & Ferreira 2016: 1019, fig. 1). © 2015 The Experimental Psychological Society. Reprinted by Permission of SAGE Publications, Ltd	26
3.1	Attribute-value pair (from Bresnan 2001: 47, fig. 2). © 2001 Joan Bresnan. Reprinted by permission of John Wiley & Sons	50
3.2	F-structure of *Lions live in the forest* (from Lenzing 2013: 29, fig. 2.2.1-6; adapted from Bresnan 2001: 46, fig. 1). Reprinted by permission of John Benjamins	51
3.3	(a) endocentric (English) and (b) lexocentric constituent structure (Warlpiri) (from Bresnan 2001: 5–6, figs 1, 3). © 2001 Joan Bresnan. Reprinted by permission of John Wiley & Sons	52
3.4	Lexical entries	55
3.5	Feature unification	56
3.6	A simplified account of mapping in LFG	56
3.7	Information exchange (from Pienemann & Lenzing 2020: 166, fig. 8.1). © 2020 Taylor & Francis. Reproduced with permission of the Licensor through PLSclear	61
3.8	XP-adjunction (from Lenzing 2013: 86, fig. 4.4-1). Reprinted by permission of John Benjamins	62
3.9	'Aux-2nd'-structure (from Lenzing 2013: 88, fig. 4.4-2). Reprinted by permission of John Benjamins	65

3.10	Linear mapping (from Lenzing 2013: 94, fig. 4.6.1-1). Reprinted by permission of John Benjamins	67
3.11	Non-linear mapping in passive constructions (from Lenzing 2013: 103, fig. 4.6.3-1). Reprinted by permission of John Benjamins	68
3.12	The *Multiple Constraints Hypothesis* (from Lenzing 2013: 8, fig. 1.3-1). Reprinted by permission of John Benjamins	70
4.1	The *Integrated Encoding-Decoding Model of SLA*	90
4.2	Birdiness ranking (from Aitchison 2012: 5, fig. 6.1). © 2012 John Wiley & Sons, Inc. Reprinted by permission of John Wiley & Sons	95
4.3	The *Online Cognitive Equilibrium Hypothesis* adapted to SLA	97
5.1	The idealized category of the passive with prototypical centre (adapted from Meints 1999b: 101, fig. 3). © 1999 Springer Nature. Adapted by permission of Springer Nature	104
5.2	Morpho-lexical operations in passives (from Lenzing 2016: 7, fig. 1). Reprinted by permission of John Benjamins	106
5.3	Principles and constraints in a- to f-structure mapping (from Lenzing 2016: 8, fig. 2). Reprinted by permission of John Benjamins	107
5.4	The English passive: feature unification and mapping processes	109
5.5	C-structure for the sentence *The cake is eaten by John*	111
5.6	Lexical entries for the auxiliary and the verb in the sentence *The cake is eaten by John*	112
5.7	One-to-many relationship in German case marking (from Pienemann 1998: 157, fig. 4.3-4). Reprinted by permission of John Benjamins	113
5.8	Many-to-one relationship in German plural marking (from Pienemann 1998: 157, fig. 4.3-5). Reprinted by permission of John Benjamins	113
5.9	Form-function relationships '-ed'/past participle	114
6.1	Picture description task: example items. © Ron Schulz	123
6.2	(a) active and (b) passive cues in the fish film	124
6.3	Example passive production task (Actor: Lola Lenzing)	125
6.4	Example sentence-picture matching: biased reversible passive *The woman is carried by the hero* (Actors: Emilia and Simon Nottbeck)	126
6.5	Example enactment task: non-reversible passive *The cage is opened by Lisa*	128
7.1	Example sentence-picture matching: non-reversible passive *The flower is watered by the woman* (Actor: Emilia Nottbeck)	141
7.2	Example sentence-picture matching: non-reversible passive *The wall is painted by the boy* (Actor: Simon Nottbeck)	142

7.3	Sentence-picture matching: ditransitive passive *The boy was brought to the doctor by the mother* (Actors: Katharina Hagenfeld; Emilia and Simon Nottbeck)	142
7.4	Direct mapping processes ditransitive passives	144
7.5	Misinterpretation of *James is saved from the tiger by Tom*	167
7.6	Sentence-picture matching learner SM04 (Actor: Sam Cosper)	202

Tables

2.1	Predictions of dedicated-workspaces hypothesis and single-workspace hypothesis	39
3.1	Feature decomposition of argument functions	54
3.2	Hypothetical hierarchy of processing procedures (adapted from Pienemann 1998: 79)	59
3.3	Processability hierarchy for English (adapted from Lenzing 2013: 85; Pienemann 2005: 24)	60
3.4	Revised labels and corresponding structural phenomena (from Pienemann, n.d.)	66
3.5	*Lexical Mapping Hypothesis* (from Pienemann, Di Biase & Kawaguchi 2005: 240)	68
3.6	Distributional analysis '3sg -s' (extract from Sub-study 3)	72
3.7	Distributional analysis '3sg -s' learner S04	72
3.8	Sample implicational scale longitudinal data	76
3.9	Sample implicational scale cross-sectional data (from Lenzing 2019: 29)	77
3.10	Sample implicational scale with deviations	78
3.11	Two approaches to error assignment: error minimization (EM) vs. *Goodenough-Edwards* (GE) approach	79
6.1	Overview of tasks	118
6.2	Tasks for oral speech production data	119
6.3	Experimental sentences: mean plausibility ratings and standard deviations	122
7.1	Overview of participants: Sub-study 1	137
7.2	Production and comprehension tasks: Sub-study 1	137
7.3	Transcription key	137
7.4	Stages of acquisition: L2 learners Sub-study 1	138
7.5	Distributional analysis of comprehension data passives: L2 learners Sub-study 1	140
7.6	Plausibility rating of biased reversible passives: Sub-study 1	141
7.7	Plausibility rating of non-reversible passives: Sub-study 1	141
7.8	Plausibility rating of symmetrical reversible passives: Sub-study 1	144
7.9	Plausibility rating of symmetrical reversible passives: Sub-Study 1	144

7.10	Overview of participants: Sub-study 2	146
7.11	Production and comprehension tasks: Sub-study 2	146
7.12	Distributional analysis of all features: L2 learners Sub-study 2 (from Lenzing 2019: 32–3)	148
7.13	Distributional analysis 'Wh-Copula S (x)': learner P03	150
7.14	Stages of acquisition: L2 learners Sub-study 2 (from Lenzing 2019: 34)	151
7.15	Argument-function mapping in passives: L2 learners Sub-study 2	154
7.16	Morpho-syntactic processing in passives: L2 learners Sub-study 2	158
7.17	Sequence of acquisition within morpho-syntactic processing	162
7.18	Summary of oral production data of passives: L2 learners Sub-study 2	163
7.19	Classifications of interpretations of passives in enactment task	164
7.20	Distributional analysis of comprehension data passives: L2 learners Sub-study 2 (Lenzing 2019: 39)	166
7.21	Plausibility rating of semantically irreversible passives: Sub-study 2	167
7.22	Plausibility rating of biased reversible passives: Sub-Study 2	169
7.23	Plausibility rating of symmetrical reversible passives: Sub-study 2	169
7.24	Overall results: PT stages, comprehension and production of passives: Sub-study 2 (Lenzing 2019: 41)	171
7.25	Overview of participants: Sub-study 3	173
7.26	Production and comprehension tasks: Sub-study 3	173
7.27	Distributional analysis of all features: L2 learners Sub-study 3	176
7.28	Stages of acquisition: L2 learners Sub-study 3	180
7.29	Argument-function mapping in passives: L2 learners Sub-study 3	183
7.30	Morpho-syntactic processing in passives: L2 learners Sub-study 3	190
7.31	Distributional analysis verbal morphology for learner SM11	194
7.32	Summary of oral production data of passives: L2 learners Sub-study 3	197
7.33	Distributional analysis of comprehension data of passives: L2 learners Sub-study 3	200
7.34	Plausibility rating of non-reversible passives: Sub-Study 3	200
7.35	Plausibility rating of biased reversible passives: Sub-study 3	202
7.36	Overall results: PT stages, comprehension and production of passives: Sub-study 3	204
7.37	Mean RTs for grammatical and ungrammatical stimuli	209
7.38	Mean RTs and results t-test/Wilcoxon signed rank test for different conditions Group 1 ($\alpha = 0.05$)	211
7.39	Mean RTs and results Wilcoxon signed rank test for different verb types Group 1 ($\alpha = 0.05$)	211

7.40	Mean RTs and results *t*-test for different conditions Group 2 ($\alpha = 0.05$)	212
7.41	Mean RTs and results Wilcoxon signed rank test for different verb types Group 2 ($\alpha = 0.05$)	213
7.42	Mean RTs and results *t*-test for different conditions Group 3 ($\alpha = 0.05$)	214
7.43	Mean RT and results *t*-test for different verb types Group 3 ($\alpha = 0.05$)	215
7.44	Gradual acquisition of processing operations in L2 passives	218

Acknowledgements

Writing this book has been a long journey, and I am indebted to many people who have supported my endeavour in various ways. A number of colleagues shared their expertise in psycholinguistics and second language acquisition with me and provided constructive feedback at various stages of this project.

I would like to thank Manfred Pienemann for the numerous fruitful discussions and his valuable comments on both theoretical and empirical issues related to my research. His extensive knowledge and his ever-curious commitment to second language acquisition research have been a great source of inspiration. I am also indebted to Howard Nicholas for a continuous exchange of ideas and perspectives on second language acquisition, his thoughtful comments on an earlier version of the manuscript, as well as his advice in all language-related aspects. I wish to thank Gerard Kempen for sharing his thoughts on grammatical coding and *Performance Grammar* with me and for patiently answering all my questions on this topic.

Special thanks are due to Anja Plesser and Katharina Hagenfeld, who supported this project in a number of ways. This includes many inspiring discussions on theoretical considerations at early stages of the project and an invaluable support in all issues related to task design and data collection, as well as their encouraging comments on a preliminary version of the manuscript.

I am grateful to the following people for their support in creating tasks for data collection and/or in assisting me in data collection and data transcription: Sam Cosper, Nadja Fakha, Olivia Geier, Birgit Göhrmann, Julia Kröger, Emilia Nottbeck, Simon Nottbeck, Carolin Stephan and Rebecca Krüll. Thanks are also due to Ron Schulz for the pictures in the first sentence comprehension task and Sabine Vahle for her work on the figures in the text as well as to Sam Cosper for proofreading the manuscript, Rômulo Luzia de Araujo for his work on the bibliography and Josephine Fisher for her work on the index.

I am greatly indebted to all the learners who participated in my study as well as their teachers who made the data collection possible. Thanks also go to the native speakers who participated in the reaction-time experiment. Parts of this project were realized during a six-month stay as a visiting scholar at Flinders University, Australia, in 2015, which was supported by a scholarship of the Heinrich-Hertz-Stiftung. I would also like to gratefully acknowledge the financial support provided by Paderborn University, Germany.

Thanks are also due to the team at Bloomsbury, Andrew Wardell and Becky Holland, as well as to three anonymous reviewers who provided helpful critical feedback on my text. Naturally, I remain responsible for all remaining errors.

Finally, I would like to thank my family for their support during the time I spent on this project. My deepest gratitude goes to my husband Peter, who constantly supported me during the various stages of my research and who encouraged me to finish this enterprise. I am also indebted to my children Benjamin and Lola, who not only kept with me during those times when I was immersed in my project but also patiently served as guinea pigs for my various tasks for data elicitation.

Abbreviations

ADJ	adjunct
ADV	adverb-first/adverb-preposing
AP	adjective/adverbial phrase
BOLD	blood oxygen level dependent
CS	coefficient of scalability
DET	determiner
DMTH	*Developmentally Moderated Transfer Hypothesis*
ERP	event-related potential
ESL	English as a second language
fMRI	functional magnetic resonance imaging
GJT	grammaticality judgement task
IFG	inferior frontal gyrus
INV	inversion
L1	first language
L2	second language
LFG	*Lexical-Functional Grammar*
MTG	middle temporal gyrus
NP	noun phrase
NUM	number
NVN	noun-verb-noun
OBJ	object
OBL	oblique
PET	positron emission tomography
PL	plural
PP	prepositional phrase

PRED	semantic feature
PT	*Processability Theory*
RT	reaction time
SG	singular
SLA	second language acquisition
SSH	*Shallow Structure Hypothesis*
SUBJ	subject
SVO	subject-verb-object
TOP	topic
UG	*Universal Grammar*
VP	verb phrase
XP	phrase of the category X
ZISA	*Zweitspracherwerb Italienischer, Spanischer und Portugiesischer Arbeiter*

Introduction

This book addresses a key issue in second language acquisition (SLA) research, namely the relation between second language (L2) production and L2 comprehension. My main aim is to investigate the interface between these two modalities in the L2 acquisition process. L2 production and comprehension are potentially linked (1) at the level of linguistic representations and (2) at the level of processing. In this book, I explore to what extent the two modalities rely on shared representations and/or shared processes. I propose the *Integrated Encoding-Decoding Model of SLA*, a model of L2 production and comprehension that focuses on grammatical coding processes and, at the same time, accounts for the influence of semantic aspects on L2 comprehension. Gaining a deeper understanding of these processes and, in particular, of the nature of the link between production and comprehension in SLA can contribute to a better understanding of the underlying mechanisms that are at work in the L2 acquisition process.

The central question underlying this endeavour is related to the cognitive architecture of human language processing and the question as to whether and how production and comprehension are interwoven. In this regard, Kempen (1999: 1) emphasizes that a fundamental question in sentence processing concerns the relation between grammatical encoding and decoding: 'Are the two modalities subserved by different types of processors, or is the same type of syntactic processing module deployed in both grammatical encoding and decoding?'

In the past, the mechanisms underlying production and comprehension have been investigated in different subfields of psycholinguistics (see e.g. Gambi & Pickering 2017; Pickering & Garrod 2013). In keeping with this, most psycholinguistic research has addressed only one of the two processes – either production or comprehension – although Gambi and Pickering (2017: 157) point out that 'many psycholinguistic tasks involve both'.

As regards the relation between production and comprehension, the traditional view is the one of a two-systems approach, assuming that the two processes operate in two different modules with two different types of information (see e.g. Clark & Malt 1984; Ruder & Finch 1987). Arguments in favour of a two-systems approach include dissociations in production and comprehension abilities in patients with aphasia (e.g. Kolk 1998) as well as asymmetries in production and comprehension in language acquisition (e.g. Clark 1993; Clark & Hecht 1983; Spenader, Smits & Hendriks 2009). It is only recently that researchers have engaged with the issue of potential interfaces between production and comprehension and have proposed more integrated accounts that focus on overlaps in the resources humans can draw on in the two modalities (see e.g. Kempen, Olsthoorn & Sprenger 2012; Pickering & Garrod 2013). A key motivation for proposing an integrated account of production and comprehension is the 'nature of language use in dialogue' (Gambi & Pickering 2017: 173), which is characterized by rapid switches between speaking and listening between and within turns in a conversation. In addition, an integrated account of production and comprehension constitutes a parsimonious solution to the question of how the architecture of human language processing can be conceptualized.

Clearly, production and comprehension are not considered to be based entirely on the same processes. As Hendriks (2014: 15) observes:

> A first and very salient difference between producing and comprehending language is the fact that the physical process of speaking – i.e., producing speech sounds by contracting the muscles in one's chest, larynx and vocal tract in a coordinated way – is different from the physical process of listening – i.e., perceiving a stream of noise and identifying speech sounds in this continuous stream.

A further disparity relates to the directional difference in the information flow in the two modalities. Whereas the production process involves mappings from meaning to form, the comprehension process requires mappings from form to meaning. However, these differences do not exclude the possibility of shared resources in production and comprehension. In this vein, proponents of an integrated view of language production and comprehension emphasize the similarities of the two processes and explore the possibility of overlaps at different levels of representation (e.g. semantic, syntactic or sound-based representations) as well as in language processing.

0.1 Linking production and comprehension in L2 acquisition

Naturally, the importance of investigating shared resources in production and comprehension is not restricted to human language processing in general or the acquisition of a person's first language (L1) but also applies to the L2 acquisition process. In this book, I argue for an integrated perspective on production and comprehension in SLA. Taking a psycholinguistic perspective on SLA, I propose a model of the interface between production and comprehension in L2 acquisition with one main focus being the processes involved in grammatical encoding and decoding. In addition, I also consider some key semantic aspects that have been shown to play a major role in the comprehension process. In particular, these are lexical semantics, event probability and prototypicality effects. In order to account for the influence of these semantic factors on the L2 comprehension process, the proposed *Integrated Encoding-Decoding Model of SLA* integrates a component that captures the relation between semantic and syntactic processing in SLA.

The model is based on the following theoretical cornerstones: The view of language production follows to a large extent the one outlined by Levelt (1989, 1999) and Levelt,

Roelofs and Meyer (1999). The perspective on language comprehension adopted in my approach is the *Good-Enough Approach to Language Comprehension* (see e.g. Christianson et al. 2001; Ferreira 2003; Ferreira & Patson 2007) and its extension, the *Online Cognitive Equilibrium Hypothesis* (Karimi & Ferreira 2016). The basis for my proposed relationship between production and comprehension comes from the notion of a *shared grammatical workspace* as developed by Kempen (1999) and Kempen, Olsthoorn and Sprenger (2012), which is further supported by research in neuroimaging (Menenti et al. 2011; Segaert et al. 2012). As regards the relation between syntactic and semantic processing in comprehension, I adopt the *Online Cognitive Equilibrium Hypothesis* (Karimi & Ferreira 2016) to SLA. The theoretical perspective on SLA underlying my hypotheses is *Processability Theory* (PT) (Pienemann 1998; Pienemann & Lenzing 2020) and the *Multiple Constraints Hypothesis* (Lenzing 2013, 2015b).

The key hypotheses of the model are that (1) there is one single syntactic processor underlying both grammatical coding processes in L2 acquisition and (2) the same processing procedures are involved in grammatical encoding and decoding. This shared grammatical coder develops stepwise in accordance with the predictions spelled out in PT. I further hypothesize that production and comprehension also share resources at the level of linguistic representations. Based on the claims of the *Multiple Constraints Hypothesis*, I assume that the L2 learner's mental grammatical system for both grammatical encoding and decoding is initially highly constrained at the different levels of linguistic representation. The *Integrated Encoding-Decoding Model of SLA* is complemented by the adaptation of the *Online Cognitive Equilibrium Hypothesis* (Karimi & Ferreira 2016) to SLA in order to incorporate some of the key semantic aspects that have been shown to influence the comprehension process. This approach specifies the relation between semantic and syntactic processing in SLA. Its core claim is that, in principle, there are two routes in L2 processing, a semantic and a syntactic route. I hypothesize that the syntactic route encompasses the processing procedures required for syntactic operations. This route is claimed to be initially underdeveloped in SLA, and L2 learners are assumed to rely on the semantic route at the beginning of their L2 acquisition process. In line with research findings on comprehension processes in L1 and L2 acquisition, I assume that semantic processing can override syntactic processing in comprehension and that this applies in particular to the early stages of L2 acquisition, when learners have not yet developed the necessary processing prerequisites for syntactic processing.

The *Integrated Encoding-Decoding Model* and the adaptation of the *Online Cognitive Equilibrium Hypothesis* to SLA are examined in relation to empirical data that were collected in three thematically related cross-sectional studies focusing on the acquisition of the English passive in L2 learners of English with a German background, at different stages of L2 acquisition. I propose a developmental sequence for the L2 acquisition of English passive constructions that is based on an analysis of the English passive in terms of PT and *Lexical-Functional Grammar* (LFG) (see e.g. Bresnan 2001). In addition, I specify minimal requirements for the production and comprehension of English passives that I test in the empirical study. The data obtained in the study consist of oral production and comprehension data of the passive that are examined in relation to each learner's stage of acquisition.

0.2 Outline

To set the context for my theoretical considerations concerning the interface between production and comprehension in L2 acquisition, Chapter 1 explores the architecture of human language processing. In my view, an understanding of some of the core processes in human language processing in general is a prerequisite for gaining insights into the processes underlying L2 acquisition. In speech production, the major focus is on Levelt's model of sentence generation (Levelt 1989, 1999, 2000), as I adopt key aspects of his model in my hypothesized shared coder in L2 acquisition. As regards speech comprehension, I first introduce the major theoretical approaches to sentence comprehension that engage with the question as to how the processing of syntactic and semantic information is related. This is then followed by a presentation of the core claims of the *Good-Enough Approach to Language Comprehension* and the *Online Cognitive Equilibrium Hypothesis* (Karimi & Ferreira 2016), which forms the theoretical cornerstone of my approach to model the relation between semantic and syntactic processing in L2 acquisition.

Chapter 2 engages with different perspectives on the relation between production and comprehension in language processing. In a first step, I critically examine some of the major arguments put forward in favour of a dual-processor architecture. This is followed by a discussion of arguments that support a single-processor architecture in language processing. In the next step, I outline Kempen and colleagues' notion of a *shared grammatical workspace* and present evidence from both behavioural and neuroimaging studies that support this view.

Chapter 3 introduces the perspective on SLA adopted in this book. Firstly, an account of the core aspects of PT is provided. This includes an introduction to key psychological features in language processing, an introduction to LFG – the grammatical formalism in PT – and the core mechanisms underlying the PT hierarchy of processing procedures. A further aspect relates to the processes involved in the acquisition of discourse-pragmatic structures such as the passive. Secondly, the chapter introduces the *Multiple Constraints Hypothesis* that engages with the constraints of the initial L2 mental grammatical system. This is followed by a presentation of three major methodological principles underlying the data analysis in PT-based research, namely the distributional analysis, the emergence criterion and implicational scaling. In a final step, the chapter provides a critical discussion of studies that investigate L2 comprehension within the PT framework.

In Chapter 4, I introduce the *Integrated Encoding-Decoding Model of SLA*. I first provide an overview of the core claims of the model and present the proposed grammatical coding processes in L2 production and comprehension. Next, I discuss key semantic aspects that influence comprehension processes, namely lexical semantics, event probability and prototypicality effects. I then outline my approach to the relation between syntactic and semantic processes in L2 comprehension and present the adaptation of the *Online Cognitive Equilibrium Hypothesis* to SLA.

Chapter 5 engages with the English passive as a test case for my hypotheses. This includes an introduction of key characteristics of English passive constructions, a discussion of relevant semantic aspects in the comprehension of the passive as well as a detailed LFG-based analysis of English passive constructions. In a further step, I analyse English passive constructions in terms of PT and propose a developmental sequence for the acquisition of the English passive in L2 acquisition in both production and comprehension. This includes a specification of the minimal requirements for producing and comprehending passive structures.

In Chapters 6 and 7, the details of the empirical study are presented. Chapter 6 provides an overview of the study design and its methodology. In a first step, the different tasks used in the data elicitation process in the three sub-studies are introduced. These include oral speech production tasks to determine the L2 learners' stages of acquisition, tasks to elicit oral speech production data of English passive constructions as well as comprehension tasks that focus on the learners' comprehension of passive structures.

Chapter 7 presents empirical evidence for (1) the proposed developmental sequence of acquisition of English passives in production and comprehension and (2) the hypotheses of the *Integrated Encoding-Decoding Model of SLA* and the adaptation of the *Online Cognitive Equilibrium Hypothesis* to SLA. The chapter contains a summary and discussion of the results of the data analysis. In a first step, the results of the analysis of the data obtained in Sub-study 1 are presented. These include linguistic profile analyses of the learner data to determine the learners' stages of acquisition and an analysis of the comprehension data of English passive constructions. The comprehension data are examined in relation to the learners' stages of acquisition. In Sub-study 2, the data analysis focuses on (1) the L2 learners' linguistic profiles, (2) their production of English passive constructions and (3) their comprehension of passives. The passive production and comprehension data are then related to the L2 learners' stages of acquisition. The same type of analysis is presented for the data of Sub-study 3. In addition, the results of a sentence-matching reaction-time experiment implemented in Sub-study 3 are presented. These results shed light on morpho-syntactic processing in the comprehension of passive constructions. Finally, the results of the data analyses are discussed with regard to the hypothesized L2 developmental sequence of the English passive and in view of the *Integrated Encoding-Decoding Model of SLA* and the adaptation of the *Online Cognitive Equilibrium Hypothesis* to SLA. It will be demonstrated that the data provide support for the proposed shared resources in L2 production and comprehension.

By way of conclusion, the closing chapter provides a summary of the key issues discussed in the book and considers both the significance and the limitations of the research findings.

1

The architecture of human language processing

This chapter engages with core aspects of human language processing. In order to be able to investigate potential relationships between language production and language comprehension in L2 acquisition, it is crucial to gain a deeper understanding of the processes underlying human language processing in general. Therefore, the chapter introduces the theoretical approaches to language production and comprehension that are relevant for the *Integrated Encoding-Decoding Model of SLA*. In a first step, the processes involved in language production are presented. The view on language production that I adopt in the model is mainly based on Levelt's model of language generation (e.g. Levelt 1989, 1999). In a second step, I introduce major approaches to language comprehension. In this regard, the focus is on the *Good-Enough Approach to Language Comprehension* (e.g. Ferreira 2003) and its extension, the *Online Cognitive Equilibrium Hypothesis* (Karimi & Ferreira 2016), as some of their core assumptions are integrated in the *Integrated Encoding-Decoding Model of SLA*.

1.1 Speech production: Levelt's model of language generation

Speech production theories focus on how humans transform ideas they want to convey into a linguistic form. This process covers the retrieval of words in the mental lexicon as well as the syntactic, morphological and phonological encoding of the various elements in the intended message to be able to produce intelligible overt speech. A central part of sentence production consists of the processes of *grammatical encoding*: They cover (1) the retrieval of lexical and syntactic forms that express the non-linguistic message and (2) the determination of the actual morphological forms and the assembly of constituent structure. Thus, Ferreira, Morgan and Slevc (2018: 432) argue that 'it is only a minor indulgence to claim that to understand why and how grammatical encoding carries out its duties is to understand a significant part of the why and how of language itself'.

Approaches to language production in general and grammatical encoding in particular differ in their underlying theoretical assumptions concerning the architecture of the language processing system. In the psycholinguistic literature, a common distinction is between connectionist approaches to speech production (e.g. Chang 2002; Dell 1986; Dell, Chang & Griffin 1999) and approaches that assume a modular architecture of the human processing system (Garrett 1982; Levelt 1989;

Levelt, Roelofs & Meyer 1999). However, the line separating these two perspectives is becoming increasingly blurred, as the two approaches have influenced each other over time: Kormos (2006: 6) points out that models with a modular architecture increasingly incorporate connectionist aspects, in particular in modelling lexical access (see e.g. Levelt 1999, 2000; Levelt, Roelofs & Meyer 1999). Connectionist accounts, on the other hand, have adopted aspects of modularity, in that the system is assumed to be globally modular but locally interactive (see e.g. Dell & O'Seaghda 1991; Goldrick 2007).[1]

Although there is considerable debate in the field concerning the exact conceptualization of the different processes involved in language production, there seems to be a consensus on some core aspects of sentence generation. This concerns, for instance, the assumption that there are three main steps in language production, namely conceptualizing, formulating and articulating (see e.g. Griffin & Ferreira 2006: 21; Grosjean 2013: 51; Levelt 1999: 88; Pickering, Branigan & McLean 2002: 586). These stages are independent in that each has its own type of representation and works on its own characteristic input.

Levelt's model of language generation (see e.g. Levelt 1989, 1999, 2000) provides a detailed account of these three stages in language production. The model constitutes the psycholinguistic basis of *Processability Theory* (PT), and some of its core assumptions form a central part of the *Integrated Encoding-Decoding Model* presented in Chapter 4. This concerns in particular the psychological aspects of language generation and the processes involved in grammatical encoding.

1.1.1 A blueprint for the speaker: An introduction

Levelt's (1989, 1999) model of sentence generation, the *Blueprint for the Speaker*, is arguably the most influential account of speech production in the field of psycholinguistics. According to Kormos (2006: 7), the model is also 'the most widely used theoretical framework in L2 speech production research'. Initially articulated in 1989, the blueprint has been continually enhanced and expanded in order to incorporate advances in psycholinguistic research that have provided more information on the language production process. This applies in particular to a revised conceptualization of the process of lexical access in speech production (see Levelt, Roelofs & Meyer 1999) but also includes slightly revised labels for the different components (see Levelt 1999).

This chapter introduces the core components of the blueprint as well as those developments of the theory that are central to an understanding of the perspective on the development of language production in SLA taken in this book. For the sake of compatibility with the theoretical approaches to SLA based on Levelt's model, that is, PT and its extension, the *Multiple Constraints Hypothesis*, reference is made to its initial conceptualization and the related terminology (Levelt 1989). However, the chapter also introduces relevant revisions of the model, including modifications in both the area of grammatical encoding and the mental lexicon (e.g. Bock & Levelt 1994; Levelt 1999, 2000; Levelt, Roelofs & Meyer 1999).

The *Blueprint for the Speaker* is depicted in Figure 1.1. It covers the processes from the initial concept a speaker intends to express to the actual articulation of the speaker's utterance. The model is modular in nature and consists of a number

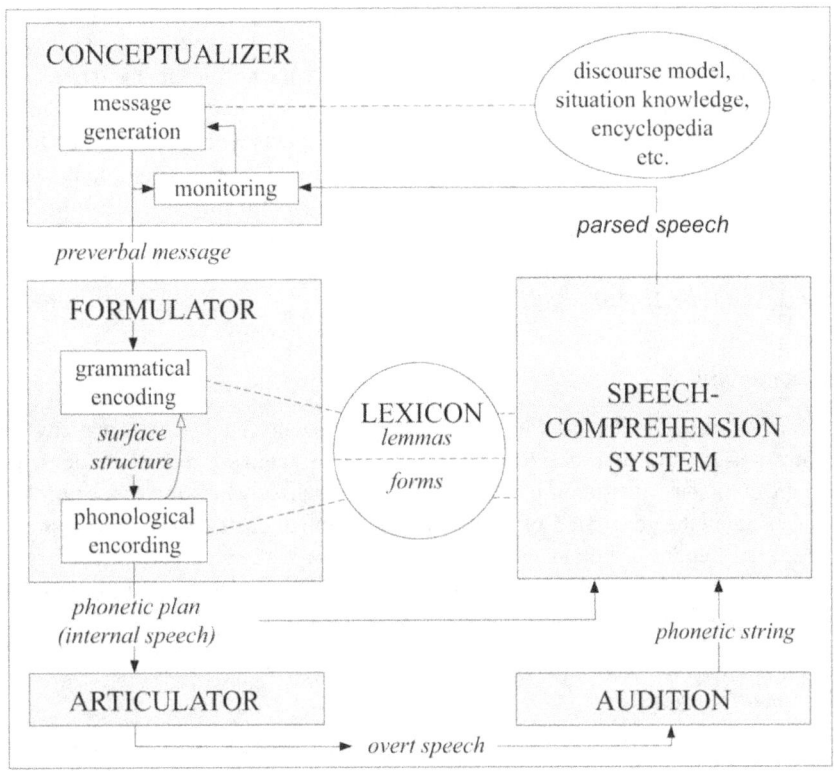

Figure 1.1 A blueprint for the speaker (from Levelt 1989: 9, fig. 1.1). © 1989 Massachusetts Institute of Technology, by permission of The MIT Press.

of interrelated processing components. These are the *conceptualizer*, the *formulator*, the *articulator*, the *audition* and the *speech comprehension system*. Speech generation starts in the conceptualizer. It is here that the message a speaker intends to convey is conceived, which involves the selection and ordering of the information as well as perspective-taking. The output of the conceptualizer is the preverbal message. In a next step, the preverbal message is transformed into a linguistic structure. This takes place in the formulator and involves both the retrieval of lexical information and the grammatical encoding of the message. The output of the grammatical encoder, the surface structure, is then given a phonological shape, which results in the phonetic plan or internal speech. In a final step, the phonetic plan is executed by the articulator, resulting in overt speech (see Levelt 1989: 8–13).

Processing components as autonomous specialists

Levelt (1989: 4) conceptualizes the processing components as 'relatively autonomous specialists'. He argues that each component is a specialist that works (relatively) autonomously on a specific kind of input and produces a specific kind of output. The output of one component serves as input to the next component. For instance, the grammatical encoder takes the preverbal message as characteristic input and translates the conceptual structure into a surface form. The encoder contains specialized procedures to retrieve lemmas from the mental lexicon as well as syntactic building procedures. The characteristic output – the surface structure – is the input to the phonological encoder. The algorithms of the specific components are assumed to be executed in real time. Another tenet of the model is that there is no exchange of information between the components and no feedback from components down the line (Levelt 1989: 15–16).

Automaticity

A further characteristic of the processing components is their automaticity. In contrast to controlled processing, the execution of automatic processes does not require conscious attention. Apart from the conceptualizer, which involves controlled processing as the generation of a communicative intention relies on awareness and conscious attention, all other processing components are assumed to operate largely automatically (Levelt 1989: 21). This view of processing can account for its high speed as well as its efficiency (see Levelt 1989: 22).

Incremental processing

One core assumption underlying Levelt's model is that language generation is *incremental*. This means that processing components are triggered by fragments of characteristic input. Processors can thus work on the incomplete output of the previous processing component. This architecture allows for parallel processing in a stage model: The different components can work in parallel on different parts of the utterance or, as Levelt (1999: 88) puts it: '[T]he various processing components are normally simultaneously active, overlapping their processing as the tiles of a roof. When we are uttering a phrase, we are already organizing the content for the next phrase, etc.' Levelt (1989: 27) points out that incremental processing is only possible when processing takes place automatically.

1.1.2 Conceptualizer

The conceptualizer is the locus of message generation. Levelt emphasizes that message generation does not occur in isolation but has to be seen in the context of social and communicative interaction (Levelt 1999: 83–4), as language use can be viewed as some kind of joint action (see also Clark 1996). Thus, when conceptually preparing a message, the speaker draws on various kinds of knowledge sources, including the exercise of social competence.

The generation of the conceptual message involves the planning of the communicative intention including its sequencing into subgoals and the selection of the type of information to be expressed (e.g. assertions, declarations, questions) (Levelt 1989: 107). In sequencing the communicative intention, the speaker is confronted with what is called the *linearization problem*, which consists of 'deciding what to say first, what to say next, and so on' (Levelt 1989: 138). The sequencing or, in other words, the linearization of propositions is guided by the principle of natural order, stating that the information to be expressed should be sequenced 'according to the natural order of its content' (Levelt 1989: 138). When expressing events, the natural order relates to the chronological order in which the events occur. The default interpretation of propositions expressing an event is to assume that the order in which the events are presented corresponds to the chronological order in which they occurred. Deviations of the natural order should ideally be marked explicitly in order to facilitate mutual understanding of the message, as in example (1), in which the preposition *after* indicates a deviation from the natural order of events.

(1) She took off her boots after she climbed the mountain.

In example (1), the second event (she climbed the mountain) occurs before the first one (she took off her boots), which poses a processing problem for the speaker. The linearization problem and the resulting processing difficulties are central to PT, the theory of SLA adopted in this book, as it is assumed that linearization poses a major challenge for L2 learners. Therefore, the linearization problem will be taken up again in Section 3.1 in the context of L2 acquisition and processing.

Conceptualizing additionally involves the assignment of an *accessibility status* to the referents in the conceptual message, which indicates whether referents have been previously introduced in the discourse or whether they can be assumed to be known by the interlocutor. The message is then assigned a propositional format and perspective. Furthermore, the mood of the message is determined, that is, whether it is declarative, interrogative or imperative (Levelt 1999: 93). The output of the *conceptualizer* is the *preverbal message*, which serves as the characteristic input for the next component, the *formulator*.

1.1.3 Formulator

In the formulator, a conceptual structure is transformed into a linguistic structure. The translation of the preverbal message into an articulatory plan is achieved by the process of grammatical encoding. As this process forms the heart of the formulator and is central to both PT and the *Integrated Encoding-Decoding Model*, the focus of this section is on grammatical encoding. The second process taking place in the formulator – phonological encoding – will not be introduced (for details, see e.g. Levelt 1999).

According to Levelt (1999: 94), grammatical encoding exhibits the following three properties: 'it takes preverbal messages as input, it produces surface structures as output, and it has access to the mental lexicon'. In formalizing the process of grammatical encoding, Levelt (1989) draws on aspects of Kempen and Hoenkamp's (1987) *Incremental Procedural Grammar* and an early version of LFG (Bresnan 1982).[2] The process of grammatical encoding can be divided into two major types of processing – functional processing and positional processing (see also Garrett 1980, 1982, 1988) – and is illustrated in Figure 1.2.

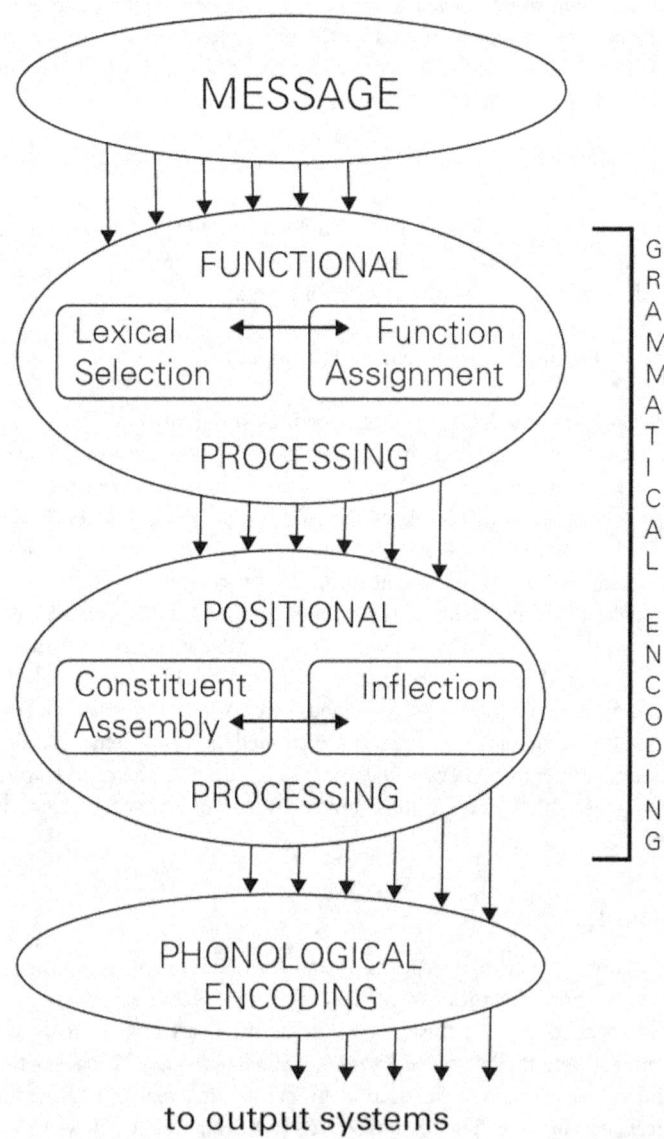

Figure 1.2 Grammatical encoding (from Bock & Levelt 1994: 946, fig. 1). © 1994 Academic Press.

Whereas functional processing encompasses the selection of suitable lexical concepts as well as the assignment of grammatical functions, in positional processing, the constituent structure is generated including morphological inflections (Bock & Levelt 1994: 946). Finally, the output of grammatical encoding serves as input to phonological encoding.

Functional processing

The first step in functional processing is lexical selection. A core tenet of Levelt's model is that speech generation is lexically driven, and he argues that 'the lexicon is the essential mediator between conceptualization and grammatical and phonological encoding' (Levelt 1989: 181).

Since Levelt's initial conceptualization of his model in 1989, the field has seen important advances in theory development of lemma access (see e.g. Roelofs 1992a, b, 1993; Levelt, Roelofs & Meyer 1999), which were incorporated into Levelt's (1999) revised model. The process from lexical selection to the actual phonological encoding of a word is framed in the computational model WEAVER ++ (Levelt, Roelofs & Meyer 1999). The core of the model is formed by lexical networks consisting of three different levels that represent different types of information. A fragment of a lexical network is presented in Figure 1.3 with the example item *select*. The first level, the *conceptual stratum*, includes conceptual information about the lexical item. The conceptual node SELECT stands for the meaning of the verb *select* with its two slots X and Y representing the two arguments the verb takes, that is, the agent that selects and the patient/theme that is selected. The conceptual node is linked to other concept nodes that are related to the concept SELECT. They can be both lexical and non-lexical. The labelled links express the relations between the concepts. An important characteristic of this approach is its non-decompositional character: Lexical concepts are not decomposed into sets of semantic features but are represented as undivided wholes (Levelt, Roelofs & Meyer 1999: 4).

In the process of lexical selection, the concepts that best match the conceptual message are activated and spread their activation to semantically related concepts. In Figure 1.3, the conceptual node SELECT spreads its activation to the concepts CHOOSE and ELECT. The conceptual node SELECT is also linked to one lemma at the second level, the *lemma stratum* or *lemma level*. The activated lexical concept (SELECT in the example above) spreads some of its activation to the lemma it is related to (*select*). The process of lexical selection 'is a statistical mechanism, which favors the selection of the highest activated lemma' (Levelt, Roelofs & Meyer 1999: 4).

Once a lemma is selected, its syntactic properties are activated, such as its syntactic category, for example noun or verb. Additionally, the values of the lemma's diacritic parameters, including its inflectional features for number, person, tense and/or mood, are set. The syntactic information then becomes available for further grammatical encoding. To be more specific, the lemma's syntax activates the syntactic building procedures involved in grammatical encoding. For instance, the category N (noun) calls the noun phrase procedure, which builds the corresponding noun phrase, the category V (verb) activates the verb phrase procedure, and so on. These procedures are seen as part of the procedural knowledge stored in the grammatical encoder (Levelt 1989: 11).

14 *The Production-Comprehension Interface in Second Language Acquisition*

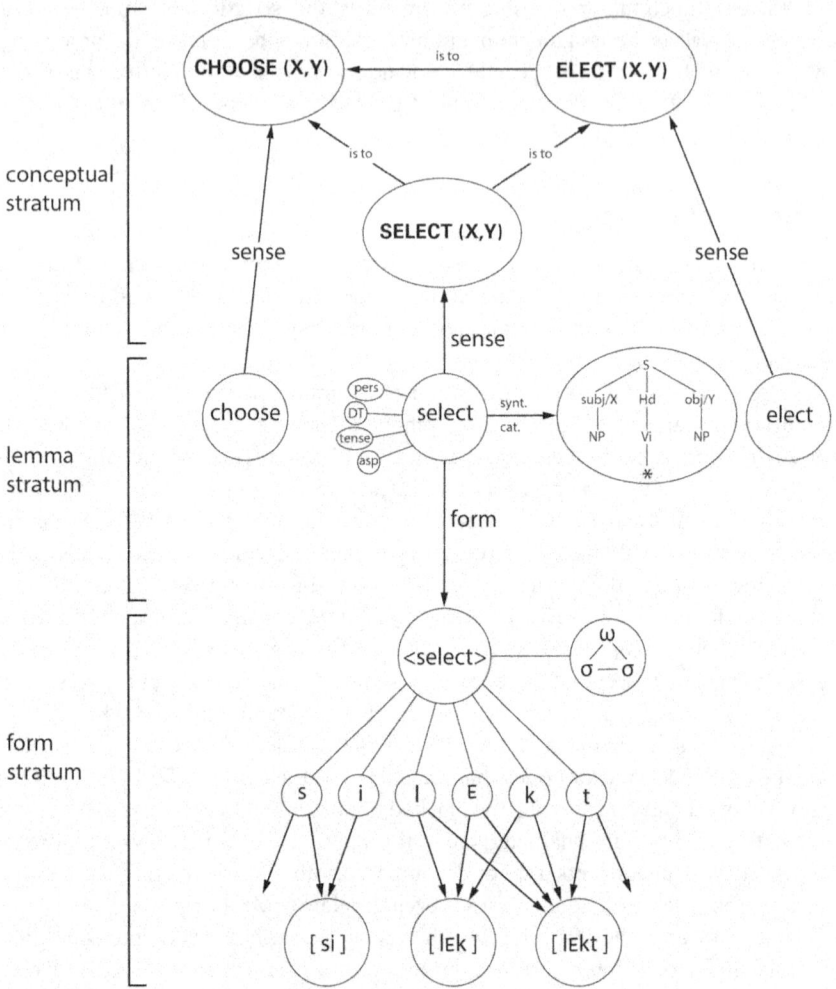

Figure 1.3 Fragment of a lexical network (from Levelt 1999: 97, fig. 4.4). © Oxford University Press, 1999. Reproduced with permission of the Licensor through PLSclear.

The third level of the lexical network introduced in Figure 1.3 is the *form stratum* containing information about the morpho-phonological form of the respective lexical item. At this level, both morpheme and segment nodes are represented (Levelt, Roelofs & Meyer 1999: 6).

The lexical network introduced above exhibits a number of general design properties. First of all, it constitutes a 'feed-forward activation-spreading network' (Levelt, Roelofs & Meyer 1999: 6). Whereas activation spreading between the conceptual and the lemma stratum is modelled as being bidirectional, the information flow between lemma and form stratum is unidirectional. As far as the latter is concerned, activation only spreads forward and there are no backward links from the form to the lemma level (see Levelt 1999: 227). This partially interactive network architecture with an interlink between conceptual and lemma stratum and a strict feed-forward relation between lemma and form stratum also has implications for the relation between the processes in word production and perception. Levelt (1999: 226) argues that 'there are good reasons for assuming that conceptual and lemma strata are shared between production and perception, hence their interconnections are modelled as bidirectional. But the form stratum is unique to word production; it does not feed back to the lemma stratum'.

The processing stages of the network are strictly serial, and the network is additionally characterized by the absence of inhibitory links between the nodes both within and between the different strata, although there is competition in the process of node selection between activated nodes. Finally, a *binding-by-checking* mechanism ensures that activated segments of words are produced in the right order by preventing the selection of inappropriate lemmas and incorrect word form nodes (Levelt, Roelofs & Meyer 1999: 6–7). Empirical support for the model of the lexical network comes from reaction-time experiments, in particular from picture-naming as well as picture- and word-categorizing experiments (see Glaser & Düngelhoff 1984; Roelofs 1992a, b, 1993).

After lexical selection has taken place and the lemma is activated by the conceptual message, the second step in functional processing is function assignment, that is, the assignment of grammatical functions (e.g. subject, object) to the activated lemmas. Bock and Levelt (1994: 961) point to the necessity to separate grammatical function assignment from lexical selection, since the same words can be assigned different grammatical functions in different sentences (e.g. *The boy kissed the girl* vs. *The girl kissed the boy*). They further observe that the assignment of grammatical functions has to be viewed separately from the assembly of constituent structure. One core assumption in grammatical function assignment is that grammatical functions are assigned only once and are maintained throughout the process of grammatical encoding, resulting in a one-to-one correspondence between the underlying grammatical functions assigned at the level of functional processing and those at the surface level assigned during positional processing (Bock & Levelt 1994: 962). This assumption is in line with LFG, the theory of syntax adopted in this book, and it contrasts with traditional conceptualizations of a deep structure in psycholinguistics.

As for the question of what kind of information controls the assignment of grammatical functions, Bock and Levelt (1994: 964) claim that both thematic or event roles and attentional roles dominate this process. Related to this is the insight that the verb plays a central role in function assignment, as its argument structure specifies both the number and types of arguments it takes. This is in turn crucial for the mapping process between thematic roles and grammatical functions (see Section 3.2). The view of a 'verb-centered control of function assignment' (Bock & Levelt 1994: 967) is supported empirically in numerous studies that also provide evidence for the related assumption that the clause forms a core unit in functional processing (see e.g. Ford 1982; Ford & Holmes 1978; Holmes 1988).

To sum up, functional processing includes both lexical selection and function assignment. Lexical selection yields a set of lemmas that best match the conceptual message. In function assignment, grammatical functions are assigned to the lemmas based on the argument structure of the verb.

Positional processing

The second type of processing present in grammatical encoding is positional processing. This involves the sequencing of elements and the assembly of the actual constituent structure of an utterance. Constituent structure is hierarchically organized and the process of its assembly is controlled by the syntactic information present in the lemmas as well as the grammatical functions assigned in functional processing. The assembly of constituent structure or, as Bock and Levelt (1994: 969) put it, the 'frame' of an utterance, is guided by two core principles, namely incremental processing and unification. Specialized building procedures work in parallel on parts of the sentence triggered by fragments of the message, and the principle of unification ensures that the fragments built by the syntactic building procedures in the encoding process are linked together. As mentioned earlier in this section, this perspective draws on the assumptions made in Kempen and Hoenkamp's (1987) *Incremental Procedural Grammar* about (1) the incremental, left-to-right approach to sentence generation and (2) the existence of a number of syntactic procedures that work in parallel on fragments of the sentence. This view on processing is also adopted in PT, the theory of SLA underlying the *Integrated Encoding-Decoding Model*.

The details of this process are illustrated with the example sentence *A child gave the mother the cat* (adapted from Levelt 1989: 273–4). In a first step, the conceptual message is generated in the conceptualizer. The structure of the message underlying the example sentence is given in Figure 1.4.

As outlined in the section 'Functional processing', once a fragment of the message matches a conceptual node in the lexical network, it is activated and spreads its

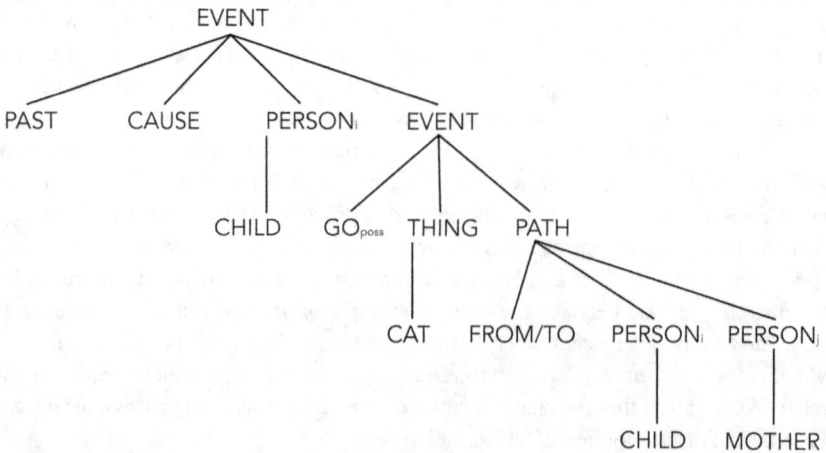

Figure 1.4 Structure conceptual message (from Levelt 1989: 164, fig. 5.1). © 1989 Massachusetts Institute of Technology, by permission of The MIT Press.

activation down to 'its' lemma in the lemma stratum. In the example sentence, the accessibility status of the referent CHILD in the conceptual message is '− accessible' and the status of the two referents MOTHER and CAT is '+ accessible'. Once the corresponding lemma is activated, its syntactic properties become available.

In a second step, the syntactic category of the lemma CHILD (noun) calls a so-called *categorical procedure*, 'a building instruction for the phrasal category in which the lemma can fulfill the function of head' (Levelt 1989: 238). This type of procedure can be called by nouns, verbs, adjectives/adverbs and prepositions and can build NPs, VPs, APs and PPs. In the case of the lemma CHILD, the NP procedure is called. The categorical NP procedure checks the conceptual message for additional material to fill complements and/or specifiers as well as for values for diacritic parameters. In the example of the lemma CHILD, the NP procedure inspects the accessibility status, which is '− accessible', and retrieves the diacritic parameter 'singular'.

The NP procedure then calls so-called functional procedures, which are subroutines that work in parallel. In the case of the example sentence, one subroutine consists of the functional procedure DET, which calls the lemma 'A', which partly occurs on the basis of the accessibility status '− accessible'. This involves so-called *functorization rules*, which govern the insertion of functors, that is, functions words, such as articles or prepositions. The value of the parameter NUMBER is also transferred to a subroutine, which inserts it in the lemma CHILD. The results of the functional procedures are delivered to the respective categorical procedure, in this case the NP procedure. In the selection of the lemma 'A', the process of feature unification also plays a crucial role: The value of the diacritic feature 'singular' of the head of the phrase (CHILD) is matched with the value of the diacritic feature of the lemma 'A'. As Pienemann (1998: 67) points out in this context, '[t]he value of the diacritic feature is "stored" by the categorical procedure until it is "delivered" to the modifier.'

At this point, the NP still lacks a grammatical function. The *functional destination* is assigned by the categorical procedure or by a higher-order procedure. Functional destinations of a phrase are determined by language-specific *appointment rules* (see Kempen & Hoenkamp 1987: 216). In the case of the NP *the child*, 'the default destination for the output of the NP procedure is "subject of S"' (Levelt 1989: 240). The NP_{subj} then calls the S-procedure, a higher-order categorical procedure specialized in building sentences. The values of the diacritic parameters are stored in the S-procedure and the message is checked for its mood. In the example sentence, the message does not exhibit a mood marker, which leads to a 'default declarative constituent order', so that the NP *a child* receives the leftmost slot and occurs in sentence-initial position. The case is different for questions. In this case, the presence of a mood marker in the message leads to a different word order (Levelt 1989: 240).

The construction of the remaining parts of the sentence follows the same steps that were outlined for the construction of the noun phrase (for more details, see Levelt 1989: 240–6). The result of grammatical encoding is the surface structure. As mentioned in this section, the principle of unification plays a crucial role in the process of syntactic composition, as it ensures the formation of grammatically well-formed sentences (see also Section 3.2.5). The notion of the unification of features is also of central importance in LFG, the theory of grammar underlying both PT and its extension, the *Multiple Constraints Hypothesis*, as well as the *Integrated Encoding-Decoding Model of SLA*.

1.1.4 Self-monitoring and the speech comprehension system

Although Levelt's model of language generation is first and foremost a model of speech production, it also addresses the issue of speech comprehension. In the initial version of the blueprint, Levelt conceptualizes the processors involved in language production and comprehension as separate modules, although he maintains that 'there are no doubt intimate connections between the speaking system and the listening system' (Levelt 1989: 477). To account for self-monitoring processes, he developed the *Perceptual Loop Theory of Self-Monitoring*. In this account, self-monitoring is seen as taking place in the comprehension system, which is conceptualized as being separate from the production system (Levelt 1989: 476).

The claim that speech production and comprehension processes operate in distinct components coincides with the traditional perspective in psycholinguistics to view production and comprehension processes as mechanisms operating in separate entities (see e.g. Gambi & Pickering 2017). The *Perceptual Loop Theory* is generally regarded as a strong argument in favour of a dual-processor architecture in language production and comprehension (see Kempen 1999; see also Section 2.1). However, since the first articulation of Levelt's *Blueprint for the Speaker*, a shift in focus can be observed in that recent perspectives on language processing focus on commonalities rather than on differences. This general shift is also reflected in Levelt's more recent publications (Levelt 2000, 2001; Levelt, Roelofs & Meyer 1999), where he has somewhat modified his initial position of strictly separated systems and addresses the question of which areas of speech processing are shared between the two commonalities.[3] Focusing on word generation, Levelt, Roelofs and Meyer (1999: 7) argue for a shared perceptual and production network between the lemma level and the conceptual level: '[T]he perceptual and production networks coincide from the lemma level upwards'. Levelt (1999: 113) generalizes this claim to all types of processing in the lemma/conceptual strata domain for reasons of consistency. In the shared perception/production network, feedback can flow bidirectionally, namely from lexical concepts to lemmas as well as from lemmas to lexical concepts. As for the question of shared syntax in production and comprehension, Levelt (2001: 246) refers to research by Kempen (2000) and Vosse and Kempen (2000) and states that '[i]t would contribute to this grand unification to make the further claim that grammatical encoding and grammatical decoding are one. This is exactly the step taken by Kempen (2000; see also Vosse and Kempen 2000) […]. Although this is a well-argued and attractive proposal, its empirical consequences need further scrutiny.'

To sum up, the focus of Levelt's model of sentence generation is clearly on the sentence production process. Although his blueprint includes a speech comprehension component, Levelt does not elaborate on the details of the sentence comprehension process. Recent developments of the theory indicate a shift from the initial strict separation between production and comprehension processes towards potential interlinks between the two modalities.

1.2 Language comprehension

This section engages with the cognitive architecture of sentence comprehension. As a first step, some of the major approaches to sentence comprehension will be introduced to set the scene for the discussion of the perspective adopted in the *Integrated Encoding-Decoding Model of SLA*, namely the *Good-Enough Processing Model* (Christianson et al. 2006; Ferreira & Patson 2007) as well as its extension, the *Online Cognitive Equilibrium Hypothesis* (Karimi & Ferreira 2016).

Generally speaking, models of sentence comprehension investigate 'how people obtain a particular syntactic analysis for a string of words and assign an interpretation to that analysis' (Pickering 1999: 123). Similar to sentence production, sentence comprehension is also a fast and efficient process, and researchers agree that it is highly incremental (see e.g. Just & Carpenter 1980; Kempen 2000; Pickering 1999). This means that, in comprehension, words are encountered sequentially and analysed straightaway. Evidence supporting incrementality in sentence comprehension comes from a number of studies looking at so-called garden-path effects that occur when processing temporarily ambiguous sentences. Probably the most famous example of this kind of ambiguity that metaphorically leads listeners 'down the garden-path' is the sentence *The horse raced past the barn fell* (Bever 1970). In keeping with the notion of incremental processing, when the word *raced* occurs in the input, it is initially assigned the role of the main verb. Only when the listener encounters *fell*, do they realize that the word *raced* constitutes a past participle form as part of a reduced relative clause.

There is a consensus in the field that processing takes place in an incremental fashion and that the process of both syntactic and semantic analysis of sentence fragments encountered in the input takes place very rapidly without any major delay. However, the question remains as to how exactly syntactic and semantic analyses are related and what kind of information the sentence processor initially has access to. The theoretical approaches that have dominated the field for a long time are commonly divided into modular and interactive models of processing (see e.g. van Gompel & Pickering 2007). These models differ in their assumptions about the exact interplay between syntactic and semantic information and the proposed time course of processing. The core claim underlying modular models of processing is that due to the task-specificity of the different modules involved in sentence processing, syntactic processes occur separately from semantic and/or discourse processes. In interactive models, on the other hand, it is assumed that all types of information are initially available and influence parsing decisions.

1.2.1 Modular models

Probably the most influential modular model of sentence processing is the *Garden-Path Model* (see e.g. Frazier 1987, 1990; Frazier & Rayner 1982), a two-stage model of sentence processing which postulates that initial parsing decisions are based on syntactic information derived from word category information. It is only at a later stage that non-syntactic information, such as semantic and context information, becomes available for processing. In temporarily ambiguous sentences, the parser initially adopts a single syntactic analysis. This analysis is based on specific parsing heuristics that account for garden-path effects in processing temporarily ambiguous sentences, as in example (2) (Frazier 1987: 562):

(2)
    a) The girl knew the answer by heart.
    b) The girl knew the answer was in the book.

The parser processes the sentence incrementally and analyses fragments of available input. When the parser encounters the NP *the answer*, there are two possible analyses: Within an overall main clause analysis, the NP could be assigned the patient/theme argument of the verb *know* and be analysed as an object, as is the case in example (2a). Alternatively, the parser could adopt a subordinate clause analysis. In this case, the NP would be processed as the subject of a reduced relative clause, as in example (2b). According to the parsing heuristics proposed in the *Garden-Path Model*, the parser initially favours the main clause analysis, as it is 'simpler' in that it requires fewer nodes. In example (2a), the main clause analysis is compatible with the following input and therefore it does not cause any processing difficulties. In example (2b), however, processing difficulties arise once the parser encounters *was*, the verb in the subordinate clause. The initial parse turns out to be incorrect and has to be revised by a process referred to as reanalysis. In this process, the main clause analysis is revised in favour of the reduced relative clause analysis (see Frazier 1987: 562). Reanalysis most commonly occurs when the analysis adopted by the parser is incompatible with incoming syntactic information that is encountered at a later stage (van Gompel & Pickering 2007: 291). As observed by Pickering and Traxler (1998), semantic factors can also cause reanalysis. This is the case when the initially favoured analysis turns out to be semantically implausible. Evidence for the proposed parsing heuristics and the notion of reanalysis comes from studies by, for example, Clifton, Speer and Abney (1991); Ferreira and Clifton (1986); Frazier (1987); Frazier and Rayner (1982); Mitchell and Holmes (1985); and Rayner and Frazier (1987).[4]

1.2.2 Interactive models

In contrast to modular approaches to sentence processing, interactive models propose that the information the processor initially has access to is not restricted to syntax but includes other types of resources, such as semantics, discourse context and frequency. As all possible sources of information influence the parsing process at every point in time, a core assumption underlying interactive approaches is that the parser is not restricted to one single syntactic analysis but instead is capable of building multiple alternative analyses in parallel (see van Gompel & Pickering 2007: 292).

The most prominent interactive models are so-called *constraint-based models* (see e.g. MacDonald & Seidenberg 2006; MacDonald, Pearlmutter & Seidenberg 1994; McRae, Spivey-Knowlton & Tanenhaus 1998; Trueswell, Tanenhaus & Garnsey 1994). They claim that the multiple structural alternatives are ranked according to a number of different factors, such as plausibility or frequency, so that the analysis that is most likely to be correct receives more activation and the analyses that are less likely receive less activation. In interactive accounts, no reanalysis takes place in temporarily ambiguous sentences. Instead, processing difficulties occurring in syntactically ambiguous sentences are claimed to be due to competition of two approximately equally activated structural analyses at the point of disambiguation. Most constraint-based models are lexicalist in nature (see e.g. MacDonald & Seidenberg 2006) and assume that the lexical representation of a word includes syntactic information, such as the word's grammatical function. The core prediction of constraint-based models is that information other than syntactic cues influences the parsing process right from the beginning, which results in different weightings of structural alternatives. Therefore, possible constraints, such as semantic information, discourse context or frequency are isolated in constraint-based studies in order to examine whether they have any influence on the parsing process.

Studies investigating the initial influence of semantic cues on sentence parsing yielded mixed results. Whereas a study by Trueswell, Tanenhaus & Garnsey (1994) supports the notion of semantic cues influencing the initial parse, the results of the studies by Ferreira and Clifton (1986), Rayner, Carlson and Frazier (1983) or Clifton et al. (2003) suggest the opposite. Other cues, such as discourse context, seem to have a measurable influence on sentence processing (Altmann & Steedman 1988; Altmann et al. 1998; Crain & Steedman 1985). The picture is less clear, however, when it comes to frequency effects: Trueswell (1996) and Tabor and Tanenhaus (1999) found support for frequency effects on initial parsing decisions. However, in studies by Kennison (2001) and Pickering, Traxler and Crocker (2000) lexical frequency did not affect parsing (see also van Gompel & Pickering 2007: 294).

Overall, there is conflicting evidence for both models: Although there is some support for the assumption that processing occurs in two stages, the *Garden-Path Model* cannot account for discourse effects on sentence processing. On the other hand, the fact that the parser seems to prefer the simpler analysis and not necessarily the semantically more plausible structure poses problems for constraint-based approaches (see e.g. Traxler 2012: 171). Thus, there seems to be a consensus that non-syntactic information plays a major role in sentence processing and that this information can be integrated very rapidly into the analysis pursued by the parser (see e.g. Pickering 1999: 145; van Gompel & Pickering: 2007: 301). However, the questions remain (1) whether the information is integrated at the very beginning of the parsing process or whether it is slightly delayed and (2) whether this process conforms to the assumptions made by constraint-based approaches (see Pickering 1999: 147). In particular, the latter point applies to the question of whether processing difficulties are due to competition or reanalysis. Again, the existing evidence is somewhat inconclusive, as both assumptions are supported by empirical evidence. Pickering and van Gompel (2006: 474) point out that '[m]ost studies showing evidence for processing difficulty during syntactic ambiguity resolution are consistent with either assumption'.

Although the modularity-interaction debate has dominated much of the research on sentence processing, in recent approaches the focus has shifted towards other issues influencing the parsing process, such as working memory capacity (see Just & Carpenter 1992) or the processing of structurally complex sentences – for example, different types of relative clauses (see Gordon, Hendrick & Johnson 2001, 2004; for an overview, see van Gompel & Pickering 2007 and MacDonald & Hsiao 2018).

1.2.3 Some alternative approaches

Other approaches to sentence comprehension have refined and modified earlier proposals or combined aspects of both. This applies, for instance, to the *Construal Hypothesis* (Frazier & Clifton 1996), a modified version of the *Garden-Path Model*. The *Construal* account views parsing essentially as a two-stage process. At the same time, however, it delineates specific circumstances that allow for the influence of contextual information on the initial parsing process (for details, see Frazier & Clifton 1996).

An approach that integrates aspects of both modular and interactive models is the *Unrestricted Race Model* (van Gompel, Pickering & Traxler 2000, 2001; van Gompel et al. 2005). This hybrid model seeks to account for the conflicting evidence yielded in studies of sentence processing. Similar to constraint-based approaches, it is assumed that multiple sources of information can determine which syntactic analysis is initially adopted. The strictly incremental parser initially attempts to build multiple structural analyses in parallel, and all structures that adhere to the grammar of the particular language receive some activation from the information present in the input. In the case of syntactic ambiguity, the alternative structures 'are engaged in a race' (van Gompel, Pickering & Traxler 2000: 623): The analysis that receives the most support by the different sources of information is constructed fastest, and only this analysis is then adopted by the parser. As in two-stage models, the parser pursues only a single analysis. The *Unrestricted Race Model* exhibits a further characteristic of two-stage models: Unlike constraint-based approaches, which assume that processing difficulties in ambiguous sentences are due to competition, the *Unrestricted Race Model* predicts reanalysis in cases where the adopted syntactic structure is incompatible with later information (van Gompel et al. 2005: 227). The assumptions of the model are supported by studies by Traxler, Pickering & Clifton (1998), van Gompel, Pickering & Traxler (2000) and van Gompel et al. (2005).

The *Unrestricted Race Model* is critically discussed in Vosse and Kempen (2009), who opt for 'a "modularized", less monolithic version of a parallel-interactive speed race model of ambiguity resolution' (Vosse & Kempen 2009: 6) to account for van Gompel and colleagues' empirical findings. In this scenario, a conceptual and a syntactic processor work in parallel on processing input sentences. The two types of processors interact with each other so that incompatible analyses can be discarded. If, in the end, a processor fails to come up with an acceptable analysis, reanalysis takes place (Vosse & Kempen 2009: 4). The notion of a syntactic and a non-syntactic processor operating in parallel is also put forward by Kuperberg (2007), who, based on findings of a number of event-related potential (ERP) studies, claims that 'the language processing system engages at least two interactive but dissociable routes or streams to comprehension' (Kuperberg 2007: 44). These include a semantic memory-based system and a combinatorial system that is sensitive to morpho-syntax.

1.2.4 The *Good-Enough Approach to Language Comprehension*

The idea of two interacting processors operating in parallel in distinct but related processing routes is also put forward in the *Good-Enough Approach to Language Comprehension* (Christianson et al. 2006; Ferreira 2003; Ferreira & Patson 2007;

Ferreira, Christianson & Hollingworth 2001) and its recent extension, the *Online Cognitive Equilibrium Hypothesis* (Karimi & Ferreira 2016). Ferreira and colleagues question the assumption underlying serial as well as parallel models of sentence processing that 'utterances are compositionally built up from words clustered into hierarchically organized constituents' (Ferreira, Bailey & Ferraro 2002: 11). They argue that, in comprehension, 'language processing is not always compositional' (Ferreira, Bailey & Ferraro 2002: 12). Instead, listeners frequently rely on shallow, 'good-enough' representations that are often incomplete. These superficial representations are in line with the plausibility of real-world events but do not necessarily reflect the actual input (Ferreira, Engelhardt & Jones 2009: 413). The notion of non-compositionality in language processing is supported by a number of research findings. Ferreira, Bailey & Ferraro (2002: 11–12) point to the 'Moses illusion' (Erickson & Mattson 1981), which constitutes a famous example of shallow processing. Erickson and Mattson (1981: 541) observed that when people in an experiment are asked the question, 'How many animals of each sort did Moses take on the ark', the majority of the participants failed to detect the inconsistency in the sentence (i.e. that it was Noah and not Moses) and answered 'Two' (for similar results, see Barton & Sanford 1993).

Research supporting the hypothesis of *good-enough* representations explored misinterpretations of garden-path sentences and passive sentences. The studies engaging with garden-path sentences investigated whether the initial misanalysis is completely erased after reanalysis and the related question of whether the sentence is in the end understood correctly (see Christianson et al. 2001; Ferreira, Christianson & Hollingworth 2001). This is illustrated with the sentence in example (3) (taken from Christianson et al. 2001: 394).

(3) While Anna dressed the baby spit up on the bed.

This sentence constitutes a temporarily ambiguous sentence that creates a garden-path effect: If the sentence is presented visually without commas, listeners initially interpret *the baby* as the object of *dressed* and revise their initial analysis when they encounter *spit up* (see Christianson et al. 2001). Generally, it is assumed that once reanalysis takes place, the initial parse is fully revised. Strikingly, the results by Christianson and colleagues indicate that this does not always seem to be the case. In their study, participants were visually presented with temporarily ambiguous sentences as in example (3) and they were asked to answer two types of comprehension questions after reading, which relate to the subject of the subordinate clause and the subject of the main clause. This is illustrated in example (4) for example sentence (3):

(4)
    a) Did the baby spit up?
    b) Did Anna dress the baby?

The first question aimed to investigate whether the parser successfully revises the initial analysis of the NP *the baby* as object of the subordinate clause and correctly interprets the NP as the subject of the main clause. Christianson and colleagues found that the participants correctly answered the first type of question with *yes*. However, a second finding was that the second question type was incorrectly answered with *yes* approximately 60 per cent of the time. This indicates that the majority of the participants retained parts of their initial analysis and kept the interpretation that Anna dressed the baby, which results in an incorrect understanding of the sentence (for similar results, see also Ferreira, Christianson & Hollingworth 2001). Christianson et al. (2001: 372) argue that 'initial thematic role assignments were surprisingly resistant to revision' and that this applies in particular to cases where the semantic plausibility is in line with parts of the initial analysis. This means that the initial representation lingers and only partial reanalysis takes place, which leads to a representation where the baby is assigned both the object of *dressed* and the subject of *spit up*.

The second type of experiments that lends support to the *Good-Enough Approach* focuses on the misinterpretation of passive sentences (see e.g. Ferreira 2003; Ferreira & Stacey 2000; Ferreira, Bailey & Ferraro 2002). The question underlying these experiments is the following: 'Are people ever tricked by simple, but implausible, passive sentences?' (Ferreira, Bailey & Ferraro 2002: 13). In a study by Ferreira and Stacey (2000), participants were visually presented with both plausible and implausible sentences in their active and in their passive form. The participants were asked to judge whether the sentences are plausible or not. The data analysis showed that implausible active sentences were generally judged as implausible (95 per cent) and both plausible actives and plausible passives were regarded as plausible (95 per cent for actives and 92 per cent for passives). Implausible passives such as *The dog was bitten by the man*, however, were rated as implausible in merely 74 per cent of all cases (Ferreira & Stacey 2000: 16). When participants were asked to identify the agent and the patient of the action depicted in the sentences, they were most accurate in the active conditions (99 per cent) and more accurate in the plausible passive condition (88 per cent) than in the implausible passive condition (74 per cent) (Ferreira & Stacey 2000: 24). Overall, the results indicate a tendency to interpret implausible passive sentences as actives. Ferreira, Bailey & Ferraro (2002: 13) comment on the results as follows:

> Thus, when people read or hear a passive sentence, they use their knowledge of the world to figure out who is doing what to whom. That interpretation reflects the content words of the sentence more than its compositional, syntactically derived meaning. It is as if people use a semantic heuristic rather than syntactic algorithms to get the meaning of difficult passives.

Reporting on the results, Ferreira (2003: 192) argues that, in sentence comprehension, both parsing heuristics and syntactic algorithms are involved and suggests that 'the language comprehension system uses simple heuristics to process sentences, and somehow coordinates the output of those heuristics with the products of more rigorous syntactic algorithms'. She identifies the following two main heuristics in language processing: Firstly, the N V N (Noun Verb Noun) strategy states that the subject is interpreted as a proto-agent and the object as a proto-theme. Secondly, the plausibility strategy specifies that the parser adopts 'the semantic analysis that is most consistent with world knowledge' (Ferreira 2003: 192).

Further support for the finding that plausibility cues strongly influence language processing and that semantic processing occurs in parallel to syntactic processing comes from an ERP study by Kim and Osterhout (2005). Their research findings indicate that, in certain conditions, semantic processing guides the language comprehension process. Kim and Osterhout (2005: 214) propose a 'dual route' in language processing and argue that their data appear to be consistent with a system of parallel, independent syntactic and semantic processing mechanisms.[5]

The finding that, in comprehension, linguistic representations are often imprecise is further supported by studies by, for example, Klin et al. (2006), Levine, Guzman and Klin (2000) and Swets et al. (2008) (see also Karimi & Ferreira 2016).

1.2.5 The *Online Cognitive Equilibrium Hypothesis*

Since its initial articulation, the *Good-Enough Approach* has been further developed and extended to the *Online Cognitive Equilibrium Hypothesis* (Karimi & Ferreira 2016), an approach to language processing which aims to model the interplay between processing heuristics and deep syntactic algorithms. Karimi and Ferreira investigate the driving force 'that influences depth of processing' (Karimi & Ferreira 2016: 1017). Although the authors argue that 'sentence processing proceeds through a heuristic process in which a noun-verb-noun syntactic template is quickly mapped into an agent-verb-patient thematic structure' (Karimi & Ferreira 2016: 1015), they make clear that this does not rule out parallel algorithmic processing. Instead, they assume that heuristic processing occurs in parallel to algorithmic processing and may even precede the latter. In their model, they draw on work by Piaget (1952, 1977, 1985), in particular the notion of *cognitive equilibrium*. Piaget's theory, which primarily focuses on cognitive development, proposes that two main processes are involved in humans' adaptation to their environment, namely assimilation and adaptation. Assimilation refers to the process of integrating information encountered in the environment into pre-existing schemata (cognitive structures). Adaptation, on the other hand, involves modifications or changes of existing schemata to incorporate new information. Both assimilation and adaptation are essential processes for cognitive development and growth. Ideally, a balance between assimilation and adaptation is achieved, a state referred to by Piaget as *(cognitive) equilibrium*. An imbalance between the two processes leads to a state of disequilibrium. The aim of the cognitive system is to restore equilibrium as fast as possible, as '[e]quilibrium is a necessary condition toward which the organism constantly strives' (Wadsworth 1989: 16).

The authors apply Piaget's notion of cognitive equilibrium to language processing, arguing that, in language processing, 'equilibrium is the default and desired cognitive state' and that the input to the processing system triggers a disequilibrium, as the new information needs to be processed and integrated into existing schemata in order to restore cognitive equilibrium: 'processing a sentence(s) can be viewed as entering a state of disequilibrium and then moving towards a state of equilibrium' (Karimi & Ferreira 2016: 1018).

Karimi and Ferreira (2016: 1018) propose two general principles related to the *Online Cognitive Equilibrium Hypothesis*:

1. The cognitive system attempts to maximize equilibrium *at the earliest opportunity*.
2. Once at equilibrium, the language processing system prefers to stay in that state as long as possible and as long as there is no strong reason for abandoning that state.

Why does the parser sometimes rely on processing heuristics instead of deep syntactic algorithms? According to the two principles of the *Online Cognitive Equilibrium Hypothesis*, the system's aim is to reach equilibrium as soon as possible and to stay in the state of equilibrium as long as possible. In some cases, equilibrium is achieved fastest by relying on shallow processing instead of deep processing, and applying heuristics allows the system to stay longer in that state (Karimi & Ferreira 2016: 1018).

The model underlying the *Online Cognitive Equilibrium Hypothesis* is shown in Figure 1.5. As illustrated in Figure 1.5, the authors propose that both processing routes, that is, the heuristic route and the algorithmic route, are activated at the same time. However, as heuristic processing is assumed to be faster than algorithmic processing, the system reaches an 'interim output' (Karimi & Ferreira 2016: 1018) via the heuristic route. This interim output then influences the still-ongoing algorithmic parsing process. Karimi and Ferreira (2016: 1018–19) consider this process as crucial in arriving at shallow representations and they maintain that 'the formation of an interim output by heuristic route [*sic*] causes the algorithmic route to become confirmatory in nature, leading to good-enough final representations'. Whereas processing heuristics mainly rely on semantic information and are therefore claimed to proceed in a top-down fashion, algorithmic processing is based on linguistic knowledge and processing takes place in a bottom-up way.

According to this approach, the achievement of cognitive equilibrium is not an all-or-nothing process. Instead, different degrees of equilibrium can be reached based on

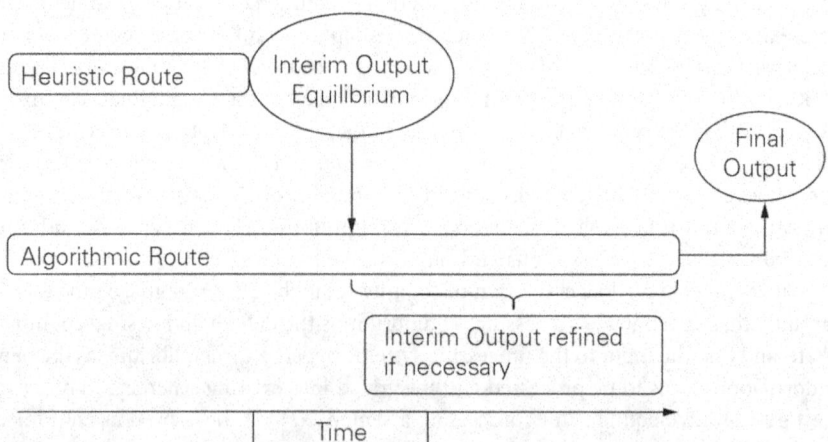

Figure 1.5 The model of language processing according to the *Online Cognitive Equilibrium Hypothesis* (from Karimi & Ferreira 2016: 1019, fig. 1). © 2015 The Experimental Psychological Society. Reprinted by Permission of SAGE Publications, Ltd.

the interim output. These depend on various factors, such as the person's certainty about the accuracy of the output, the strengths of the representations as well as task demands (Karimi & Ferreira 2016: 1019).

The *Online Cognitive Equilibrium Hypothesis* has been successfully applied to both inter- and intrasentential processing (for research on intrasentential processing and underspecification of representations, see the discussion in this section as well as Christianson, Luke & Ferreira 2010; for intersentential processing, see e.g. Cook 2014; Poesio et al. 2006). Karimi and Ferreira show that their model is consistent with a number of 'established psycholinguistic findings' (Karimi & Ferreira 2016: 1030). One such finding is that, in language processing, predictive processes are involved, so that 'upcoming information is preactivated before they even appear in the unfolding linguistic input' (Karimi & Ferreira 2016: 1030). These predictive operations are often attributed to probabilistic issues, such as frequency effects (see e.g. Jaeger 2010; McClelland 1998). The explanation of predictability in language processing underlying the *Online Cognitive Equilibrium Hypothesis* differs in this respect. As the aim of the heuristic route is the achievement of cognitive equilibrium, it draws on all the information that is available, which is then related to existing schemata. In this process, an 'entire event representation' (Karimi & Ferreira 2016: 1031) can be accessed by the parsing heuristic before the actual linguistic input is fully available. The interim output then maps its contents onto algorithmic processing, which leads to predictions about upcoming linguistic input. Karimi and Ferreira (2016: 1031) claim that, in this scenario, predictions do not yield any additional processing load: 'Prediction does not require resources under OCE [Online Cognitive Equilibrium]; indeed, an interesting prediction of the OCE is that resources would be required to *inhibit* the generation of a prediction if the output of the heuristic route is sufficiently compelling.'

A second phenomenon that can be explained in terms of the *Online Cognitive Equilibrium Hypothesis* is the garden-path effect. According to the hypothesis, in a temporarily ambiguous sentence such as *While Anna bathed the baby played in the crib*, the parser's aim to reach equilibrium leads to the initial interpretation of the NP *the baby* as an object instead of the subject of the main clause. In this way, equilibrium is reached as soon as the NP is encountered in the input, and an interim output can be constructed. The correct assignment of the subject role to the NP *the baby* would delay the creation of an interim output and equilibrium would only be reached at a later stage (Karimi & Ferreira 2016: 1032).

The *Online Cognitive Equilibrium Hypothesis* also offers an explanation for other phenomena, such as attachment preferences in globally ambiguous sentences by humans with different working memory spans, the resolution of ambiguous pronouns or lingering representations in garden-path sentences (see Karimi & Ferreira 2016: 1033–4). The processing of complex sentences provides a further testing ground for the *Online Cognitive Equilibrium Hypothesis*: Karimi and Ferreira hypothesize that, when processing complex sentences, humans rely more on the heuristic route to attain equilibrium, and the interim output is created far earlier than the output of the algorithmic route (Karimi & Ferreira 2016: 1029).

To sum up, the *Online Cognitive Equilibrium Hypothesis* and its underlying model of language processing constitute a framework that specifies how shallow semantic/

heuristic and deep syntactic algorithmic processing interact. By proposing that the attainment of online cognitive equilibrium is the driving force in language processing, the model is capable of explaining the creation of underspecified representations via the heuristic route. At the same time, the proposed architecture of the language processing system allows for the formation of full linguistic representations via the deep algorithmic processing route.[6] Karimi and Ferreira demonstrate that their model can explain a number of psycholinguistic findings. These relate to the impact of predictive operations in processing, the occurrence of garden-path effects or differences in attachment preferences of ambiguous relative clauses. The psychological plausibility of this approach to sentence processing is a major reason for its incorporation into the *Integrated Encoding-Decoding Model of SLA*.

2

The relation between production and comprehension in language processing

As discussed in the Introduction and Chapter 1, in recent decades, much research has been devoted to some of the core issues related to language production and comprehension processes, and the results of numerous studies provide many insights into how humans produce and understand language.

This chapter engages with the relation between production and comprehension in human language processing. As the overall goal of this book is to model interfaces between production and comprehension in SLA, the relation between the two modalities in human language processing is considered to be of crucial importance. According to Kempen (1999: v),

> [a] fundamental question regarding the cognitive architecture of human syntactic processing concerns the relationship between its two main modalities: grammatical encoding (formulating) and grammatical decoding (parsing). Are they subserved by different types of syntactic processor (i.e. modules operating on very different principles), or is the same type [of] processing module, a *grammatical coder*, deployed in both parsing and formulating? In the latter case, our cognitive system may contain two exemplars of this module (one for parsing, one for formulating), or one exemplar could subserve both modalities, presumably in time-sharing mode. (italics original)

Traditionally, the mechanisms of production and comprehension have largely been studied separately, as the standard assumption in linguistics and cognitive psychology is that these processes occur in two different modules with two different types of operations (see e.g. the discussion in Gambi & Pickering 2017; Kempen, Olsthoorn & Sprenger 2012: 347–8; Meyer, Huettig & Levelt 2016; Pickering & Garrod 2007: 105–6). Proponents of the view that there are two separate systems involved in production and comprehension include for instance Clark and Malt (1984), Chapman and Miller (1975) and Ruder and Finch (1987). However, this view has recently been challenged by proponents of a more integrated view of syntactic processes in production and comprehension (e.g. Garrett 2000; Kempen, Olsthoorn & Sprenger 2012; Pickering & Garrod 2004, 2007, 2013; Segaert et al. 2012).

According to Kempen (1999: 1), the standard viewpoint in the psycholinguistic community favours the dual-processor hypothesis, with the processors sharing a single grammar and lexicon. This view is based on a number of arguments that are traditionally put forward to support the notion of a *dual-processor architecture*, that is, an architecture of the language processing system that strictly separates between encoding and decoding processes (see also Gambi & Pickering 2017: 158). However, as will be shown in the ensuing critical discussion of some of the popular arguments used in favour of a dual-processor architecture, these arguments do not withstand scrutiny and thus do not rule out the possibility of shared processes in production and comprehension. In fact, they are also compatible with a single-processor architecture, which is a more parsimonious conceptualization of human language processing.

2.1 A critical look at the dual-processor architecture

Kempen (1999: 5) names four core issues that traditionally support the view of two distinct processing systems in production and comprehension:

1. task requirements
2. self-monitoring
3. findings from neurolinguistics
4. findings from language acquisition

Although the four issues are used to support a dual-processor view, a critical examination of the key arguments underlying these issues shows that they are also compatible with a more integrated account of comprehension and production.

2.1.1 Task requirements

Although, in principle, both syntactic encoding and decoding focus on the assembly of syntactic structures, they face different task requirements (Kempen 1999: 5). This is also observed by Thornton and MacDonald (2003: 756) who argue that

> [t]hough they [production and comprehension] may be affected in the same way by similar information, production and comprehension are fundamentally different tasks, and the behavior of each will likely vary as a function of differing task demands.

For instance, in decoding, the resolution of lexical and syntactic ambiguity plays a crucial role, as the decoder works on sequences of lemmas in the input. According to Thornton and MacDonald (2003: 756), 'ambiguity resolution is less of a concern in production, because speakers already know the meaning of what they are producing, potentially minimizing the influence of linguistic ambiguity in the production system'. In grammatical encoding, on the other hand, a major focus is on the combinability of lemmas and on determining word order (see Kempen 1999: 5).

However, differences in task requirements in the two modalities do not imply that both processes are entirely separate. Moreover, they do not rule out a 'single-processor' architecture. Kempen (1999: 13) argues that although '[i]t cannot be denied that grammatical encoding and decoding have to meet diverging desiderata [...], this observation alone does not entail that different types of mechanisms are necessary to fulfil them'. In this context, he points to the possibility of a single mechanism that is able to rapidly switch between the two modalities (see Section 2.3 for details).

Self-monitoring

A second argument put forward by proponents of the dual-processor architecture is related to self-monitoring. The fact that speakers are able to self-monitor and repair their utterances in speech production is commonly regarded as evidence for the existence of two distinct processing systems, as it is assumed that self-monitoring involves the comprehension system. This is, for instance, the case in Levelt's *Perceptual Loop Theory of Self-Monitoring* (see Section 1.1.4).

Although humans' capability of self-monitoring is commonly regarded as a particularly strong argument in support of a dual-processor view, self-monitoring does not rule out a single-processor architecture per se. Indeed, it can also be plausibly integrated into a single-processor architecture. Kempen (1999: 11) discusses the possibility that self-monitoring could be accomplished by a single processor that switches rapidly between the two modalities encoding and decoding. In addition, he claims that self-monitoring does not necessarily need to be based on parsing operations. Kempen, Olsthoorn and Sprenger (2012: 371–2) further elaborate on a conceptualization of self-monitoring within a single-processor architecture. The core ideas in this concern are that (1) self-monitoring and self-repair are viewed as an 'optimization process' that takes place continually during sentence generation and (2) during this process of optimization the current structure is available to both phonological encoding and overt pronunciation. The crucial difference to perception-based approaches to self-monitoring such as the *Perceptual Loop Theory* is that monitoring is assumed to be production-based so that the 'dynamic self-monitoring process does not involve grammatical decoding of a word string that has just been grammatically encoded' (Kempen, Olsthoorn & Sprenger 2012: 372). The notion of a production-based monitor is also put forward by Nozari, Dell and Schwartz (2011). This conceptualization of self-monitoring is compatible with a single-processor architecture (see also the discussion in Gambi & Pickering 2017).

2.1.2 Findings from neurolinguistics

Early research findings in the field of aphasia led to the distinction of the two brain regions Broca's and Wernicke's area in relation to speech processing. Based on patients' sites of lesions and their specific language processing impairments, the two areas were assigned different functions in language processing. The traditional view that prevailed for a long period of time was to associate Broca's area with production and Wernicke's area with comprehension processes respectively (see e.g. Gazzaniga, Ivry & Mangun 2002: 384–5). Naturally, the allocation of two different language processes (i.e. production and comprehension) to two different brain regions supported the idea of a dual-processor architecture. A further argument in this vein relates to (rare) cases of aphasic patients who show dissociations between grammatical encoding and decoding. These patients suffer from problems in grammatical encoding but have apparently unimpaired parsing capabilities (see e.g. Kolk 1998).

However, since the 1970s, research in the field of neurolinguistics has investigated the role of Broca's area in language processing in greater detail, producing several crucial findings. First of all, Broca's area seems to be more diverse than initially thought and is now seen as a 'heterogeneous patch of cortex and not a uniform cortical entity' (Hagoort 2006: 243). As far as aphasic symptoms are concerned, what is termed Broca's aphasia not only results in impairments in language production but also includes syntactic deficits in comprehension (see e.g. Blumstein 1995; Kolk & Friederici 1985). What is more, the sites of lesions in aphasic patients do not match their processing impairments in a one-to-one fashion and a number of exceptions to the classic association between sites of lesions and aphasic symptoms have been reported (e.g. Basso et al. 1985; Willmes & Poeck 1993). Research findings further suggest that (1) Broca's area is not restricted to language processing but includes other types of processing such as musical sequences (see e.g. Maess et al. 2001) or the rhythm and imagery of motion (see e.g. Binkofski et al. 2000; Friederici 2002; Schubotz & von Cramon 2001) and that (2) syntactic processing forms merely a part of language-specific processes taking place in this area (Hagoort 2006: 246). Hagoort (2006: 248) proposes that different kinds of unification processes take place in parts of what he calls 'Broca's complex' that integrate words into larger structural units. These processes include, but are not restricted to, syntax.

These more recent findings are all compatible with a single-processor architecture, as they imply that 'this cortical region [Broca's area] subserves aspects of grammatical encoding as well as decoding' (Kempen 1999: 12; see also Friederici 1998; Segaert et al. 2012). According to Kempen, Olsthoorn and Sprenger (2012: 370), research findings suggest that the same neural circuits are involved in structure formation in the two modalities (see e.g. Hagoort 2005; Ullman et al. 2005). Finally, the cases of dissociation between agrammatic production and agrammatic comprehension do not necessarily imply the existence of two separate processing systems for the two modalities. Instead, the dissociations can be explained in terms of differences in the ability to access the relevant syntactic information (Kempen 1999: 11).

2.1.3 Findings from language acquisition

A final argument in favour of a dual-processing architecture is related to the finding that production and comprehension abilities do not seem to develop simultaneously in language acquisition. Kempen (1999: 6) refers to studies by Bates, Bretherton and Snyder (1988) and Bates, Dale and Thal (1995), revealing that '[c]orrelations between productive and receptive measures of language proficiency tend not to be very high'. Although it is a common finding that production skills emerge later than comprehension skills (see e.g. Benedict 1979; Gertner, Fisher & Eisengart 2006), this asymmetry in language acquisition is by no means unidirectional. Hendriks (2014) reviews a number of studies providing evidence for an inverse order of acquisition, in that production of certain structures precedes their comprehension (e.g. Chan et al. 2009; Chapman & Miller 1975; Thal & Flores 2001). The reason for these dissociations is yet unclear, and a number of different explanations have been proposed, such as differences in accessing syntactic information in the two modalities, lack of pragmatic knowledge, limitations in processing capacity and different task demands (see Hendriks 2014: 34–5). But do these dissociations necessarily imply a dual-processor architecture? Kempen (1999: 12) argues that 'as long as alternative interpretations […] cannot been [sic] eliminated, the developmental dissociation between language comprehension and production is a poor argument in favour of dual-processor models'. In this context, Gambi and Pickering (2017: 158) point out that 'dissociations and asymmetries are in principle compatible with some degree of sharing [of production and comprehension processes], as long as there are subcomponents of production that are not used in comprehension and vice versa'.

To conclude, a critical review of the traditional arguments supporting the view of production and comprehension as separate processes shows that these arguments do not necessarily exclude alternative perspectives on this issue. Instead, they are also compatible with a more integrated view of language processing. In keeping with this, the dual-processor approach has recently been challenged by advocates of a more integrated view of comprehension and production processes. These include, for instance, Garrett (2000), Kempen (1999, 2000), Kempen, Olsthoorn and Sprenger (2012), Menenti et al. (2011), Pickering and Garrod (2007, 2013) and Segaert et al. (2012). Naturally, these accounts differ to a certain extent in their theoretical perspective on this issue. Pickering and Garrod (2013: 332), for instance, claim that humans can draw on production processes in comprehension and vice versa: '[W]e propose that comprehension processes are routinely accessed at different stages in production, and that production processes are routinely accessed at different stages in comprehension.' In their integrated approach to production and comprehension processes, they view language production as a form of action and comprehension as a form of perception or, to be more precise, as a form of *action perception*. The finding that action and perception processes are tightly interwoven is applied to the domain of language processing. Pickering and Garrod elaborate on a forward model of this type of action and action perception at different levels of linguistic representation, which serves to explain the ability of humans to predict both themselves and each other (Pickering & Garrod 2013). Kempen, Olsthoorn and Sprenger (2012) propose a so-called *shared grammatical workspace*, 'a single architecture for the online assemblage and short-term storage of grammatical structures' (Kempen, Olsthoorn & Sprenger 2012: 345).

Despite the differences in the conceptualization of the relation between the two modalities, what these accounts have in common is that they do not assume the existence of two entirely separate processes involved in production and comprehension. Instead, they view the two processes as intertwined and, thus, focus on a potential interlink between them. This integrated view of language processing is supported by a number of theoretical arguments as well as empirical data.

2.2 Arguments in favour of a single-processor architecture

A unitary view of sentence processing has been proposed by Kempen (1999, 2000) and further developed and empirically tested by Kempen, Olsthoorn and Sprenger (2012). They put forward the hypothesis of a *shared grammatical workspace* involved in both production and comprehension; that is, they propose the existence of one single syntactic processor which is involved in syntactic decoding and encoding. Kempen (2000: 38) envisages this idea as follows: 'Suppose that [...] our cognitive system has a single processing mechanism for syntax assembly that is used for *constructing* syntactic structures (grammatical encoding in sentence production) as well as for *reconstructing* syntactic structures (parsing, grammatical decoding in sentence comprehension).'

He argues that this shared system relies on two different types of information in grammatical encoding and decoding and thus operates in two different 'processing contexts' (Kempen 2000: 38). In encoding, the processor relies on the lexico-syntactic information which is associated with the respective conceptual structure or message. In decoding, the information derives from the strings of words occurring in the input. Both processes – grammatical encoding and grammatical decoding – involve mappings between meaning and form or, to be more specific, 'mappings between nonlinguistic communicative intentions and lemma strings that underlie spoken, written, or signed linguistic expressions of such intentions' (Kempen, Olsthoorn & Sprenger 2012: 347). The underlying idea of Kempen and colleagues' unitary approach to syntactic processing is that, despite the 'directional difference', the mapping operations between the communicative intention and the linguistic expression are very similar (Kempen, Olsthoorn & Sprenger 2012: 347–8). Following Kempen (2000: 39–40), both modalities share the following characteristics: lexical guidance; sensitivity to conceptual factors; direct mapping between conceptual (thematic) and syntactic relations; incremental processing; determinism; and similar empirical profiles.

Lexical guidance

In encoding as well as decoding, lexical items or lemmas are indispensable for syntactic structure building. In encoding, lemma retrieval makes the syntactic information available that is necessary for the activation of syntactic building procedures (see e.g. Kempen & Hoenkamp 1987; Levelt 1989). Lemmas also play a crucial role in grammatical decoding: They are retrieved by the parser on the basis of the lexemes encountered in the input, and the syntactic information that is present in the lemmas' entries allows for syntactic structure building. This view is also supported by MacDonald et al. (1994), who argue that syntactic ambiguity resolution is lexical in nature.

Sensitivity to conceptual factors

In grammatical encoding, conceptual structures form the input of the formulator. In decoding, the syntactic parser makes recourse to the conceptual system to check the parse tree in terms of plausibility (see e.g. Kempen 1996, 1999).

Direct mapping between conceptual (thematic) and syntactic relations

In both coding processes, the mapping between conceptual and syntactic relations takes place directly without any intermediate steps. For instance, when encoding or decoding passive structures, no transformations are assumed to take place (see e.g. Bock, Loebell & Morey 1992; Slobin 1966).

Incremental processing

Both encoding and decoding processes are incremental: 'Syntactic trees grow from left to right, in tandem with the unfolding of a conceptual message (in formulating) or a string of words (in parsing)' (Kempen 2000: 39). The incremental nature of the speech production process was outlined in the section on positional processing. In comprehension, there is a consensus that syntactic processing also takes place in an incremental fashion and that the parser starts constructing the syntactic tree on the basis of the fragments encountered in the input (see Section 1.2).

Determinism

In production, the formulator transforms a particular preverbal/conceptual message into one sentence. In comprehension, the parser produces one analysis as the final result of the parsing process. Kempen (1999: 8) argues that '[b]oth modules commit themselves to a single outputstructure [*sic*] at an early stage'. In temporarily ambiguous sentences, this commitment to a single structure can lead to the need for reanalysis (see Section 1.2). Kempen (1999: 8) also points out that this kind of determinism relates to the output of syntactic processing and does not rule out that the parser considers multiple alternative structures *during* processing, as is, for instance, the case in constraint-based models of parsing (see Section 1.2.2).

Similar empirical profiles

Several studies have shown that both encoding and decoding are sensitive to experimental manipulation (e.g. syntactic priming) and seem to respond in a similar fashion in the following areas:

1. Preferences for specific lexical or subcategorization frames seem to affect both production and comprehension. Many verbs have more than one lexical frame, that is, they can be used transitively or intransitively. In these cases, speakers of a language show lexical frame preferences. The preferences can be assessed in free production tasks, where participants are asked to form sentences using verbs that have more than one lexical frame. Thus, speakers prefer to use the verb *teach* in its transitive form, but they apply the verb *perform* more often in its intransitive form (Kempen 1999: 8). The same type of lexical frame preferences can be found in sentence comprehension: Research findings show that sentences are easier to understand when the structure reflects the lexical frame preferences (see e.g. Clifton, Frazier & Connine 1984; MacDonald, Pearlmutter & Seidenberg 1994).
2. Syntactic priming has been observed in both research on oral and written production (see e.g. Bock 1986; Pickering & Branigan 1999) and research on comprehension (e.g. Branigan 1995; van Gompel et al. 2006). In a study on

syntactic priming in production, Bock (1986: 378) observed that 'speakers tend to repeat the syntactic forms of sentences in subsequent utterances that are minimally related in lexical, conceptual, or discourse content'. For instance, after reading out a sentence with a prepositional dative construction, such as *The rock star sold some cocaine to an undercover agent*, participants were more likely to use prepositional dative constructions in picture description than double-object datives, as in *The governess made the princess a cup of tea* (examples taken from Bock 1986: 360–1). A study on structural priming by van Gompel et al. (2006) showed that priming effects also occur from comprehension to production. Van Gompel and colleagues investigated temporarily ambiguous sentences such as *While the man was visiting the children who were surprisingly pleasant and funny played outside*. The results of the study indicate that participants produced more transitive sentences after the exposure to temporarily ambiguous sentences than after the exposure to unambiguous sentences that were disambiguated by a comma. According to the authors, this indicates that the initial transitive analysis remains activated (see also Bock et al. 2007).
3. Studies on agreement errors in speech production reveal the occurrence of so-called *attraction errors*. Complex noun phrases, for instance *The label on the bottles* (Bock & Miller 1991), sometimes trigger agreement errors on the finite verb (*are* instead of *is*). Speakers seem to be influenced by the local instead of the head noun in processing agreement (see also Bock & Cutting 1992). The same type of subject-verb agreement error has been observed in comprehension (Nicol, Forster & Veres 1997). It is assumed that there is an 'agreement checking component' in comprehension, which is sensitive to the same factors as in production (Kempen 2000: 39).
4. Both production and comprehension are sensitive to 'structural complexity effects' (Kempen 2000: 39). Sentences that are structurally complex are more difficult to understand and occur less frequently in oral and written speech (see e.g. Gibson & Pearlmutter 1994; Keenan 1987).

In light of the above considerations, Kempen (1999: 13) opts for a single processor for grammatical encoding and decoding as the most parsimonious solution. He observes that this view has implications concerning the assumptions made about a grammar component in sentence processing. In contrast to the conceptualization of a separate declarative representation of grammatical knowledge, he proposes the existence of a *Performance Grammar* (Kempen 1999: 15), 'a performance-oriented representation that is immediately tractable (i.e. without intermediate compilation steps) by the sole syntax assembly mechanism – or the sole type of syntax assembly mechanism – available to language users'. This type of grammar meets a number of key criteria to achieve psychological plausibility: First of all, *Performance Grammar* is lexical in nature. In the mental lexicon, lexical items are related to *lexically anchored building blocks*, 'more or less elaborate syntactic structures that can be retrieved as a whole' (Kempen 1999: 15). The segments that are stored in fixed combinations in the mental lexicon are also referred to as 'lexical frames' (Kempen 1999: 24) or, in later versions, as 'treelets' (Kempen 2014: 119). In grammatical encoding and decoding, the treelets are then assembled into larger syntactic structures in the *Unification Space*, the single coder where grammatical encoding and decoding take place.

A second feature of *Performance Grammar* is *conceptual-syntactic synchrony*. Thematic relations at the conceptual level constitute the counterpart to functional relations within lexically anchored building blocks at the level of syntax. The correspondences between the two domains – synchronization links – are assumed to operate bidirectionally, so that, in production, activation spreads from conceptual to syntactic building blocks and, in comprehension, activation spreads from syntactic blocks to thematic relations (Kempen 1999: 16).

A further component is the *linearization component*. This parsing mechanism relates to the notion of incremental processing and attaches new material to 'the right-hand flank of the current tree' (Kempen 2000: 16). Furthermore, the parser ensures that functional relations are encoded before positional processing takes place (see also Section 1.1.3). The assembly of the treelets in both encoding and decoding is established via *unification links* (U-links) in the *Unification Space*, resulting in a single syntactic structure. Apart from feature unification, linearization rules play a crucial part in combining the treelets to form larger syntactic structures (see Kempen 2014). The *Unification Space* is seen as distinct from but heavily interacting with the mental lexicon. Whereas the frames or treelets associated with the lemmas in the mental lexicon are language-specific, the unification mechanisms are claimed to be universal (Kempen personal communication).

As mentioned in Chapter 1, the grammatical theory underlying the theory of SLA and the *Integrated Encoding-Decoding Model of SLA* proposed in this book is *Lexical-Functional Grammar* (LFG), which also constitutes a non-derivational, lexicalist grammar. Some elements of *Performance Grammar* are inspired by LFG as well as by other grammatical theories (Kempen 1999: 19); however, the details of the formalism underlying *Performance Grammar* and the *Unification Space* clearly differ from these approaches. Despite these differences, a fair share of the core ideas of *Incremental Procedural Grammar* (Kempen & Hoenkamp 1987), which forms a basis for Levelt's (1989) view of grammatical encoding and thus also plays a crucial role in PT, is still considered to be valid (Kempen personal communication).[1] Thus, I argue that the core tenets of *Performance Grammar* are, in principle, also compatible with the theoretical framework of the *Integrated Encoding-Decoding Model of SLA*. This applies in particular to the following aspects of *Performance Grammar*:

1. its lexicalist nature;
2. the assumption of incremental processing;
3. the notion of feature unification; and
4. the existence of linearization rules.

2.3 A *shared grammatical workspace*

The idea of a single-processor architecture is further elaborated on by Kempen, Olsthoorn and Sprenger (2012: 348), who argue that 'grammatical encoding and decoding could be accomplished by SHARED processing resources – by a single exemplar of all, or all important, parts of the cognitive resources' (small caps in original). They hasten to add that a *shared grammatical workspace* does not imply that grammatical encoding and decoding can take place simultaneously. In their view, simultaneous processing in production and comprehension could only occur in a *dedicated-workspaces architecture*, when the two tasks are executed by two distinct processing resources. If grammatical encoding and decoding are subserved by the same cognitive processing resources, task-switching is required, as some kind of alternation between the two different tasks would need to take place.

> A dedicated-workspaces architecture predicts that encoding and decoding processes are able to assemble, during overlapping time intervals, two different grammatical forms – one being decoded, the other encoded –, and that they can do this without the need to switch, within those intervals, between the tasks and between the grammatical forms involved in the tasks. The hypothesis of a single shared workspace, in contrast, predicts that concurrent assemblage of two differing grammatical forms – one by the encoder, one by the decoder – requires switching between tasks and between grammatical forms involved. (Kempen, Olsthoorn & Sprenger 2012: 348)

Kempen and colleagues tested the predictions deriving from the competing processing architectures (dedicated-workspaces vs. shared-workspace architecture) in an empirical study with native speakers of Dutch in a university context. The experiments in the study involve the notion of *grammatical multitasking*, that is, 'grammatical encoding and grammatical decoding in overlapping timespans' (Kempen, Olsthoorn & Sprenger 2012: 348). The design of the experiments sought to require rapid alternations between encoding and decoding. This was done in order to figure out (1) whether encoding and decoding processes assemble two different grammatical forms without switching between the tasks and the different grammatical forms or (2) whether it is indeed the case that switching between tasks and between different grammatical forms does occur, as is predicted by the hypothesis of a single shared workspace.

In the experiments, the participants worked on a so-called *paraphrasing task*, where they had to read fragments of sentences and to immediately paraphrase them. The underlying logic of the experimental setup is that it triggers grammatical multitasking: Whereas reading the fragment leads to a process of decoding, the activity of paraphrasing the same fragment triggers an encoding action. Hence, in reading and paraphrasing an entire sentence, the participants switched frequently between decoding and encoding. Example sentences are given in example (1).[2] All experimental sentences included a quoted main clause with the first-person personal pronoun *I* as subject NP. In some trials, the conjunction *that* was presented in a salient way to indicate that, in paraphrasing the sentence, the direct main clause had to be transformed into indirect speech, as in example (1b).

(1)
    a) The angry/headmaster/complained:/
       'I have/seen/a nasty cartoon/of/myself/in/the hall.'

b) The angry/headmaster/complained/
 that/<u>he had</u>/seen/a nasty cartoon/of/<u>himself</u>/in/the hall.
c) *The angry/headmaster/complained:/
 'I have/seen/a nasty cartoon/of/himself/in/the hall.'

The crucial element in the experiment is the reflexive pronoun. Whereas some sentences contained a correct reflexive pronoun (e.g. *myself* in example (1a)), others, such as example (1c) included an incorrect pronoun (*himself*). During the trials, response latencies related to the production of the reflexive pronouns were measured, as these were viewed as crucial for the hypothesis to be tested.

Following the dedicated-workspaces hypothesis, encoding and decoding processes construct and work on separate grammatical forms. A switch between the two modalities includes a switch between two different grammatical forms. In the sentences in example (1), the first-person value of the subject (the personal pronoun *I*) is assumed to remain present once it is decoded and is matched with the value of the reflexive pronoun later in the decoding process. The shared-workspace hypothesis, however, assumes that 'the two modalities work with the same (token-identical) grammatical form-under-construction' (Kempen, Olsthoorn & Sprenger 2012: 351). In the process of encoding, the value of the subject's feature for person is overwritten from first to third person. This value is then matched with the value of the reflexive pronoun in the decoding process (as in *The angry headmaster complained that **he** had seen a nasty cartoon of **himself** in the hall*). Kempen, Olsthoorn and Sprenger (2012: 351) argue that, according to the shared-workspace hypothesis, 'CORRUPTING AN INPUT SENTENCE LIKE (1A) BY CHANGING THE CORRECT MYSELF TO INCORRECT HIMSELF, AS IN (1C), WILL NOT BE NOTICED BY THE DECODING PROCESS' (small caps in original).

The two hypotheses about the cognitive architecture of the encoding and decoding modalities yield different predictions with regard to the response latencies in the different input sentences of the paraphrasing task. These are summarized in Table 2.1 (see Kempen, Olsthoorn & Sprenger 2012: 377).

Table 2.1 Predictions of dedicated-workspaces hypothesis and single-workspace hypothesis.

	dedicated-workspaces hypothesis		single-workspace hypothesis	
input sentence	1(a) I ... myself	1(c) I ... *himself	1(a) I ... myself	1(c) I ... *himself
expectancy violation during decoding	no	yes	yes	no
output sentence	He ... himself	He ... himself	He ... himself	He ... himself
repair during encoding	yes	no	yes	no
source of response delay	repair	violation	violation & repair	–

Note. The asterisk indicates that the reflexive pronoun is incorrect, specifically, its person feature does not agree with the person feature of its antecedent.

In their study, Kempen and colleagues distinguish between two types of response delays, namely 'expectancy violation' during decoding and 'repair' during encoding. According to the dedicated-workspaces hypothesis, response delays in paraphrasing grammatically correct input sentences, as in example 1(a), are due to a 'repair' during encoding. In this condition, the reflexive pronoun has to be changed from first to third person, that is, from *myself* to *himself*. In paraphrasing ungrammatical stimuli where the reflexive pronoun does not match the subject pronoun, as in example (1c), response delays occur due to 'expectancy violations', that is, the noticing of the mismatch between the subject pronoun and the reflexive pronoun. The single-workspace hypothesis, on the other hand, predicts that response delays only occur in the case of grammatical reflexive pronouns, as in example (1a), as matching reflexive pronouns trigger both an expectancy violation and a repair action in the paraphrasing task. As both decoder and encoder work on the identical grammatical structure, the reflexive pronoun *myself* triggers an expectancy violation in the decoding process. This yields a repair in the encoding process. In the case of ungrammatical reflexive pronouns, however, no response delay is expected, as the mismatch is not noticed by the parser. Therefore, the single-workspace hypothesis predicts that reaction times are shorter in the case of ungrammatical stimuli than in the case of a grammatical stimuli.[3]

The results of the study provide support for Kempen and colleagues' shared workspace hypothesis: In the paraphrasing task, reaction times were shorter when the reflexive pronoun matched the one that was intended in the output, such as in example (1c). On the other hand, reaction times were longer when both input and output reflexives did not match (as in example (1a)).

Kempen, Olsthoorn and Sprenger (2012: 369) maintain that '[t]his evidences that the two modalities of grammatical performance are not completely independent: When processing the same communicative intention concurrently, they work with one and the same (more precisely: token-identical) linguistic expression of that intention. This suggests that the grammatical encoding and decoding processes command the same, shared workspace for the assembly and short-term storage of grammatical forms.' However, they point out that this does not exclude the possibility to keep both encoded and decoded structures apart, as in simultaneous interpreting. In this case, the grammatical coder deals with two structures simultaneously. These are structurally different but entail essentially the same meaning. Drawing on Salvucci and Taatgen's (2008) approach to *threaded cognition*, Kempen, Olsthoorn and Sprenger (2012: 369) argue that, in the case of simultaneous interpreting, the grammatical workspace creates separate *threads* and switches between them. The high cognitive processing load related to such a switching between separate threads reflects the processing load in simultaneous translation tasks. Overall, the authors conclude that 'our multitasking experiments suggest that grammatical encoding and grammatical decoding are subserved by a shared workspace for the assemblage and temporary storage of grammatical forms. Additional observations reported in the psycholinguistic literature indicate that the resemblance between the two modalities of grammatical performance does not stop here; the overlap between their cognitive processing resources may be considerable, in fact' (Kempen, Olsthoorn & Sprenger 2012: 375).

2.3.1 Evidence from structural priming experiments

Further support for shared processes in production and comprehension comes from studies on syntactic priming effects related to the two modalities. Several studies show that comprehension has an immediate effect on production. For instance, Bock et al. (2007) investigated the structural persistence, that is, the 'structure-specific influence of an experienced syntactic pattern on later episodes of comprehension and production' (Tooley & Bock 2014: 102) of auditorily presented sentence primes to the persistence of primes that were produced. The results of their study indicate structural persistence both within and across modalities. Van Gompel et al. (2006) found priming effects from comprehension to production that were related to an incorrect comprehension of garden-path sentences. Further evidence for '[p]arity at the semantic and lexico-syntactic levels' (Gambi & Pickering 2017: 159) comes from studies yielding priming effects between comprehension and production in dialogue tasks (Branigan, Pickering & Cleland 2000; Cleland & Pickering 2003).

A study by Tooley and Bock (2014) examined structural persistence in priming in both reading comprehension and spoken production. Previous research on priming effects seemingly revealed a difference in structural persistence in production and comprehension: Studies engaging with structural priming in comprehension indicate that persistence effects are most reliable when the same verb is used in the prime and the target sentence (see e.g. Pickering, McLean & Branigan 2013). This is illustrated in example (2) (taken from Tooley & Bock 2014: 103):

(2)
 a) prime: The man watched by the woman was tall and handsome.
 b) target: The mouse watched by the cat hid under the table.

In production studies, structural persistence is shown to be abstract and its occurrence seems to be independent of lexical support (Bock & Griffin 2000; Luka & Choi 2012; see the discussion in Tooley & Bock 2014: 103). These differences were generally taken to hint at different processing mechanisms involved in comprehension and production. However, Tooley and Bock (2014: 103) argue that

> despite its appeal, the claim remains tenuous. Its support comes from contrasts between production and comprehension priming in distinct experiments where the initial priming experiences, and just about everything else, differ. There are differences in prime presentation techniques, in tested structures, and in the depth of processing required by the tasks. […] The upshot is that existing research on structural persistence offers precious little evidence for fundamental differences in the syntactic components of speaking and understanding. What evidence there is comes from experiments that lack an essential element: A manipulation of modality.

In order to be able to make precise claims about similarities and/or differences in underlying processing mechanisms in the two modalities, in their study, Tooley and

Bock used 'the same priming procedure, the same sentences and sentence structures, and the same participants, at the same time' (Tooley & Bock 2014: 104). Their results show that, in both modalities, structural priming led to abstract structural persistence. This means that structural persistence occurred in both modalities regardless of whether or not the same verb was used in the prime and the target sentence (Tooley & Bock 2014: 112). Tooley and Bock (2014: 116) conclude that their results are 'consistent with a language processing system in which comprehension and production operate in similar ways and on similar principles'.

2.3.2 Evidence from neuroimaging studies

Apart from study results on structural priming, there is also neurobiological evidence for shared resources in production and comprehension. Neuroimaging studies that have addressed the issue of potential overlaps between production and comprehension in the brain and the related question of to what extent the neuronal infrastructure underlying linguistic processing in both modalities overlap include the ones by Awad et al. (2007) and by Stephens, Silbert and Hasson (2010). Awad and colleagues investigated brain activation in production and comprehension of narrative speech by using positron emission tomography (PET) scans. The study by Stephens, Silbert and Hasson addressed the issue of speaker-listener interaction and examined the brain regions involved in successful engagement in communication. The results of both studies indicate an extensive overlap in brain activity for speaking and listening; however, as pointed out by Menenti et al. (2011: 1174), the results have to be treated with caution, as '[t]hese common activations in speaking and listening modalities, though compelling, are hard to interpret because results were based on comparison between complex speaking and listening tasks and very simple baseline tasks. In addition, in the positron emission tomography study, different modalities were investigated with radically different tasks.'

A further neuroimaging study providing evidence of overlapping brain regions in both production and comprehension processes is the one by Wilson et al. (2004), who examined the role of motor areas in speech perception that are also involved in speech production. Focusing on syllable perception, the results of their study suggest that speech perception involves the motor system that is also employed in production processes (Wilson et al. 2004: 702). However, these results are limited to the area of phonological perception and production.

Two more recent functional magnetic resonance imaging (fMRI) studies (Menenti et al. 2011; Segaert et al. 2012) also investigated the overlap of neuronal infrastructure underlying linguistic processes in production and comprehension. Their studies provide support for a unitary system for the processing of syntax. Although study design and experimental stimuli of both studies partially overlap, their focus is (slightly) different. Whereas the study by Menenti et al. (2011) investigated the different levels of linguistic processing (semantic, lexical and syntactic), the study by Segaert et al. (2012) focused on syntactic encoding and decoding. To be more precise, it investigated whether syntactic processing in language production and language comprehension is subserved by the same neurobiological system and, in particular, whether the two modalities share the same neuronal substrate.

Both studies employed a so-called fMRI adaptation paradigm. FMRI adaptation effects occur when a repeated stimulus leads to changes of activation in those areas of the brain which are sensitive to the properties of the specific stimulus. The underlying idea of the paradigm is that 'neurons in a neuronal population generally respond less strongly when the stimulus property is repeated, that fewer neurons in a neuronal population respond, and that neuronal activity of the neurons peaks earlier' (Segaert et al. 2012: 1664).

The design of Menenti and colleagues' study aimed to disentangle lexical, semantic and syntactic processes at the sentence-level by looking at fMRI adaptation effects in response to the three areas across production and comprehension. Their study consisted of two experiments, one focusing on production (the speaking experiment) and one on comprehension (the listening experiment). Twenty-two participants took part in the production experiment and twenty-four participants carried out the comprehension experiment. All participants were native speakers of Dutch. The structures in focus in both experiments were active and passive transitive sentences. In the speaking experiment, participants were presented transitive verbs, followed by a picture depicting two actors performing the respective action. For instance, the subjects saw the verb *strangle* on the projection screen, which was followed by a picture of a woman strangling a man. In order to induce the production of passive sentences, the so-called stoplight paradigm was employed: The actors were coloured either red or green and, in the passive condition, subjects were asked to start with the green actor (patient) when describing the action. In the listening experiment, a sentence-picture matching paradigm was used. Subjects saw pictures of an action and at the same time listened to a sentence describing an action. The subjects had to decide whether the sentence they had heard matched the action depicted in the picture. The participants performed the tasks while lying in a magnetic resonance scanner. The brain regions where the fMRI adaptation effects were expected were scanned during task performance.

The study results show an overlap of brain areas for all three types of linguistic processing: Response adaptation effects were measured in relation to the repetition of semantic, syntactic and lexical content across the two modalities. The only exception relates to word processing: Here, one brain area showed repetition suppression for word production but not for comprehension (Menenti et al. 2011: 1178–9). Menenti et al. (2011: 1179) conclude that '[t]he neuronal infrastructure underlying sentence-level semantic, lexical, and syntactic processes in speaking and listening is largely shared. For semantic and syntactic representation, we found no brain areas showing a differential effect between modalities. Language production and comprehension are two facets of one language system in the brain.'

The study by Segaert et al. (2012) also employed an fMRI adaptation paradigm. In addition to the features included in the study by Menenti et al. (2011), they investigated adaptation effects both within and across the two language processing modalities to test whether the same neuronal populations are involved in the two processes. If fMRI adaptation effects are also present between modalities, one could conclude that neuronal populations are shared between the two modalities under investigation, as 'fMRI adaptation is assumed to be a consequence of a modulation within the same neuronal population' (Segaert et al. 2012: 1664). It is only then that one could speak of 'a shared neuronal substrate' (Segaert et al. 2012: 1664).

The underlying idea of the study is as follows: If it is indeed the case that production and comprehension of syntactic structures share the same neuronal population, then adaptation effects should be observable in one modality when syntactic processing takes place in the other modality. In order to test the hypothesis that the same neuronal substrate operates in language production and comprehension, syntactic priming effects within and across the two language modalities were examined and syntactic adaptation effects were compared within and between language modalities. This was achieved by investigating the neuronal substrate of syntactic encoding as well as syntactic decoding processes by means of fMRI. Specifically, it was examined whether comparable syntactic fMRI adaptation effects within one modality and between modalities can be observed (Segaert et al. 2012: 1664).

In their study, twenty-four native speakers of Dutch participated. The participants completed production and comprehension tasks. They were presented photographs as well as auditory sentence descriptions of transitive events, such as *kissing* or *helping*. The experimental design included the following four factors:

1. Syntactic repetition: the syntactic structure of the sentence was either novel or repeated compared to the preceding sentence.
2. Modality repetition: the processing modality (speaking/listening) was either novel or repeated.
3. Target modality: changes in the processing modality (listening vs. speaking).
4. Target structure: both active and passive structures were elicited.

This design allowed for the examination of fMRI adaptation effects both within and across modalities. During task performance, the participants' entire temporal and frontal lobes were scanned, as the fMRI adaptation effects were expected in these regions.

The results of the study lend strong support to the hypothesis that the same neuronal substrate subserves syntactic encoding and decoding processes: It was found that a syntactic adaptation effect occurred in several brain regions (left MTG [middle temporal gyrus], left IFG [inferior frontal gyrus] and supplementary motor area); that is, particular regions in the brain were less activated for sentences with the same underlying syntactic structure than the preceding one. A further observation relates to syntactic adaptation in the different processing modalities investigated in the study. The results indicate that the same amount of syntactic adaptation occurred across processing modalities and within processing modalities. This finding is seen as crucial evidence for the claim that the same neuronal substrate is involved in both production and comprehension (Segaert et al. 2012: 1668).

Segaert et al.'s (2012: 1662) conclusion that syntactic processing in production and comprehension seems to be subserved by the same neurobiological system provides strong support for integrated production-comprehension models, such as the one proposed by Kempen, Olsthoorn and Sprenger (2012). Although Segaert et al. (2012: 1669) state that their findings do not exclude differences between the two modalities grammatical encoding and decoding, such as directional differences, they conclude that 'there is an extensive amount of overlap in syntactic decoding and encoding. There are good arguments and evidence that the workspace for the assembly and short-term storage of syntactic structures is shared between processing modalities.'

To sum up, there is ample evidence for the hypothesis of the existence of a shared workspace in grammatical encoding and decoding. This single-processor architecture is not only a parsimonious solution to the question of how human grammatical coding can be conceptualized; it is also supported by recent research findings in psycholinguistics and neurolinguistics. The single-processor architecture for human grammatical coding forms one theoretical cornerstone of the *Integrated Encoding-Decoding Model in SLA*. A second theoretical cornerstone of the model is a psychologically and typologically plausible theory of SLA, namely PT as well as its extension, the *Multiple Constraints Hypothesis*.

3

The view on second language acquisition: *Processability Theory* and the *Multiple Constraints Hypothesis*

Processability Theory (PT) (see e.g. Pienemann 1998; Pienemann, Di Biase & Kawaguchi 2005; Pienemann & Lenzing 2020) is a psycholinguistic theory of SLA that focuses on the development of L2 processing capacities. Initially, PT addressed the developmental problem (Pienemann 1998), whereas the extended version of PT (Pienemann, Di Biase & Kawaguchi 2005) and recent developments of the theory (Lenzing 2013) also begin to engage with the logical problem (see Pienemann & Lenzing 2020: 164). The developmental problem deals with the question of why L2 learners follow a universal path in the acquisition of specific morpho-syntactic structures, whereas the logical problem addresses the question of what constitutes the origin of linguistic knowledge, or, in other words, 'how learners come to know what they know if their knowledge is not represented in the input' (Pienemann & Lenzing 2020: 164).

It is a well-attested finding from SLA research that L2 learners acquire specific morpho-syntactic structures in a universal sequence regardless of their first language (for early studies, see e.g. Clahsen 1980; Huang & Hatch 1978; Meisel, Clahsen & Pienemann 1981; Pienemann 1981; Ravem 1968; Wode 1976). Ortega (2009: 34) observes that '[t]here is robust evidence that L1 transfer cannot radically alter the route of L2 acquisition' and argues that 'there are developmental solutions for a given area of the grammar that L1 and L2 learners must naturally and universally traverse on their path to final competence in that area. Although the details for how L1 and L2 learners do this may differ, in the most general sense the developmental constraints are undeniable in both L1 and L2 acquisition.'

In PT's explanation for the developmental path in L2 acquisition, recourse is made to 'some of the key psychological aspects of human language processing because describable developmental routes are, at least in part, caused by the architecture of the human language processor' (Pienemann 1998: 4). The theory's point of departure is the concept of learnability. The underlying rationale is that a definition of learnability as a 'purely logico-mathematical problem' is limited in that '[s]uch a perspective ignores the fact that this problem has to be solved, not by an unconstrained computational device, but by a mind that operates within human psychological constraints' (Pienemann 1998: 1). According to PT, the system has to meet two requirements in order for real-time speech production to take place: fast word order retrieval and automatized mechanisms for language production, so that 'acquisition has to be viewed as the process of automatisation of linguistic operations' (Pienemann 1998: 5).

The language processor constrains the structural options that are available to an L2 learner at a given point in time. The ability to produce a linguistic structure depends on the capability of the language processor to process that structure. This means that the necessary processing procedures have to be available to the learner (see Pienemann 1998: 4–9). The processing procedures form part of the core construct in PT, a universal processability hierarchy. This hierarchy consists of the above-mentioned processing procedures, which are hierarchically ordered and implicationally related, so that 'each procedure is a necessary prerequisite for the following procedure' (Pienemann 1998: 6). Developmental patterns in L2 acquisition are claimed to be the result of the hierarchical arrangement of underlying processing procedures. A further hypothesis of the theory is that both L2 development and L2 variation are constrained by processability. In this way, predictions about L2 developmental trajectories can be made (Pienemann & Lenzing 2020: 162).

The perspective on language processing adopted in PT is based on Levelt's (1989) model of speech processing (see Section 1.1). The 'representational correlates' (Pienemann 2015: 127) to the processing requirements spelled out in Levelt (1989, 1999) are defined within *Lexical-Functional Grammar* (LFG) (see e.g. Bresnan 2001), which is incorporated in PT as its grammatical formalism.

3.1 Key psychological factors in language processing

The following four psychological premises are central to PT's perspective on 'the processing environment within which the learning of language takes place' (Pienemann 2005: 3; see also Levelt 1989).

  i. Processing components are relatively autonomous specialists which operate largely automatically;
 ii. Processing is incremental;
iii. The output of the processor is linear, while it may not be mapped onto the underlying meaning in a linear way;
 iv. Grammatical processing has access to a grammatical memory store. (Pienemann 2005: 3–4)

3.1.1 Premise 1

The conceptualization of processing components as autonomous specialists makes it possible to account for the high speed in language processing (see Levelt 1989: 20–1; Section 1.1.1). PT assumes that the execution of automatic processes, in particular grammatical encoding, does not involve intention or conscious awareness.

A characteristic that further increases processing speed is the task-specificity of autonomous specialist processing components.

3.1.2 Premise 2

As outlined in Section 1.1.1, the underlying idea of incremental processing is that conceptualizing, formulating and articulating can run in parallel, as 'the next processor can start working on the still-incomplete output of the current processor' (Levelt 1989: 24). The processing components are activated by fragments of characteristic input, that is, increments of the message to be uttered.

3.1.3 Premise 3

The natural chronology of events is not necessarily reflected in an utterance's surface structure. As pointed out in Section 1.1.2, this relates to the *linearization problem*, that is, the speaker's decision about how to sequence their communicative intention (Levelt 1989: 138). However, as pointed out by Pienemann (2005: 5), the linearization problem is not limited to the ordering of the propositions that are expressed by the speaker but also operates at the morpho-syntactic level. An example of linearization at the level of morpho-syntax is subject-verb agreement, as in example (1):

(1) Peter plays the piano.

In order to achieve subject-verb agreement and to correctly insert the agreement marker, the information concerning the subject's person and number marking needs to be temporarily stored and to be matched with the information about person and number contained in the lexical entry of the verb. Crucially, the storage of grammatical information differs from the storage of propositional content (Pienemann 2005: 5).

3.1.4 Premise 4

Owing to the different nature of their processing, propositional content and grammatical information are assumed to rely on two different types of memory stores. Propositional content is temporarily stored in working memory, which is the locus of 'temporary attentive processes' (Pienemann 2005: 6), and has only a limited capacity. Grammatical information, which is processed automatically, is buffered in a grammatical memory store. This store is highly task-specific, and 'specialised grammatical processors can deposit information of a specific nature' (Pienemann 2005: 6).

3.2 Lexical-Functional Grammar

LFG (see e.g. Bresnan 2001; Dalrymple 2001; for a summary, see Lenzing 2013) constitutes the grammatical framework implemented in PT and in the proposed

Integrated Encoding-Decoding Model of SLA. It is a generative theory of grammar, that is, one of its central aims is to formalize the mental representations underlying linguistic knowledge. The theory was conceptualized in the late 1970s by Kaplan and Bresnan as an alternative approach to the Chomskyan framework that was criticized for its lack of typological and psychological plausibility. In line with this, a major aim in the initial design of LFG was to provide a theory of grammar that is psychologically plausible (Bresnan & Kaplan 1982: xxiii).

In contrast to the Chomskyan framework, LFG constitutes a non-transformational approach to grammar. It is a constraint-based theory of syntax, in that different aspects of linguistic structure are realized by different but related levels of linguistic representation. LFG is also considered to be a unification grammar, its main focus being on the unification of lexical features in the process of sentence generation. A further characteristic of LFG is its lexicalist approach to syntax and the related claim that grammars are lexically driven. The core of the theory is formed by its parallel projection architecture with three independent levels of linguistic representation that exist in parallel and are related to each other by specific linking or mapping principles. The three levels are (1) functional structure (f-structure), (2) constituent structure (c-structure) and (3) argument structure (a-structure). At each of the three levels of representation, different types of linguistic knowledge are encoded. This is seen as being essential for the generation of a potentially infinite number of grammatically well-formed sentences.

3.2.1 Functional structure

The level of f-structure is concerned with the abstract functional organization of language. F-structure encodes universal aspects of grammar. It contains (1) grammatical functions, such as subject or object, and (2) a set of functional features that denote the grammatical properties of a word, for example person, number or tense (Lenzing 2013: 27). According to Bresnan (2001: 94), the grammatical functions in f-structure are 'the "relators" from c-structure to a-structure'. Information encoded at f-structure level is formally represented in terms of attribute-value pairs, as shown in Figure 3.1.

Attributes and values can be of different types: Attributes can consist of symbols, indicating either functional relations or features such as TENSE, NUM (number) or PRED, which represents syntactically relevant semantic aspects of linguistic elements

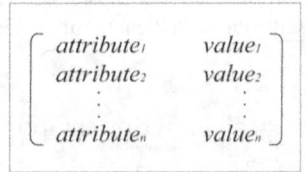

Figure 3.1 Attribute-value pair (from Bresnan 2001: 47, fig. 2). © 2001 Joan Bresnan. Reprinted by permission of John Wiley & Sons.

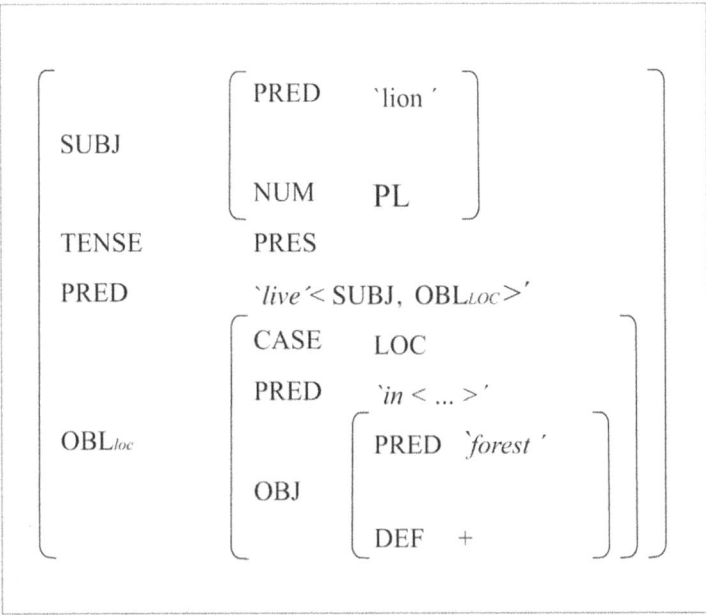

Figure 3.2 F-structure of *Lions live in the forest* (from Lenzing 2013: 29, fig. 2.2.1-6; adapted from Bresnan 2001: 46, fig. 1). Reprinted by permission of John Benjamins.

(see Falk 2001: 13). Values, on the other hand, can realize three different types of information. They can consist of symbols (e.g. PL for plural), semantic forms ('lion') or whole f-structures. The formal representation of f-structure is illustrated in Figure 3.2 based on the example sentence *Lions live in the forest*.

A number of functional well-formedness conditions apply to ensure the grammaticality of the generated sentences. For instance, the *uniqueness condition* specifies that 'every attribute has a unique value' (Bresnan 2001: 47) and thus ensures that each attribute is assigned a unique value.

3.2.2 Constituent structure

The second level representing syntactic aspects of language is c-structure. It is here that the surface syntactic organization of phrases is encoded and the relation between words in phrases and sentences is depicted in terms of phrase structure trees. C-structure is considered to be language-specific. In LFG, a general distinction is made between endocentric and lexocentric languages (Bresnan 2001: 98–112). Endocentric languages, such as English, are characterized by their hierarchical c-structures. Lexocentric languages, on the other hand, exhibit flat c-structures and the grammatical relations are specified by morpho-lexical means, such as case or agreement morphology. A case

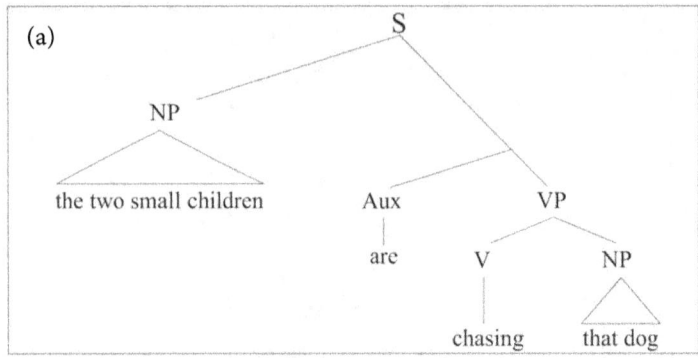

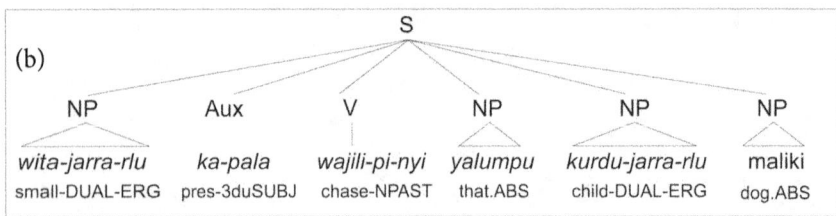

Figure 3.3 (a) endocentric (English) and (b) lexocentric constituent structure (Warlpiri) (from Bresnan 2001: 5–6, figs 1, 3). © 2001 Joan Bresnan. Reprinted by permission of John Wiley & Sons.

in point is Warlpiri, an Australian Indigenous language (for details, see Lenzing 2013: 34–9). The two types of c-structure are illustrated in Figure 3.3 for the sentence *The two small children are chasing that dog*.

In keeping with the lexicalist premises of LFG, the theory claims that the process of word formation does not take place at the syntactic level. This is captured in the c-structure principle of *lexical integrity*, which states that '[m]orphologically complete words are leaves of the c-structure tree and each leaf corresponds to one and only one c-structure node' (Bresnan 2001: 92). This means that the formation of words and the formation of phrases and sentences constitute two different processes. In contrast to transformational theories, c-structure positions can only be filled by morphologically complete words and not by affixes (Bresnan 2001: 92).

3.2.3 Argument structure

A-structure forms the link between lexical semantics and syntactic structure. Bresnan (2001: 304) describes the content of a-structure as follows: 'On the semantic side, argument structure represents the core participants in events (states, processes) designated by a single predicator. [...] On the syntactic side, argument structure represents the minimal information needed to characterize the syntactic dependents of an argument-taking head." A-structure contains the following three types of information (Bresnan 2001: 307):

1. the predicator and its argument roles
2. the hierarchical ordering of the argument roles in terms of their relative prominence
3. the syntactic classification of the argument roles

This is illustrated in examples (2)–(4) that are further explained in this section.[1]

(2) place <x　　　　y　　　　　z >
　　　　　(agent)　　(theme)　　(locative)
　　　　　[–o]　　　 [–r]　　　　[–o]
　　　　　John placed the plate　on the table.

(3) hit　 <x　　　　y>
　　　　　(agent)　　(patient)
　　　　　[–o]　　　 [–r]
　　　　　The girl　 hit　the boy.

(4) freeze <x>
　　　　　(theme)
　　　　　[–r]
　　　　　The lake freezes.

In LFG, the existence of a hierarchy of thematic roles is presumed. This hierarchy structures the thematic roles of the predicator (see Bresnan 2001: 307). It is ordered from left to right reflecting the relative prominence of the thematic roles as shown here (for the notion of a thematic hierarchy, see also Jackendoff 1972).

Thematic hierarchy:
Agent > beneficiary > experiencer/goal > instrument > patient/theme > locative

In examples (2) and (3), the lexical semantics of the (x) argument corresponds to the thematic role of agent, the most prominent role of the two predicators *place* and *hit*. The (y) argument in both sentences is ordered to the right of (x) and takes the thematic role of theme in (2) and patient in (3). The least prominent role of the predicator *place* is the (z) argument, which is a locative in lexical semantics. In example (4), the only argument (x) corresponds to the thematic role of theme (see Bresnan 2001: 307; Lenzing 2016: 5–6).

Although all (x) arguments are the most prominent thematic roles in the predicators' a-structure, there are differences concerning their syntactic properties. These differences are captured at the syntactic side of a-structure. The syntactic side

Table 3.1 Feature decomposition of argument functions.

	−r	+r
−o	subj	obl$_\theta$
+o	obj	obj$_\theta$

of a-structure contains specific syntactic features that constrain the mapping of arguments onto grammatical functions in functional structure. The syntactic classification of arguments is based on the observation that the relation between arguments and grammatical functions is constrained: Certain thematic roles can only be mapped onto a limited set of grammatical functions and certain grammatical functions can only be filled by specific thematic roles. For instance, the roles *patient* and *theme* can only be mapped onto the subject (SUBJ) or object (OBJ) function. On the other hand, the SUBJ function is not restricted as to the types of thematic roles it can take.

The basic argument functions in f-structure, SUBJ, OBJ, oblique (OBL$_\theta$) and secondary object (OBJ$_\theta$) are classified according to the features [±r] (thematically restricted or not) and [±o] (objective or not) (Bresnan 2001: 308) (see Table 3.1). The argument functions that are thematically restricted receive the feature [+r], whereas those that can take any thematic role are classified as [−r]. Thus, the SUBJ and OBJ function are classified as [−r], as they are not restricted in terms of thematic roles. The OBJ$_\theta$ and OBL$_\theta$ functions are classified as [+r], as they can take only certain thematic roles. The features [+o] and [−o] refer to object-like and non-object-like functions. Both OBJ and OBJ$_\theta$ are classified as object-like functions and are therefore [+o]. The SUBJ and the OBL$_\theta$ function are classified as [−o], as they are non-object-like functions (see Bresnan 2001: 308; Dalrymple 2001: 204).

The mapping operations between arguments at a-structure and grammatical functions at f-structure level are formalized in *Lexical Mapping Theory*, which is outlined in Section 5.2.1.

3.2.4 The lexicon

As mentioned in Section 3.2, LFG constitutes a lexicalist approach to syntax. The assumption that grammars are lexically driven implies that the mental lexicon plays a crucial role in the overall architecture of the mental grammar. In line with this, it is hypothesized that the lexicon contains a substantial amount of grammatical information, and 'words, or lexical elements, are as important as syntactic elements in expressing grammatical information' (Bresnan 2001: 14).

The lexical entries provide information about the word's meaning, its form and its syntactic category. This is illustrated in the example entries for the NP *a dog* (see Figure 3.4).

To unify the information encoded at the different levels of representation, LFG proposes two major processes, namely feature unification and mapping operations. Feature unification relates to the transfer of grammatical information at the level of

a, D	DEFINITE = -
	NUMBER = SG
	PERSON = 3
dog, N	PRED = 'dog'
	NUMBER = SG
	PERSON = 3

Figure 3.4 Lexical entries.

constituent structure. The transfer of both grammatical and semantic information between argument and functional structure and between constituent and functional structure is guided by specific mapping principles.

3.2.5 Feature unification and mapping principles

The unification of features at the level of constituent structure is exemplified with the NP *a dog*. In the process of generating the NP, the diacritic features of the determiner *a* and the noun *dog* have to be matched. The lexical entries are annotated for the respective diacritic features. As shown in Figure 3.5, the lexical entries for *a* and for *dog* are annotated for number and person, and the respective value is 'singular' and '3rd person' in both cases. In order to generate a grammatical sentence, this grammatical information has to be matched within the phrase.

Feature unification constitutes one of the core processes in LFG. According to Falk (2001: 17), the merit of feature unification is that

> [i]t allows us to represent together features that belong to a single conceptual part of the syntactic structure of the sentence even if the features come from several places in the actual syntactic structure.

The concept of feature unification is one main reason why LFG was adopted as the grammatical formalism in PT (see Pienemann 1998: 97).

The second key mechanism in LFG to linearize the grammatical information at the different levels of representation consists of specific mapping principles that unify the semantic and syntactic information encoded in a-, f- and c-structure. The 'linking' (mapping) principles relate (1) arguments (agents, patients, etc.) at a-structure level to grammatical functions (subjects, objects, etc.) in f-structure and (2) constituents (e.g. NPs) in c-structure to grammatical functions. A simplified account of the mapping processes aligning the different levels of representation is given in Figure 3.6.

When generating the sentence *John likes ice cream*, the agent argument at a-structure level is mapped onto the subject function in f-structure. In addition, the sentence-initial NP in c-structure (*John*) is also mapped onto the subject. In this process, the syntactic features at a-structure level are unified with the syntactic specifications of the grammatical functions (see also Section 5.2.1). In the example

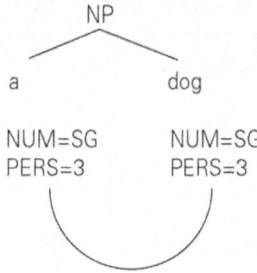

Figure 3.5 Feature unification.

A-structure	like <agent		patient/theme>	semantic side
	[-o/-r]		[-r]	syntactic side
	⇩		⇩	
	[-o/-r]		[-r]	
F-structure	SUBJ		OBJ	
	⇧		⇧	
C-structure	John	likes	ice cream	

Figure 3.6 A simplified account of mapping in LFG.

sentence *John likes ice cream* the mapping process is linear, as there is a one-to-one correspondence between arguments, grammatical functions and constituents (see Pienemann, Di Biase & Kawaguchi 2005: 224). However, the relationship between the three levels of representation is not necessarily linear, and it is this non-linearity that constitutes a challenge for L2 learners. This will be further explained in Section 3.5.

LFG's mathematically well-defined formalism accounts for its psychological and typological plausibility. As stated in Section 3.2, one of the key aims in the initial conceptualization of LFG was to develop a psychologically plausible theory of grammar 'that would not only account for observed patterns of linguistic behaviour but would also provide insight into the mental representation of language' (Dalrymple 2001: 430). Falk (2001: 8) observes that a non-derivational design of grammar has a major impact on its psychological plausibility. He argues that '[n]onderivational theories are more plausible as psychological and computational models of human language than derivational theories. Transformational theories are, by the nature of what a transformation is, nonlocal theories of syntax. However, human language processing is local.'

LFG meets a number of psycholinguistic constraints in language processing, such as creativity, finite capacity and universality (for further details, see Dalrymple 2001: 430; Kaplan & Bresnan 1982: xxxix–xlviii). The theory has further been successfully incorporated as grammatical formalism in work on child language acquisition (Pinker 1982, 1984, 1989) and second language acquisition (e.g. Lenzing 2013; Pienemann 1998; Pienemann, Di Biase & Kawaguchi 2005). The parallel architecture of LFG enables the theory to account for configurational as well as non-configurational languages, and the grammatical framework has been applied in a number of studies on a wide range of typologically diverse languages (see Lenzing 2013: 54).

To sum up, LFG is considered to be a psychologically and typologically plausible theory of grammar, which is characterized by its mathematically well-defined formalism. LFG constitutes a nonderivational approach to syntax. A related claim is that grammars are lexically driven. The theory's architecture consists of three parallel levels of linguistic representation that are related to each other by functional constraints, formalized in terms of feature unification and mapping principles. Its psychological and typological plausibility was a main reason for the incorporation of LFG as grammatical formalism in PT.

3.3 The processability hierarchy

This section engages with the core of PT – the processability hierarchy. The processability hierarchy is based on the concept of incremental language processing by Levelt (1989) and Kempen and Hoenkamp (1987). To recall, Levelt proposes a number of processing procedures that are activated in a particular sequence in the process of sentence generation (see the section 'Positional processing' in Chapter 1).

A crucial insight in this context is that the process of incremental language generation proposed by Levelt only applies to mature speakers and that the situation is different for second language learners. Pienemann (1998: 73) argues that '[w]hile even beginning second language learners can make recourse to the same *general* cognitive resources as mature native language users, they have to create language-specific processing procedures' (italics in original). The development of these processing routines is assumed to take place within the overall architecture of the human language processor. It is important to note at this point that, in principle, Levelt's model of language generation can also account for L2 processing. This has been demonstrated by De Bot (1992), who adapted the model to bilingual processing and hypothesized the existence of separate formulators for each language (De Bot 1992: 14). PT adopts the notion of language-specific processing components and Pienemann (1998: 74) proposes the following language-specific processing devices that L2 learners have to acquire in the course of SLA:

1. word order rules
2. syntactic procedures and their specific stores

3. diacritic features in the lexicon
4. the lexical category of lemmata
5. functorization rules

Pienemann (2005: 11) states that 'word order rules are language-specific and there is no *a priori* way of knowing for the language learner how closely related L1 and L2 are' (italics in original). The same applies to the diacritic features in the mental lexicon. Features such as number, gender, tense and case are clearly language-specific. In this context, I have argued in Lenzing (2013: 82) that, initially, the L2 lexicon is not fully annotated, which applies to both the lexical items' syntactic category and their respective diacritic features. The syntactic procedures responsible for phrase structure building and the temporary storage of grammatical information are also conceptualized as being language-specific. Pienemann (2005: 11) maintains that '[g]iven that diacritic features are language-specific and that these are stored in syntactic procedures, L1 procedures are not equipped to handle the specific storage task required by the L2'. Both the lexical category of lemmata and functorization rules are considered to be language-specific and therefore also form part of the L2 learning task.

The core idea of the processability hierarchy is that the language-specific processing resources have to be acquired by the learner in order to be able to generate sentences in the L2. Pienemann (2005: 13) claims that

> [t]hese processing resources are interrelated in two ways. (1) They feed into each other in the temporal event of language generation, i.e. one is utilised before the other. (2) The information processed and generated in one is required in the other. In this way these resources form a hierarchy. If one building block of the hierarchy is missing, the top cannot be reached.

The processing procedures that form the PT hierarchy are the ones that are activated successively in the process of incremental language generation:

 i. the lemma,
 ii. the category procedure (lexical category of the lemma),
 iii. the phrasal procedure (instigated by the category of the head),
 iv. the S-procedure and the target language word order rules,
 v. the subordinate clause procedure – if applicable. (Pienemann 2005: 9)

Pienemann hypothesizes that, in L2 acquisition, the processing procedures are acquired in the same sequence in which they are activated in the speech production process. The procedures are hierarchically ordered and implicationally related, so that each lower procedure is a prerequisite for the acquisition of the next higher one.

The hierarchy of processing procedures is shown in Table 3.2. The labels t_1–t_5 refer to different time points in the development of an L2 learner's interlanguage.

Table 3.2 Hypothetical hierarchy of processing procedures (adapted from Pienemann 1998: 79).

	t_1	t_2	t_3	t_4	t_5
S'-procedure (Embedded S)	–	–	–	–	–
S'-procedure	–	simplified	simplified	interphrasal information exchange	interphrasal information exchange
Phrasal procedure (head)	–	–	phrasal information exchange	phrasal information exchange	phrasal information exchange
Category procedure (lex. categ.)	–	lexical morphemes	lexical morphemes	lexical morphemes	lexical morphemes
Word/lemma	+	+	+	+	+

The PT hierarchy postulates five distinct stages in the development of the L2 processor. At the first stage, no language-specific processing procedures are present and the L2 learners' mental lexicon is not annotated for any language-specific syntactic information. It is for this reason that no syntactic building procedures can be activated. Also, no transfer of grammatical information can take place at this stage of acquisition. In terms of processing, learners can map conceptual structures onto single words and formulae. The second stage is characterized by the annotation of the L2 lexical items for their syntactic category. This enables the call of the category procedure and leads to the activation of lexical morphemes. At this stage of development, however, no exchange of grammatical information within or across constituents can take place (see Pienemann 1998: 83–4). At stage 3, the activation of the phrasal procedure allows for 'the storage and unification of diacritic features, e.g. between the head and its modifier' (Lenzing 2013: 83). This forms the prerequisite for the production of phrasal morphemes. The acquisition of both S-procedure and appointment rules at stage 4 enables the L2 learner to build sentences. This includes the transfer of grammatical information at the sentence level and the production of interphrasal morphemes. Pienemann (1998: 84) hypothesizes that '[o]nce the Appointment Rules are present and the S-procedures are complete interphrasal morphemes can be produced and word order can be structured syntactically according to L2 constraints'. In a final step, the subordinate procedure is acquired at stage 5. This leads to the learner's ability to distinguish between main and subordinate clauses (see Pienemann 1998: 85–6).

3.4 Applying the processability hierarchy to L2 English

The proposed development of the processing procedures and the resulting PT hierarchy is claimed to be valid cross-linguistically. In this section, it will be applied to the syntactic and morphological development of L2 English (see Pienemann 1998: 171–2). English contains an additional procedure, namely the verb phrase procedure located at stage 4. This results in six stages of development that will be further explained in this section. The developmental schedule of English as an L2 is given in Table 3.3.

In the acquisition of morphology, PT distinguishes between three different types of morphemes: (1) lexical morphemes, (2) phrasal morphemes and (3) interphrasal morphemes (see Pienemann 1998: 8). This is illustrated in Figure 3.7.

Lexical morphemes, such as the '-ed' in *talk**ed***, are assumed to be acquired at stage 2. The lemma contains the information about the item's syntactic category (verb), which leads to the activation of the category procedure, as well as the relevant diacritic features, in this case the feature 'past'. The diacritic feature is present in one constituent only, which means that no feature unification occurs at this stage of development.

The case is different for phrasal morphemes (e.g. the 'plural -s' as in the NP *two kids*). Here, grammatical information has to be exchanged within the phrase. Applied to the example noun phrase *two kids*, this means that the feature 'plural' present in the lexical entries of the DET *two* and the N *kids* has to be unified (see Pienemann 1998: 171). This operation requires the phrasal procedure to be in place. In keeping with this, phrasal morphemes occur at stage 3.

Finally, the production of interphrasal morphemes requires the exchange of grammatical information across constituent boundaries. This applies, for instance,

Table 3.3 Processability hierarchy for English (adapted from Lenzing 2013: 85; Pienemann 2005: 24).

Processing procedures	Information exchange	Morphology	Syntax
6. subordinate clause procedure	main and subordinate clause		Cancel inversion I wonder what he wants.
5. S-procedure	interphrasal information exchange	inter-phrasal morph. SV-agreement *The mouse* plays volleyball	Neg/Aux-2nd-? Why doesn't he go home? Aux-2nd What do you collect?
4. VP-procedure	interphrasal information exchange	phrasal morphemes Tense agreement *has* seen	Wh-copula S (x) What is your number? Copula S(x) Are there boots?
3. phrasal procedure	phrasal information exchange	phrasal morphemes Det + N agreement *two ears*	Adverb-First Today he stay here. Wh-SV(O)-? What you like? Do-SV(O)-? Do you have a sun?
2. category procedure	no information exchange	lexical morphemes Plural -s (*pets*) Past -ed (*play**ed***)	Canonical word order SVO The mouse play volleyball.
1. word/lemma access	no information exchange	invariant forms	formulae

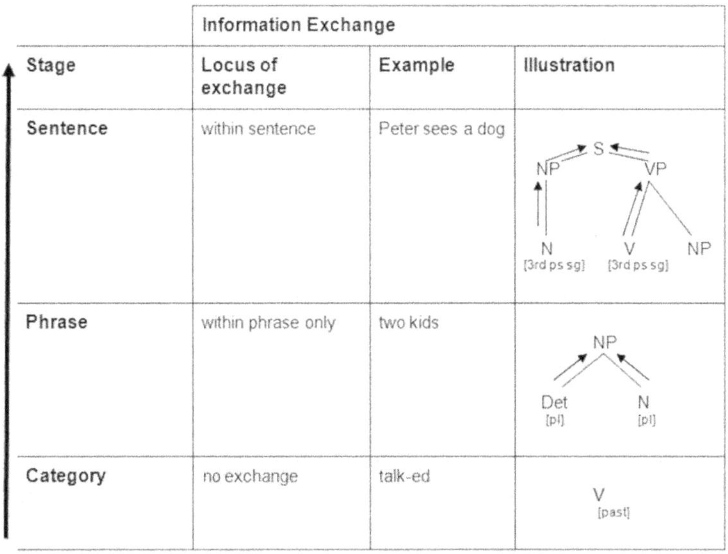

Stage	Information Exchange		
	Locus of exchange	Example	Illustration
Sentence	within sentence	Peter sees a dog	S → NP VP; N [3rd ps sg], V [3rd ps sg], NP
Phrase	within phrase only	two kids	NP → Det [pl] N [pl]
Category	no exchange	talk-ed	V [past]

Figure 3.7 Information exchange (from Pienemann & Lenzing 2020: 166, fig. 8.1). © 2020 Taylor & Francis. Reproduced with permission of the Licensor through PLSclear.

to subject-verb agreement (e.g. the insertion of the '3sg -s' in the sentence ***Peter sees a dog***). In this case, the features for person (3rd) and number (singular) have to be unified between the subject and the verb. This unification process across constituents requires the acquisition of the S-procedure. Therefore, subject-verb agreement marking ('3sg -s') is predicted to occur at stage 5.[2] According to Pienemann (2005: 25), 'the observed sequence of acquisition (lexical before phrasal before inter-phrasal morphemes) is predicted by the processability of the morphological structures under investigation'.

Within the PT framework, the development of syntax can be accounted for in terms of LFG and its core process of feature unification. The syntactic structures that L2 learners are able to produce at the different stages of L2 acquisition can be captured by language-specific word order rules and underlying feature unification processes. L2 learners of English start out with canonical SVO word order. According to Pienemann (1998: 172), canonical SVO word order can be derived directly from c-structure rules:

(R1) S → NP_{subj} V (NP_{obj}) (ADJ) (S)

Canonical word order does not require an exchange of grammatical information and does not involve any feature unification processes. At this stage of acquisition, L2 learners cannot make recourse to the full S-procedure. Instead, they rely on a simplified version, which means that constituents are not processed as phrases. This simplified version is based on the direct mapping of conceptual structures onto linguistic form:

agent   action   patient
N   V   N

Therefore, this syntactic structure is predicted to occur at stage 2 of the PT hierarchy (Pienemann 1998: 173).

In the course of L2 acquisition, the word order rules are modified and annotated in specific ways to allow words of a particular category to be placed in a specific position in the sentence. The occurrence of Wh-words and adverbs in sentence-initial position is accomplished by (R2):

(R2) S' → (XP)   S
$$\begin{Bmatrix} wh =_c + \\ adv =_c + \end{Bmatrix}$$

This modification of (R1) (XP-adjunction) specifies that only adverbs and Wh-words can occur in focused position. The combination of the two rules (R1) and (R2) enables the learner to produce sentences as in Figure 3.8.

A further modification of (R1) allows for the production of 'Do-SV(O)-?' structures:

(R3) S → ($V_{aux=c\ 'do'}$) NP_{subj} V (NP_{obj}) (ADJ) (S)

In terms of LFG, the constraint equation[3] aux = $_c$ 'do' specifies that the initial V position can only be filled by the auxiliary *do*. This enables the learner to produce Do-SVO-? question forms (e.g. *Do you play volleyball?*).[4] The types of structures generated by rules (R2) and (R3) occur at stage 3 (phrasal procedure), as the specific positions in the sentence have to be processed as phrases (see Pienemann 1998: 174).

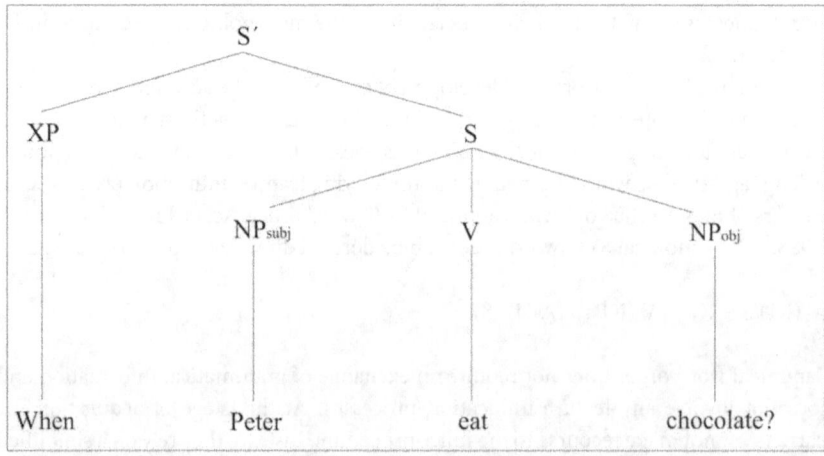

Figure 3.8 XP-adjunction (from Lenzing 2013: 86, fig. 4.4-1). Reprinted by permission of John Benjamins.

In a next step (stage 4), the constraint equation aux =$_c$ 'do' is generalized to aux =$_c$ +, which allows for all auxiliaries to appear in the initial V position. Pienemann (2005: 27) argues that '[t]his form of the rule then describes the *positional* facts of yes/no inversion, while the morphological forms of AUX and V are untouched'.[5]

A further feature that learners are, in principle, able to process at stage 4 is tense agreement. In order to achieve this type of agreement, the learners' lexical entries have to be annotated for specific values, which have to be unified between the lexical verb and the auxiliary (see Pienemann 1998: 174–5, 2005: 27–8). This is illustrated with the example entries in example (5) (adapted from Pienemann 1998: 174):

(5)
seen: V,   PRED = 'see' (SUBJ, OBJ)
              PARTICIPLE = PAST
              INF = +
              AUX = –

has: V,   PRED = 'have, V-COMP (SUBJ)'
              TENSE = PRES
              ASPECT = PERF
              AUX = +
              NUM = SG
              PERSON = 3rd
              V-COMP PARTICIPLE =$_c$ PAST
              V-COMP INF =$_c$ +

In order for learners to produce the sentence *He has seen him*, the lexical entry for the lexical verb has to be annotated for INF = + and PARTICIPLE = PAST, and the entry for the auxiliary has to be annotated for the constraint equations V-COMP PARTICIPLE =$_c$ PAST and V-COMP INF =$_c$ +. These features have to be unified between the lexical verb and the auxiliary. This type of unification requires the verb procedure to be in place and is therefore located at stage 4. Pienemann (1998: 175) argues that the INF value ensures that 'the complement does not define any tense'. This constraint equation rules out the generation of sentences with tensed verb forms, such as examples (6)–(7) (taken from Pienemann 1998: 175):

(6) He has sees him.
(7) He has see him.

However, as pointed out by Pienemann (1998: 175) and as will be shown in Sections 7.2.2 and 7.3.3, these kinds of forms are produced by L2 learners. The production of these forms can be due to two reasons. One reason could be that the learner has not reached the respective stage of acquisition to be able to achieve agreement between the auxiliary and the lexical verb (i.e. stage 4). A second potential reason is the lexical nature of the learning process: As the lexicon is annotated gradually, not all lexical entries are necessarily annotated for the past participle at the same point in time. As further discussed in Section 5.2.2, I argue that, at stage 4, learners are, in principle, able to perform the agreement operation. However, owing to the gradual annotation of the L2 lexicon, this type of agreement constitutes a gradual process.

In passive sentences, the same kind of feature unification process as described in this section takes place, that is, the lexical entry of the lexical verb has to be annotated for INF = + and PARTICIPLE = + and the auxiliary has to be annotated for the respective constraint equations. I claim that this process is also acquired by learners at stage 4. Owing to the lexical nature of the acquisition task, the agreement between the auxiliary and the lexical verb is also acquired in a gradual fashion. This is exemplified in examples (8)–(10) with examples of passive structures produced by stage 4 learners in the study presented in Chapters 6 and 7. As can be seen in examples (8)–(10), L2 learners at stage 4 produce both target-like forms (as in example (10)) and non-target-like forms (as in examples (8) & (9)) of the English passive. This can be explained by the incomplete annotation of their L2 mental lexicon.

(8) The green fish was eating from the purple fish. (learner SM09)
(9) The man was pushes from the woman. (learner P04)
(10) The girl is kissed by the woman. (learner G09)

'Aux - 2nd' question forms (e.g. *What do you collect?*) are located at stage 5, as they require a modification of (R2) and (R3):

(R4) S' → (XP) S
$$\left\{ \begin{array}{l} wh =_c + \\ adv =_c + \\ Sent\ Mood =_c Inv \end{array} \right\}$$

Rule (R3) is extended as follows:

(R5) S' → (V) S
$$\left\{ \begin{array}{l} aux =_c + \\ Root =_c + \\ Sent\ Mood =_c Inv \end{array} \right\}$$

The constraint equations in (R5) ensure that (1) only auxiliaries occur in the initial V position (aux =$_c$ +), (2) the sentence mood is inversion (Sent Mood =$_c$ Inv) and (3) inversion occurs only in matrix sentences (Root =$_c$ +). In addition, the constraint equations in (R4) specify that, when both rules are combined, auxiliaries only occur in initial V position when Wh-words or adverbs appear in XP-position (wh =$_c$ +, adv =$_c$ +) (see Pienemann 1998: 175). The interplay between the two rules is illustrated in Figure 3.9.

The type of structure shown in Figure 3.9 is predicted to occur at stage 5 of acquisition, as it requires the unification of features across constituent boundaries, that is, at the sentence level. The grammatical information contained in the equation

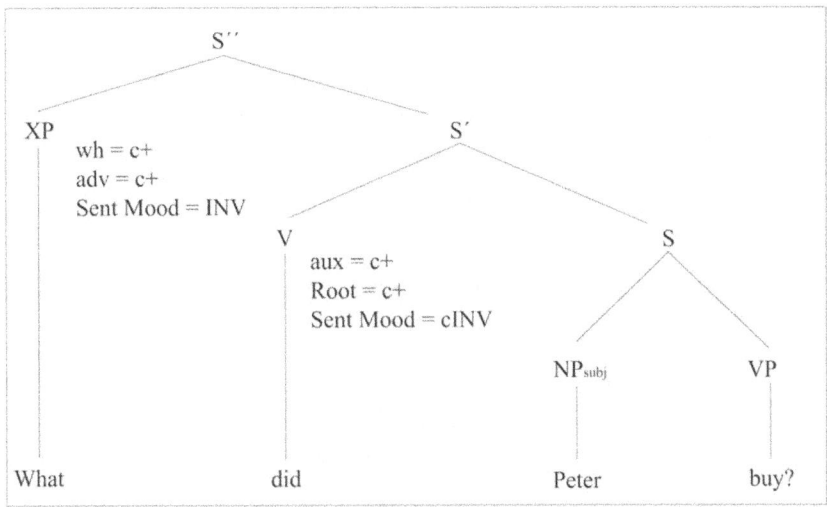

Figure 3.9 'Aux-2nd'-structure (from Lenzing 2013: 88, fig. 4.4-2). Reprinted by permission of John Benjamins.

'Sent Mood = Inv', which is appended to the XP in (R4), has to be unified with that of the constraint equation 'Sent Mood = $_c$Inv' appended to V in rule (R5). This process of interphrasal information exchange requires the S-procedure (see Pienemann 1998: 175).

Finally, rule (R6) generates 'Cancel inversion' structures that are located at stage 6:

(R6) S → (COMP)$_{Root = -}$ NP$_{subj}$ (V)$_{INF = +}$ (V)$_{INF = -}$ (NP$_{obj1}$) (NP$_{obj2}$) (ADJ)

In this linear c-structure assumed for the generation of Cancel inversion structures, the annotation (Root = −) is appended to the complementizer, which allows for the distinction of subordinate clauses from matrix clauses, as in *I asked if he could come home* (example taken from Pienemann 1998: 176). Similar to the acquisition of tense agreement, the acquisition of Cancel inversion is assumed to be a gradual process due to the lexical nature of the acquisition process (Pienemann 1998: 176).

In Table 3.4, the processability hierarchy is applied to L2 English, including a number of revised labels for the different phenomena. The PT hierarchy has been applied to and empirically tested on English as an L2 as well as on a number of typologically different second languages (see Lenzing 2013: 90–1).

To sum up, the universal hierarchy of processability can be applied to L2 English as well as to typologically different languages by formalizing the processing requirements for morpho-syntactic structures in LFG. In this way, the theory can account for the acquisition of specific morpho-syntactic structures and predict L2 developmental trajectories.

Table 3.4 Revised labels and corresponding structural phenomena (from Pienemann, n.d.).

Stage	Phenomena	Examples
6	Cancel Aux-2nd	I wonder *what* he wants.
5	Neg/Aux-2nd-?	Why *didn't* you tell me? Why *can't* she come?
	Aux-2nd-?	Why *did* she eat that? What *will* you do?
	3sg -s	Peter like*s* bananas.
4	Copula S (x)	*Is* she at home?
	Wh-copula S (x)	*Where* is she?
	V-particle	Turn it *off*!
3	Do-SV(O)-?	*Do* he live here?
	Aux SV(O)-?	*Can* I go home?
	Wh-SV(O)-?	*Where* she went? *What* you want?
	Adverb-First	*Today* he stay here.
	Poss (Pronoun)	I show you *my* garden. This is *your* pencil.
	Object (Pronoun)	Mary called *him*.
2	S neg V(O)	*Me no* live here./I don't live here.
	SVO	Me live here.
	SVO-Question	You live here?
	-ed	John play*ed*.
	-ing	Jane go*ing*.
	Plural -s (Noun)	I like cat*s*.
	Poss -s (Noun)	Pat*'s* cat is fat.
1	Words	Hello, Five Dock, Central
	Formulae	How are you? Where is X? What's your name?

3.5 Mapping processes

The focus of PT is not limited to constituent structure and the exchange of grammatical information using feature unification to account for the acquisition of specific morpho-syntactic structures. In an extended version of PT (Pienemann, Di Biase & Kawaguchi 2005), further LFG principles were incorporated to account for the linguistic non-linearity of a range of linguistic phenomena, such as the passive.

The linearization problem does not only apply to propositional content and to grammatical information at the level of c-structure. It is also relevant to the linking of the information encoded in a-, f- and c-structure. Pienemann, Di Biase and Kawaguchi (2005: 201) maintain that the relationship between these three levels is not necessarily linear, as there is considerable surface structure variation, such as active and passive forms, or affirmative sentences and questions. This is accounted for by different mapping principles between the different levels of linguistic representation outlined in Section 3.2.5.

A core hypothesis of PT is that at the beginning of the SLA process, the relationship between the three levels of representation (a-, f- and c-structure) is linear (see Figure 3.10). The linear mapping between the different levels of representation results in *Unmarked Alignment*, which is assumed to be the initial state of L2 development (see Pienemann, Di Biase & Kawaguchi 2005: 145; Pienemann & Lenzing 2020: 172). At this stage of

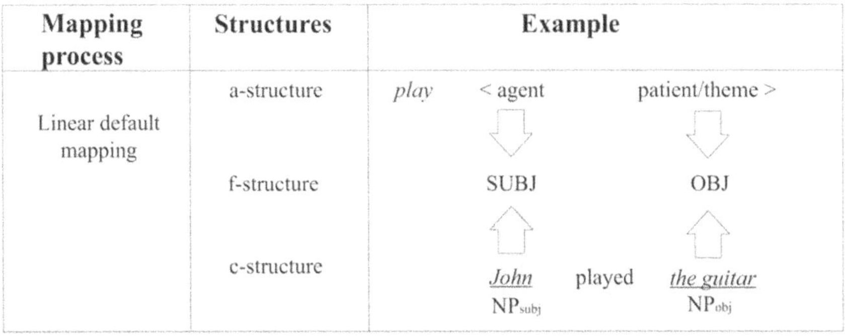

Mapping process	Structures	Example		
Linear default mapping	a-structure	*play*	< agent ⇓	patient/theme > ⇓
	f-structure		SUBJ ⇑	OBJ ⇑
	c-structure		<u>John</u> NP$_{subj}$ played	<u>the guitar</u> NP$_{obj}$

Figure 3.10 Linear mapping (from Lenzing 2013: 94, fig. 4.6.1-1). Reprinted by permission of John Benjamins.

development, the S-procedure is simplified, which constrains the structural options L2 learners have to a N(oun)-V(erb)-N(oun) word order where the agent is mapped onto the subject (first N) and the patient/theme argument onto the object function (second N). Clearly, there are other structural options to express an intended message, such as passive constructions or the topicalization of objects. However, these non-canonical structures lead to changes in the relation between arguments, grammatical functions and constituents, and involve different kinds of non-linear mapping processes between the different levels of representation. L2 learners have to acquire additional processing resources in order to be able to produce these forms. In line with this, in PT the acquisition process is seen as 'the cumulative adaptation of the interlanguage to the specific linking principles of the L2' (Pienemann, Di Biase & Kawaguchi 2005: 232; see also Lenzing 2013: 95).

A structure that constitutes a deviation from the linear default mapping between arguments and grammatical functions is the passive (see Figure 3.11). According to an LFG-based analysis, the non-linearity in passive constructions applies to the relation between a-structure and f-structure. The agent in a-structure is no longer mapped onto the subject in f-structure. Instead, it is the patient/theme argument that is mapped onto the subject function and that is realized as the initial noun phrase in the sentence. The agent is mapped onto the grammatical function oblique and is expressed as a prepositional phrase at the level of c-structure. In terms of processing, the non-linear mapping between a-structure and f-structure is more complex than processing canonical sentences with default linear mapping operations (see Pienemann, Di Biase & Kawaguchi 2005: 245).

Other structures that exhibit a non-linear relation between arguments and grammatical functions are exceptional verbs, such as *receive*, and complex predicates, for instance causative constructions (for details, see Pienemann, Di Biase & Kawaguchi 2005: 244–5). The increasingly complex relationship between arguments and grammatical functions is accounted for in the *Lexical Mapping Hypothesis*. This hypothesis is based on LFG principles specifying the detailed mapping operations between a-structure and f-structure captured in *Lexical Mapping Theory* (see Section 5.2.1) and makes predictions concerning the processability and the acquisition of structures involving non-linear a- to f-structure mapping, such as the passive. The

a- to f-structure mapping	Structures	Example
Non-default mapping. (single clause) passive	a-structure	play <agent patient/theme>
	f-structure	SUBJ OBL_ag
	c-structure	The guitar was played by John.

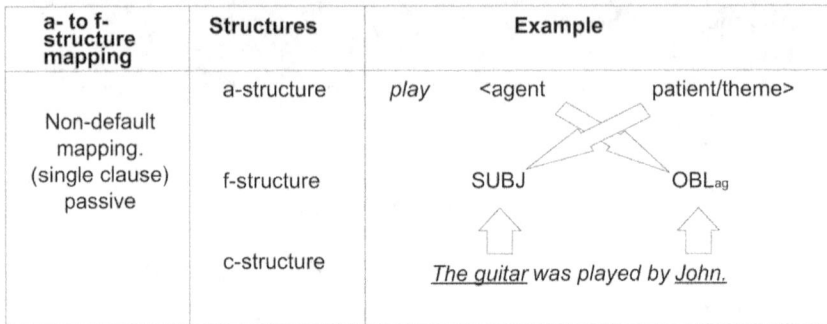

Figure 3.11 Non-linear mapping in passive constructions (from Lenzing 2013: 103, fig. 4.6.3-1). Reprinted by permission of John Benjamins.

Table 3.5 *Lexical Mapping Hypothesis* (from Pienemann, Di Biase & Kawaguchi 2005: 240).

a- to f-structure mapping	Structural outcomes
Non-default, complex mapping	Complex predicates, e.g. causative (in Romance languages, Japanese, etc.), raising, light verbs
↑	↑
Non-default mapping (single clause)	Passive Exceptional verbs
↑	↑
Default mapping, i.e. Most prominent role is mapped onto subject	Canonical order

predictions are summarized in Table 3.5 (for further details, see Pienemann, Di Biase & Kawaguchi 2005: 244; Lenzing 2013: 102–6).

The incorporation of LFG's mapping principles that relate the three levels of linguistic representation – a-structure, f-structure and c-structure – in PT widens the scope of the theory: In this way, the theory can account for L2 developmental trajectories of discourse-pragmatic structures such as the passive (for details on the mapping processes between f- and c-structure, see Pienemann, Di Biase & Kawaguchi 2005).

PT not only engages with the developmental dimension of L2 acquisition but also addresses the issue of individual learner variation. Pienemann (2015: 130) comments on the relation between L2 development and L2 variation as follows:

> [T]he processability hierarchy determines universal levels of processability for specified morphological and syntactic features, which serve to predict developmental trajectories of L2s through a shared set of common stages for these features. At the same time, many other linguistic features of the interlanguage are available at many different developmental stages and take up an orderly position within a nondevelopmental (variational) dimension, quite similar to linguistic variation in fully developed languages.

The variational dimension of PT is formally modelled in the notion of *Hypothesis Space* (for details, see Pienemann 1998: 231–4). PT explains both L2 learners' developmental trajectories for specific morpho-syntactic structures and L2 learners' interlanguage variation in terms of the architecture of the human language processor. However, this perspective on L2 acquisition does not imply that L2 development is fully predetermined. Instead, it is based on minimal assumptions concerning the L2 initial state: 'PT makes minimal assumptions about innate linguistic structures. Rather than assuming sets of universal principles, it assumes only that the basic notion of constituency and the one-to-one mapping of semantic roles (such as agent, patient, etc.) is a given, and all other formal aspects of grammar follow from this' (Pienemann 2015: 134). This view on innate prerequisites for language acquisition clearly challenges strong nativist premises, as, for instance, adopted in Chomsky's *Universal Grammar* (UG). The question of what kind of linguistic resources are present in the L2 initial state is addressed by the *Multiple Constraints Hypothesis* (Lenzing 2013), a conceptual extension of PT that engages with the L2 learner's initial mental grammatical system and its development.

3.6 The initial L2 mental grammatical system: The *Multiple Constraints Hypothesis*

The *Multiple Constraints Hypothesis* uses LFG as grammatical formalism to model the mental grammatical system of learners at the beginning of the L2 acquisition process. It proposes a number of testable hypotheses concerning the constraints of the L2 initial mental grammatical system. The core premise of the *Multiple Constraints Hypothesis* is that, at the beginning of the L2 acquisition process, the L2 mental grammatical system is not fully developed. In line with this, I assume in the *Multiple Constraints Hypothesis* that the mental grammatical system is initially restricted and that these restrictions affect both syntactic and semantic representations. This means that beginning L2 learners can only draw on a restricted set of linguistic resources. The constraints postulated by the *Multiple Constraints Hypothesis* are formalized in LFG and apply to the different levels of linguistic representation (a-structure, f-structure and c-structure). The *Multiple Constraints Hypothesis* is summarized in Figure 3.12.

In what follows, the constraints at the different levels of linguistic representation are briefly summarized.

1. Argument structure
The *Multiple Constraints Hypothesis* proposes that the initial restrictions at a-structure level affect both its semantic and its syntactic side. The constraints on the semantic side of a-structure restrict the types of argument roles that are present in the L2 learner's lexical entries. As far as the syntactic side is concerned, I assume that it is initially not fully annotated for its syntactic features. However, in LFG, these syntactic features are a crucial prerequisite for the mapping operations relating arguments at a-structure to grammatical functions at f-structure level. Missing syntactic features on the syntactic side of a-structure result in the L2 learner's inability to map arguments onto grammatical functions. What follows from this is that L2 learners in the initial state have to rely on direct mapping operations from arguments to surface form (see Lenzing 2013: 8).

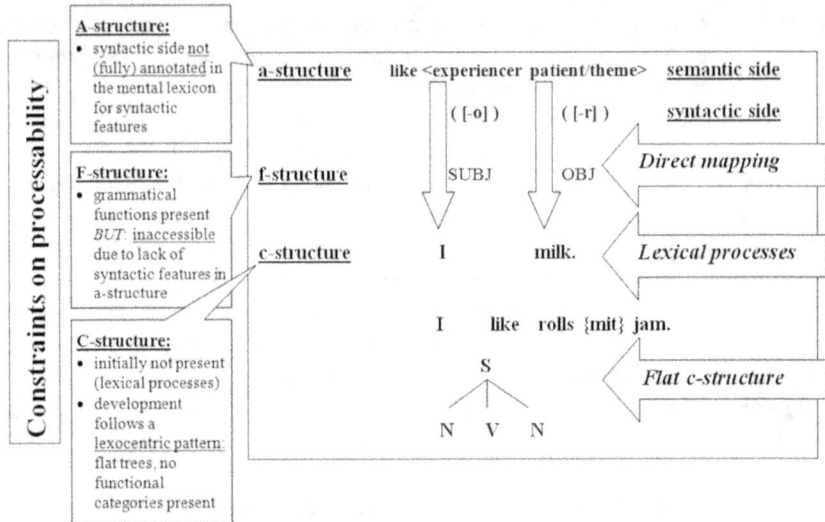

Figure 3.12 The *Multiple Constraints Hypothesis* (from Lenzing 2013: 8, fig. 1.3-1). Reprinted by permission of John Benjamins.

2. Functional structure
In LFG, grammatical functions are regarded as primitives (see Dalrymple 2001: 39). The *Multiple Constraints Hypothesis* adopts this perspective and hypothesizes that the universal grammatical functions encoded at f-structure level are present in the L2 learner's mental grammar in the L2 initial state. However, the functions are initially not accessible due to the lack of syntactic features in a-structure. This means that '[i]t is the successive annotation of a-structure for syntactic features in the course of L2 development that makes the grammatical functions accessible' (Lenzing 2019: 17).

3. Constituent structure
In the *Multiple Constraints Hypothesis*, I propose that c-structure is not present in the initial L2 mental grammatical system (see Lenzing 2013: 9). I claim that the utterances of beginning L2 learners are not generated by c-structure processes but instead are based on lexical processes. The claim that c-structure emerges gradually is in line with the predictions of PT. I argue that the emergence of c-structure develops stepwise from a simplified c-structure following a lexocentric pattern to a more hierarchical endocentric structure (Lenzing 2013: 9).

4. The lexicon
The lexicon is assumed to be gradually annotated (e.g. for the lexical item's syntactic category, such as noun or verb). This hypothesis implies that, initially, not all verbs are annotated for the type and number of arguments they take (Lenzing 2013: 9).

As outlined in Section 3.2.5, the two core processes that relate the semantic and syntactic information present at the different levels of linguistic representation in

LFG are feature unification and mapping operations. In the *Multiple Constraints Hypothesis*, I argue that these processes cannot operate in the L2 initial state, as essential features are missing. I propose that, instead, the constraints on the L2 mental grammatical system result in lexical processes and direct mapping operations from a-structure onto surface form, bypassing f-structure (Lenzing 2013: 155). I further hypothesize that the development of the L2 mental grammatical system proceeds in line with the predictions of PT. In Lenzing (2013), I demonstrate that the initial constraints outlined in this section are relaxed successively in the course of L2 development such that learners have more and more linguistic resources available as learning progresses.

The *Multiple Constraints Hypothesis* was tested on oral speech production data (Lenzing 2013). I argue that the constraints spelled out in the *Multiple Constraints Hypothesis* also apply to L2 comprehension, as L2 learners draw on the same mental grammar in both modalities. The assumption that L2 learners access the same mental representations in production and in comprehension is in line with the view of most theorists of lexico-syntactic parity in both modalities (see Gambi & Pickering 2017).

3.7 Methodological principles in PT-based research

In order to investigate developmental trajectories in L2 speech production (and comprehension), a number of key methodological principles are applied in PT-based data analysis. This section introduces three key methodological principles underlying this kind of data analysis. These are (1) the distributional analysis, (2) the emergence criterion and (3) implicational scaling. The three principles are also central to the methodology of the empirical study presented in Chapter 6.

3.7.1 Distributional analysis

A thorough description of the dynamics of L2 development that enables researchers to establish a linguistic profile of an L2 learner's interlanguage grammar requires a detailed analysis of the respective learner's data sample. This can be accomplished by means of distributional analyses of the morpho-syntactic structures occurring in the data sample. As Pienemann (1998: 139) observes, fine-grained distributional analyses of learner data can 'determine which contexts or even which linguistic items are related to which particular interlanguage rules'. He argues that obligatory contexts of the target language do not necessarily apply to the learner's interlanguage, which might operate only on a subset of the features and categories that the target language is sensitive to (Pienemann 1998: 138). As an example, he points to the inflectional morpheme '3sg -s': Whereas the target language is sensitive to categories and features such as tense, number, person, verb, subject and voice in the application of agreement marking, this is not necessarily the case for a learner's interlanguage. This is reflected in the following utterances produced by learners participating in my study:

(11) The green fish was eats from the pink fish (learner P07)
(12) The carrot eatings from the mother (learner P05)
(13) The childrens rides of the *roler* (scooter)? (learner P06)

These utterances show that the feature '3sg -s' is not applied in a target-like fashion by the three learners, as the learners' interlanguage is not sensitive to the above-mentioned features to the same extent as the target language.

In PT-based research, the distributional analysis of specific morpho-syntactic structures occurring in an L2 learner's data sample is considered to be a suitable means to create a linguistic profile of the learner and to determine their stage of L2 acquisition. To accomplish this, the speech sample is analysed with particular focus on the occurrence of developmental features, that is, those morphological and syntactic features that indicate an L2 learner's development. This procedure is illustrated in Table 3.6 with the feature '3sg -s' that occurs at stage 5 of the PT hierarchy.

In Table 3.6, the '+' indicates the presence of the '3sg -s' morpheme and the '–' denotes its absence in obligatory contexts in the speech samples of five different learners (S01, S02, S03, S04, S05). The table shows that learner S04 applies the '3sg -s' morpheme in three obligatory contexts but fails to do so in three other contexts.

In addition to the distributional analysis of the type displayed in Table 3.6, more fine-grained analyses of the learner data can be carried out to investigate in which contexts the respective feature is actually applied by the learner. The analysis displayed in Table 3.7 reveals that learner S04 applies the morpheme under investigation with three different verbs. In addition, it can be seen that the '3sg -s' is not applied in all obligatory contexts.

A further distinction between (1) the application or non-application of a particular feature in obligatory contexts and (2) the use of the feature in non-target-like contexts provides insights into the invariant occurrence of particular forms and can contribute to the identification of formulaic sequences in the learner's interlanguage (see Lenzing

Table 3.6 Distributional analysis '3sg -s' (extract from Sub-study 3).

Stage	Phenomenon	S01	S02	S03	S04	S05
5	3sg -s	0	+2/ –6	+3/ –1	+3/ –3	+3

Table 3.7 Distributional analysis '3sg -s' learner S04.

S04	Mr. Lee starts working at eight.	+
	Mr. Lee wakes up at seven fort(/) fifteen.	+
	He gets coffee at seven forty.	+
	Mr. Lee stop working at five o'clock.	–
	Mr. (/) Mr. Lee help his kids with homework at seven (/) eight o'clock.	–
	Mr. Lee go to bed at eleven o'clock.	–

2013). This is exemplified in example (14) with the 'plural -s (Det + N agr)' structure (stage 3) produced by a 'stage 2' learner in the context of body parts (taken from Roos 2007: 158–9):[6]

(14)

C09	My monster have got five teeth?
	My monster has got two eyes.
	(Hmhm) (ehm) my monster has got (ehm) one nose?
	(Ehm) my monster has got (ehm) two ears?
	One legs.

At first glance, it seems as if learner C09 has acquired feature unification at the phrasal level, as he produces the 'plural -s (Det + N agr)' structure with lexical and morphological variation (*two eyes – one nose*). However, in her detailed analysis of data collected in a primary school context, Roos shows that learners produce noun phrases in the context of body parts as invariant units, as they occur as fixed expressions in the learners' textbooks. She further observes that nouns that relate to body parts often occur in their plural forms in the learners' textbooks (Roos 2007: 158–9). This is mirrored in learner C09's non-target-like utterance *one legs*.

3.7.2 The emergence criterion

A crucial question in (second) language acquisition research is how to operationalize *acquisition* in order 'to be able to define **when** a specific morphological or syntactic structure can be considered to have actually been acquired by the learner' (Lenzing 2013: 151, bold and italics in original).[7] Sayehli (2013: 23) notes that '[t]he operational definition of "acquisition" used in a study will affect the interpretation of data and the delimination of developmental stages'. This is by no means a trivial task, and there is no consensus in SLA research on how to define and measure acquisition. A widely used criterion to determine acquisition is the *accuracy criterion*, which has a long history in both L1 and L2 language acquisition research. In his seminal L1 acquisition study, Brown (1973) applied a 90 per cent accuracy criterion to the data, which means that he considered a morpheme as acquired when the child produced it correctly in 90 per cent of all contexts in which it was required in the L1 grammar. In studies on L2 acquisition, the accuracy criterion has been applied with different cut-off points, ranging from 60 per cent (e.g. Vainikka & Young-Scholten 1994) to 90 per cent (e.g. Dulay & Burt 1974).

The use of accuracy criteria is discussed controversially in the literature. Pallotti (2007: 362) observes that 'choice of the criterion level seems rather arbitrary and no author has provided convincing theoretical reasons for maintaining that a certain threshold is a more valid indicator of acquisition than another'. This arbitrariness in the choice of accuracy rates crucially influences the respective study outcome: The application of different accuracy criteria to the same data set yields different acquisition orders (see e.g. Glahn et al. 2001; Hatch & Farhady 1982). Pienemann (1998: 59) critically remarks that '[t]here is no guarantee that the accuracy of morpheme insertion will increase steadily in relation to any two morphemes or in relation to any two learners. On the contrary, it is quite likely and well attested in empirical studies that accuracy rates develop with highly variable gradients in relation to grammatical items and individual learners.'

Although accuracy criteria are still applied in some SLA studies, the insight that the order of accuracy does not necessarily reflect the order of acquisition (see e.g. Meisel, Clahsen & Pienemann 1981) and that, therefore, accuracy cannot be regarded as a valid measure of an L2 learner's linguistic development had already developed in the early 1980s. It was in particular the research conducted by the ZISA (*Zweitspracherwerb Italienischer, Spanischer und Portugiesischer Arbeiter*) group that initiated a shift in perspective in that the group took a learner-oriented perspective instead of the at that time predominant focus on accuracy in terms of the target language. Instead of regarding the development of learner language as a uniform and linear process that is reflected in accuracy orders, the ZISA research group proposed a view of L2 development as a multidimensional process. This shift in perspective led to a focus on *emergence* instead of accuracy (see Meisel, Clahsen & Pienemann 1981).

According to the *emergence criterion*, a linguistic structure is considered to be acquired if it occurs productively in a learner's interlanguage, which means that the learner is, in principle, able to produce the structure. Pienemann (1998) adopts Meisel and colleagues' approach to view the emergence of linguistic features as an indicator for a learner's developmental stage. Taking a processing perspective on L2 acquisition, he argues that the point of emergence of a particular linguistic structure reflects the point in L2 acquisition when a specific processing procedure can be carried out by the L2 learner:

> From a speech processing point of view, emergence can be understood as the point in time at which certain skills have, in principle, been attained or at which certain operations can, in principle, be carried out. From a descriptive viewpoint one can say that this is the beginning of an acquisition process, and focusing on the start of this process will allow the researcher to reveal more about the rest of the process. (Pienemann 1998: 138)

When applying the emergence criterion to actual learner data, it is crucial to differentiate between a learner's *productive* use of a linguistic feature and its occurrence as an *unanalysed chunk* that is stored as a holistic item in the learner's mental lexicon. This distinction is particularly important when the criterion is applied to morphological features, and the evidence that is required to determine the productive use of a structure is different for morphological features than for syntactic ones.

In the area of syntax, a structure is considered to be used productively if it occurs with lexical variation in the speech sample. In order to be able to differentiate between the use of formulaic sequences and productive structures in a learner's interlanguage, a syntactic structure is considered to be acquired when the learner's speech sample contains at least three different realizations of the respective structure (see Pienemann, Keßler & Liebner 2006: 78; Lenzing & Pienemann 2015: 109).

In the area of morphology, the situation is different. To be able to determine whether a particular morphological feature is used productively or as part of a formulaic sequence, the distributional analysis of the learner data has to focus on both lexical and morphological variation. Pienemann (1998: 133) illustrates this with the example of the acquisition of subject-verb agreement in *he goes*:

> To be sure that 'he goes' is a genuine case of productive SV-agreement one has to ascertain that both, subject and verb vary morphologically and lexically: unless 'he goes' co-occurs with 'I go' etc. there is no reason why 'he-goes' may not be a single lexical item in the learner's lexicon. This means that the simple occurrence of 'he goes' alone is not a sufficient indicator of the emergence of SV agreement.

Thus, to consider the '3sg -s' morpheme as acquired, the following two conditions have to be met: (1) the morpheme has to occur with different lexical verbs in the data sample (e.g. *follow-s, eat-s, open-s, kick-s*) and (2) the lexical verb has to occur with different suffixes (e.g. *go-ing, go-Ø*). In addition, a fine-grained distributional analysis and the test of the null hypothesis that the '3sg -s' occurs only in target-like contexts reveal whether the feature is also present in non-target-like contexts in the speech sample, as would be the case in *I goes* and *we goes* (see Pienemann 1998: 144; Lenzing 2013: 153).

The emergence criterion is considered to be far less arbitrary than accuracy criteria (see e.g. Sayehli 2013: 22). Pallotti (2007: 365) maintains that 'Pienemann's detailed treatment of the emergence criterion constitutes an exception and a significant improvement in the field of SLA research. The notion is theoretically well-founded and many of the methodological problems involved in its operationalization are convincingly worked through.' However, the emergence criterion has also been subject to criticism. This concerns the difficulties associated with unambiguously determining the first *productive* use of a structure to ensure that the learner uses the structure systematically. Glahn et al. (2001: 398) argue that this applies in particular to cross-sectional studies, which leads them to conclude that 'this criterion is not always easy to apply in practice'. A related issue concerns the identification of formulaic sequences, which is crucial in order to be able to distinguish between unanalysed chunks and learners' productive use of a specific structure (see e.g. Pallotti 2007: 367).[8] These difficulties might be one of the reasons why the criterion has been applied in slightly different forms and with different 'threshold levels' in various SLA studies (see e.g. Baten 2013; Baten & Verbeke 2015; Di Biase & Kawaguchi 2002; Sayehli 2013; Spinner 2013; Zhang 2004), which potentially renders a direct comparison of research results problematic.[9]

Despite these potential difficulties related to its practical application, the emergence criterion is considered to be an extremely useful instrument in investigating developmental sequences in SLA. As pointed out by Nicholas, Lenzing and Roos (2016) it enables the researcher (1) to determine when a learner can process and produce specific morphological or syntactic structures, (2) to assign a learner to a particular developmental stage in the PT hierarchy and (3) to trace a learner's interlanguage development over time.

3.7.3 Implicational scaling

The third major methodological principle that is introduced in this section is *implicational scaling*, which is used in SLA research to capture the dynamics of the L2 acquisition process and to identify regularities in interlanguage development. As Rickford (2002: 142) notes, '[i]mplicational scales represent an important device for revealing structure in variability, and for demonstrating that what some linguists might dismiss as random or free variation is significantly constrained'.

There are at least two different traditions of implicational analyses, which are based on two independent starting points in scientific research. One such point is commonly associated with the seminal paper by Guttman (1944) on scalogram analysis, which was applied in social and psychological assessment as a method to quantify qualitative data. The underlying idea of scalogram analysis is that, when attempting to measure attitudes or public opinions, people's responses to sets of items can be ordered in such a way that predictions concerning people's behaviour are possible. The second tradition is the use of implicational scaling in linguistics. Implicational scaling was introduced to the field of linguistics independently of its use in social and psychological assessment by the sociolinguist DeCamp in 1968 in a study on Jamaican Creole development (see DeCamp 1971). Since then, implicational scaling has been used in a great number of studies on sociolinguistic variation (e.g. Akers 1981; Bickerton 1971, 1973; Bailey 1973a, b; Labov 1973; Lameli 2004; Rickford 1991; Sankoff 1973) as well as in studies on L2 acquisition (e.g. Andersen 1978; Bayley 1999; Di Biase 2008; Ellis 2008; Itani-Adams 2007; Kawaguchi 2016; Lenzing 2013; Meisel, Clahsen & Pienemann 1981; Nagy, Moisset & Sankoff 1996; Pienemann 1998; Trofimovich, Gatbonton & Segalowitz 2007; Trudgill 1986), and constitutes a standard tool in PT-based analysis.

In linguistics, implicational scales can reveal hierarchical patterns in the acquisition or use of specific linguistic features (Rickford 2002: 143). This means that linguistic features can be ordered in such a way that the presence of feature x in a data sample implies the presence of feature y, but not vice versa. In the field of SLA, implicational scaling provides a valuable means to describe L2 development and to identify systematic patterns in the L2 interlanguage (see e.g. Trofimovich, Gatbonton & Segalowitz 2007). It is an advantage of this method that it can be applied to both longitudinal as well as cross-sectional data, as is illustrated in Tables 3.8 and 3.9 (see also Pienemann 1998: 134–5). Table 3.8 depicts the occurrence of the linguistic features a, b, c and d in a fictitious data sample of an L2 learner obtained in a longitudinal study.

Table 3.8 Sample implicational scale longitudinal data.

feature	time 1	time 2	time 3	time 4
a	1	1	1	1
b	0	1	1	1
c	0	0	1	1
d	0	0	0	1

Table 3.9 Sample implicational scale cross-sectional data (from Lenzing 2019: 29).

feature	learner 1	learner 2	learner 3	learner 4
a	1	1	1	1
b	0	1	1	1
c	0	0	1	1
d	0	0	0	1

It serves to demonstrate the applicability of implicational scaling to L2 acquisition research: In this example, the features a–d are acquired in a cumulative fashion, which means that if a data sample contains feature b, it should also contain feature a, but not the other way around.

Implicational scaling can also be applied to learner data obtained in a cross-sectional study (Hatch & Farhady 1982: 176). This is exemplified in Table 3.9. In this implicational scaling matrix, the linguistic features under investigation are again presented vertically and the learners are presented horizontally. The features are ordered in an implicational fashion, which makes it possible to describe regularities in the acquisition of particular interlanguage features.

However, as pointed out by Guttman (1944: 140), 'perfect scales are not to be expected in practice'. Indeed, deviations from the expected patterns are often found when analysing actual data samples, which raises the question as to when an implicational matrix can be considered to be valid. This 'deviation from perfection' (Guttman 1944: 140) is measured by the *coefficient of reproducibility* (sometimes also called *index of reproducibility*), which assesses the degree of scalability of the data. This is commonly calculated by taking the ratio of the actual errors to the maximum number of opportunities for errors (Rickford 2002: 154).

$$IR = 1 - \frac{\text{Total number of errors}}{\text{Total number of opportunities for error}} = 1 - \frac{\text{Total number of errors}}{\text{No. cols.} \times \text{No. rows}}$$

This procedure is demonstrated in the following based on the example presented in Table 3.10. The implicational table (Table 3.10) contains one deviation from the expected pattern: In the data sample of learner 4, there is no instance of feature a, although the sample contains the features b, c and d. Applying the formula introduced here, this table would result in a coefficient of reproducibility of 0.94. Following Hatch and Lazaraton (1991: 210), the coefficient of reproducibility should be higher than 0.90 for a scale to be valid.[10]

Menzel (1953) introduced an additional coefficient to scalogram analysis – the coefficient of scalability (CS). This coefficient is intended to overcome a limitation

Table 3.10 Sample implicational scale with deviations.

feature	learner 1	learner 2	learner 3	learner 4
a	1	1	1	*0
b	0	1	1	1
c	0	0	1	1
d	0	0	0	1

of the coefficient of reproducibility: The coefficient is sensitive to extreme marginal distributions of items and categories so that there are cases where a high coefficient of reproducibility can be achieved even though the data are randomly distributed (see Menzel 1953: 269). The CS measures 'predictability of the scale relative to the level of prediction afforded by consideration of the row and column marginals' (Guest 2000: 351). It is calculated by the following formula (McIver & Carmines 1981: 50):

CS = 1 − (scale errors/marginal errors)

As far as the level of acceptance of the CS is concerned, Menzel (1953: 279) points out that '[i]ts exact value must await practical experience' but suggests that it should be 'somewhere between .60 and .65'. The level of 0.60 has generally been adopted as an indicator for the scalability of an implicational table (see e.g. Dunn-Rankin 1983: 107; Hatch & Lazaraton 1991: 212), although McIver and Carmines (1981: 50) point out that this level of acceptance 'is only a rule of thumb; a CS of .60 has no explicit theoretical justification'.

As mentioned in this section, the origins of implicational scaling in linguistics differ from those in sociology and psychology, and the actual methodology used in variationist and SLA research developed independently from its application in socio-psychological research. Although there is a great deal of overlap in the two fields in applying this methodology to empirical data, the two traditions differ in their understanding of what actually constitutes an error in an implicational matrix.

There are basically two approaches to error assessment in implicational scaling, which have repercussions on the interpretation of the results. The first one is the so-called *minimization of error* approach, which can be characterized as follows:

> According to minimization of error, the number of errors is the least number of positive responses that must be changed to negative or negative responses that must be changed to positive in order for the observed pattern to be transformed into an ideal response pattern. (McIver & Carmines 1981: 42)

The second approach, developed by Goodenough (1944) and Edwards (1948), is based on the assumption that 'items should in fact be perfectly reproducible from a subject's responses' (McIver & Carmines 1981: 44). This form of error counting is also called the *deviation from perfect reproducibility* or *Goodenough-Edwards* technique. This approach measures the number of responses that deviate from the predicted pattern in that it assigns ideal response patterns to the participants, which are based on the number of their *positive* responses (McIver & Carmines 1981: 44).

This difference is illustrated with the example of a participant who scored positively on two out of four items in a study measuring social attitudes. In this case, the ideal response pattern would be (+ + − −). However, in the example, the participant's response pattern is not perfect, as the participant scored negatively on the first item, which yields the pattern (− + + −). According to the *minimization of error* approach, the first negative response would be counted as one error, as it constitutes a deviation from the implicational pattern. The *Goodenough-Edwards* technique, however, would count two errors, as two items would have to be changed to arrive at the ideal pattern (− + + −) → (+ + − −).

As illustrated in Table 3.11, when the response pattern deviates from an ideal scale, the two methods of error assessment yield different results. Table 3.11 compares the two approaches to error assignment on a number of different response patterns and reveals that the *Goodenough-Edwards* technique to error assignment results in a greater number of errors than the *minimization of error* approach: In this technique, not only the deviations of the pattern from a perfect implicational scale in general are counted but all deviations from a perfect score based on the number of positive results.

When investigating the actual application of the two techniques in empirical linguistic research, it can be seen that it is the *minimization of error* approach that is predominantly used in the linguistic tradition of implicational scaling. This applies to both early and more current variationist studies (e.g. Bickerton 1973; Lameli 2004; Rickford 1979, 1991; Trudgill 1986) as well as SLA research (e.g. Andersen 1978; Dittmar 1980; Ellis 2008; Keßler & Pienemann 2011; Pienemann 1998; Spinner 2011; Trofimovich, Gatbonton & Segalowitz 2007).

In keeping with this tradition, the *minimization of error* approach is also adopted in the analysis presented in this book. However, in some recent studies in the PT framework, the *Goodenough-Edwards* technique was applied to the data (e.g. Buyl 2019; Sayehli 2013; Spinner 2013; see also Section 3.8). Thus, when attempting to compare results from different studies, it has to be kept in mind that both approaches

Table 3.11 Two approaches to error assignment: error minimization (EM) vs. *Goodenough-Edwards* (GE) approach.

Response pattern				Assignment of error	
				EM	GE
+	+	+	+	0	0
+	+	+	−	0	0
+	+	−	+	1	2
+	−	+	+	1	2
−	+	+	+	1	2

yield different results and that therefore, the results from the different studies might not be comparable in a one-to-one fashion.

3.8 Studies investigating L2 comprehension within the PT framework

This section engages with studies investigating L2 comprehension from a PT perspective. Although, in principle, the theory holds that 'at any stage of development the learner can produce and comprehend only those second language (L2) linguistic forms which the current state of the language processor can handle' (Pienemann & Lenzing 2020: 162), in the past PT has primarily engaged with constraints on L2 speech production. However, it is now widening its focus to include speech comprehension processes, and in the past few years a number of studies have engaged with the question of whether PT can account for comprehension processes in L2 acquisition (Buyl 2015, 2019; Buyl & Housen 2013, 2015; Keatinge & Keßler 2009; Spinner 2013; Spinner & Jung 2018, 2019). The studies differ in their methodology and yield mixed results: Whereas the results of both Keatinge and Keßler (2009) and Buyl and Housen (2013, 2015) indicate that the sequence of acquisition in L2 comprehension follows the predictions of PT for L2 speech production, the studies by Spinner (2013), Spinner and Jung (2018, 2019) and Buyl (2015, 2019) do not show any systematicity in the L2 comprehension data.

The study by Keatinge and Keßler (2009) investigated the L2 acquisition of English passive structures in both production and comprehension by learners with different L1 backgrounds. The authors hypothesize that the L2 comprehension of English passives is constrained by processability and that passives are understood earlier than they are produced, so that there is a gradual development from perception to production (see Keatinge & Keßler 2009: 75–6). Keatinge and Keßler analysed speech production data of sixty-two English as a second language (ESL) learners with different L1s and comprehension data of thirty-three ESL learners with German as L1 at different stages of L2 development. They employed different communicative tasks to elicit speech production data in order to determine the participants' stages of acquisition, and the fish film (Tomlin 1995; see also Section 6.3) and a sentence completion task to elicit the production data of passive structures. To obtain comprehension data, they used a semantic decision task and a sentence-picture matching task. Keatinge and Keßler claim that the L2 learners in their study are able to produce passive structures in a target-like way at stage 6 and can both produce pseudo-passives and comprehend passive structures from stage 4 onwards.[11] The results of the study indicate that English passive sentences are understood before they can be produced, and Keatinge and Keßler (2009: 91) thus conclude that '[i]t is evident that the acquisition of comprehension skills is one or two stages further developed than the productive skills'.

Keatinge and Keßler's study provides interesting insights into the L2 acquisition of English passives. However, a number of questions arise concerning theoretical as well as methodological issues. Firstly, the authors do not provide any details about the theoretical motivation of their claims. In particular, they do not specify the processing prerequisites for the L2 comprehension of passives. Secondly, Keatinge and Keßler do not provide a detailed distributional analysis of the production and comprehension data and the analysis presented in the study is based on the comprehension data of merely ten learners. A further point of criticism relates to the fact that no acquisition criterion is specified in the study. The comprehension data are presented in percentage terms, which suggests that Keatinge and Keßler used an accuracy criterion. However, as observed by Buyl and Housen (2015: 535), the level of accuracy for a comprehended structure to be considered as acquired is not defined in their study. To summarize, Keatinge and Keßler argue that their study results show that the processing procedures underlying PT can account not only for L2 production but also for L2 comprehension. However, owing to the theoretical and methodological limitations mentioned here this claim is of limited value with regard to the question of a potential interface between L2 production and comprehension.

Spinner (2013) also investigated whether PT's processing mechanisms can account for L2 comprehension data. She presents the results of three related studies that aim at 'determining the extent to which the mechanisms described by Pienemann's (1998, 2005) PT for production are also operative in reception' (Spinner 2013: 707). The first study focused on L2 comprehension. Sixty-four ESL learners and forty native speakers carried out a timed audio grammaticality judgement task (GJT) that included fourteen morpho-syntactic structures from stage 2–6 of the PT hierarchy: plural -s, past -ed and possessive -s (stage 2); object pronouns, possessive pronouns and adverb-first structures (stage 3); Wh-Copula questions, copula questions, phrasal verbs (stage 4); 3sg -s, Aux2nd questions and Neg/Aux2nd questions (stage 5); Cancel Aux2nd and tag questions (stage 6); as well as passives. In the second study, a subgroup of the same participants took part in a speech production task that aimed to elicit production data for a PT-based analysis. In the third study, sixty-three ESL university students completed a revised version of the timed audio GJT. The data analysis is based on both mean accuracy scores and implicational scaling. Spinner defines emergence in L2 comprehension in terms of an 80 per cent accuracy criterion. The results indicate that, whereas the production data are scalable and confirm the sequence of acquisition predicted by PT, the comprehension data fail to show any systematicity. The latter applies to both the mean accuracy scores and the implicational analysis.

However, Spinner points out that the results do not necessarily imply that L2 production and comprehension rely on completely separate processing mechanisms. Instead, she argues that the findings could be due to specific factors that are unique to comprehension, such as potential difficulties to aurally perceive suffixes such as the '3sg -s' or the 'past -ed', which could be 'particularly problematic if the phonotactic system of the L1 disallows these sequences' (Spinner 2013: 732). In addition, Spinner discusses potential limitations of the use of the GJT. She observes that the GJT might tap into metalinguistic awareness instead of implicit knowledge. Although the timed version of the GJT was used in the study to overcome these limitations, Spinner points out that it cannot be ruled out that the learners relied on metalinguistic knowledge (Spinner 2013: 733). A crucial question related to her observation is whether GJT tasks target language processing or rather language competence/representation. Spinner also addresses the issue of redundancy in comprehension, that is, the possibility that L2 learners rely on lexical and semantic cues in interpreting structures instead of on potentially redundant grammatical information. In my view, the issue of redundant grammatical markers and 'shallow processing' in comprehension is one of the core differences between the two processing modalities (see also Chapter 4).

A theoretical limitation of the study relates to the classification of the structure 'tag question' as a 'stage 6' structure. Tag questions are not included in the PT hierarchy, and the theoretical motivation underlying the inclusion and classification of the 'tag question' structure in the study is not made clear.[12] A further weakness of the study relates to the way the data are analysed. Firstly, the use of group mean scores is of limited value in investigating the question of whether the acquisition of the L2 comprehension of grammatical features follows the same sequence as in L2 production, as group mean scores do not allow for any conclusions concerning individual learner development (see e.g. Long & Sato 1984). The ensuing implicational analysis, intended to overcome this limitation, also suffers from methodological flaws. Firstly, no full distributional analysis is provided. Instead, the implicational table merely indicates whether a structure has emerged according to the accuracy criterion applied to the data. In a second implicational table, the data were collapsed into five categories based on the stages of acquisition (Spinner 2013: 719). The application of an accuracy criterion to the data and the conflation of items in the implicational analysis might obscure potential patterns in the L2 comprehension data.

Spinner and Jung (2018, 2019) also focused on the question of whether production and comprehension skills emerge simultaneously in L2 acquisition. They conducted a self-paced reading study with sixty-one ESL learners with various L1 backgrounds as well as twenty-one native speakers. The learners completed an oral interview and a self-paced reading task, and the native speakers served as the control group in the self-paced reading task. The interview was designed to elicit oral production data for a PT-based analysis. The self-paced reading task contained six morpho-syntactic structures from stage 2 to stage 6 of the PT hierarchy to elicit comprehension data and included both grammatical and ungrammatical items. The underlying rationale of self-paced reading tasks is that inferences about language processing can be drawn from differences in reading times. Longer reading times are interpreted as reflecting processing difficulties, whereas shorter reading times are related to facilitation in processing (Jegerski 2014: 24). Applied to SLA research, it is assumed that learners who have acquired a specific grammatical feature are sensitive to ungrammaticalities related to this feature. This sensitivity to an ungrammatical sentence slows down the reading process. Spinner and Jung assume that native speakers and learners who have acquired a particular structure should exhibit shorter reading times on grammatical sentences than on ungrammatical sentences that contain the grammatical item in question.

In Spinner and Jung (2018), the learners were allocated to three different groups, a 'high-level' group, a 'mixed' group and a 'low-level' group. Whereas the 'high-level' learners had acquired two 'stage 5' structures in production, the 'mixed level' learners had acquired only one of the structures, and the 'low level' learners did not show evidence of the acquisition of any of the 'stage 5' structures. In a first step, the study design was chosen to investigate the question of whether the 'high-level' group learners were able to detect ungrammaticalities related to 'stage 5' structures in the self-paced reading task. The results indicate that the learners did not demonstrate sensitivities to the ungrammaticalities present in the 'stage 5' structures in the self-paced reading task. A further analysis of the reaction-time data of all learners that included structures at lower stages of acquisition yielded mixed results, as sensitivities to structures at lower stages could be detected in the data (Spinner & Jung 2018: 312). According to Spinner and Jung (2018: 315), 'there was some support for an order of acquisition in receptive data as predicted by PT, albeit one that follows production after a delay'. Based on these findings, they consider the possibility that 'the same basic procedures could function in comprehension after a delay' (Spinner & Jung 2018: 312).

In Spinner and Jung (2019), the reaction-time data obtained in the self-paced reading task were analysed in the form of an implicational analysis, that is, the data of the individual participants were plotted on an implicational scale. This methodology is highly unusual, as data obtained in reaction-time experiments are traditionally analysed statistically based on pooled data. Depending on the underlying research question, the analysis is based on either individual or group mean scores to be able to identify patterns in the data and to attain statistically robust results (see e.g. Jegerski 2014; Jiang 2012).

The implicational analysis in Spinner and Jung (2019) indicates that the ESL data of the self-paced reading task are not scalable. This leads Spinner and Jung to conclude that the sequence in which specific morpho-syntactic structures emerge in oral speech production is not reflected in the self-paced reading data. In a further step, the oral production data were analysed, resulting in a nearly perfect implicational scale. The analysis of the production and comprehension data was then combined to compare individual learners' oral production and their individual self-paced reading results. Overall, this comparison did not yield a high percentage of matching scores, which shows that, with this type of analysis, no strong relationship between learners' performance in production and their performance on the self-paced reading task is found.

Spinner and Jung's study takes an innovative approach in that it investigates comprehension by means of a self-paced reading task and in this way avoids the use of accuracy scores. However, the methodology used in the study raises a number of questions. A first case in point relates to the question of whether the modality involved in the self-paced reading task might influence its outcome. Beginning L2 learners do not necessarily rely on automatized reading skills (see e.g. Verhagen 2009: 92). In addition, it might be the case that the learners' L1 reading directionality mode has an effect on the task results (see Spinner & Jung 2018: 314). A further issue concerns the analysis of the reaction-time data. First of all, the data were conflated in that the reaction times for the different grammatical structures occurring at a particular stage were amalgamated. The data obtained at different points in the reading process (region of primary interest and spillover region) were also combined in the analysis.

Secondly, the results were obtained by plotting the individual learners' reaction-time data on an implicational scale, which raises the possibility that outliers and individual deviations distorted the overall results. This is mirrored in the results of the native speakers: The implicational analysis of their individual reaction-time data yields a coefficient of reproducibility of 0.87, which is just below the score that Hatch and Farhady (1982) consider to be an indicator for a scalable table (0.90). This finding supports the assumption that plotting individual learners' reaction-time data on an implicational scale might not be a suitable means to gain insights into potential systematic patterns in L2 acquisition.

Buyl and Housen investigated the development of L2 comprehension within the PT framework in a longitudinal (Buyl & Housen 2013) as well as in a cross-sectional study (Buyl & Housen 2015). The data in both studies were partly collected within the context of the *Early Language and Intercultural Acquisition Studies* (ELIAS) project (Kersten et al. 2010). The participants were seventy-two francophone child L2 learners of English who were enrolled in an immersion programme in the French-speaking part of Belgium. The focus of both studies was on six different morpho-syntactic structures located at stage 2 (poss -s, plural -s agreement, negation, SVO) and stage 5 of the PT hierarchy (3sg -s, copula agreement) respectively.[13] To elicit the comprehension data, the ELIAS Grammar Test was used, a sentence-picture matching task developed within the ELIAS project. The task consists of three pictures per item (correct/incorrect/distractor), and the participants have to match an aurally presented prompt that includes a particular grammatical phenomenon with the corresponding picture that represents the prompt.

Buyl and Housen are well aware of the fact that the emergence criterion used in analysing oral production data cannot be applied to comprehension data in a one-to-one fashion. In searching for a potential solution to this methodological problem, they discuss the possibility to apply different 'emergence/acquisition criteria' (Buyl & Housen 2015: 535) to the data. An important issue in this concern is the factor of chance performance in the comprehension data when using a sentence-picture matching task. Buyl and Housen (2015: 535) observe that '[i]n a three-choice task, participants have one chance out of three to arrive at a correct reply merely by guessing, and this for every of the six test items for a given grammatical phenomenon. When setting a criterion, we must therefore establish whether the probability that a participant meets this criterion is above chance performance.' Taking these considerations into account, Buyl and Housen argue that a participant's score of 5/6 structures or 6/6 structures, which would equal an 80 per cent accuracy criterion, rules out chance performance. However, to provide a more complete picture of the participants' performance in the comprehension task, they also include data analyses for all lower scores (3/6–4/6 structures in the 2013 study and 1/6–4/6 structures in the 2015 study). In both studies, the data were analysed in terms of implicational scaling, and Buyl and Housen state that the results support the claim that the order of acquisition of specific grammatical phenomena in L2 comprehension reflects the order of acquisition found in oral speech production. Those learners who have acquired one or both 'stage 5' structures had also acquired at least some of the 'stage 2' structures. This order seems to hold across all acquisition criteria that were applied in the analysis (1/6–6/6 structures) and applies to both the cross-sectional and the longitudinal data.

Overall, the studies yield interesting results. This concerns in particular the operationalization of different acquisition criteria with respect to L2 comprehension data. However, the authors point to a potential limitation of the task design. This relates to the question of whether the prompts in the ELIAS Grammar Test serve to trigger the processing of particular grammatical phenomena or whether the comprehension of the prompts can also be accomplished by relying on non-linguistic information. For instance, the aural prompt targeting the 'possessive -s' is the sentence *The girl is feeding the boy's dog*. The three pictures the participant can choose from show (1) a girl feeding a boy, (2) a girl, a boy and a dog that are not involved in an action (distractor item) and (3) a girl feeding a dog that belongs to a boy. The question that arises is whether a participant who points to the correct picture necessarily processes the 'possessive -s'. It could also be the case that the learner merely understands the words *girl, feed* and *dog* and relates these words to the event depicted in the picture.

The study by Buyl (2015) engaged with 'the receptive acquisition of English morphology among adult learners of English as a second language' (Buyl 2015: 139). She employed a self-paced reading task that targets six morphological structures located at five different stages of the PT hierarchy. The rationale of the self-paced reading task in her study is the same as the one in the study by Spinner and Jung discussed in this section.

Buyl's analysis is twofold: In a first step, the data were analysed at the group level in order to explore which of the ungrammaticalities in the task led to processing difficulties by the L2 learners. In a second step, the individual learners' reaction-time data were analysed in terms of implicational scaling. As in the study by Spinner and Jung (2019), a learner is considered to be able to process a particular structure when the reaction time for an ungrammatical stimulus is longer than the one for a grammatical stimulus, which is taken as an indicator that the ungrammaticality led to processing difficulties. The results of the analysis at the group level reveal that, in some conditions, the reaction times were significantly shorter for the ungrammatical stimuli than for the grammatical ones. Buyl (2015: 159) thus argues that these findings are not in line with the predictions of PT. The analysis of the individual reaction-time data indicates that the data are not scalable and do not reflect the sequence of acquisition predicted by PT for oral production data. On this basis, Buyl (2015: 163) concludes that

> [a] – very tentative – conclusion for PT theory development would be that receptive and productive grammar acquisition are independently developing processes, and that the mechanisms which PT hypothesises to govern productive grammar acquisition do not shape the developmental pattern of receptive grammar acquisition. Whether this is because the PT mechanisms do not apply to receptive grammar acquisition at all, or whether their effect is limited due to other processes and factors at work in grammar acquisition is of course too early to say.

Investigating the question of whether the methodology employed in the study truly sheds light on receptive grammar processing, Buyl observes that a problem that applies to all receptive grammar tasks is to fully determine whether learners rely on grammatical processing in task performance. She points out that results might be influenced by lexical and/or pragmatic issues or by general aspects related to attention (Buyl 2015: 162). This issue is crucial to all studies investigating comprehension processes and also affects the methodological considerations of the empirical study in this book.

Apart from these issues that arguably apply to a certain degree to most if not all other types of comprehension tasks, the methodological challenges of using a self-paced reading task pointed out in the discussion of the study by Spinner (2013) also apply to the present study. In addition, the exploratory study presented in Buyl (2015) does not include a native speaker control group. Therefore, there is no clear benchmark with which the non-native speaker results can be compared.

In a further study, Buyl (2019) elicited L2 comprehension data by means of a timed written GJT, again focusing on the acquisition of morphological structures in L2 reception. Sixty-one adult L2 learners of English and nineteen native speakers took part in the study. The morphological structures included in the task were the same ones as in Buyl (2015). Buyl included both the grammatical and the ungrammatical items in her analysis and conducted separate implicational analyses for the two categories. As in the studies by Buyl (2015) and Buyl and Housen (2013, 2015), different operationalizations of acquisition were used, and the cut-off points were determined as 30 per cent, 50 per cent and 80 per cent accuracy respectively. Buyl calculated both the coefficient of reproducibility and the CS (see Section 3.7.3). She concludes that the different implicational scales show no developmental systematicity and argues that her study does not support the hypothesis that L2 receptive processing is governed by the mechanisms spelled out in PT.

However, a closer inspection of her data set reveals that this claim does not apply to all the implicational scales in her study. For instance, in the scales for the grammatical items, the coefficient of reproducibility is above 0.90 for the accuracy criteria of 30 per cent and 50 per cent. In the case of the 80 per cent criterion, the coefficient of reproducibility is just below the threshold level (0.89). The CS, however, is always below the threshold of 0.60, as most participants have reached stage 4 or higher. In my view, this does not necessarily imply that the data violate the predictions of PT. It simply shows that there are not sufficient learners at lower stages to be able to calculate a meaningful CS. This applies, for instance, to the implicational analysis for grammatical items using an accuracy criterion of 50 per cent: The coefficient of reproducibility for this implicational table is 0.98, as the data of fifty-eight out of sixty-one participants show a pattern that is in line with PT. The data of merely three participants yield a pattern diverging from this developmental systematicity. However, as the great majority of learners (fifty) has already acquired stage 5 according to the applied criterion, the data do not offer valuable clues about the sequence of acquisition of structures of lower stages and yield a low CS.

A potential limitation of the study relates to the use of a written GJT to elicit comprehension data. Apart from the question of whether a GJT targets language processing or taps into language competence/representation, the use of a written task raises further issues: Can the processing of aural and written stimuli be compared and can it be assumed that both processes rely on the same processing resources?

To sum up, the existing studies investigating L2 comprehension processes from a PT perspective employed different methodological approaches to shed light on the question of whether the acquisition of grammatical features in L2 comprehension follows the same sequence as in L2 production. The studies yield different results, which might at least in part be due to methodological issues. Despite some interesting observations, for instance related to the question of what constitutes an appropriate acquisition criterion in L2 comprehension, and innovations in data elicitation within the PT framework, the studies also exhibit some methodological limitations. A further issue concerns theoretical considerations: What has so far been lacking in the examination of potential interfaces between production and comprehension within the PT framework is an attempt to model their exact relation based on (1) psycholinguistic insights and evidence and (2) a detailed LFG analysis of the processes involved in the production and the comprehension of particular morpho-syntactic structures.

In this book, I aim to address this gap by presenting a theoretically motivated model of the interface between production and comprehension that is based on recent psycholinguistic research findings. This *Integrated Encoding-Decoding Model of SLA* is tested against empirical data for the L2 acquisition of English passive constructions.

4

The *Integrated Encoding-Decoding Model of SLA*

This chapter introduces the *Integrated Encoding-Decoding Model of SLA*. The model offers a solution to the unresolved question of how production and comprehension are related in L2 acquisition. Its focus is twofold: First of all, it models the relation between L2 grammatical encoding and decoding. A second focus is on the influence of semantic factors on the L2 comprehension process. The *Integrated Encoding-Decoding Model* reflects the influence of a number of theoretical approaches related to different aspects of language processing and language acquisition. These theoretical approaches are combined and partly reshaped in a model of L2 comprehension and production that is psychologically plausible and at the same time parsimonious following the principle of Occam's razor.

As regards language production, I follow to a large extent the view put forward by Levelt (1989, 1999) and introduced in Section 1.1. Taking an integrated view on language production and comprehension processes, I adopt the notion of a *shared grammatical workspace* proposed by Kempen, Olsthoorn and Sprenger (2012). This single-processor architecture is a more parsimonious solution than a dual-processor architecture and can account for a number of empirical findings in language processing research (see Section 2.3). The theoretical perspective on SLA and the L2 initial state is the one spelled out in PT (Pienemann 1998; Pienemann & Lenzing 2020) and the *Multiple Constraints Hypothesis* (Lenzing 2013). To account for semantic aspects of L2 comprehension and to enable the modelling of the relationship between semantic and syntactic processing in SLA, the *Integrated Encoding-Decoding Model* includes a component that adapts ideas presented in the *Online Cognitive Equilibrium Hypothesis* (Karimi & Ferreira 2016) (see Section 1.2.5).

4.1 An overview of the *Integrated Encoding-Decoding Model of SLA*

A key claim of the *Integrated Encoding-Decoding Model* is that, in L2 syntactic encoding and decoding, L2 learners draw on essentially the same resources, which are constrained by (1) the architecture of the human language processor and (2) the underdeveloped L2 mental grammatical system. The syntactic coding component constitutes one core aspect of the *Integrated Encoding-Decoding Model*, and the following hypotheses are central to this component of the model:

1. There is one single syntactic processor underlying both grammatical encoding and grammatical decoding processes in L2 acquisition. This processor develops stepwise in accordance with the predictions of PT.
2. The L2 learner's mental system for both grammatical encoding and decoding is initially highly constrained at the different levels of linguistic representation postulated in *Lexical-Functional Grammar* (LFG), as proposed in the *Multiple Constraints Hypothesis*.

A second key component focuses on semantic processing and engages with the relation between semantic and syntactic processing in L2 comprehension. I argue that semantic processing can override syntactic processing and that L2 learners can draw on shallow processing in L2 comprehension. As semantic aspects play a crucial role in language processing in general and in comprehension processes in particular, I integrate key semantic factors, such as lexical semantics and event probability, in the overall design of the model. The relation between semantic and syntactic processing in L2 comprehension is modelled by adapting the *Online Cognitive Equilibrium Hypothesis* (Karimi & Ferreira 2016) to SLA (see Section 4.3). The core components of the *Integrated Encoding-Decoding Model* are presented in Figure 4.1.

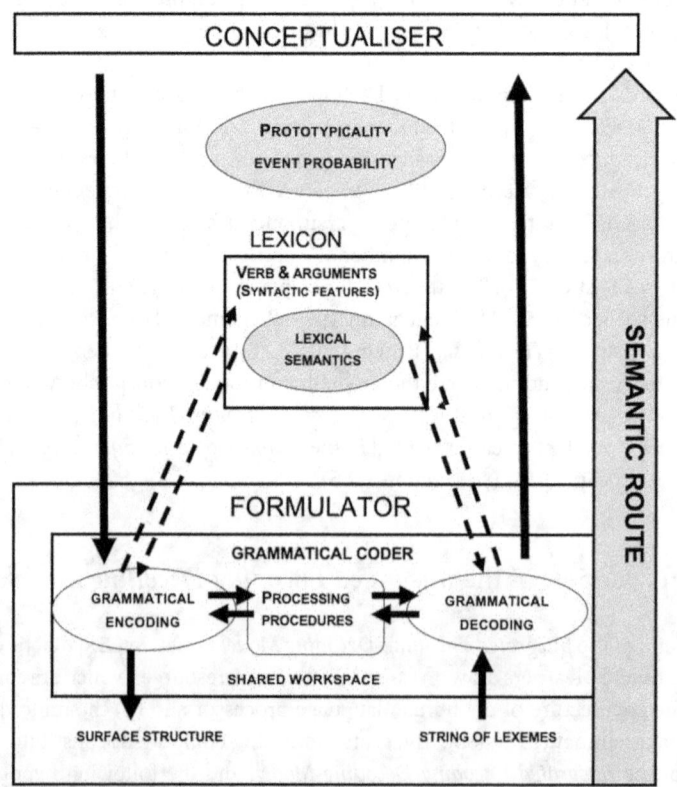

Figure 4.1 The *Integrated Encoding-Decoding Model of SLA*.

As mentioned earlier in this section, the fundamental assumptions concerning language production proposed by Levelt also apply to the model presented here, for example the incrementality of the sentence generation process, the assumption that processing components operate automatically or that a grammatical memory store is involved in grammatical processing (see Section 1.1.1). The *Integrated Encoding-Decoding Model* also adopts aspects of the architecture of Levelt's blueprint, including some of the processing components (conceptualizer, lexicon and – at least parts of – the formulator).

However, the formulator is modified in one crucial aspect: In contrast to Levelt (1989), who initially conceptualized the speech comprehension system as a distinct component that is separate from the formulator, I claim that production and comprehension rely on (partially) the same resources. Therefore, I adopt the notion of a *shared grammatical workspace* by Kempen, Olsthoorn and Sprenger (2012). In the *Integrated Encoding-Decoding Model*, the shared workspace is realized as a *grammatical coder*, which constitutes a part of the formulator. This grammatical coder forms one core of the model, and I argue that both syntactic encoding and decoding processes take place in this shared workspace. In Figure 4.1, the directional difference between the two processes is captured by the arrows to and from the conceptualizer. In grammatical encoding, the preverbal message generated in the conceptualizer is transformed into a surface form, whereas in grammatical decoding, the string of lexemes encountered in the input is transformed into a conceptual message. Notwithstanding this directional difference, I argue that the same processing mechanisms are involved in the two syntactic processes. This conceptualization of the architecture of language processing in SLA has the advantage that it can account for a number of empirical findings in psycholinguistic and neurolinguistic research (see e.g. Menenti et al. 2011; Segaert et al. 2012; Tooley & Bock 2014). What is more, a single-processor architecture is a more parsimonious approach to model the relation between comprehension and production than a dual-processor architecture (see also Kempen 1999).

I claim that the processes taking place in the grammatical coder are based on the processing procedures spelled out in Levelt (1989) and adopted in PT to account for L2 acquisition. In L2 acquisition, these are claimed to be acquired in a stepwise fashion (see Pienemann 1998), and I hypothesize that this gradual acquisition applies to production (encoding) as well as comprehension (decoding). This means that, similar to the syntactic encoding process, the decoding process is also constrained by processability. In order to be able to syntactically parse linguistic input, L2 learners have to have acquired the respective processing procedures. In line with this, I assume that syntactic parsing also involves the core operations spelled out in LFG, namely feature unification and mapping operations.

A further hypothesis of the model is that L2 learners draw on the same mental grammatical system as a resource in both encoding and decoding. As argued in the *Multiple Constraints Hypothesis* (see Section 3.6), this grammatical system is highly constrained at the beginning of the L2 acquisition process, and the constraints apply to the different levels of linguistic representation outlined in LFG. I hypothesize that these constraints affect both grammatical encoding and decoding, such that the same constraints that restrict the L2 production process also apply to the grammatical decoding process. As there is a directional difference between encoding and decoding, the direct mapping process in decoding proceeds from surface form to conceptual structure. The grammatical functions are not accessible due to the lack of syntactic features at a-structure and the lack of c-structure annotations. This means that, in grammatical decoding, L2 learners initially also rely on lexical processes and direct mapping operations. Similar to the production process, the gradual annotation of the lexicon and in particular the annotation of the syntactic side of a-structure enables the L2 learners to draw on the grammatical functions at f-structure in syntactic parsing.

In the model depicted in Figure 4.1, L2 speech production begins in the conceptualizer. Fragments of the generated preverbal message enter the formulator, and, in particular, the grammatical coder. It is here that the grammatical encoding of the intended message takes place. In this process, recourse is made to the processing procedures spelled out in Levelt (1989) as well as to the information stored in the L2 mental lexicon, which is indicated by the arrows to and from the mental lexicon to the grammatical coder in Figure 4.1. The result of the encoding process is the surface structure.

As discussed in Section 3.3, a core claim of PT is that the processing procedures are acquired stepwise in L2 acquisition. This implies that, initially, the L2 learner's grammatical coder is not fully developed. In the *Multiple Constraints Hypothesis*, it is further assumed that the L2 mental lexicon is annotated in a gradual fashion. Owing to these constraints, L2 learners initially rely on direct mapping operations from concepts/arguments to surface form.

The comprehension process starts with a string of lexemes that the L2 learner encounters in the input. This input string is decoded in the shared grammatical coder. I argue that, as in encoding, the processing procedures are also involved in the decoding process. In addition, the parser draws on the information present in the L2 mental lexicon, which is indicated by the bidirectional arrows between the lexicon and the grammatical decoding component in Figure 4.1. An alternative route to syntactic processing in L2 comprehension is the semantic route, which is represented by the grey arrow in the figure. I claim that L2 learners use semantic cues, such as lexical semantics, prototypicality and event probabilities in comprehension, and that these factors crucially influence the L2 semantic processing in the semantic route. Therefore, these factors are also marked in grey in Figure 4.1. The use of the semantic route applies in particular to early L2 learners who cannot draw on the processing procedures required for full morpho-syntactic processing, as their L2 grammatical coder is initially underdeveloped. The dual route in L2 comprehension – syntactic and semantic – and the relation between semantic and syntactic processing in L2 comprehension is further discussed in Section 4.3.

4.2 Semantic aspects in comprehension

This section introduces some of the core semantic factors that influence the (L2) comprehension process, such as lexical semantics, event probability and prototypicality.

In a next step, the adaptation of the *Online Cognitive Equilibrium Hypothesis* (Karimi & Ferreira 2016) to SLA is presented, which complements the *Integrated Encoding-Decoding Model* in that it models the relation between syntax and semantics in L2 comprehension.

Naturally, in both (L2) production and comprehension learners do not rely exclusively on syntactic processing but also draw on semantic information. This applies in particular to the comprehension process. Semantic cues form a crucial part of the resources humans draw on in comprehension, and these cues are particularly important in the early stages of L2 comprehension, when the L2 syntactic processor is still underdeveloped. In the *Integrated Encoding-Decoding Model* of L2 processing, different types of semantic resources are integrated, which have been shown to influence the L2 comprehension process. This applies to *lexical semantics*, *event probability* and the notion of *prototypicality*.

4.2.1 Lexical semantics and event probability

Both lexical semantics and event probability influence the (L2) comprehension process, albeit in different ways. VanPatten (1996: 36) makes the following distinction between lexical semantics and event probability: 'Lexical semantics refers to the constraints on a situation imposed by the semantics of the verb involved. […] An event probability refers to the likelihood that a given situation exists in the real world, even though lexical semantics allows it.'

He illustrates the concept of lexical semantics with the verb *kick*, which requires the agent to be animate and to have legs to do the kicking action. This renders sentences like *The fence kicked the horse* (VanPatten 2020: 113) and *The snake kicked the koala* semantically anomalous. In the first sentence, the agent is inanimate and, in the second sentence, the agent is animate but has no legs to carry out the action.

The following two sentences demonstrate the concept of event probability:

(1) The cat ate the mouse.
(2) The mouse ate the cat.

In terms of lexical semantics, both sentences are possible (in both cases, the agent is animate and is capable of eating). However, the event probability of the sentence in example (1) is much higher than the one of example (2), as the event described by the first sentence is far more plausible than the one in the second sentence. In this context, VanPatten (2020: 113) observes that '[w]ith event probabilities, either noun may be capable of the action but one is more likely. With lexical semantics, it is the case that only one noun is capable of the action.'

Figure 4.1 has the two types of knowledge located in different kinds of stores: Information about lexical semantics is part of lexical knowledge and is therefore stored in the lexicon. On the other hand, knowledge about event probabilities forms part of the speaker's declarative world knowledge, similar to what Levelt refers to as *situational knowledge* and *encyclopaedic knowledge* (Levelt 1989: 9–11).

Lexical semantics and event probabilities play an important role in sentence comprehension, and research findings show that these semantic factors can override syntactic processing. This kind of *shallow processing* has been observed in first as well as second language acquisition (for L1 acquisition, see Bates et al. 1984; Slobin 1966; for L2 acquisition, see Clahsen & Felser 2006, 2018; VanPatten 1996, 2020). As discussed in Section 1.2.4, it also occurs in native speaker sentence processing (e.g. Ferreira, Bailey & Ferraro 2002; Sanford & Sturd 2002).

As these findings show that comprehension is not only constrained by syntactic processing but also considerably influenced by semantic resources, these resources are included in the *Integrated Encoding-Decoding Model* and are also addressed in the empirical study.

4.2.2 Prototypicality

A further aspect that seemingly influences comprehension in language acquisition is the *prototypicality* of structures encountered in the input. The notion of linguistic prototypicality originates in research in the 1970s by Rosch and colleagues on the structure of natural categories (see e.g. Rosch 1978, 1988; Rosch & Mervis 1975; Mervis & Rosch 1981). Categorization by prototype challenged the classical Platonic view of categorization, which defined membership to a category in terms of a set of necessary and sufficient features (see Givón 1986). In linguistics, this classical approach is evident in the componential model of semantic analysis, which was popular within the framework of transformational grammar (see e.g. Katz & Fodor 1963). The prototype approach is based on the insight that 'the classical theory fails to predict the referential range of at least some words in everyday use' (Taylor 2003: 43), as categories can exhibit fuzzy boundaries (see e.g. Labov 1973; Wittgenstein 1953). Rosch (1975a: 544) observes that

> categories are not – as many research traditions in psychology, linguistics, and anthropology imply – logical, bounded entities, membership in which is defined by an item's possession of a simple set of criterial features, in which all instances possessing the criteria attributes have a full and equal degree of membership. Rather, many natural categories are internally structured into a prototype (clearest cases, best examples) of the category with nonprototype members tending towards an order from better to poorer examples.

The categorization of items in terms of typicality traits implies that category membership is not an all-or-nothing phenomenon. Instead, category membership is graded and categories have fuzzy boundaries. The prototypes, the best examples of a category, serve as cognitive reference points in relation to other category members (Rosch 1975a: 545). According to Radden (2008: 7), '[p]rototypes are those members of a category that are felt to be the best, i.e. the most central, salient and typical subcategories or individuals of their category'. The notion of prototypicality is exemplified with the category *birds* in Figure 4.2.

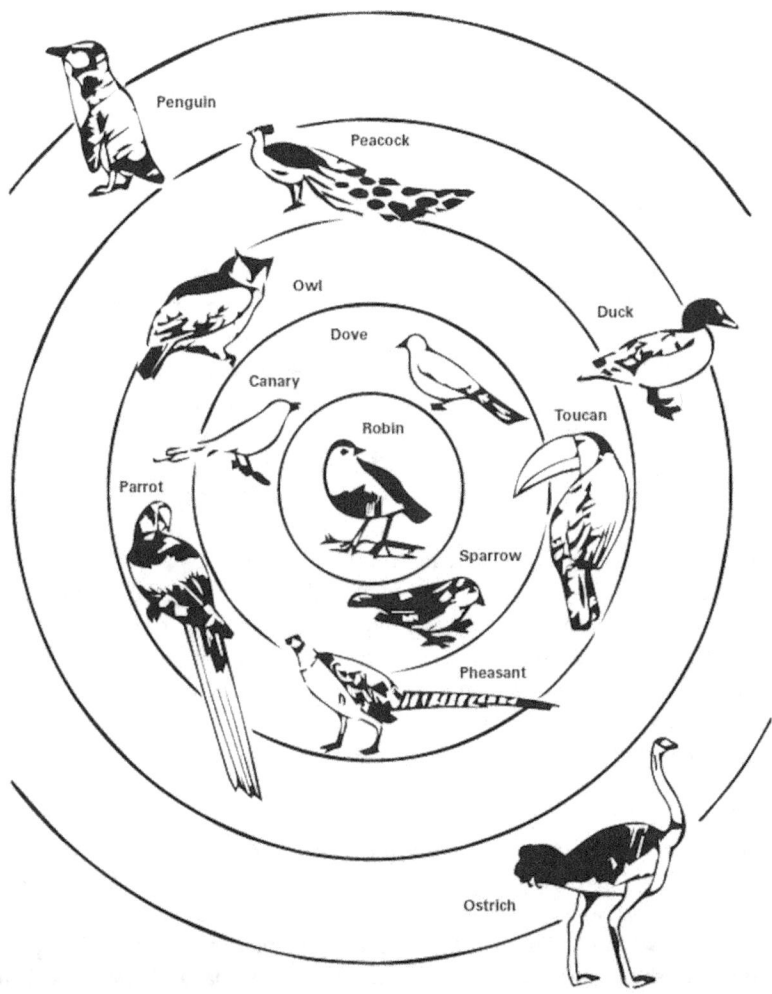

Figure 4.2 Birdiness ranking (from Aitchison 2012: 5, fig. 6.1). © 2012 John Wiley & Sons, Inc. Reprinted by permission of John Wiley & Sons.

Figure 4.2 is based on the results of Rosch's (1975b) study on the cognitive representations of semantic categories. The type of bird that is considered to be the most prototypical exemplar of the category *bird* – the robin – is placed at the centre of the circle. Less prototypical exemplars of birds, such as the penguin or the ostrich, are depicted at the margins. Figure 4.2 shows the graded nature of categories, with good examples of the category that share a large number of attributes depicted in the inner circle and poorer examples of the category that share only a few attributes with the more central category members occurring at the periphery (see Rosch & Mervis 1975). There is a wide range of evidence supporting the notion of prototypes. Following Radden (2008: 7), '[p]rototypes have been shown to display a number of "prototype effects" in experiments: they are rated as the best examples of a category, have the shortest reaction time in verifying them, are associated with the most attributes, and are mentioned first in naming tasks.'

Since the 1980s, the concept of prototypes has been widely adopted in linguistics (see e.g. Lakoff 1987; Langacker 1987; Taylor 2003; Wierzbicka 1985) and extensively applied to linguistic categorization (see e.g. Taylor 2003).[1] The question of the origin of prototypicality effects, however, still seems to be a contested issue. Rosch (1975c: 182) names inherent properties of human perception as one potential reason for some prototypicality effects. In her research on the natural categories colours and forms, she identifies perceptual salience as a core feature of prototypicality (Rosch 1973: 330). In this context, Taylor (2003: 56) argues that '[t]he prototypicality of focal colours very probably has a natural basis in the neurology of colour perception; in a sense, colour categories pre-exist their linguistic encoding.' However, he points out that, while this might be true for natural categories, other explanations have to be sought for artefactual categories, as '[t]here can be no question of a neurological basis to the perception of prototypical cups or furniture' (Taylor 2003: 56).

A further feature that is often associated with the notion of prototypicality is frequency. The underlying idea is that the more often humans encounter a particular item or word, the more likely it is for the concept or word to achieve prototypical status. Although intuitively appealing, there does not seem to be a one-to-one correspondence between prototypicality and frequency of occurrence, and many researchers do not regard frequency as a major influence on typicality effects (see e.g. Rosch, Simpson & Miller 1976; Stolz, Lestrade & Stolz 2014; but, for a different view, see Ibbotson & Tomasello 2009; N. C. Ellis 2012).

In this book, I adopt the view of prototypicality outlined in Meints (1999a: 69), who applies this concept to the linguistic category of the English passive. In general, she sees 'idealised prototypes as an orientational help in an (also idealised) cognitive category model'. In her work on the L1 production and comprehension of English passive constructions, she includes a number of semantic, conceptual and pragmatic factors characterizing the passive, such as focus, reversibility, event probability, affectedness and animacy as well as transitivity (see Section 5.1).

4.3 The relation between semantics and syntax in L2 comprehension

When attempting to integrate semantic aspects of language processing in the *Integrated Encoding-Decoding Model of SLA*, the question arises as to how semantic and syntactic processing are related in L2 parsing. As discussed in Section 1.2, a number of different perspectives on parsing have been proposed in the psycholinguistic literature, and the existing evidence is inconclusive as to how exactly semantic and syntactic parsing are

The Integrated Encoding-Decoding Model of SLA

related. The approach to sentence parsing adopted in this book is the *Online Cognitive Equilibrium Hypothesis* (Karimi & Ferreira 2016), which proposes a dual route in processing to account for instances of non-compositional language processing and the possibility of shallow processing in native speakers. As mentioned in Section 1.2.5, the core claim of the model is that, once an incoming input triggers a cognitive disequilibrium in the processing system, both the heuristic and the algorithmic processing route are activated in parallel in order to restore cognitive equilibrium as fast as possible. The interim output of the heuristic route influences algorithmic processing and is refined if necessary.

This model of sentence processing fits well with the overall assumptions of the *Integrated Encoding-Decoding Model of SLA*, and I argue that the proposed gradual development from semantic to syntactic processing in L2 acquisition can be explained by adapting Karimi and Ferreira's approach to sentence parsing to SLA. The adaptation of the *Online Cognitive Equilibrium Hypothesis* to SLA is presented in Figure 4.3.

As can be seen from Figure 4.3, I assume that, in principle, the two routes – the heuristic route and the algorithmic route – operate in parallel in L2 parsing. The heuristic route includes the two main parsing heuristics identified by Ferreira (2003: 192; see Section 1.2.4), namely (1) the N V N strategy, that is, the mapping of a 'noun-verb-noun syntactic template [...] into an agent-verb-patient thematic structure' (Karimi & Ferreira 2016: 1015), and (2) the plausibility strategy, which in essence states that the semantically most plausible analysis will be adopted by the parser. In addition, I hypothesize that related semantic aspects, such as prototypicality and lexical semantics, also play a crucial role in heuristic processing.

A further modification of Karimi and Ferreira's model concerns the algorithmic route, where syntactic processing takes place: I argue that, in L2 acquisition, the algorithmic route is the locus of PT's processing procedures. As outlined in Chapter 3, these procedures are acquired stepwise in the L2 acquisition process, and I hypothesize that the processing procedures also constrain the L2 syntactic parsing process. In keeping with these assumptions, I claim that – similar to L1 processing – L2 learners can, in principle, activate the heuristic route and the algorithmic route in parallel in L2 parsing. However, the algorithmic route is initially underdeveloped and L2 syntactic

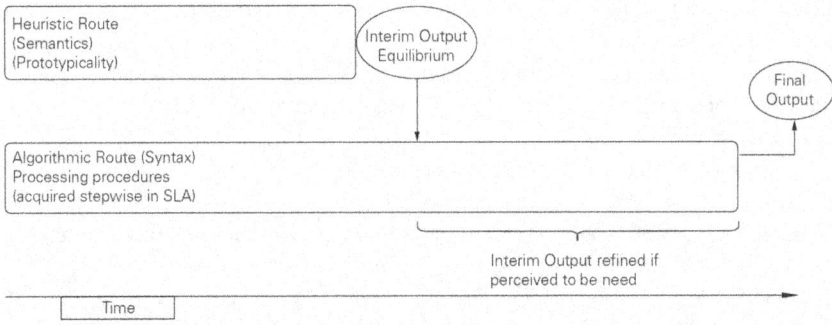

Figure 4.3 The *Online Cognitive Equilibrium Hypothesis* adapted to SLA.

parsing is constrained in terms of processability. As beginning L2 learners lack the necessary processing procedures for deep algorithmic processing, they primarily rely on semantic processing and direct mapping operations instead. Thus, initially, the interim output from the heuristic route is not further refined by the algorithmic route and constitutes the final output. The stepwise acquisition of L2 processing procedures and the gradual development of the L2 mental grammatical system enable the learner to successively rely on syntactic processing in L2 parsing. The increase in processing resources results in refinements of the interim results of the heuristic route by means of syntactic processing.

The conceptualization of L2 parsing in terms of a dual-pathway model is, in principle, compatible with the core claims of the *Shallow Structure Hypothesis* (SSH) by Clahsen and Felser (2006, 2018). Comparing studies on grammatical processing in adult native speakers, child L1 and adult L2 learners, Clahsen and Felser observed striking differences between native speakers and adult L2 learners in real-time processing. The SSH claims that 'unlike native speakers, even highly proficient L2 speakers tend to have problems building or manipulating abstract syntactic representations in real time and are guided more strongly than native speakers by semantic, pragmatic, probabilistic, or surface-level representation' (Clahsen & Felser 2018: 693–4). A further claim of the SSH is that 'grammatical constraints may be less robust in the L2 than in the L1 and that L2 processing tends to rely more on nongrammatical information than on the grammatical route to interpretation than L1 processing' (Clahsen & Felser 2018: 701). However, the claim that learners do not make use of syntactic information in the same way as native speakers do does not necessarily imply that L2 speakers do not have access to syntactic processing. Clahsen and Felser (2018: 697) argue that the L1/L2 processing differences can be understood as being gradual rather than binary oppositions and maintain that many of the observed differences between L1 and L2 processing can be accounted for by multiple-pathway models, pointing out that 'the models may well need refinement'.

The assumption that semantic and syntactic processing occur in parallel and that native speakers and L2 learners do not always rely on deep syntactic processing but also on shallow processing and underspecified representations implies that not all grammatical structures occurring in the input are necessarily processed. In L2 acquisition, this applies, for instance, to grammatical structures such as the '3sg -s' (John cook**s**) or the 'past -ed' marker in cases where a content word encodes the same meaning (e.g. **Yesterday**, John cook**ed** dinner.). This is captured in some of VanPatten's (1996, 2020) input processing principles, such as the *Lexical Preference Principle* or the *Preference for Nonredundancy Principle* (see e.g. VanPatten 2020: 108–9).[2] In the same vein, I argue that the auxiliary 'do' in 'Aux-2nd' structures, such as *What does Peter buy?*, will probably initially not be processed by L2 learners, as the auxiliary carries no intrinsic meaning in this particular construction. Thus, the question arises as to which grammatical structures are necessarily processed by L2 learners and are therefore suitable to test the hypothesis of a *shared grammatical workspace* in SLA and the related assumptions of the *Integrated Encoding-Decoding Model* sketched out in Section 4.1. As a possible solution to this problem, I chose to investigate the acquisition of passive constructions by L2 learners of English.

5

The English passive as a test case for the *Integrated Encoding-Decoding Model of SLA*

This chapter engages with English passive constructions, as the L2 acquisition of these structures is investigated in the empirical study in Chapter 7. In a first step, the chapter provides an introduction to some of the key characteristics of English passive constructions. Next, semantic aspects that influence the comprehension of English passives are presented. This is then followed by an LFG-based analysis of the English passive. In a final step, I outline my hypotheses concerning the processes involved in the L2 acquisition of passive constructions.

The active-passive alternation in English involves a change in voice. The same action can be described in two ways, which usually does not change the reported facts (but, for exceptions, see Quirk et al. 1985: 166) (examples taken from Quirk et al. 1985: 159):

(1) The butler murdered the detective.
(2) The detective was murdered by the butler.

This periphrastic form of the passive contains a form of the auxiliary *be* that is followed by the past participle of the main verb. English passives can, however, also be formed with *get*, as in example (3):

(3) He *got run over* (by a lorry).

Get-passives differ from be-passives in that they occur mostly without an expressed animate agent (see e.g. Carter & McCarthy 1999; Svartvik 1966). Furthermore, they occur more frequently in informal than in formal style (Quirk et al. 1985: 161). Some cases of get-constructions are classified as *resulting copulas*. These forms are labelled *pseudo-passives* by Quirk et al. (1985: 161), as they do not allow for an expression of the agent, as in example (4):

(4) I have to get dressed before eight o'clock.

Other forms of the pseudo-passive include constructions with the verbs *become, grow* and *seem*.[1]

In general, sentences that contain a transitive verb (e.g. *kick, play, see*) can be expressed in passive voice, as in example (5), whereas sentences with intransitive verbs cannot be passivized, as in example (6) (but, for exceptions to this rule, see Quirk et al. 1985: 162):

(5) The dog was seen by John.
(6) *The dog was slept.

In passivization, the agent by-phrase is considered to be optional, and according to Quirk et al. (1985: 1164–5) 'four out of five English passive sentences have no expressed agent. This omission occurs especially when the agent is irrelevant or unknown.' They point to a number of structural voice constraints, such as restrictions on the passivization of prepositional verbs or constraints related to the passivization of sentences with clauses as objects. A further constraint applies to the frequency with which active and passive forms occur in both oral speech and written texts. In general, active forms occur far more often than passives. However, there is considerable variation in the use of the passive depending on differences in text types and the type of prose that is used.

In the classification of English passives, a common distinction is made between *actional* or *dynamic* passives and *statal* or *stative* passives (e.g. Huddleston 1984; Kibort 2004). These are illustrated in examples (7) and (8):

(7) The vase was broken by John.
(8) The vase was already broken.

Whereas actional passives focus on a particular event that took place, statal passives 'attribute to their subject the property of being in the state resulting from a certain event' (Kibort 2004: 166). Kibort observes that, if the by-phrase is removed from sentence (7), the resulting sentence *The vase was broken* can belong to either of the two categories. According to her, the distinction between actional and statal passives closely corresponds to the one between *verbal* and *adjectival* passives (Kibort 2004: 167). In verbal passives, the passive participle is commonly analysed as head of the verb phrase, that is, as the main verb (see e.g. Bresnan 1982). In adjectival passives, on the other hand, the passive participle is often analysed as an adjective (but, for a different analysis of adjectival passives, see Kibort 2004).

Taking the different forms of English passive constructions into consideration, Quirk et al. (1985: 167) propose the 'passive gradient', which can be understood as a scale with true or central passives at one end and pseudo-passives at the other:

I. Central passives with or without expressed agents:
   These passives have a direct active-passive relation with either personal or impersonal agents.
   (*This violin was made by my father. This difficulty can be avoided in several ways.*)

II. Semi-passives:
Semi-passives exhibit both verbal and adjectival properties, i.e. they have active counterparts but have certain adjectival properties, such as the possibility to modify the participle with *quite, rather* or *more*.
(*Leonard was interested in linguistics.*)
III. Pseudo-passives:
These passives have no active counterpart and no possibility to add an agent.
(*The building is already demolished. The modern world is getting more industrialized.*)
(see Quirk et al. 1985: 167–71)

The empirical study investigates the L2 acquisition of those constructions that are labelled *central passives* by Quirk et al. (1985). The trial sentences used in the experiments all consist of central passives with expressed agents to be able to explore the acquisition of the underlying linguistic non-linearity between arguments at a-structure level and grammatical functions in f-structure in comprehension: The agent argument at a-structure level is not related to the subject function in f-structure, as is the case in active voice. Instead, the patient/theme argument is mapped onto the subject function and the agent is optionally realized as an oblique and expressed by means of a prepositional phrase.

Processing the non-linearity between arguments and grammatical functions in passive constructions is non-redundant in comprehension, as non-linear argument-function mapping is crucial in order to understand who does what to whom in the event expressed in a passive sentence. I hypothesize that, if the L2 learner has not acquired this mapping process, they rely on default mapping operations and interpret the initial NP as the agent argument (see Section 5.2.2). The initial assignment of the initial NP to the agent in passive constructions potentially leads to misinterpretations. In this scenario, the passive sentence *The man is kissed by the woman* is processed as 'man' (agent) 'kiss' (predicate) 'woman' (patient) and thus interpreted as an active sentence (*The man kisses the woman*).[2] Indeed, research in both L1 and L2 acquisition shows that, initially, learners tend to interpret passive sentences as active constructions and assign the sentence-initial noun phrase the agent function (for L1 acquisition, see e.g. Bever 1970; Hill 1998; Lempert 1978; Maratsos 1974; for L2 acquisition, see e.g. VanPatten 1984, 2020; Wang 2011).

5.1 Semantic factors influencing the comprehension of the passive

As discussed in Section 4.2, semantic factors play a crucial role in the comprehension process and this also applies to the comprehension of the passive. In such circumstances, the default interpretation of the first NP as agent can be overridden by semantic factors, in particular by lexical semantics, event probabilities and the overall prototypicality of the specific passive construction. This implies that, for certain passive constructions, comprehension may not be delayed by grammatical processing issues.

A semantic factor that influences the comprehension of passive constructions is related to the notion of reversibility and the general distinction that is made between reversible and non-reversible passives. In reversible passive constructions, both the subject NP (patient/theme) and the oblique NP (agent) are animate, as in example (9).

(9) The boy was kissed by the girl.

In the reversible passive construction in example (9), an exchange of agent and patient/theme would result in a logically possible meaning (*The boy was kissed by the girl* – *The girl was kissed by the boy*). In contrast, in non-reversible passives, as in example (10), the patient/theme in subject position is not animate.

(10) The door was opened by the boy.

In this case, a role reversal is not possible: As the patient/theme in subject position is not animate, lexical semantics does not allow for this kind of exchange (*The door was opened by the boy* – **The boy was opened by the door*). Research in L1 acquisition reveals that children acquire non-reversible passive constructions earlier than reversible passives (e.g. Bates et al. 1984; Hakuta 1982; Slobin 1966).

Event probabilities also crucially influence the comprehension of passive constructions. This is exemplified in examples (11) and (12):

(11)
    a) The baby was fed by the mother.
    b) The mother was fed by the baby.

(12)
    a) The boy was hugged by the girl.
    b) The girl was hugged by the boy.

Examples (11a) and (11b) illustrate cases of high and low event probability. Clearly, it is far more likely that the baby would be fed by the mother (11a) than the other way around (11b).

Examples (12a) and (12b) constitute instances of a 'neutral' event likelihood, as both events are considered to be equally likely to take place. Research findings in L1 acquisition indicate that, in comprehension, passives with high event probability are understood before passives with 'neutral' event likelihood (e.g. Bloom 1974; Chapman & Kohn 1978; Clark 1980). According to VanPatten (2020: 113–14), both lexical semantics and event probabilities also have an impact on L2 comprehension. He argues that the two types of semantic cues can override the default interpretation (first NP = agent). Applied to examples (11) and (12), it would be expected that L2 learners comprehend the passive construction in (11a) before the ones in (12a) and (12b).

A related factor that seemingly has an impact on the comprehension process of passive structures is their prototypicality. Research by Meints (1999a, b) investigated the L1 acquisition in production and comprehension of English passive constructions. Drawing on research on the internal structures of categories, Meints (1999a, b) views the English passive as a graded category with fuzzy boundaries that exhibits typicality effects. She argues that the English passive is 'a category which possesses an internal and graded structure with the canonical action event as its prototype and other kinds of passives as more peripheral members' (Meints 1999a: 69).

In determining the prototypicality of passive constructions, she includes a number of factors that in her view contribute to the typicality of different passive structures. These are 'the character of patient, agent, action and transitivity, focus, reversibility and event-probability' (Meints 1999a: 71). She argues that prototypical passive constructions should include the following factors:

1. The patient is
    - affected,
    - animate or inanimate, and
    - focused.

2. The action incorporates
    - a high degree of action,
    - punctuality,
    - direct physical contact, and
    - shows a visible result.

3. The agent is
    - acting,
    - animate, and
    - defocused.

According to Meints, the prototypical passive encompasses a transitive scene with focus on the patient. Ideally, the structure is 'semantically irreversible' (Meints 1999a: 71), a concept that incorporates the notions of reversibility and event probability introduced in this section. The idealized category of the passive is illustrated in Figure 5.1.

The non-reversible construction *John was run over by the lorry* is considered to be a prototypical passive, as it constitutes a transitive construction that focuses on the patient, displays a highly actional punctual action and is non-reversible (for the related notion of *semantic transitivity*, see Hopper & Thomson 1980). The sentence *John was seen by Mary* is also a transitive sentence with focus on the patient. However, it constitutes a reversible passive and contains a perception verb. Therefore, it is regarded as being a less prototypical construction occurring at the margins of the category passive.

The semantic, pragmatic and conceptual factors included in Meints's (1999a, b) conceptualization of the prototypical category passive have been shown to influence the L1 acquisition process of the English passive (for reversibility, see e.g. Slobin 1968; for event probability, see Strohner & Nelson 1974; for action vs. perception verbs, see Maratsos et al. 1985; for affectedness of agent and patient, see Hopper & Thomson

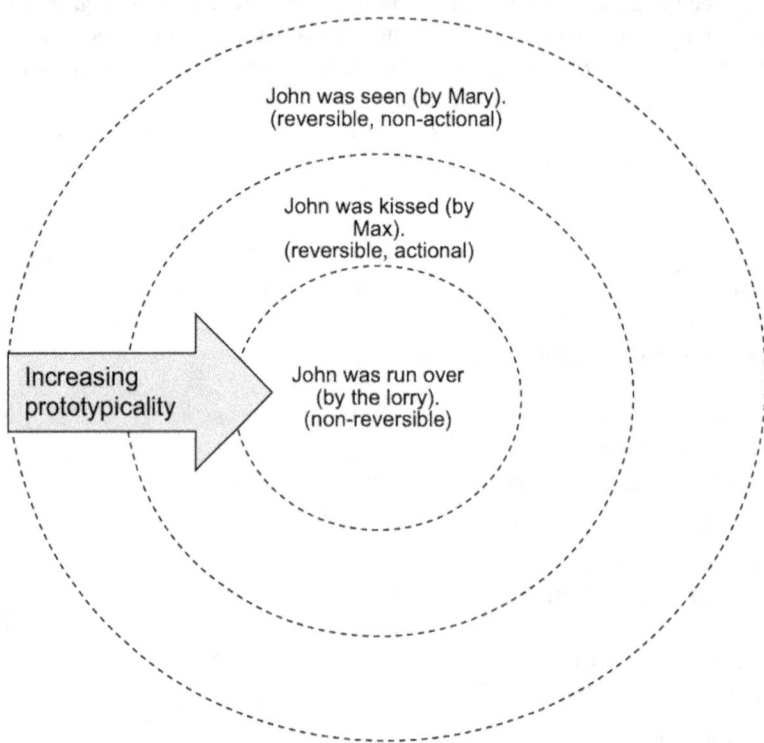

Figure 5.1 The idealized category of the passive with prototypical centre (adapted from Meints 1999b: 101, fig. 3). © 1999 Springer Nature. Adapted by permission of Springer Nature.

1980; Pinker, Lebaux & Frost 1987; for transitivity, Corrigan 1986; Marchman et al. 1991). Her own research on the L1 acquisition of English passives indicates that (1) children comprehend English passive structures earlier than they produce them and that (2) children acquire prototypical passives earlier than less prototypical forms in both production and comprehension. Meints (1999a: 73) points out that

> [t]he internal structure of the action expressed by the verb played a crucial role in the comprehension and production of the English passive. The higher the degree of implicit actionality and punctuality of the action, the more obviously the action brings about a visible result, and the more direct the contact between patient and agent, the more the production and the comprehension of the passive is facilitated.

To sum up, semantic factors play a crucial role in comprehension in general and, naturally, this also applies to the comprehension of English passive constructions. This is mirrored in the L1 acquisition of passive structures. Research findings suggest that the initial comprehension of prototypical passives, including the factors of non-reversibility and biased event probability, reflects semantic processing. In these cases, learners do not rely on full syntactic processing in order to correctly interpret the sentence. Applying these findings to the L2 acquisition of English passives, I claim that semantic processing also plays a crucial role in L2 comprehension and I assume that, in L2 acquisition, the comprehension of non-reversible passives and passives with biased event probability occurs at an earlier stage than the comprehension of reversible passives. I also argue that such examples do not test claims about the existence of unitary syntactic processing in L2 acquisition.

As semantic factors play a crucial role in the acquisition process, I aimed to incorporate some influential semantic factors in the design of my empirical study on the L2 acquisition of English passive constructions in production and comprehension. In keeping with this, the tasks encompass passive constructions that differ in terms of reversibility and event probability.

5.2 The English passive in LFG

In order to investigate the L2 acquisition of the English passive in both modalities and to be able to make claims about shared syntactic processing procedures involved in the production and comprehension of the passive, it is essential to first assign the structure to a specific stage of acquisition in terms of the PT hierarchy. This, in turn, requires a detailed LFG analysis of English passive constructions with regard to both feature unification and mapping processes.

The core tenets of LFG were briefly introduced in Section 3.2, where I pointed out that the theory constitutes a non-derivational approach to syntax. In keeping with this, passivization is conceived as a non-transformational process in LFG. Bresnan (2001: 26) argues that both active and passive verb forms have the same predicate-argument structure. The difference between the two is an alternative set of grammatical functions that are lexically associated with the arguments. The details of this mapping operation between arguments and grammatical functions are formalized in *Lexical Mapping Theory*, which was first introduced by Bresnan and Kanerva (1989).

5.2.1 *Lexical Mapping Theory*

Lexical Mapping Theory focuses on the relations between arguments and grammatical functions. According to Bresnan and Kanerva (1989: 22), *Lexical Mapping Theory* consists of the following four major components: '(a) hierarchically ordered semantic role structures, (b) a classification of syntactic functions along two dimensions, (c) principles of lexical mapping from semantic roles to (partially specified) functions, and (d) well-formedness conditions on lexical forms.'

The first two components – the hierarchy of thematic roles and the classification of syntactic functions – were introduced in Section 3.2.3. The third one – the mapping from thematic roles to syntactic functions – is governed by the following three principles of lexical mapping (Bresnan & Kanerva 1989: 25):

1. intrinsic role classifications
2. morpho-lexical operations
3. default classifications

The intrinsic role classifications are assumed to be universal and apply cross-linguistically (Bresnan & Kanerva 1989: 26). They consist of three principles that relate the intrinsic meaning of the semantic roles to specific syntactic functions. The *agent encoding principle* specifies that the intrinsic value of the agent role is constrained to [–o]. In this way, the agent can only be encoded as subject or oblique. The *theme encoding principle* states that the value of the patient/theme role is unrestricted [–r], so that the patient/theme is realized as either subject or object. The locative encoding principle specifies that the locative is encoded as a non-objective function, receiving the feature [–o].

The morpho-lexical operations affect lexical argument structure in that the operations add or suppress thematic roles. Bresnan and Kanerva assume that, in the case of passivization, a morpho-lexical operation suppresses the highest thematic role in a-structure, the logical subject (the agent in Figure 5.2). In this scenario, the lower unrestricted role (the patient) is mapped onto the SUBJ function.

Once the morpho-lexical operations have taken place and a-structure has been built up in a morpho-lexical way, default classifications apply that specify that the highest thematic role is mapped onto the SUBJ function. All thematic roles that are lower in the thematic hierarchy are realized as non-subjects. This means that the highest thematic role ($\hat{\theta}$) is classified as unrestricted and assigned the feature [–r]. All other roles that are lower in the thematic hierarchy are classified as restricted and are assigned the feature [+r] (Bresnan & Kanerva 1989: 27). Bresnan and Kanerva (1989: 28) further specify that 'all default classifications apply to a role only if it is not already specified for an incompatible value of the default feature'. Finally, two well-formedness conditions on lexical form apply that further constrain the mapping from arguments to grammatical functions.

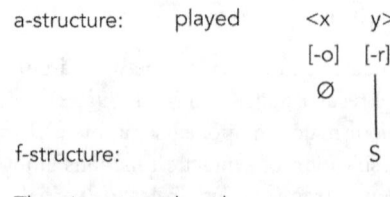

The piano was played.

Figure 5.2 Morpho-lexical operations in passives (from Lenzing 2016: 7, fig. 1). Reprinted by permission of John Benjamins.

The subject condition: Every lexical form must have a subject.

Function-argument biuniqueness: In every lexical form, every expressed lexical role must have a unique syntactic function, and every syntactic function must have a unique lexical role. (Bresnan & Kanerva 1989: 28)

Figure 5.3 illustrates the mapping operations between arguments and grammatical functions as proposed in *Lexical Mapping Theory*. As can be seen from Figure 5.3, in the sentence *John placed the plate on the table*, the verb *place* takes three arguments (x, y & z). These are assigned the thematic roles *agent*, *theme* and *locative*. The first principle of *Lexical Mapping Theory*, the *intrinsic role classification*, specifies that the agent argument is assigned the feature [–o]. The theme argument is classified as [–r] and the locative is classified as [–o]. The *default classification* specifies that the highest thematic role, the agent, receives the feature [–r] and the locative receives the feature [+r]. Finally, the well-formedness conditions on lexical form apply. In this case, the function-argument biuniqueness condition assigns the theme to the OBJ function (see Lenzing 2016: 8).

To sum up, in *Lexical Mapping Theory*, the relation between arguments and grammatical functions is governed by a number of precisely spelled out principles and conditions. The principles introduced in this section have been adopted within the PT framework to account for the acquisition of structures requiring non-linear mapping operations between arguments and grammatical functions, such as passivization.

Current LFG accounts formalize passivization in terms of some version of *Lexical Mapping Theory*. However, a number of different approaches have been proposed within the LFG framework that differ in their view on the number of lexical entries as well as the exact details of the mapping processes involved in passivization (e.g. Bresnan 2001; Dalrymple 2001; Falk 2001; Kibort 2004, 2005). For instance, Falk (2001: 94) views the suppression of the logical subject as the core process in passivization and argues that there are two lexical entries, one for the active and one for the passive form. Bresnan (2001) and Dalrymple (2001) do not specifically comment on the question of the number of lexical entries but share Falk's account of the suppression of the logical subject.

place	<x	y	z >	
	(agent)	(theme)	(locative)	
	[-o]	[-r]	[-o]	intrinsic role classification
	[-r]		[+r]	default classification
	SUBJ	SUBJ/OBJ	OBL$_\theta$	
		OBJ		function/arg. biuniqueness
	John placed	the plate	on the table.	

Figure 5.3 Principles and constraints in a- to f-structure mapping (from Lenzing 2016: 8, fig. 2). Reprinted by permission of John Benjamins.

The approach that I adopt in my account of the processes involved in the L2 acquisition of English passives is the one proposed by Kibort (2004, 2005). Her account differs from the standard LFG analysis of passivization, which is based on the suppression of the logical subject argument. Kibort views passivization as a 'demotional operation', where the thematically highest argument is not suppressed but 'demoted' to the lower grammatical function of oblique. In this way, the passive operation 'is captured at the syntactic level or argument structure' (Kibort 2004: 71), thus leaving the semantic side unaffected. Instead of suppressing the thematically highest argument, this underspecified argument is restricted in terms of its syntactic classification, 'specifying that it must map onto a restricted grammatical function characteristic of obliques' (Kibort 2004: 363).

The view of passivization as a demotional operation instead of a 'promotional' one, in which the lower argument that is usually mapped onto the object position becomes 'promoted' to the subject position, has several advantages. The semantic side of a-structure is preserved and the number of arguments is the same in active and passive constructions. According to Kibort (2004: 362), the standard LFG analysis of passivization is problematic in that the analysis does not account for the potential realization of the agent argument as an adjunct in a straightforward way. She points out that the suppressed agent argument cannot receive any syntactic specifications and cannot be mapped onto a syntactic argument. By formalizing passivization as a 'demotional' operation, the semantic side of the predicate is preserved. This also means that there is no need for two separate lexical entries, as changes in voice merely affect the syntactic side of a-structure. In my opinion, this account is much more plausible than assuming changes to the argument structure as such (i.e. also to the semantic side) and/or the conceptualization of the active/passive alternation as involving two separate lexical entries.

5.2.2 Processing the English passive in L2 acquisition

My hypotheses concerning the acquisition of the passive constitute a modification of the formalization of the passive in PT by Pienemann, Di Biase and Kawaguchi (2005), which is based on the principles of *Lexical Mapping Theory*. My modified account of this formalization integrates Kibort's (2004, 2005) view of passivization as a morpho-lexical operation on argument structure. This is further complemented by allocating the different processes involved in passivization to the different components present in the language generation process.

The processes that form the prerequisite for a target-like production of passive constructions are illustrated in Figure 5.4 with the example sentence *The cake was eaten by John*. In this account of passivization, I distinguish between processes that occur in the lexicon and processes that take place in the formulator.

Processes taking place in the lexicon

I assume that the following two major processes occur in the lexicon:

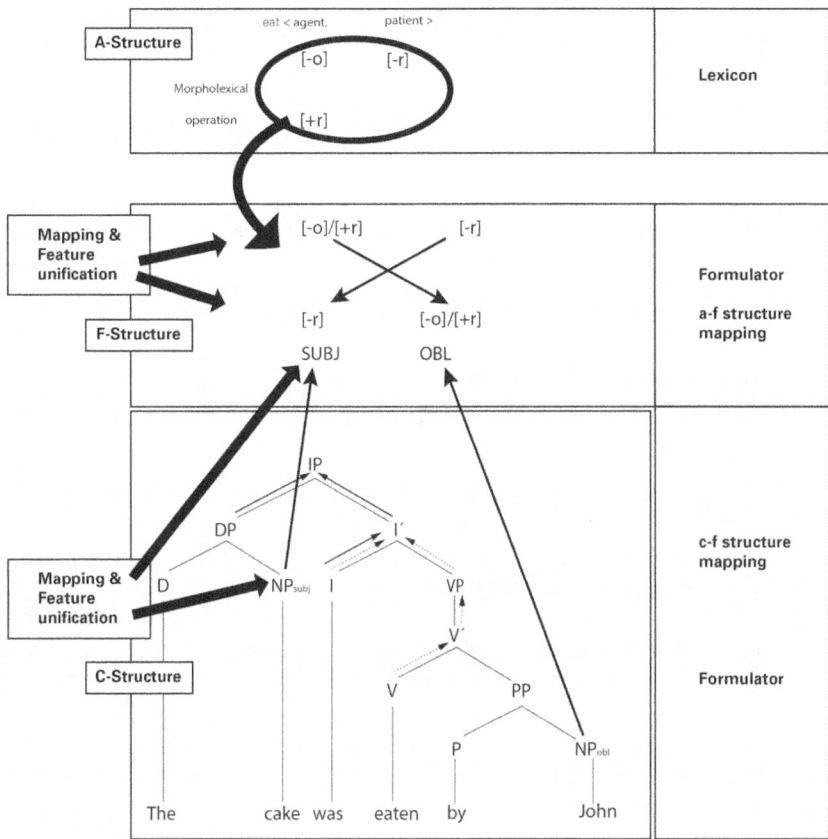

Figure 5.4 The English passive: feature unification and mapping processes.

1. the annotation of arguments for syntactic features
2. the morpho-lexical operation to demote the highest argument

A first requirement in passivization is the annotation of the syntactic side of a-structure for the relevant syntactic features [±o] and [±r]. These are essential to map arguments onto grammatical functions at f-structure level. In the example in Figure 5.4, the agent argument (*John*) receives the feature [−o], and the patient/theme argument (*the cake*) receives the feature [−r]. In a second step, the underspecified agent argument is demoted by adding a restriction to it (see Kibort 2004). In the example sentence, the agent argument is restricted by the feature [+r], which is added by a morpho-lexical operation. I argue that both processes – the annotation of arguments for syntactic features and the morpho-lexical operation that demotes the highest argument by adding a restriction – occur in the lexicon.

As regards the question of at what stage in the L2 acquisition process the two processes are acquired, I propose that these processes cannot be allocated to a specific stage, as they cannot be captured in terms of PT's processing procedures. In the *Multiple Constraints Hypothesis* (see Section 3.6), I argued that the annotation of the L2 learner's mental lexicon for syntactic features constitutes a gradual process and that initially, the L2 learner's entries in the mental lexicon lack a full annotation of the syntactic side of a-structure, which results in an inability to map arguments onto grammatical functions. In the case of passivization, the morpho-lexical operation sketched out in this section depends on the full annotation of a-structure for its syntactic features. In line with this, I claim that this gradual annotation is part of individual learner variation and cannot be explained in terms of the acquisition of the processing procedures spelled out in PT.

Processes taking place in the formulator

I hypothesize that, in passivization, the following mapping and feature unification operations take place in the formulator:

- non-linear mapping operation between arguments and grammatical functions (feature unification between syntactic classification of arguments and corresponding grammatical functions)
- linear mapping operation between constituents and grammatical functions
- annotation of c-structure rules for grammatical functions
- feature unification within the verb phrase

The non-linear mapping process between a- and f-structure present in passivization aligns the arguments with the grammatical functions by unifying the syntactic features assigned to the arguments with the syntactic classifications of the grammatical functions. In Figure 5.4, the syntactic features of the agent argument (*John*) ([−o/+r]) are unified with the syntactic features of the grammatical function oblique ([−o/+r]), and the feature of the patient/theme argument (*the cake*) ([−r]) is unified with the feature of the subject function ([−r]).

The unification process underlying the mapping of arguments onto grammatical functions again depends on the annotation of the syntactic side of a-structure. Therefore, I argue that it cannot be allocated to a specific PT stage but instead its acquisition constitutes a gradual process. However, I assume that non-linear argument-function mapping does not take place before the L2 learner has reached stage 3. From a theoretical perspective, stage 3 allows the learner to assign lexical items a syntactic category and to process phrases. In my view, assigning lexical items a syntactic category is a crucial prerequisite for lexical mapping, as learners need to access the syntactic information associated with the lexical item. In particular, this applies to the syntactic information of the verb and its corresponding arguments. The syntactic realization of the verb's arguments at the level of c-structure requires at least the phrasal procedure to be in place if arguments are not mapped directly onto surface form. As discussed in Section 3.5 passive constructions cannot be realized by relying on direct mapping processes due to their underlying non-linearity. From an empirical perspective, I have shown in Lenzing (2013) that learners at the first two stages of acquisition have problems with syntactically realizing the arguments that are required by the respective verbs in constructions that involve non-linear mapping processes (apart from formulaic use of these structures). I have argued that these processing difficulties arise because the L2 learner's a-structure is not fully annotated, which leads to the inaccessibility of grammatical functions at f-structure level.

A second process that takes place in the formulator is the mapping between c- and f-structure. In passivization, this process is linear, that is, the first NP is mapped onto the subject. Again, I hypothesize that, in order to perform this mapping operation, the phrasal procedure needs to be in place to build the respective NPs and PPs. This procedure is acquired at stage 3 of L2 acquisition. Applied to the example in Figure 5.4 this operation ensures that the first NP (*the cake*) is mapped onto the subject and that the PP (*by John*) is mapped onto the oblique function.

At c-structure level, a further prerequisite for the target-like production of the English passive is the feature unification process within the verb phrase. As discussed in Section 3.4, in PT, the VP procedure is acquired at stage 4 (Pienemann 2005: 24). To achieve agreement between the auxiliary and the participle in English passive constructions, the information about the feature 'participle' has to be matched between the auxiliary and the verb. This is illustrated in Figure 5.5 using the example sentence *The cake is eaten by John*.

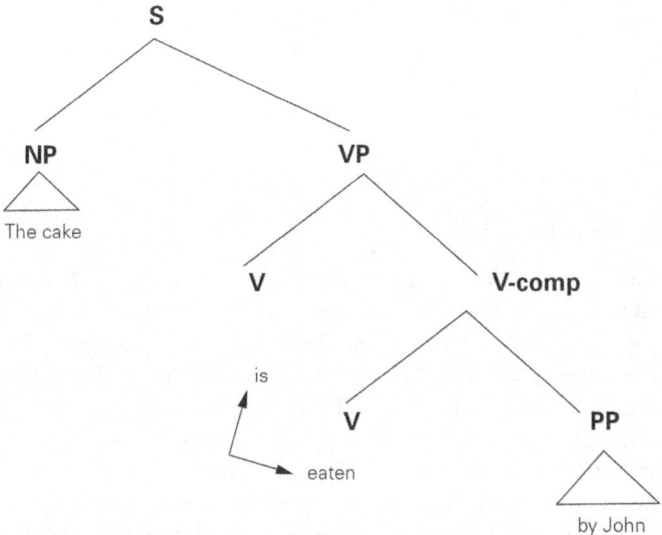

Figure 5.5 C-structure for the sentence *The cake is eaten by John*.

is: V, PRED = 'be', V-Comp (SUBJ)
TENSE = PRESENT
AUX = +
NUM = SG
PERSON = 3rd
V-COMP PARTICIPLE = $_c$PAST

eaten: V, PRED = 'eat (SUBJ), (OBL)'
PARTICIPLE = PAST

Figure 5.6 Lexical entries for the auxiliary and the verb in the sentence *The cake is eaten by John*.

As shown in Figure 5.6, the full lexical entry *is* contains the constraint equation V-COMP PARTICIPLE = $_c$PAST that specifies that the V-COMP contains a past participle. This feature has to be unified to generate a grammatically well-formed passive sentence. In order to be able to produce target-like passives, the L2 learner's mental lexicon has to be annotated for the respective features (in this case, the specification of the past participle). The constraint equation V-COMP PARTICIPLE = $_c$PAST rules out sentences like examples (13)–(15):

(13) *The cake is eat by John.
(14) *The cake is eats by John.
(15) *The cake is eating by John.

However, as postulated in the *Multiple Constraints Hypothesis*, the L2 learner's mental lexicon is gradually annotated, which implies that the respective lexical entries are initially not fully annotated for the relevant constraint equations. It is indeed the case that sentences such as examples (13)–(15) frequently occur in early learner language (see Chapter 7).

Form-function relationships

A further aspect in processing English passive constructions relates to the acquisition of the language-specific form-function relationships in verb morphology. Pienemann (1998: 154–5) argues that, in L2 morphological processing, it is important to distinguish between two aspects, namely (1) the processing procedures that are required in different kinds of affixation processes and (2) the 'learning of morphological forms in relation to their functions'. He considers these two kinds of processes to be different and claims that 'the learning of the morphological form of the affix constitutes a task that is different from managing the information distribution in the affixation process where diacritic features have to be exchanged within different grammatical structures'.

Pienemann distinguishes between different kinds of complex form-function relationships that deviate from a one-to-one relation between form and function. In Figures 5.7 and 5.8, one-to-many relationships and many-to-one relationships are illustrated.

The example of the German morpheme 'e' as a case marker shows that there are cases where one morpheme marks a number of diacritic features. In this example, the morpheme 'e' marks the dative when the noun is masculine or neuter and singular. In many-to-one relationships, one feature is marked by several morphemes. This is, for instance, the case in the plural marking of German nouns, as illustrated in Figure 5.8.

The morphological marking of the past participle in English includes both one-to-many and many-to-one relationships (see Figure 5.9). On the one hand, the past participle can be marked with several inflectional morphemes depending on the verb. In addition, the morpheme '-ed' also marks the past tense.

Whereas the acquisition of the VP procedure at stage 4 in principle enables the L2 learner to process the unification of the features present in the lexical entries of both auxiliary and verb, the L2 learner additionally has to acquire the form-function relations involved in the affixation of the past participle. In line with Pienemann (1998), I argue that this task is not dependent on the processing procedures and therefore its acquisition constitutes a gradual process that is subject to individual learner variation.

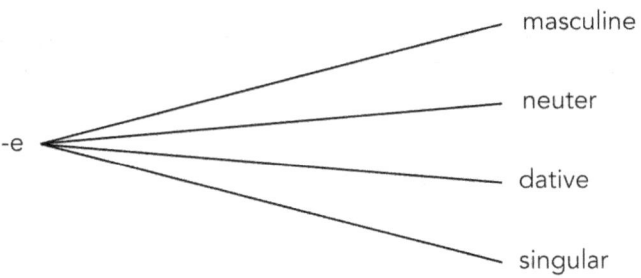

Figure 5.7 One-to-many relationship in German case marking (from Pienemann 1998: 157, fig. 4.3-4). Reprinted by permission of John Benjamins.

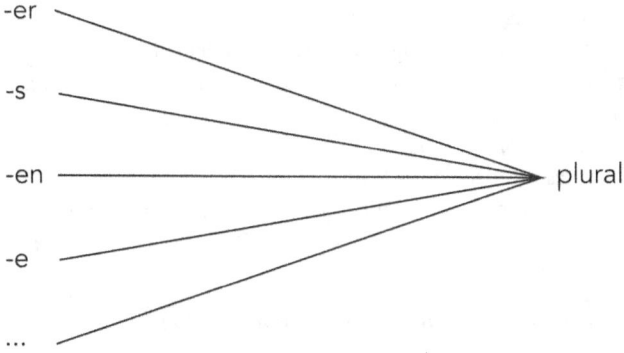

Figure 5.8 Many-to-one relationship in German plural marking (from Pienemann 1998: 157, fig. 4.3-5). Reprinted by permission of John Benjamins.

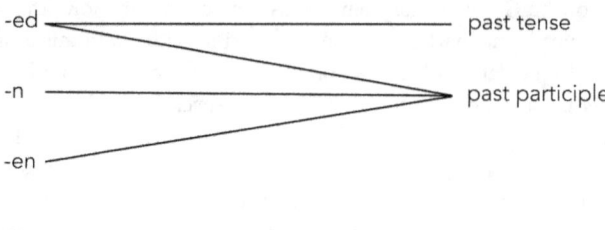

Figure 5.9 Form-function relationships '-ed'/past participle.

I assume that the process of acquiring the form-function relationships involved in the affixation of the past participle proceeds gradually from stage 4 onwards, when the VP procedure is in place.

On the basis of this LFG/PT-based analysis of the English passive, I argue that the passive cannot be assigned a single PT stage. I have shown that (1) the different processes sketched out in this chapter and illustrated in Figure 5.4 are acquired at different stages of acquisition and that (2) not all processes can be explained in terms of the processes assumed to underlie the PT stages, that is, feature unification and mapping operations.

Hypothesized L2 developmental sequence of English passives

I hypothesize that the initial restrictions constraining the underdeveloped L2 syntactic processor result in the following proposed sequence of both encoding and decoding of English passives:

1. Shallow processing/linear argument-function mapping:
   - the first noun phrase is assigned the role of agent or experiencer
   - syntactic features are missing in the lexicon.
2. Non-linear argument-function mapping:
   - the first noun phrase is assigned the role of patient/theme
   - syntactic features become involved in unification processes of argument-function mapping.
3. Morpho-syntactic processing:
   - incorporates the c-structure level
   - incorporates both feature unification within the VP and form-function relationships.

Minimal requirements production and comprehension

As far as the production and the comprehension of the English passive are concerned, I claim that they are based on partially different processes. I hypothesize that differentiation between production and comprehension of the passive occurs because different minimal requirements apply rather than because of differences in processing procedures. I propose specific minimal requirements for the production (encoding) and the comprehension (decoding) of the passive that are needed in order to produce or to comprehend a specific structure. These minimal requirements are based on the theoretical assumptions outlined in this chapter. I argue that comprehension does not occur before production due to an advance in processing procedures but rather because of different minimal requirements.

Based on the analysis of the processes involved in the English passive sketched out in this chapter I assume that the following three requirements at the different levels of linguistic representations have to be met in order for L2 learners to be able to *produce* English passive constructions.

1. Non-linear argument-function mapping (gradual process, not before stage 3)
2. Feature unification within the VP (stage 4)
3. Form-function relationships (gradual process, beginning at stage 4)

I argue that, despite a substantial overlap in processing resources, the requirements for the *comprehension* of English passives are slightly different from those for production. A main difference relates to semantic aspects in parsing, which play a crucial role in comprehension (see Section 4.2). In line with the adaptation of the *Online Cognitive Equilibrium Hypothesis* to SLA, I argue that, in some cases, semantic factors can override syntactic processing in comprehension. As regards the comprehension of passive constructions, this applies to non-reversible passives and passives with high event probabilities. I assume that semantic processing is particularly prominent in early L2 acquisition, when learners have not yet acquired the relevant syntactic processing procedures. Otherwise, as in production, the learners have to acquire non-linear argument-function mapping, which I assume to be a gradual process. Full syntactic processing in the comprehension of English passive constructions requires the verb phrase procedure to be in place (stage 4), as L2 learners have to process the verb construction (be + past participle) in order to comprehend the sentence as having passive voice. In contrast to the production of passives, I argue that the acquisition of form-function relationships is not a necessary prerequisite for the comprehension process. The minimal requirements for the comprehension of English passive constructions can be summarized as follows:

1. Non-linear argument-function mapping (gradual process, not before stage 3)
2. Feature unification within the VP (stage 4)
    Semantic processing can override syntactic processing

These considerations form the basis for investigating the relation of grammatical encoding and decoding in the production and comprehension of L2 English passives across different developmental stages in the empirical study.

6

The study: Methodological considerations

The study presented in this book consists of a series of three thematically related sub-studies that form a whole. The sub-studies are cross-sectional in design and examine different aspects of the L2 acquisition process in both production and comprehension. Overall, a total of eighty-one learners of English in a school-based context in Germany at different stages of L2 development participated in the three studies.

As the sub-studies are thematically connected, there are a number of general methodological considerations that are relevant to all three of them. This applies in particular to the experimental design of the studies and the tasks used for data collection. In all three sub-studies, L2 oral speech production data as well as L2 comprehension data were elicited. The data collection focused on the following three aspects of L2 acquisition:

1. the learners' stages of acquisition according to *Processability Theory* (PT)
2. the learners' acquisition of English passives in speech production
3. the learners' acquisition of English passives in speech comprehension

The oral speech production data were collected for the following two purposes: They served (1) to determine the L2 learners' developmental stages and (2) to investigate the L2 learners' ability to produce English passive constructions at the different stages of acquisition. In a similar vein, the comprehension data focused on the L2 learners' ability to comprehend English passive constructions. In this way, the study aims to relate the individual L2 learners' developmental stage to their production and comprehension of passive constructions.

Different kinds of tasks were developed to shed light on the various aspects involved in the L2 acquisition of production and comprehension. An overview of the tasks used in the three sub-studies is given in Table 6.1. The first sub-study – Sub-study 1 – served as a pilot study to test the production and comprehension tasks designed to elicit English passive constructions. Owing to several limitations of the passive production task, only the comprehension data were considered in the analysis of the L2 acquisition of passive constructions in Sub-study 1 (see Section 6.3 for more details).

Table 6.1 Overview of tasks.

Type of data	Tasks	Sub-study
Oral speech production I: stages of acquisition	Communicative tasks	1, 2 & 3
Oral speech production II: passive	Picture description task	1*
	Fish film	2 & 3
	Film clips	
Comprehension passive I: general	Sentence-picture matching task	1 & 3
	Enactment task	2
Comprehension passive II: morpho-syntactic processing	Sentence-matching reaction time experiment	3

Note. * not included in analysis.

6.1 Oral speech production tasks I: Stages of acquisition

In order to be able to establish linguistic profiles of the L2 learners' interlanguage grammars and to determine their stages of acquisition, for each learner a data sample of their spontaneous oral speech production was collected and analysed within the PT framework. The speech samples were elicited with three different *communicative tasks*. These tasks are considered to be the most effective means to elicit spontaneous oral speech production data that exhibit the necessary data density to establish a learner's interlanguage profile.

There is no general consensus among researchers and language teachers as to an exact definition of the term *task*, and various definitions of the term exist in the literature.[1] However, two defining features are recurrent in the various existing definitions. Firstly, a task should be *goal-oriented*. This means that, in carrying out the task, participants should arrive at a specific outcome. Secondly, a task should involve *work* or *activity*, so that participants are actively involved in working on the task (see Pica, Kanagy & Falodun 1993: 11).

Communicative tasks constitute a specific type of task that incorporates the notions of *interactional activity* and *communication goal*. According to Pica, Kanagy and Falodun (1993: 13), the two concepts relate to the idea that the task should encourage participants to engage in meaningful interaction and to negotiate towards mutual comprehension to arrive at a meaningful outcome. A further core characteristic of communicative tasks is their focus on meaning. Nunan (1989: 10) argues that a communicative task is '[a] piece of […] work which involves learners in comprehending, manipulating, producing or interacting in the target language while their attention is primarily focused on meaning rather than form. The task should have a sense of completeness, being able to stand alone as a communicative act in its own right.'

Pica, Kanagy and Falodun (1993: 17) suggest a number of conditions that communicative tasks used for research purposes should meet in order to be efficient.

1. Each interactant holds a different portion of information which must be exchanged and manipulated in order to reach the task outcome.
2. Both interactants are required to request and supply this information to each other.
3. Interactants have the same or convergent goals.
4. Only one acceptable outcome is possible from their attempts to meet this goal.

The first two conditions relate to the notion of an *information gap*, which means that each participant holds information the other one does not have. This information needs to be exchanged in order to complete the task. An information gap in a task is regarded as a central element in triggering authentic communication.

In the design of the tasks used in the present study, the criteria outlined above were taken into consideration. In this way, the tasks provided a context for spontaneous oral speech production. Additionally, they aimed at the production of specific morpho-syntactic structures that are relevant for a PT-based analysis, such as different types of question forms or the '3sg -s' feature. In order to achieve this end, the task design was based on a number of tasks that had been empirically tested in the context of the PT framework (see e.g. Lenzing 2013; Pienemann 1998; Pienemann & Mackey 1993; Roos 2007), as these have shown to be the most effective means of profiling a learner's interlanguage.

The tasks that were employed in the data collection of the study to establish the L2 learners' interlanguage profiles are summarized in Table 6.2. As can be seen from Table 6.2, the tasks aimed at the production of different kinds of question forms, affirmative and negative statements, the fronting of adverbs, and specific morphemes such as the '3sg -s' or the 'plural -s'. These morpho-syntactic structures are relevant for determining the L2 learners' respective developmental stages.

Table 6.2 Tasks for oral speech production data.

Tasks for data elicitation		
1. Habitual actions	**2. Picture differences**	**3. Role play: Meet a Martian**
Targeted structures: – declarative sentences – third person sg -s – adverb fronting	Targeted structures: – question forms – declarative sentences	Targeted structures: – question forms – declarative sentences
Subjects were each given a set of pictures. The pictures relate to a couple, one set depicting the daily activities of a male and the other set the activities of a female person. In an alternating fashion, the subjects described the activities of the respective person to their partner.[2]	Subjects were each given one picture. The two pictures were largely identical except for five differences. The subjects were encouraged to ask questions to find out about the differences and to give positive and negative responses.	Subjects were asked to participate in a role play. One subject was assigned the role of a Martian who had just landed on Earth with a spaceship. The other subject was assigned the role of an Earthling who met the Martian. They were then encouraged to ask their partner questions about life on Mars and life on Earth respectively.

6.2 Experimental stimuli in elicitation of passives in production and comprehension

A number of general considerations guided the selection of the stimuli used in the tasks for the elicitation of English passives in production and comprehension. As the study aimed at exploring the influence of the semantic factors of reversibility, event probability and prototypicality on the L2 acquisition process of English passives, I included the following types of experimental sentences in both production and comprehension tasks.

1) Symmetrical reversible passives

These types of passives are reversible in that both arguments can be exchanged, and the active and the passive interpretations of the stimulus sentence are equally plausible (*Santa Claus follows the pirate* vs. *Santa Claus is followed by the pirate*).

In Sub-studies 1 and 3, a further distinction was made between *actional* and *non-actional* symmetrical reversible passives: *Actional* passives contain an action verb (e.g. *kick*, as in *The boy is kicked by the girl*), whereas *non-actional* passives encompass a non-action verb (e.g. *hear*, as in *The daughter is heard by the mother*). Passive constructions with action verbs are regarded as being more prototypical than passive constructions with non-action verbs (see Meints 1999a, b), as the latter exhibit less prototypical characteristics. In L1 acquisition, reversible passives with action verbs are acquired earlier than reversible passives with non-actional verbs (see e.g. Maratsos et al. 1985; Pinker, Lebaux & Frost 1987; Sudhalter & Braine 1985).

2) Biased reversible passives

Biased reversible passives also constitute reversible passive constructions, as both arguments can be exchanged. However, in these structures, one arrangement is much more plausible than the other one. In the case of an active interpretation of the passive stimulus, the event probability is fairly low (*The cat is fed by the woman* vs. *The cat feeds the woman*). In L1 acquisition, biased reversible passives are acquired before reversible passives with equal event probability in L1 acquisition, as L1 learners rely on semantic cues in processing these constructions (see Section 5.1).

3) Non-reversible passives

In non-reversible passive constructions, one argument is animate and the other argument is inanimate, as in *The wall is painted by the boy*. Therefore, the arguments cannot be exchanged without rendering the sentence implausible, as in *The wall paints the boy*. In L1 acquisition, non-reversible passives are acquired before reversible passives. Again, L1 learners are assumed to rely on semantic cues in processing non-reversible passives (see Section 5.1).

4) Passives with three arguments

In addition to the passives that differ in terms of their reversibility, the study also encompasses passive constructions that contain three arguments, as in *The plant is put on the table by the man*. In ditransitive constructions, a simple exchange of arguments is not possible. These types of passives were included in the study to investigate whether their production and comprehension differs from the one of passive constructions with two arguments. A study that explored the L1 acquisition of ditransitive passives in comprehension is the one by O'Grady (1997). The results of O'Grady's study show that 'the comprehension of the passive version of ditransitive verbs lagged far behind all other constructions studied [actives with transitive verbs & passives with transitive verbs]' (O'Grady 1997: 214).

The semantic properties of the trial sentences used in the study were assessed in a separate study. In order to determine the plausibility of the different test stimuli and in this way to be able to differentiate between symmetrical and biased reversible passives as well as semantically implausible non-reversible passives, the study design by Ferreira (2003) was adopted. She investigated the misinterpretation of different types of English passive constructions by native speakers. To assess the plausibility of the trial sentences used in her research, she conducted a study involving 100 participants who received lists with a number of experimental and filler items. All items were presented in their active form and the participants had to rate their plausibility on a Likert scale from 1 to 7.

In the plausibility study that I conducted to assess the semantic properties of the trial stimuli, a total of 227 subjects participated. All of them were university students of English. The participants were given different lists with 28–32 trial sentences and filler items each. All experimental items were presented in their active form in order to assess the plausibility of an active interpretation of the passive trial sentences. The participants were told that some of the sentences in the list were more plausible than others and that some sentences were implausible. They were asked to read all sentences carefully and to rate each sentence on a scale from 1 to 7, where '1' meant that the sentence was extremely plausible and '7' indicated that the sentence was extremely implausible. A total of thirty-four lists were excluded from the analysis because they contained missing data. Sentences in the following six conditions were included in the analysis (based on Ferreira 2003; Ferreira & Stacey 2000: 59):

1. symmetrical, one order (*Santa Claus follows the pirate*)
2. symmetrical, other order (*The pirate follows Santa Claus*)
3. biased reversible, plausible (*The woman carries the rabbit*)
4. biased reversible, implausible (*The rabbit carries the woman*)
5. non-reversible, plausible (*James pushes the wheelbarrow*)
6. non-reversible, implausible (*The wheelbarrow pushes James*)

The final analysis included seventy sentences that were rated by fifty-six participants each. The means and standard deviations for the different conditions are presented in Table 6.3. As can be seen from the table, the sentences used in the study had the appropriate semantic properties for the experiments: The sentences in the two symmetrical versions were rated almost exactly the same (2.10 vs. 2.15). The sentences in the two conditions *biased reversible, implausible* and *non-reversible, implausible* were rated as far less plausible than in the plausible condition (4.74 and 6.37 vs. 1.99 and 1.56). For this reason, I considered the trial sentences to be appropriate exemplars for the conditions implemented in my study.

Table 6.3 Experimental sentences: mean plausibility ratings and standard deviations.

Condition	Mean	SD
symmetrical, one order (Santa Claus follows the pirate)	2.10	0.43
symmetrical, other order (The pirate follows Santa Claus)	2.15	0.43
biased reversible, plausible (The woman carries the rabbit)	1.99	0.42
biased reversible, implausible (The rabbit carries the woman)	4.74	0.58
non-reversible, plausible (James pushes the wheelbarrow)	1.56	0.33
non-reversible, implausible (The wheelbarrow pushes James)	6.37	0.48

6.3 Oral speech production tasks II: Passives

The elicitation of production data of English passive structures constitutes a methodological challenge, as there are no obligatory contexts for passive constructions. When reporting an event, a speaker is always faced with a syntactic choice. In English, a proposition can be expressed in active or passive voice respectively. The question arises as to which factors influence the speaker's selection of one of these two grammatical alternatives. One such factor is the saliency of the referents participating in an event, which is influenced by their relative size and colour. The results of several studies (e.g. Johnson-Laird 1968; Lempert 1990; Sridhar 1988) indicate that manipulating the physical saliency of the representation of the patient/theme argument, for example by employing stimuli where the patient/theme referent is larger in size than the agent referent, or by using pictures with a coloured patient/theme entity in contrast to a non-coloured agent referent, leads to an increase in the choice of passive structures.

The manipulation of perspective-taking also influences the choice of passive over active voice. Research results indicate that objects that are located to the left of the agent entity and closer to the participant than the agent are more likely to be encoded as the grammatical subject of the sentence (Altmann & Kemper 2006; Flores d'Arcais 1975; Sridhar 1989). A further aspect relates to 'global control' (Tomlin 1995: 524) of the theme or topic in discourse (see e.g. Bates & Devescoci 1989; Turner & Rommetveit 1967). The underlying idea here is that the speaker's choice between active and passive structures depends on which of the two referents is considered to be more significant in relation to the overall discourse topic. The global topic of the discourse can be influenced by using linguistic cues to draw attention to the patient/theme argument, for example by asking questions such as 'What is happening to X?' or 'What is being done to X?' (Turner & Rommetveit 1967), and studies indicate that the manipulation of the global topic results in an increase of passive structures (see e.g. Bates & Devescoci 1989; Flores d'Arcais 1975).[3]

In Sub-study 1, a pilot study to test the tasks designed for the elicitation of passive structures in production and comprehension, I employed a picture-description task that incorporated the criteria of saliency, perspective-taking and global control of the topic. The saliency of the referents was manipulated in that the patient/theme entity was bigger in size than the agent entity and was additionally coloured. As far as perspective-taking is concerned, the patient/theme entity was located at the left side of the picture. Finally, the global control of the topic was established and the attention was drawn to the patient/theme argument by asking questions such as 'What is happening to X?' Figure 6.1 presents two pictures used in the picture-description task which aimed to elicit the sentences *The train is/was pushed by the bear* and *The dragon is/was killed by the king* respectively.

The picture-description task was employed in Sub-study 1 with twenty-two L2 learners at different stages of L2 acquisition. However, the task yielded mixed results: None of the learners at the lower stages of acquisition produced passive constructions. Learners at stages 4 and 5 produced isolated instances of passive constructions. Therefore, in a follow-up study, the picture-description task was completed by four native speakers. The native speakers used the passive at variance: Not all native speakers produced passive forms, and those native speakers who used passive constructions did not apply them in all trials. Therefore, the picture-description task employed in Sub-study 1 is not considered to be an appropriate means to investigate the L2 acquisition of English passive constructions in speech production, and the production data are not further included in the analysis presented in Section 7.1. These results are in line with other research findings indicating that, although the manipulation of saliency of characters and global control of theme resulted in an increase in the production of passives by the participants in the respective experiments, a number of cases remained where participants produced active sentences in conditions that aimed to trigger passive voice (see Tomlin 1995: 525).

In Sub-studies 2 and 3, I employed two tasks to elicit production data of the passive. The first one is a computer-animated film clip designed by Tomlin (1995), the so-called fish film. Tomlin developed the fish film to test his hypothesis that a key factor in

Figure 6.1 Picture description task: example items. © Ron Schulz.

grammatical subject assignment is focal attention at the time of utterance formulation (Tomlin 1995: 527). The film is subdivided into a number of trials showing two fish in varying colours that swim towards each other. When the two fish reach each other, one swallows the other. One of the fish is visually cued by an arrow above it, and participants were instructed 'to produce on-line descriptions of the events they witnessed' (Tomlin 1997: 177) and at the same time to keep their eyes on the fish cued by the arrow. This procedure aimed at maximizing the probability that participants allocated their intention to the visually cued fish. The film includes both agent-primed and patient-primed trials. This is illustrated in Figure 6.2, which depicts two scenes from the fish film. The first one (Figure 6.2a) represents a cue for an active sentence. In agent-primed trials, participants are expected to map the agent onto the subject function and to produce sentences in active voice (*The white fish eats the black fish*). The second scene (Figure 6.2b) constitutes a cue for a passive sentence. In patient-primed trials, the patient argument is expected to be encoded as a subject, resulting in passive constructions (*The white fish is eaten by the black fish*). Tomlin's hypothesis that visual attention crucially influences word order choice is supported in an empirical study using the fish film (Tomlin 1995, 1997) as well as in a study by Gleitman et al. (2007) with a slightly different research design.

Gleitman et al. (2007: 546) point to a number of weaknesses in the design of Tomlin's fish film as a device to shed light on focal attention processes. These include the fact that attention is manipulated in an overt way by using the arrow to attract visual attention as well as an additional explicit instruction that participants should maintain the fixation on the cued entity. A further point of criticism relates to the continuous repetition of the same event (a fish eating another fish).

Despite these limitations, the fish film has been successfully used to investigate the production of passive structures in L1 acquisition (see e.g. Kim 2008) and L2 acquisition research, in particular within the PT framework (see e.g. Kawaguchi & Di Biase 2012; Keatinge & Keßler 2009; Medojevic 2014; Wang 2009, 2011). However, one of the limitations of the fish film mentioned here also applies to the purpose of this study: As the fish film consists of a series of trials depicting the same event that only varies in the colour of the fish and the focus of the arrow, it does not allow for lexical variation concerning the verb. For this reason, I used only a limited number of trials of the film in both studies and additionally employed a second task. This aimed to incorporate (1) lexical variation of the verb and, related to that, (2) the factors of reversibility and event plausibility outlined in this section.

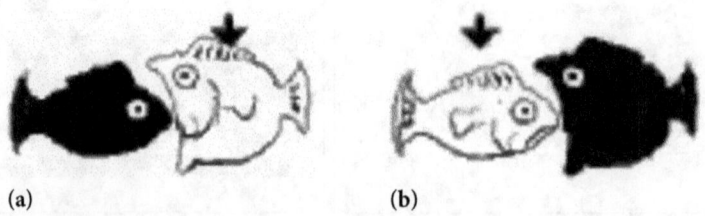

Figure 6.2 (a) active and (b) passive cues in the fish film.

The second passive production task is a film clip designed by me that consists of a number of trials depicting different events. Its design is partly based on the fish film, as I implemented an arrow as a cue to manipulate the participants' attention. In agent-primed trials, the arrow points to the agent in the event and, in patient-primed trials, the arrow points to the patient respectively. Similar to the instructions in Tomlin's (1995) study, the participants were asked to describe the event by focusing on the entity the arrow points to. The combination of the arrow as a visual cue with explicit instruction concerning the participants' focus in Tomlin's study has been criticized as being a 'rather blatant manipulation of attention' (Gleitman et al. 2007: 546). The cue might have influenced the results in that participants might have produced 'the expected findings in contravention of their behavioral tendencies under more neutral conditions' (Gleitman et al. 2007: 546). This point of criticism might be justified when engaging with the question of what exactly determines word order choice. However, the research presented here focuses on the *acquisition* of passives and the related question of whether learners are in principle *capable* of producing passive constructions. Therefore, I consider the use of overt cues a suitable means to maximize the probability that the participants' attention is on the cued entity and thereby to create contexts in which participants produce passive constructions. In keeping with this, I additionally aimed to incorporate the notions of saliency and global control of theme in the task. In the trials, the cued entity was presented in isolation with an arrow pointing at it at the very beginning of every trial before the actual event unfolded. This is illustrated in Figure 6.3 with the screenshots of two scenes cueing the sentence *The bottle is opened by the girl*. As some of the learners were at lower stages of acquisition, the verb they were supposed to use was shown in the right-hand corner of the screen.

As mentioned in Section 6.2, the production task employed in Sub-studies 2 and 3 aimed to elicit different types of passive constructions in order to take semantic factors into account that affect sentence processing. The task included the following conditions: symmetrical reversible passives (*Santa Claus is followed by the pirate*), biased reversible passives (*The cat is fed by the woman*), non-reversible passives (*The wall is painted by the boy*) and passives with three arguments (*The book is given to the girl by the boy*).

Figure 6.3 Example passive production task (Actor: Lola Lenzing).

6.4 Comprehension tasks I: Passive (general)

In the study, different types of comprehension tasks were employed to investigate the L2 acquisition of English passives in comprehension. In Sub-studies 1 and 3, a sentence-picture matching task was used, and Sub-study 2 contained an enactment task.

6.4.1 Sentence-picture matching

In sentence-picture matching tasks, participants are asked to match an aurally presented stimulus with a picture representing the event described by the sentence. This method is also known as sentence-picture verification or as sentence-picture comparison task (Jiang 2012: 216). The sentence-picture matching paradigm is frequently employed in studies investigating L1 development. This applies to studies engaging with the English passive (e.g. Miller 1962; Slobin 1966; Stromswold 2006; Turner & Rommetveit 1967) as well as other linguistic phenomena (e.g. Eisele & Lust 1996; Friedman & Novogrodsky 2004; Love, Walenski & Swinney 2009). Sentence-picture matching tasks are also employed in L2 acquisition research engaging with comprehension processes (see e.g. Buyl & Housen 2015; Grüter 2005; Keatinge & Keßler 2009; Kersten et al. 2010).

The design of the sentence-picture matching task used in the present study is similar to the ELIAS grammar test (Kersten et al. 2010, see also Section 3.8), in that, for each orally presented prompt, the participants had to choose between three different pictures. An example of the sentence-picture matching task used in the study is presented in Figure 6.4. It illustrates the pictures related to the oral prompt *The woman is carried by the hero*. One of the three pictures represents the event described in the stimulus sentence; that is, it shows a hero carrying a woman (picture 3). A second picture depicts the same event but with reversed roles, such that the woman carries the hero (picture 2). Finally, a third picture constitutes a distractor item. It displays both participants in the event but does not depict the event/action described in the sentence (picture 1). As in the production task, the trial sentences included symmetrical reversible passives, biased reversible passives, non-reversible passives and passives with three arguments.

Figure 6.4 Example sentence-picture matching: biased reversible passive *The woman is carried by the hero* (Actors: Emilia and Simon Nottbeck).

6.4.2 Enactment task

The second type of comprehension task used in the study is an *enactment task*. In this kind of task – also known as *act-out task* or *toy-moving task* (see e.g. Lust & Blume 2016) – the participants have to enact sentences that are presented to them aurally. The enactment of the sentences is accomplished by using different kinds of toys and other props.

Similar to the sentence-picture matching task, the enactment task has long been employed in language acquisition research on typologically diverse languages (e.g. Foley et al. 1997; Goodluck 1996; Somashekar et al. 1997). The methodology has been applied to investigate different linguistic phenomena, such as word order (Chan et al. 2010) or relative clauses (Flynn & Lust 1980). Enactment tasks have also frequently been used in studies investigating the acquisition of the passive by young children (see e.g. Lempert 1978; Strohner & Nelson 1974).

An advantage of applying this kind of methodology in L2 acquisition research is its non-intrusive character. This is particularly beneficial when focusing on young learners. Lust and Blume (2016: 140) point out that

> [the enactment task] allows subjects to provide any interpretation they want, without the researcher giving them a set of adult-predetermined possible interpretations. This is important because children – and impaired subjects – may have grammars that deviate from those of nonimpaired adults in ways that the researcher may have not imagined. The task does not depend on prior adult representations of a sentence's meaning. Unlike, for example, the picture judgment task, it allows the child to create his or her own interpretations of a sentence, which the adult may not have predetermined as an option.

It is exactly for this reason that the enactment task was employed in Sub-study 2: In contrast to the sentence-picture matching task, the participants do not choose between different items but have to enact the scene presented to them. In this way, instances of chance performance are reduced and the use of distractor items is not necessary. Interestingly, however, an empirical study comparing the results yielded by both sentence-picture matching and enactment tasks has shown that both kinds of tasks lead to similar results in children aged five years and older (Watermeyer 2010; Watermeyer & Kauschke 2013).

In the enactment task employed in Sub-study 2, the researcher read out a sentence to the learners and they were asked to enact the sentence they heard with selected Playmobil® figures. The learners had to choose the figures for the different scenes from a pool of props available to them. In this way, chance performance was further reduced. In potentially ambiguous cases, the learners were asked to additionally point to the Playmobil® figure that carried out the action in the enacted scene. A picture of each Playmobil® scene was taken for analysis. An example of an enacted scene in the task is presented in Figure 6.5. As in the other tasks, the experimental sentences used in the enactment task were of the four categories symmetrical reversible passives, biased reversible passives, non-reversible passives and passives with three arguments.

Figure 6.5 Example enactment task: non-reversible passive *The cage is opened by Lisa*.

6.5 Comprehension tasks II: Passive (morpho-syntactic processing)

A methodological challenge in investigating L2 comprehension processes is to differentiate between semantic and syntactic aspects of processing and to include tasks in data elicitation that tap into morpho-syntactic processing (see also Section 3.8). As pointed out in Section 6.4, both the sentence-picture matching task and the enactment task have been used extensively in studies engaging with the comprehension of passives in L1 acquisition. Applied to L2 acquisition, I argue that the incorporation of the two types of tasks that include passives with different semantic properties (symmetrical reversible, biased reversible and non-reversible passives) serves to shed light on the following issues: (1) semantic aspects in processing and acquisition and (2) the acquisition of the principled capability to process non-linear mapping operations, which is reflected by the ability to map the patient/theme argument onto the subject function.

However, the two tasks are limited in that they do not allow for an unequivocal distinction between semantic and syntactic processing and cannot account for morpho-syntactic processing. In order to be able to make statements concerning the L2 acquisition of morpho-syntactic aspects of the passive, I incorporated a sentence-matching task in the study, a reaction-time experiment that provides insights into morpho-syntactic processing operations.

6.5.1 Sentence-matching experiments: An overview

Traditionally, sentence-matching experiments have been employed in studies investigating human language processing. Participants are presented with two sentences on a computer screen, usually with a delay time between the two sentences. The sentences are either grammatical or ungrammatical, and the sentence pairs are either identical or not. The participants are asked to judge as quickly as possible whether the two sentences are identical or different and to respond by pressing one of two buttons/keys on a response box or keyboard. One button/key indicates a positive and the other one a negative response. The response latencies are measured, and the focus of analysis is on differences in the reaction times on grammatical and ungrammatical matching sentence pairs. The crucial finding in sentence-matching tasks is that native speakers are faster in matching grammatical sentence pairs (as in example (1a)) than matching ungrammatical sentence pairs (as in example (1b)) (examples taken from Jiang 2012: 203).

(1)
    a) Mary was writing a letter to her husband.
       Mary was writing a letter to her husband.
    b) *Mary were writing a letter to her husband.
       *Mary were writing a letter to her husband.

The first studies using this type of same/different matching paradigm focused on word processing and the question of whether words are processed as a string of letters or as whole units (e.g. Chambers & Forster 1975). The logic underlying the same/different matching paradigm was then applied to sentence processing by researchers such as Forster (1979), Freedman and Forster (1985) and Crain and Fodor (1987).

6.5.2 Sentence-matching experiments in L2 acquisition

Bley-Vroman and Masterson (1989) introduced the sentence-matching paradigm to L2 acquisition research using it as a supplement to a grammaticality judgement task to determine the grammaticality status of different structures in L2 learners. In their view, the reaction times obtained in sentence-matching experiments 'probe the character of the learner's grammar' (Bley-Vroman & Masterson 1989: 208). The underlying logic is as follows: The reaction-time patterns of L2 learners are assumed to differ from those of native speakers in that ungrammaticality effects that are observed in native speakers do not necessarily occur in L2 learners. The missing ungrammaticality effects for certain structures, such as sentences with incorrect subject-verb agreement, apply in particular to early L2 learners. For instance, if learners do not exhibit any differences in reaction times when they are presented with sentence pairs with correct agreement and sentence pairs with agreement violations, they are assumed not to have acquired subject-verb agreement (see also Clahsen & Hong 1995: 70).

    Since the pioneering research of Bley-Vroman and Masterson (1989), sentence-matching experiments have been employed extensively in studies on L2 acquisition (e.g. Beck 1998; Clahsen & Hong 1995; Duffield & White 1999; Duffield, Matsuo & Roberts 2007; Eubank 1993; Gass 2001; Pienemann 1998; Slabakova 1997; Verhagen 2009, 2011). As pointed out in Section 6.5.1, the initial application of sentence-matching experiments in psycholinguistic research addressed issues related to language *processing*. It seems that, in L2 acquisition research, the focus has shifted so that the sentence-matching paradigm is also used to engage with issues related to language *knowledge* or *representation*. This applies predominantly to studies within the UG framework (see e.g. Clahsen & Hong 1995; Duffield et al. 2007). In some accounts, the two dimensions – processing and representation – are seemingly conflated. For instance, Beck (1998) carried out a sentence-matching study that aimed to investigate a specific UG-based hypothesis related to L2 competence. However, elaborating on what actually happens in sentence-matching, she points out that processing operations take place in judging stimulus pairs as being identical or not (Beck 1998: 324).

Thus, the question arises as to what the sentence-matching procedure actually measures: Does the task provide insights into linguistic processing or underlying linguistic representations? I argue that sentence-matching experiments can be used to investigate language *processing* for the following reasons: First of all, the sentence-matching paradigm originates in experiments focusing on word *processing*, and researchers who used the technique to investigate the level of sentence processing also considered sentence-matching to be a *processing* task (see e.g. Freedman & Forster 1985: 127). Second, the actual measurement in sentence-matching tasks, that is, the differences in response latencies in matching grammatical versus ungrammatical sentence pairs relate to differences in *processing* grammatical and ungrammatical sentences respectively. As argued by Pienemann (1998: 220), who used sentence-matching to test the so-called *procedural skill hypothesis*, what is measured is 'the speed with which certain linguistic computations can be executed'.[4]

A further crucial issue in this respect concerns the theoretical paradigm underlying the respective studies and the related assumptions concerning linguistic representations. These clearly differ depending on the theoretical framework adopted. Most L2 studies that view sentence-matching as a means to investigate linguistic knowledge or representations were carried out within the framework of UG. Cleary, the theoretical conceptualization of linguistic representations in UG differs fundamentally from the one in an LFG-based account of the mental grammatical system, as adopted in this book. This is related to the question of in what ways processing and representations are linked and to what extent sentence-matching experiments can also contribute to a better understanding of underlying mental representations of linguistic knowledge (see also the discussion in Pienemann 1998). I argue that, in SLA, the acquisition of the relevant processing procedures to carry out feature unification and mapping processes does not occur independently of the development of the learners' L2 mental grammatical system. As outlined in the *Multiple Constraints Hypothesis*, I assume that, initially, the L2 mental grammatical system is highly constrained and that incomplete annotations of the L2 mental lexicon and, in particular, of the syntactic side of a-structure, do not allow for these processes to take place. The gradual annotations at different levels of representation and the accessibility of grammatical functions at f-structure level enable the learner to map arguments onto grammatical functions instead of relying on direct mapping processes.

In view of these arguments, I claim that sentence-matching experiments first and foremost tap into sentence processing. Taking a processability perspective on L2 acquisition, I argue that sentence-matching experiments are a suitable means to investigate the L2 acquisition of morpho-syntactic processing. I assume that the response pattern of L2 learners in sentence-matching experiments depends on both the acquired processing procedures and their L2 mental grammar.

Despite its widespread application in SLA, the sentence-matching paradigm has also faced criticism. Apart from divergent views as to how to interpret the findings in terms of underlying processes and/or representations (see also Duffield et al. 2007), the application of the technique to SLA was criticized by Gass (2001) on both methodological and empirical grounds. Gass critically examined previous L2 research using the sentence-matching paradigm and also reported on her own research. This failed to confirm previous findings, as learners showed no grammaticality effects in any structural condition. In addition, learners' reaction times in sentence-matching did not correlate with their acceptability judgements in a supplementary grammaticality judgement test. In a response to Gass's criticism, Duffield et al. (2007: 160-2) point to methodological differences in research design that might have resulted in the failure to replicate the results obtained in a large number of studies. Gass's observation that traditional grammaticality judgement tests and sentence-matching experiments did not yield the same results in her study is probably due to the fact that the two types of tasks do not tap into the same underlying processes and/or linguistic knowledge respectively.

Despite the criticism voiced by Gass (2001), the sentence-matching paradigm has been successfully applied in numerous studies and is therefore regarded as a valuable instrument to gain insights into sentence processing operations. It is for this reason that the sentence-matching paradigm was incorporated in Sub-study 3.

6.5.3 Sentence-matching experiment: Experimental design

The sentence-matching experiment in Sub-study 3 differs from the standard methodology that includes a visual/written presentation of the stimuli on a computer screen (see e.g. Jiang 2012): In the experiment in this study, the sentences are presented aurally. This design is based on the methodology adopted in a study by Verhagen (2009, 2011), who was the first to use auditory stimuli in sentence-matching in her study of the L2 acquisition of finiteness in Dutch. The use of auditory instead of written stimuli has the crucial advantage that auditory stimuli allow for an investigation of processing operations in learners who have not yet acquired automatized reading skills in their L2. This applies in particular to beginning L2 learners, where reading difficulties could potentially lead to delays in reaction times that are not related to morpho-syntactic processing. A further advantage of aurally presented stimuli relates to the overall aim of this study, which is to shed light on potential interfaces between morpho-syntactic processing in production and comprehension. As pointed out in Section 2.2, grammatical encoding and decoding involve mappings between meaning and form, and a key distinguishing factor between the two processes is their directional difference. In speech production, the study investigates the L2 acquisition of the English passive in *oral* speech production. Therefore, it seems reasonable to also engage with the acquisition of *spoken* input in comprehension. The use of written stimuli would introduce a further factor to the experimental design, as orthographic representations of a word have to be mapped onto either phonological or semantic representations of the respective word.[5]

The stimuli in the experiment consisted of English passive constructions with the two verbs *push* (in a non-reversible context) and *follow* (in a reversible context) (see examples (2) and (3)).

(2) The blue train is pushed by Polly and Jack.
(3) The old woman is followed by the big elephant.

I included non-reversible and symmetrical reversible stimuli in the experiment to investigate (1) whether in L2 acquisition, non-reversible passive constructions are comprehended earlier than reversible construction on a purely semantic basis or (2) whether the syntactic processing of non-reversible passives also occurs at an earlier stage than in reversible constructions.

In order to examine the morpho-syntactic processing of passive constructions in L2 comprehension in more detail and to investigate which syntactic aspects are involved in grammatical decoding, the ungrammatical stimuli were presented in the following three conditions:

1. Omission of the preposition:
   *The orange bike is pushed Ø the old man.
2. Omission of the auxiliary:
   *The blue train Ø pushed by Polly and Jack.
3. Omission of the *-ed* morpheme:
   *The little girl is followØ by Emily and Bill.

The experiment contained a total of forty-eight sentences, divided into twelve target sentence pairs and twelve filler sentence pairs, which results in an overall target-filler ratio of 1:1 (see Jiang 2012; Roberts 2012).[6]

Half of the target items consisted of matching grammatical sentence pairs and the other half of matching ungrammatical sentence pairs. Each sentence was presented in a matching grammatical and a matching ungrammatical condition in order to be able to make comparisons in terms of reaction times between the two different conditions. The items in the two conditions were matched in all other aspects that affect the participants' reaction times except for grammaticality. This is illustrated in examples (4) and (5) for the conditions +/− auxiliary and the verb *follow*:

(4) Matching grammatical, condition + *auxiliary*, verb *follow*
    The old woman is followed by the big elephant.
    The old woman is followed by the big elephant.

(5) Matching ungrammatical, condition - *auxiliary*, verb *follow*
   *The old woman Ø followed by the big elephant.
   *The old woman Ø followed by the big elephant.

Two sentence pairs per condition were presented, which results in six target sentence pairs with the verb *push* and six target pairs with the verb *follow*.

The filler items also consisted of six sentence pairs with the verb *push* and six pairs with the verb *follow*. They were presented in the following four conditions (examples given for *push* and *follow*):

1. Grammatical, lexically different:
   The big girl is followed by the hungry cat.
   The little girl is followed by the hungry cat.
2. Ungrammatical, lexically different:
   *The little boy is by the old woman followed.
   *The little girl is by the old woman followed.
3. Grammatical, syntactically different:
   The new car is pushed by the big boy.
   The big boy is pushing the new car.
4. Ungrammatical, syntactically different:
   *The little child was pushing the bike blue.
   *Little the child was pushing the bike blue.

The four conditions are based on the study by Verhagen (2009, 2011). In addition, in the selection of the actual filler sentences, the following observations by Jiang (2012: 204) were taken into consideration, who points out that '[i]t is desirable to include at least some non-matching items that are of the same structure as the critical stimuli. [...] In order to prevent the participants from noticing the target structure under investigation, some filler items involving a variety of different structures can be used.'

The experimental setup provided an equal number of grammatical and ungrammatical sentence pairs as well as an equal number of matching and non-matching sentence pairs to prevent any potential biases. All sentences were between nine and twelve syllables long, as is standard in sentence-matching tasks (see Gass 2001: 428), and all target stimuli were longer than seven words, in order to ensure that the sentences are processed and not memorized as chunks (see Roberts 2012: 117). All sound files were recorded by a native speaker of English.

I programmed the experiment in PsyScope and it was run on a Macintosh MacBook Air. The participants listened to the sentences via headphones. The sentences were presented consecutively with a 1,500 millisecond break between them, and the participants' grammaticality responses were recorded via a button box.[7] This procedure ensures a much more accurate time stamping than the use of the keyboard (see e.g. Freegard 2012; Roberts 2012). The participants had to press a green button for 'same' and a red button for 'different' respectively. Participants' response times were recorded from the offset of the second sentence. In order to prevent participants from pressing the button at an earlier point in time, and in this way distorting the results, at the end of the second sentence, a green exclamation mark appeared on the screen. This served as an indicator for the participants to give their response (see also Verhagen 2009: 188).

In addition to the trial items, every sentence pair was followed by a comprehension question that the participants had to answer with 'yes' or 'no' by pressing the green or the red button respectively. The use of comprehension questions in processing research aims at ensuring that participants process the sentences for meaning. This is illustrated in example (6):

(6) Matching grammatical, condition + *auxiliary*, verb *push*
The blue train is pushed by Polly and Jack.
The blue train is pushed by Polly and Jack.

Comprehension question:
Do Polly and Jack push the train?

All experimental stimuli (sentence pairs and corresponding content question) were randomized within PsyScope. Prior to the experiment, the participants received an oral as well as a written instruction and completed a short training session with a number of practice items.

7

Testing the *Integrated Encoding-Decoding Model of SLA*

The empirical research presented in this chapter aims to test the hypotheses of the *Integrated Encoding-Decoding Model of SLA* by exploring the L2 acquisition of the English passive in production and comprehension. In particular, the set of studies investigate the hypothesized developmental sequence of the English passive in L2 acquisition presented in Section 5.2.2. The proposed developmental sequence consists of the following three stages:

1. Shallow processing/linear argument-function mapping:
   - the first noun phrase is assigned the role of agent/experiencer
   - syntactic features are missing in the lexicon
2. Non-linear argument-function mapping:
   - the first noun phrase is assigned the role of patient/theme
   - syntactic features become involved in unification processes of argument-function mapping
3. Morpho-syntactic processing:
   - incorporates the c-structure level
   - incorporates both feature unification and form-function relationships

This sequence builds on an LFG/PT-based analysis of passive constructions with particular focus on the underlying feature unification and mapping operations and is hypothesized to apply to grammatical encoding as well as decoding. The claim that this sequence applies to both modalities derives from the *Integrated Encoding-Decoding Model of SLA*. The core assumptions of the model are that L2 learners draw on the same resources in grammatical encoding and decoding. I assume the existence of a single syntactic coder underlying the two processes in L2 acquisition. This processor is hypothesized to develop stepwise in accordance with the predictions of PT. This means that the L2 learners' syntactic resources are constrained by (1) the architecture of the human language processor and (2) the underdeveloped L2 mental grammatical system.

When investigating the cognitive architecture of L2 comprehension, a key issue relates to the influence of semantic information on the L2 learners' comprehension process. I argue that semantic cues are particularly important in the early stages of L2 comprehension, as the L2 syntactic processor is assumed to be still underdeveloped. To account for the influence of semantic information on L2 comprehension and to model the interplay between semantic and syntactic processing, I adopt the perspective of the *Online Cognitive Equilibrium Hypothesis* (Karimi & Ferreira 2016), which proposes a dual route in sentence processing. Its core claim is that humans have access to a semantic and a syntactic route, which operate in parallel. This means that listeners can make recourse both to shallow processing guided by event probabilities and to deep syntactic algorithms. Adapting the *Online Cognitive Equilibrium Hypothesis* to SLA, I argue that the syntactic route is the locus of the processing procedures spelled out in PT. In line with the assumption that the processing procedures also constrain the L2 syntactic parsing process, I argue that the syntactic route is initially underdeveloped such that early L2 learners rely on semantic processing in L2 comprehension.

The study aims to investigate the L2 acquisition of English passive constructions in production and comprehension in relation to the L2 learners' developmental stage. It consists of three thematically related sub-studies that are all cross-sectional in design. The data collection took place at different schools in and around Paderborn in Germany.

7.1 Sub-study 1

Sub-study 1 served as a pilot study for the passive tasks that I developed for production and comprehension. A total of twenty-one learners participated in this part of the study. These were all school-aged learners of English with a German-speaking background. The data collection took place in one school, and the learners were in grade 5 and in grade 7 and between ten and thirteen years of age. The learners had three and a half and four years of previous instruction in English.[1] Fifteen girls and six boys participated in the data collection. An overview of the learners is provided in Table 7.1.

The learners who participated in Sub-study 1 completed production and comprehension tasks (see Chapter 6 for details), which are presented in Table 7.2. The individual recording sessions lasted between 40 and 45 minutes. The communicative tasks to determine the learners' stage of acquisition were completed in pairs, as this setting reduces the learners' anxiety (Johnstone 2000: 15). The picture description task and the sentence-picture matching task were carried out with a researcher. The learners' oral speech production data were fully transcribed according to the transcription key in Table 7.3. As the analysis presented here focuses on the morpho-syntactic structures in the learners' speech samples, an orthographic transcription was chosen instead of a phonetic one.

As mentioned earlier in this section, the production data elicited with the picture description task were not included in the subsequent analysis, as the task was not considered to be an adequate means to elicit oral production data of passive constructions (see Section 6.3).

Table 7.1 Overview of participants: Sub-study 1.

Participants Sub-study 1												
Informants	I01	I02	I03	I04	I05	I06	I07	I08	I09	I10	I11	I12
Age	11	10	10	11	10	11	11	10	10	10	11	10
Sex	f	f	f	f	f	f	f	f	f	f	f	f
Grade	5	5	5	5	5	5	5	5	5	5	5	5
Informants	I13	I14	I15	I16	I17	I18	I19	I20	I21	I22		
Age	12	13	12	12	12	12	13	11	12	11		
Sex	f	m	m	f	f	f	m	m	m	m		
Grade	7	7	7	7	7	7	7	7	7	7		

Table 7.2 Production and comprehension tasks: Sub-study 1.

Type of data	Tasks
Oral speech production I: stages of acquisition	Communicative tasks
Oral speech production II: passive	Picture description task 11 target items (passive) 5 distractor items (active)
Comprehension passive I: general	Sentence-picture matching task 11 target items (passive) 5 distractor items (active)

Table 7.3 Transcription key.

Symbol	Meaning
(/)	Self-Interruption/change of structure mid-stream
(?)	Not sure
(XXX)	Incomprehensible
[text]	Simultaneous speech
{text}	Comments in languages other than English
(text)	Fillers, such as 'ehm'
(*w*)	Noticeable deviation from standard pronunciation

7.1.1 Results stages of acquisition: Sub-study 1

In Sub-study 1, the learners' stages of acquisition were determined by using Rapid Profile, a computer-assisted procedure to screen L2 learners' speech samples and to assess their level of L2 development. Rapid Profile was developed by Pienemann

Table 7.4 Stages of acquisition: L2 learners Sub-study 1

Participants Sub-study 1											
Informants	I01	I02	I03	I04	I05	I06	I07	I08	I09	I10	I11
Stage	3	2	3	3	3	2	2	2	2	2	3
Informants	I13	I14	I15	I16	I17	I18	I19	I20	I21	I22	
Stage	5	4	5	5	4	4	5	5	6	5	

(1990, 1992) from Standard Profile Analysis (Crystal, Fletcher & Garman 1976). The current version of Rapid Profile is based on the PT hierarchy for English as L2 (see Keßler 2006; Pienemann 1998). With the software, researchers can carry out profile analyses of individual learners by entering observations that relate to specific interlanguage data samples. The samples are coded online, and on the basis of the data entered by the researcher, the software computes the learners' developmental stage. Rapid Profile is considered to be a reliable procedure to determine L2 learners' stages of development (see Keßler 2006).

An overview of the participants' stages of acquisition is provided in Table 7.4. It can be seen from Table 7.4 that six learners are at stage 2 of acquisition, five learners are at stage 3, three learners have acquired features from stage 4, six learners are at stage 5 and one learner has reached stage 6 of acquisition. The learners' language development is implicational in that all learners follow the sequence of acquisition for specific morpho-syntactic features predicted by PT. None of the learners provided evidence of skipping stages.

7.1.2 Results comprehension data – passive: Sub-study 1

The comprehension data of the passive structures in Sub-study 1 were obtained by employing a sentence-picture matching task (see Section 6.4). An important question concerning the analysis of comprehension data relates to the application of an appropriate acquisition criterion to the data. In this concern, the question arises whether the notion of *emergence* in L2 speech production can be applied to L2 comprehension in a one-to-one fashion and, if so, how emergence in comprehension can be measured appropriately. Assuming that the same processing procedures underlie both L2 production and comprehension, I argue that the notion of emergence as denoting the point of acquisition of a particular processing procedure also applies to L2 comprehension. However, this does not mean that the same acquisition criterion can be applied to both processes, as chance performance is a factor in elicited comprehension data that might distort the analysis. The studies investigating L2 comprehension from a PT perspective discussed in Section 3.8

approach the operationalization of emergence in different ways, for instance by applying different cut-off points to the data.

The analysis presented here approaches this issue indirectly by combining implicational scaling of the comprehended structures with a statistical analysis of correlations between comprehension data and PT stages as determined by the analysis of L2 production data. No cut-off point is applied to the L2 comprehension data, as cut-off points are necessarily arbitrary and different cut-off points lead to different results.

The results of the data analysis in terms of implicational scaling are presented in Table 7.5. The table is laid out as follows: A '+' in a cell indicates that the learner's interpretation of a particular passive construction was target-like; A '–' in the cell marks those cases where the learner did not interpret the sentence correctly (i.e. by assigning the agent role to the patient in the event).

It can be seen that the learners' comprehension data can be plotted onto an implicational scale: The coefficient of reproducibility is 0.94 and the coefficient of scalability is 0.66, which yields a valid implicational table. The results indicate an implicational hierarchy in the acquisition of different passive constructions in L2 comprehension. This means that some constructions are understood by more learners than others and are thus assumed to be acquired earlier.

In what follows, the results will be discussed in terms of the prototypicality of the respective constructions with particular focus on the notions of event probability and reversibility.

The sentence that was comprehended in a target-like way by seventeen out of twenty-one learners is the biased reversible passive *The woman is carried by the hero*. The plausibility rating carried out by the university students displayed in Table 7.6 shows that the active interpretation of the sentence (*The woman carries the hero*) is indeed perceived as being more implausible than the intended meaning of the sentence. In line with the criteria outlined by Meints (1999a: 71), the structure can be considered a prototypical passive form. It is a transitive construction with focus on the patient. The verb denoting the action in the sentence displays the features of actionality, punctuality, direct physical contact and result. The verb *carry* denotes a punctual action which involves a direct contact between the agent (*the hero*) and the patient/theme (*the woman*) and leads to a visible result. Most importantly, the sentence constitutes a biased reversible passive.

However, somewhat unexpectedly, this passive construction was understood by more learners than the non-reversible forms *The flower is watered by the woman* (11 learners) and *The wall is painted by the boy* (8 learners). The plausibility assessment of the two non-reversible constructions shown in Table 7.7 reveals that, in these two cases, the active interpretations (*The flower waters the woman* and *The wall paints the boy*) are considered to be highly implausible (6.71 and 6.45 out of 7 respectively). In addition to their semantic irreversibility, the two sentences also display other characteristics of prototypical passives. Again, both sentences are transitive forms with focus on the patient. The action described in the sentences can be considered

Table 7.5 Distributional analysis of comprehension data passives: L2 learners Sub-study 1

Participant	101	108	103	104	107	118	106	102	114	105	109	110	117	111	120	113	119	116	115	122	121
Stage	3	2	3	3	2	4	2	2	4	3	2	2	4	3	5	5	5	5	5	5	6
The taxidriver is told a story by the passenger.	−	−	−	−	−	−	−	−	−	−	−	−	−	−	−	−	−	−	−	+	+
The boy is kicked by the girl.	−	−	−	−	−	−	−	−	−	−	−	−	−	−	−	−	−	−	−	+	+
The walker is seen by the bicycle rider.	−	−	−	−	−	−	−	−	−	−	−	−	−	−	−	−	−	+	+	+	+
The man is kissed by the woman.	−	−	−	−	−	−	−	+	−	−	−	−	−	−	+	+	+	+	+	+	+
The dog is kicked by the man.	−	−	−	−	−	−	−	−	−	−	−	−	−	+	+	+	+	+	+	+	+
The cat is fed by the woman.	−	−	−	−	−	−	−	−	+	−	−	−	−	+	+	+	+	+	+	+	+
The wall is painted by the boy.	−	−	−	−	−	−	−	−	−	−	−	−	+	+	+	+	+	+	+	+	+
The daughter is heard by the mother.	−	−	−	−	−	−	−	−	−	−	−	+	−	+	+	+	−	+	−	+	+
The flower is watered by the woman.	−	−	−	−	−	−	−	−	+	+	−	−	−	+	+	+	+	+	+	+	+
The boy is brought to the doctor by the mother.	−	−	−	−	−	−	+	−	−	−	+	+	+	−	+	+	−	+	+	−	+
The woman is carried by the hero.	−	−	−	+	+	+	+	−	+	+	+	+	+	+	+	+	+	+	+	+	+

Table 7.6 Plausibility rating of biased reversible passives: Sub-study 1.

Sentence	Mean	SD
The woman carries the hero	3.61	1.97
The hero carries the woman	1.80	1.07

Table 7.7 Plausibility rating of non-reversible passives: Sub-study 1.

Sentence	Mean	SD
The wall paints the boy	6.45	1.11
The boy paints the wall	1.54	0.91
The flower waters the woman	6.71	0.71
The woman waters the flowers	1.55	0.93

to be punctual and, in the case of *The wall is painted by the boy*, it both involves a direct physical contact between agent and patient/theme and leads to a clear result. According to these characteristics – in particular taking the plausibility rating into account – the two non-reversible constructions can be considered to be more prototypical than the passive with biased event probability. Therefore, one would expect that more learners comprehend the non-reversible passives than the biased reversible construction.

A potential explanation for this unanticipated finding is a cultural bias of the L2 learners towards the target-like interpretation in that it is perceived as absolutely unlikely that a woman carries a hero. Given the fact that the L2 learners were between ten and thirteen years old at the time of the data collection, it could be the case that they were highly influenced by (1) gender stereotypes and (2) stereotypes about the role of heroes in general, as, for example, depicted in *Superman*, *Batman* or other cartoon series.

In addition, it could be the case that the task type contributed to the fact that the majority of L2 learners understood the two non-reversible passives as active constructions. As illustrated in Figures 7.1 and 7.2, in sentence-picture matching,

Figure 7.1 Example sentence-picture matching: non-reversible passive *The flower is watered by the woman* (Actor: Emilia Nottbeck).

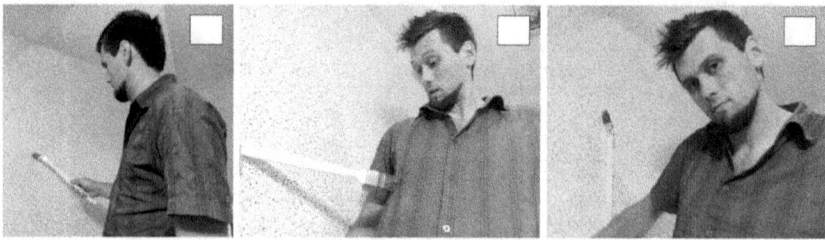

Figure 7.2 Example sentence-picture matching: non-reversible passive *The wall is painted by the boy* (Actor: Simon Nottbeck).

the implausible action is also displayed in the pictures. The situation is possibly comparable to a cartoon sequence, in which unlikely scenarios are depicted that are not necessarily matched with real-life situations by the audience. This might be a reason as to why the L2 learners considered the interpretations *The flower waters the woman* and *The wall paints the boy* as plausible.

The second sentence in the implicational table is a ditransitive construction: The sentence *The boy is brought to the doctor by the mother* was understood by eleven learners. When parsing ditransitive constructions, L2 learners cannot rely on the processing heuristic N V N proposed by Ferreira (2003) (see Section 1.2.4) and interpret the subject as proto-agent and the object as proto-patient as they do in the processing of transitive constructions.[2] In the case of the sentence *The boy is brought to the doctor by the mother* illustrated in Figure 7.3, the application of the N V N strategy could result in the interpretation *Boy brings doctor*. However, the N V N strategy does not account for the processing of the third noun *mother*. A potential solution when relying on linear mapping of arguments to surface structure could be to interpret the sentence as *Boy brings doctor to mother*. This reading is relatively implausible. What is more, this option was not included in the sentence-picture matching task, as the task was restricted to three pictures the learners could choose from.

In her analysis of prototypical passives, Meints (1999a, b) focuses on transitive constructions. Transitivity, and in particular the notion of semantic transitivity

Figure 7.3 Sentence-picture matching: ditransitive passive *The boy was brought to the doctor by the mother* (Actors: Katharina Hagenfeld; Emilia and Simon Nottbeck).

(Hopper & Thomson 1980), is considered to be a crucial characteristic of prototypical passives (see also Maratsos et al. 1985). Meints's analysis does not include passives with ditransitive verbs, and it can be observed that, in general, the acquisition of ditransitive passives has not been extensively investigated in either L1 or L2 acquisition research (for exceptions, for L1 acquisition, see O'Grady 1997; for L2 acquisition, see Wang 2011). Nevertheless, some of the criteria of prototypicality that Meints established in her study on the L1 acquisition of passives also apply to the sentence *The boy is brought to the doctor by the mother*. In this ditransitive construction, the focus is on the patient, and the verb denotes a punctual action, which involves physical contact between the agent and the patient.

The sentence *The daughter is heard by the mother* is comprehended by eight learners and constitutes an exception, as this finding cannot be explained in terms of prototypicality traits of the construction. First of all, the sentence can be classified as a symmetrical reversible passive, as can be inferred from the plausibility assessment in Table 7.8. Apart from the fact that it constitutes a transitive construction with the focus on the patient, the sentence does not display any features that are typical of prototypical passives, such as the punctuality of the action, the direct physical contact or a visible result. As the verb *hear* is a non-actional verb, it is surprising that this sentence occurs at a relatively early point in the implicational hierarchy.

The two biased reversible passives *The cat is fed by the woman* and *The dog is kicked by the man* occur next in the hierarchy in Table 7.5. These sentences display characteristics of prototypical passives in that their active interpretation is considered to be implausible. Furthermore, the action described by the sentences is punctual and involves direct physical contact.

The two forms are then followed by the three symmetrical reversible passives *The man is kissed by the woman*, *The walker is seen by the bicycle rider* and *The boy is kicked by the girl*. The main factor that influences the comprehension process of these structures seems to be their symmetrical reversibility. In all three cases, both interpretations are rated as being approximately equally likely (see Table 7.9). Other characteristics related to prototypicality, such as the degree of action denoted by the verb, do not seem to have a visible influence on the comprehension process. I argue that, in the case of symmetrical reversible passives, the learners cannot make recourse to semantic cues in comprehension but have to rely on deep algorithmic processing instead. This is mirrored in the finding that only learners at higher stages (stage 5 and 6) comprehend these structures correctly (see Table 7.5).

Finally, the ditransitive passive with a non-actional verb (*The taxi driver is told a story by the passenger*) is comprehended by two learners at stage 5 and 6 respectively. One of the learners chose the distractor item. All other learners seemed to rely on the heuristic route and a one-to-one mapping of noun phrases onto argument roles, as illustrated in Figure 7.4.

These direct mapping processes result in the interpretation *The taxi driver tells a story to the passenger*. Semantically, both options are equally plausible. Therefore, the learners have to rely on syntactic parsing algorithms in order to fully process the sentence and to arrive at the intended meaning.

Table 7.8 Plausibility rating of symmetrical reversible passives: Sub-study 1.

Sentence	Mean	SD
The daughter hears the mother	1.43	0.71
The mother hears the daughter	1.48	0.60

Table 7.9 Plausibility rating of symmetrical reversible passives: Sub-study 1.

Sentence	Mean	SD
The boy kicks the girl	1.80	1.10
The girl kicks the boy	1.71	1.00
The man kisses the woman	1.25	0.61
The woman kisses the man	1.30	0.54
The walker sees the bicycle rider	1.89	1.00
The bicycle rider sees the walker	2.02	1.10

Figure 7.4 Direct mapping processes ditransitive passives.

Apart from the results obtained by the distributional analysis of the comprehension data, a correlation analysis was conducted to investigate the correlation between the number of comprehended passive constructions and the L2 learners' PT stages. A Spearman's rank-order correlation was run to assess the relationship between the number of passive constructions comprehended by the learners and their stages of acquisition. The results show a strong positive correlation between the number of comprehended passives and the individual learners' stage of acquisition, $r_s(21) = 0.722$, $p < 0.001$ (two-tailed). These results support the claim that the procedures underlying the stages of acquisition are also involved in the L2 grammatical decoding process.

I argue that the implicational sequence of different types of passive constructions in L2 acquisition and the correlations between the number of comprehended structures and the learners' stages of acquisition reflect a gradual development from shallow or semantic processing to syntactic processing. This gradual development can be explained by the adaptation of the *Online Cognitive Equilibrium Hypothesis* to SLA. As outlined in Section 4.3, the *Online Cognitive Equilibrium Hypothesis* proposes two parallel routes to sentence parsing – the heuristic and the algorithmic route. I hypothesize that, in principle, the two routes also operate in parallel in L2 sentence parsing. However, I claim that the algorithmic route – the locus of PT's processing procedures – is initially underdeveloped and L2 syntactic parsing is constrained by processability. Initially, L2 learners lack the processing procedures required for deep algorithmic processing and therefore rely on semantic processing and direct mapping operations. It is the stepwise acquisition of L2 processing procedures and the gradual development of the L2 mental grammatical system that enable the learners to increasingly draw on the algorithmic route in sentence parsing. As pointed out in Section 4.3 and further discussed in this section, I assume that semantic aspects, such as prototypicality and lexical semantics, play a crucial role in heuristic processing.

However, not all results can be explained in terms of the prototypicality of the respective passive constructions. This applies, for instance, to the finding that the biased reversible passive *The woman is carried by the hero* was comprehended by more learners than the two non-reversible constructions *The wall is painted by the boy* and *The flower is watered by the woman*. As pointed out in this section, this unexpected result could be due to the type of comprehension task employed in the study. In order to shed light on this issue, the methodology in Sub-study 2 was refined and included an enactment task instead of a sentence-picture matching task.

7.2 Sub-study 2

Like Sub-study 1, Sub-study 2 is also cross-sectional in design. The data collection took place at three different schools with twenty-four learners from three different grades (grades 5, 8 and 9). The learners' age range was between ten and fifteen and they had received four, five and six years of instruction in English respectively. A detailed overview of the participants is provided in Table 7.10.

All learners carried out different types of tasks that aimed to elicit (1) oral speech production data to determine the individual learners' stage of acquisition, (2) oral speech production data to investigate the learners' acquisition of the English passive in production and (3) comprehension data to explore the learners' comprehension of English passives. In Table 7.11, the tasks used in Sub-study 2 are summarized. The individual data elicitation sessions lasted between 40 and 45 minutes. As in Sub-study 1, the learners worked on the communicative tasks in pairs. The passive tasks (film clip and enactment task) were carried out with a researcher. The learners' oral speech production data were fully transcribed using the transcription key in Table 7.3 and in the comprehension task, a picture of each enacted scene was taken for analysis.

As pointed out in the previous paragraph, the data analysis focused on three different aspects, namely (1) the learners' developmental stages, (2) their production of passive constructions and (3) their comprehension of passive constructions.

Table 7.10 Overview of participants: Sub-study 2.

Participants school 1								
Informants	P01	P02	P03	P04	P05	P06	P07	P08
Age	10	10	11	11	10	10	11	11
Sex	f	f	f	f	m	f	m	f
Grade	5	5	5	5	5	5	5	5
Participants school 2/3								
Informants	M01	M02	M03	M04	M05	M06	M07	B01
Age	15	15	14	14	14	13	14	15
Sex	f	f	m	m	f	m	m	f
Grade	9	9	8	8	8	8	8	9
Participants school 3								
Informants	B02	B03	B04	B05	B06	B07	B08	B09
Age	15	15	15	15	15	15	15	15
Sex	m	m	m	f	m	m	f	f
Grade	9	9	9	9	9	9	9	9

Table 7.11 Production and comprehension tasks: Sub-study 2.

Type of data	Tasks
Oral speech production I: stages of acquisition	Communicative tasks
Oral speech production II: passive	Fish film Passive film clips 9 target items (passive) 4 distractor items (active)
Comprehension passive I: general	Enactment task 12 target items (passive) 4 distractor items (active)

7.2.1 Results stages of acquisition: Sub-study 2

I determined the L2 learners' developmental stages by means of a full distributional analysis of their individual oral speech production data. This provides in-depth insights into the learners' acquisition process and allows for a fine-grained distinction between formulaic sequences and productive learner utterances. In a second step, I applied the emergence criterion to the morphological and syntactic structures produced by the learners in order to examine whether the structures under investigation had been acquired by the learners. In this way, their stages of acquisition could be precisely determined. The full distributional analysis of the learner data is presented in Table 7.12.

The figures given in Table 7.12 indicate (1) how often a particular morpho-syntactic feature was produced by the individual learners (indicated by a '+') and (2) how often a feature was not applied in an obligatory context (indicated by a '−'). The morpho-syntactic features that occurred in an invariant form in the L2 learners' speech samples, which are therefore classified as formulaic sequences, are presented in parentheses.

The definition and identification of formulaic sequences in the learners' speech samples are based on the approach to classify formulaic sequences outlined in Lenzing (2013). I view formulaic sequences from a processing perspective and argue that formulaic utterances are memorized as whole units and stored as chunks in the L2 learner's mental lexicon. This implies that the formulaic sequences in the learner data are not the result of syntactic processes but the outcome of lexical processes. Therefore, formulaic sequences are classified as 'stage 1' structures, as, apart from lemma access, no further processing prerequisites are needed in order to produce these forms. In this approach, the term *formulaic sequences* is used as a cover term, and these sequences are further subcategorized into *formulae* and *formulaic patterns* (see Lenzing 2013: 163). The structures that can be assigned to the L2 learners' textbooks and/or are commonly introduced already at primary school level in Germany are considered to be *formulae*. These include structures such as *What's your name?* or *Where are you from?*.[3] Formulaic patterns, on the other hand, are those forms that consist of an unanalyzed unit and an open slot that is filled with different lexical material.

The identification of formulaic sequences in the learner data is based on detailed distributional analyses of the individual learners' speech samples and the test of the null hypothesis (see Lenzing 2013: 165). The test of the null hypothesis includes an examination of all instances of parallel word sequences that offer variations on the claimed formulaic sequence. In this way, it can be determined whether a particular sequence of words occurs invariantly in a learner's speech sample and is thus considered to be formulaic, or whether it is also used productively, that is, whether it occurs with variation in the L2 learner's speech sample.

This procedure is exemplified in Table 7.13, which illustrates the distributional analysis of all 'Wh-Copula S (x)'-structures produced by learner P03. The detailed distributional analysis shows that the invariant formulaic pattern 'What's your favourite X' occurred in the learner data, whereas no variations of this pattern were attested. A further characteristic of formulaic patterns is that they can occur either as well-formed utterances in the learner data (e.g. *What's your favourite hobby?*) or as non-target-like, idiosyncratic utterances (e.g. *What's your favourite eat?*).

After having determined all instances of formulaic sequences in the learner data, I applied the emergence criterion to the data presented in the distributional analysis in Table 7.12 to determine the learners' stages of acquisition. These are summarized in Table 7.14. The '+' (acquired) in the respective cells indicates that a learner has acquired structures of a particular stage according to the emergence criterion, whereas the '−' (not acquired) indicates that this is not the case. In those instances where learners produced structures of a particular stage, but not in sufficient contexts in order to be considered as acquired, the plus sign occurs within parentheses '(+)'.

Table 7.12 Distributional analysis of all features: L2 learners Sub-study 2 (from Lenzing 2019: 32–3).

		School 1								School 2							School 3								
Stage	Phenomena	P01	P02	P03	P04	P05	P06	P07	P08	M01	M02	M03	M04	M05	M06	M07	B01	B02	B03	B04	B05	B06	B07	B08	B09
6	Cancel Aux-2nd									+1 −1							+1	+7				+2			+2
5	Neg/Aux-2nd-?																								
	Aux-2nd-?	+2			+2	+1		+2	(+2)	+1 (+3)	+1			+2	+4	+1	+1	+7	+2	+2		+9	+1		+2
	V2/INV				+1			+1		+1			+1					+2			+1	+1			
	3sg −s	+6 −1	+4 −3	+1 −6	−5	+3	−6	+4	+1 −3	+1 −10	+1 −3	+1 −4	+2 −7	+7 −6	+2 −7	−8	+8	+8 −2	+4 −1	+9	+5 −5	+9	+3 −5	+4 −7	+7 −2
4	Copula S (x)	+5	+6	(+6)	(+5)	+2	+1			+3		+6	+6	+7	+7	(+6)	+16	+17	+22	+9	+16	+10	+5	+7	+8
	Wh-copula S (x)	+1	+9	(+3)	(+1) (+3)	+1 (+1)	(+1)	+2 (+1)	(+4)	+9 (+14)	+2	+4	+4		+1	+7		+3	+2	+2		+6	+3	+2	+1
	V-particle																								
3	Verb-First													+1		+1	+5	+2	+4	+6	+10	+5	+1	+1	
	Do-SV(O)-?					+1		(+2)	(+2)	+1		+4		+9	+4		+5	+2	+4	+6		+5	+11	+1	+1
	Aux SV(O)-?				+1	+1					+1						+1	+2			+2				
	Wh-SV(O)-?									+9	+1		+1						+1			+1	+5		
	Adverb-First	+17	+11	+1		+3	+2	+10	+8	+13	+11	+9	+8	+6	+17	+12	+9	+9	+9	+9	+8	+10	+14	+14	+12
	Poss (Pronoun)	+2	(+12)	+9				+1	+4	+6	+4	+7	+5			+4	+7	+3	+3	+2		+6	+13	+6	+13

Stage	Phenomena	School 1								School 2							School 3								
		P01	P02	P03	P04	P05	P06	P07	P08	M01	M02	M03	M04	M05	M06	M07	B01	B02	B03	B04	B05	B06	B07	B08	B09
	Object (Pronoun)																						+2		
	Plural-s (Det + N agr.)	+3	+3	(+3)	+1			+1	+4 −1			+1		+1				+2		+1	+3	+4			
	Have-Fronting	(+3)					(+2)	(+9)	(+9)	+1		(+2)			+1	+1	+5			+1	(+3)			+1	+1
2	S neg V(O)																								
	SVO	+13	+15	+9	+8	+15	+11	+24	+17	+28	+2	+9	+8	+9	+3			+2	+1	+1	+1	+2	+2	+2	+6
	SVO-Question									+2				+1				+1	+1		+5	+2	+2		
	-ed								+1		+1														
	-ing		+1			+3 −1	+2					+3 −1	+2		+4	+1	+3	+5	+2	+2	+5	+3	+2 −1	+2	
	Plural-s (Noun)	+3	+1							+5	+1	+2	+2	+3		+2	+5	+10	+2	+6	+6	+6	+6	+2	+2
	Poss-s (Noun)	+1								+6															
1	Words	+23	+14	+4	+3	+6	+7	+11	+20	+24	+20	+11	+11	+11	+24	+4	+1	+2	+9	+2	+7	+5	+5	+13	+5

Table 7.13 Distributional analysis 'Wh-Copula S (x)' – learner P03.

What's your favourite X?	3
• What's your favourite N? (What's your favourite hobby?)	2
• What's your favourite V? (What's your favourite eat?)	1
Null Hypothesis:	–
What's his/her favourite X?	0
What are his/her/your favourite X?	0
What's your/her/his X?	0
What Ø X?	0
What is X?	0
What are X?	0

As can be seen from Table 7.14, three learners are at stage 2, three learners have acquired features of stage 3, fourteen learners have acquired features of stage 4, three learners are at stage 5 and one learner has reached stage 6. The table also reveals that some learners produce a limited number of structures from a higher stage. Of the three learners at stage 3, two produce a limited number of 'stage 4' and 'stage 5' structures. Nine 'stage 4' learners produce a few 'stage 5' structures and one 'stage 4' learner additionally uses a limited number of 'stage 6' structures. Finally, one 'stage 5' learner also produces 'stage 6' structures, albeit in insufficient contexts to be considered as acquired. This is illustrated with the case of learner P04, who produces two instances of syntactic 'stage 3' structures and nine instances of morphological 'stage 3' features. Thus, at first glance, it could be assumed that she has acquired stage 3. However, the detailed distributional analysis shows that these structures do not exhibit sufficient lexical and/or morphological variation to be considered as acquired in terms of the emergence criterion.

The two syntactic 'stage 3' structures produced by learner P04 are presented in example (1).

(1)

	P04	Can you play computer games? (Aux SV(O)-?)
		Have you got a pet? (Have-Fronting)

Learner P04 produces one 'Aux SV(O)-?' and one 'Have-Fronting' question form. The occurrence of these single forms does not meet the emergence criterion. In addition, the question *Have you got a pet?* is likely to constitute a formula, as it is introduced in Unit 2 in the textbook *Playway 3* (Gerngross & Puchta 2008a). The question form *Can you X?* occurs in Unit 7 in *Playway 3* (*Can you play football? Can you play tennis?*

Table 7.14 Stages of acquisition: L2 learners Sub-study 2 (from Lenzing 2019: 34).

Stage	P01	P02	P03	P04	P05	P06	P07	P08	M01	M02	M03	M04
6	–	–	–	–	–	–	–	–	–	–	–	–
5	(+)	(+)	–	–	(+)	–	(+)	–	–	–	–	–
4	+	+	–	–	(+)	–	(+)	+	+	+	+	+
3	+	+	–	(+)	+	–	+	+	+	+	+	+
2	+	+	+	+	+	+	+	+	+	+	+	+
1	+	+	+	+	+	+	+	+	+	+	+	+

Stage	M05	M06	M07	B01	B02	B03	B04	B05	B06	B07	B08	B09
6	–	–	–	–	+	–	–	–	(+)	–	–	(+)
5	(+)	+	–	(+)	+	(+)	(+)	(+)	+	(+)	(+)	+
4	+	+	+	+	+	+	+	+	+	+	+	+
3	+	+	+	+	+	+	+	+	+	+	+	+
2	+	+	+	+	+	+	+	+	+	+	+	+
1	+	+	+	+	+	+	+	+	+	+	+	+

Can you ride a horse?) and possibly constitutes a formulaic pattern. However, as it is not clear which textbook was used in P04's primary school, this remains a tentative assumption.

The distributional analysis of the nine morphological structures occurring in the data of learner P04 is shown in example (2).

(2)

> P04   What's **your** favourite book?
> What's **your** favourite sport?
> What's **your** favourite colour?
> What's **your** name?
> Is in **your** picture a bike with a flower?
> Is in **your** picture a {Bank} (*bench*) with a mother?
> Is in **your** picture twelve pupil?
> Is in **your** picture a {was heißt Schild?} (*how do you say sign?*)
> Is in **your** picture a bike?

The results of the analysis reveal that (1) learner P04 only produces the possessive pronoun *your* and (2) the pronoun solely occurs in the two formulaic patterns *What's your X?* and *Is in your picture X?*. In line with the emergence criterion, the invariant occurrence of one morphological form without lexical or morphological variation does not reflect the productive use of this kind of 'stage 3' structure.

The distributional analysis of all learner data presented in Table 7.12 reveals that twelve 'stage 3' and 'stage 4' learners (P01, P02, P05, P07, M05, B01, B03, B04, B05, B07, B08 and B09) produced three or more instances of the '3sg -s' structure. However, as this structure does not occur with sufficient lexical and morphological variation in their speech samples, it cannot be unambiguously determined whether the learners have acquired stage 5. This is exemplified in example (3) with the data of 'stage 4' learner P02.

(3)

P02	At one o'clock Mr Lee **eats** at work.	
	At quarter past seven Mr Lee **gets** up.	
	At five o'clock Mr Lee **works**.	
	At five (/) half past six Mr Lee **eats** with his family.	
	At eight o'clock Mr Lee **do** the homework with his sons.	
	At 20 past seven Mr Lee **drink** a tea.	
	At five to nine Mr Lee **go** to the {Arbeit} (/) the work.	

The speech sample of learner P02 contains four instances of the '3sg -s' structure, and the morpheme occurs with lexical variation (*eat, get, work*). However, there are no instances of morphological variation (e.g. *eating, eat*Ø) in the learner data. Thus, the data do not meet the emergence criterion and, due to the limited contexts, it cannot be clearly determined whether learner P02 has acquired the respective stage of acquisition. Furthermore, the analysis shows that learner P02 has not fully mastered the application of the '3sg -s': There are three instances of its non-application in obligatory contexts in the learner data. A further finding relates to the occurrence of the 'stage 2' structure 'SVO'. The distributional analysis shows that not all learners produce sufficient instances of 'stage 2' structures to meet the emergence criterion (see e.g. learner M02 or learner B02). However, these learners all produce a sufficient amount of Adverb-First structures (stage 3). As this structure includes canonical word order (ADV **SVO**), the structure 'SVO' is also considered to be acquired when a learner produces a sufficient number of Adverb-First structures to meet the emergence criterion.

On the whole, the results of the distributional analyses indicate that the development of the L2 learners is in line with the predictions made by PT. The learners' language development is implicational and all learners follow the same sequence of acquisition for specific morpho-syntactic features. None of the learners showed evidence of having skipped stages.

7.2.2 Results production data – passive: Sub-study 2

The L2 learners' oral speech production data for passive constructions were analysed according to (1) the learners' acquisition of non-linear argument-function mapping and (2) their acquisition of morpho-syntactic processing. This was done in order to test my hypotheses concerning the L2 acquisition of passive structures. I argue that multiple processes are involved in the L2 acquisition of the English passive, and it is for this reason that the passive cannot be assigned a single PT stage. I hypothesize that the initial constraints on the underdeveloped L2 processor result in the following sequence of acquisition of English passives: *linear argument-function mapping → non-linear argument-function mapping → morpho-syntactic processing* (see Section 5.2.2).

In order to test the hypothesized sequence for oral speech production of the passive, the L2 learners' production data obtained in the two passive tasks were analysed by means of distributional analyses focusing on (1) argument-function mapping and (2) morpho-syntactic processing.

Argument-function mapping

The results of the distributional analysis of the L2 learner data in terms of argument-function mapping are summarized in Table 7.15. The table is laid out as follows: The first two columns contain information on the individual learners and their stage of acquisition, and the remaining two columns provide information on their acquisition of non-linear argument-function mapping in the fish film task (column 3) and the passive film task (column 4). The figures given in the table denote how often non-linear argument-function mapping occurred in the respective contexts. A '–' indicates the non-occurrence of non-linear argument-function mapping, a '(+)' denotes that non-linear argument-function mapping occurred in the learner data, albeit not in all contexts, and a '+' indicates the occurrence of non-linear argument-function mapping in all contexts.

The distributional analysis reveals that two out of three learners at stage 2 do not produce utterances with non-linear argument-function mapping (learner P03 and P06). This applies to both the fish film and the passive film task. Learner P03 consistently relies on active forms in the fish film. She produces 'It's a X' constructions in both active and passive contexts. This is exemplified in example (4):

(4)

P03	It's a blue fish and it's a food from the green fish. *(The blue fish is eaten by the green fish.)*
	It's a red fish and it's a eat from the blue fish. *(The red fish is eaten by the blue fish.)*
	It's a red fish and it's eat the white fish. *(The red fish eats the white fish.)*

The data suggest that the structure used by learner P03 constitutes a formulaic pattern: First of all, it is used in a (nearly) invariant form – the only alternation present in the data is between 'It's a X' and 'It's X'. Secondly, the structure occurs in a target-like way (*It's a blue fish*) as well as in non-target-like constructions (*It's a eat from the blue fish*).

In the passive film task, learner P03 produces a range of different structures to solve the task. These include structures with missing subjects as in example (5), N(oun)-V(erb)-N(oun) constructions with a linear agent-verb-patient order as in example

Table 7.15 Argument-function mapping in passives: L2 learners Sub-study 2.

Stage	Learner	Non-linear argument-function mapping	
		Fish film	Passive film
6	B02	(+) (5/6)	+ (9/9)
5	B06	+ (6/6)	+ (9/9)
	M06	+ (6/6)	+ (9/9)
	B09	+ (6/6)	+ (9/9)
4	M03	+ (6/6)	+ (9/9)
	B03	+ (6/6)	+ (9/9)
	B08	+ (6/6)	+ (9/9)
	B07	+ (6/6)	+ (9/9)
	B01	+ (6/6)	+ (9/9)
	B04	(+) (4/6)	+ (9/9)
	M01	+ (6/6)	+ (9/9)
	M02	(+) (3/6)	+ (9/9)
	P01	– (0/6)	+ (9/9)
	M07	+ (6/6)	(+) (8/9)
	B05	(+) (4/6)	(+) (8/9)
	P02	+ (6/6)	(+) (7/9)
	M04	+ (6/6)	(+) (6/9)
	M05	+ (6/6)	(+) (6/9)
3	P07	+ (6/6)	+ (9/9)
	P08	+ (6/6)	+ (9/9)
	P05	+ (6/6)	(+) (8/9)
2	P04	+ (6/6)	+ (9/9)
	P06	– (0/6)	– (0/9)
	P03	– (0/6)	– (0/9)

(6) and utterances where this order is reversed after a prompt by the researcher as in example (7). However, as can be seen in the examples, in these cases, there is no further indication of passivization, such as the occurrence of a preposition, an auxiliary or changes in verb morphology.

(5) *missing subject*

P03	puts the glass on the table (er) bottle
	(*The bottle is put on the table by the woman.*)
	in the math book show
	(*The homework was shown to the mother by the girl.*)

(6) *linear agent-verb-patient order*

P03	The woman push the man.
	(*The man is pushed by the woman*).
	The woman eat a carrot.
	(*The carrot is eaten by the woman*).

(7) *reversed order after prompt by researcher*

P03	The woman eat a carrot.
	(*The carrot is eaten by the woman*).
Researcher	{versuch mal mit der carrot anzufangen}
	(*try to start with the carrot*)
P03	The carrot eat a woman.

In two cases, learner P03 produces interim forms that differ from the 'reverse order' strategy used in the example in (7) in that they contain a preposition. These are again only produced after a prompt by the researcher that the learner should try to start with the entity the arrow points to. Interestingly, the learner initially inserts a form of the German auxiliary *werden* (*to get*) in her aim to solve the task.

(8)

P03	The man push (/) {nee} (*no*) the man the man {wird} (*gets*) a man push (/) {nee} (/) the man (/) the woman push the man.
Researcher	{Versuch mal den Satz mit the man anzufangen}
	(*try to start the sentence with the man*)
P03	The man (/) {weiß ich nicht} (*I don't know*) the man {wird} (*gets*) the man push from the woman.
	The man hug from the woman.

It could be argued that these two instances constitute cases of non-linear argument-function mapping. However, as learner P03 mostly relies on other structures, such as the 'reverse-order' strategy, in solving the task and as these structures were only produced after the researcher's prompt to start with the entity the arrow points to, I argue that they do not constitute genuine cases of non-linear argument-function mapping. In addition, on the basis of merely two occurrences of a structure in the learner's speech sample, no conclusions can be drawn about its acquisition.

The second 'stage 2' learner whose speech sample does not exhibit non-linear argument-function mapping is learner P06. In completing the fish film task, learner P06 simply reverses the two arguments as part of a 'reverse-order' strategy. She produces a series of active sentences in both active and passive contexts, which leads to misleading descriptions of those scenes where the arrow points to the fish that is being eaten.

(9)

P06	The blue fish eat a green fish.	passive context
	(*The blue fish is eaten by the green fish.*)	
	The green fish eat a purple fish.	
	(*The green fish is eaten by the purple fish.*)	
	The purple fish eat a white fish.	active context
	(*The purple fish eats the white fish.*)	

In the passive film task, learner P06 also mostly relies on the 'reverse-order'-strategy, as shown in example (10):

(10)

P06	Piano play the woman.
	(*The piano is played by the woman*).
	Carrot eat a woman.
	(*The carrot is eaten by the woman.*)
	The book give a boy.
	(*The book is given to the boy by the girl.*)

I argue that these instances do not constitute cases of non-linear argument-function mapping. Instead, the learner is cued to start with the entity the arrow points to and simply inserts the two arguments in the N V N matrix in the order in which they appear in the passive film. This assumption is supported by the fact that the sentences produced by the learner are implausible.

Finally, learner P06 produces four semantically ill-formed structures that contain a preposition, as in *The woman hug for the man* (*The woman is hugged by the man*). It could be argued that the use of a preposition indicates non-linear argument-function mapping. However, the four structures that contain a preposition are semantically ill-formed and can only be understood by taking the context into account. I therefore argue that they do not constitute cases of non-linear argument-function mapping but can also be classified as instances of the 'reverse-order' strategy employed by learner P06 to solve the task.

The third 'stage 2' learner (P04) is able to perform non-linear argument-function mapping operations in the fish film task as well as in the passive task (see example (11)):

(11)

P04	The drink is put on the table.
	(*The bottle is put on the table by the woman.*)
	The man was pushes from the woman.
	(*The man is pushed by the woman.*)
	The carrot is eat.
	(*The carrot is eaten by the woman.*)
	The book is give to the boy.
	(*The book is given to the boy by the girl.*)

At first glance, these examples suggest that non-linear argument-function mapping can be acquired at stage 2. However, as indicated in Table 7.12, learner P04 also produces a few 'stage 3' structures. Although the limited number of such occurrences does not permit any firm conclusions as to the acquisition of these structures, it could indeed be the case that this learner is at an early point in the acquisition of stage 3.

Table 7.15 shows that the acquisition of non-linear argument-function mapping takes place in a gradual fashion. With the potential exception of P04, this mapping process is acquired by the learners at stage 3. The structures produced by them are characterized by (1) the use of a preposition, which can be target-like or non-target-like, and, in the majority of cases, by (2) some form of the auxiliary. At this stage, the learners either do not use any morphological marking or produce idiosyncratic verb forms, as discussed in more detail in the next section.

The learners who are at stage 4 of acquisition also produce argument-function mapping in the majority of contexts. However, the data show that, despite the strong cues for passives, the contexts for the production of passive constructions allow for other solutions. Learner P01, for instance, produces no passive forms in completing the fish film task, although she starts with the fish the arrow points to. Instead, she uses a creative solution:

(12)

P01	The red fish is in the mouth from the blue fish.
	(*The red fish is eaten by the blue fish.*)
	The blue fish is in the mouth from the green fish.
	(*The blue fish is eaten by the green fish.*)

In the passive film task, however, she produces non-linear argument-function mapping in all trials that cue the passive form, albeit without an auxiliary.

(13)

P01	The carrot eat from a girl.
	(*The carrot is eaten by a girl.*)
	Lola's mum hug from Lola's father.
	(*Lola's mum is hugged from Lola's father.*)

On the whole, the data analysis indicates that the acquisition of non-linear argument-function mapping takes place in a gradual fashion and occurs from stage 3 onwards. This finding supports my hypotheses concerning the acquisition of non-linear argument-function mapping (see Section 5.2.2).

Morpho-syntactic processing

The results of the distributional analysis of morpho-syntactic processing evident in the learner data are provided in Table 7.16. The data in the table are restricted to the passive

Table 7.16 Morpho-syntactic processing in passives: L2 learners Sub-study 2.

Stage	Learner	Morpho-syntactic processing	
		Auxiliary	Verb morphology
6	B02	+ (9/9)	+ (8/8)
5	B06	(+) (7/9) (2*)	(+) (7/8)
	M06	+ (9/9)	(+) (7/8)
	B09	+ (9/9)	(+) (2/8)
4	M03	+ (9/9)	+ (8/8)
	B03	(+) (8/9) (5**)	+ (8/8)
	B07	+ (9/9)	+ (8/8)
	B01	+ (9/9)	+ (8/8)
	M01	+ (9/9)	(+) (6/8)
	M04	(+) (7/9)	(+) (6/8)
	B08	+ (9/9)	(+) (5/8)
	B04	(+) (8/9)	(+) (5/8)
	M05	(+) (6/9)	(+) (5/8)
	B05	(+) 8/9	(+) (4/8)
	M02	(+) (8/9)	(+) (3/8)
	M07	(+) (8/9)	(+) (3/8)
	P02	(+) (6/9)	– (0/8)
	P01	– (0/9)	– (0/8)
3	P07	+ (9/9)	– (0/8)
	P05	(+) (6/9)	– (0/8)
	P08	– (0/9)	– (0/8)
2	P04	+ (9/9)	– (0/8)
	P06	– (0/9)	– (0/8)
	P03	– (0/9)	– (0/8)

Note. *there's a x, **get-passive.

film task, as there is no lexical variation in the fish film task. The first two columns in the table provide information on the L2 learners' stage of acquisition. The figures given in the third column show how often the auxiliary is produced by the respective learners, and the figures in the fourth column indicate the instances of target-like verb morphology in the individual learners' speech samples. One of the trials contains the verb *put* with its unaltered participle form. Therefore, morpho-syntactic processing is only observable in eight out of nine contexts in the learner data. A '+' denotes the target-like production of the auxiliary and/or the respective verb morphology, and a '–' indicates that the respective feature was absent in the learner data. If the feature was produced in some of the contexts, the respective cell is marked with a '(+)'. The asterisks in the third column mark alternative constructions: One asterisk indicates the use of the pattern *There's a x* (learner B06) and two asterisks mark the occurrence of the *get*-passive (learner B03). These constructions will be further discussed in the course of this section. The dotted line in the table shows the implicational acquisition of auxiliaries and verbal morphology.

Table 7.16 reveals that, with the exception of P04, the learners begin to produce auxiliaries in passives from stage 3 onwards. Full morpho-syntactic processing in passive constructions does not occur before the learners have reached stage 4, as evidenced by the production of target-like verb morphology. Only the production of target-like verb morphology indicates the acquisition of feature unification within the verb phrase, which occurs at stage 4 of the PT hierarchy (see Section 3.4). Both processes – the insertion of an auxiliary and target-like verb morphology – seem to be acquired gradually by the L2 learners.

As discussed in the previous section, the speech samples of the two 'stage 2' learners P06 and P03 do not contain any instances of non-linear argument-function mapping. In keeping with this, both learners do not produce any auxiliaries or verbal morphology. The speech sample of the third 'stage 2' learner (P04) contains auxiliaries in all passive trials (see Table 7.16). However, as pointed out in the previous section, it could be the case that P04 is at an early point in the acquisition of stage 3. As regards verbal morphology, learner P04 produces one instance of the feature '3sg -s' (*The man was pushes from the woman*) and uses uninflected verb forms in all other trials.

'Stage 3' learner P08 relies on her L1 German and consistently inserts the German auxiliary verb *werden* (to get) in her utterances:

(14)

P08	The red fish {wird gefressen was heißt das?} (*is eaten, how do you say that?*)
Researcher	{Versuch mal} (*have a try*)
P08	{Hmh keine Ahnung} (*no idea*)
Researcher	{Sag mal einfach was du was du denkst} (*just tell me what you think*)
P08	The green fish {wird} (*get*) eat by the pink fish.
	A rabbit {wird} (*get*) carry by Lola's mom.
	Lola's father {wird} (*get*) push away by Lola's mom.

As can be seen in example (14), she produces uninflected verb forms in all passive trials. The other two 'stage 3' learners (P05 and P07), on the other hand, seem to experiment with verbal morphology: They produce different kinds of idiosyncratic forms, as illustrated in examples (15) and (16).

(15)

P05	The white fish is eating from the black fish.
	The book is showing from a child and a mother.
	The mother {oder} (*or*) the carrot eatings from the mother.
	The rabbit is carry from the mother.
	The piano play from the mother.

Learner P05 frequently employs the suffix '-ing'. Interestingly, he also produces the form *eatings* in *The carrot eatings from the mother*. As he leaves out the auxiliary, it could be the case that he attaches the '-s' as a '3sg -s' marker. A further observation relates to the learner's production of the auxiliary. It is inserted in all passive forms related to the fish film but is not applied in all passive constructions in the passive film task.

As exemplified in example (16), learner P07 produces verbs with different inflectional suffixes in his passive constructions. These include the '-ing' as well as the '3sg -s' suffix. The variability in his application of verbal morphology is particularly evident in the case of the verb *eat*, which occurs with substantial morphological variation in P07's interlanguage: The learner's passive constructions include the forms *was eat-ing*, *was eat-s* and *was eatø*.

(16)

	P07	The red fish was eating from the blue fish.
		The green fish was eats from the pink fish.
		The carrot was eat from Lola's mom.
		The bottle was puts from {wer ist das?} (*who's that?*) (…) from Lola's mom of the table.
		Lola's dad was pushes from Lola's mom.

These findings support the hypothesis of the successive acquisition of morpho-syntactic aspects in English passive constructions. Interestingly, both learner P05 and learner P07 also produce a limited number of stage 4 and stage 5 structures, albeit in insufficient contexts to be able to determine whether they have acquired a higher stage than stage 3.

Apart from one 'stage 4' learner (P01), who does not produce any auxiliary in the passive trials, all learners from stage 4 onwards insert a form of the auxiliary *to be*. The majority of these learners (except for P01 and P02) also employs target-like verb morphology in at least some of the passive trials. Learner B07, for instance, applies target-like verb morphology in all contexts. However, he does not produce target-like subject-verb agreement in a consistent manner and produces forms such as *The rabbit were cuddled by the girl*. Other learners, such as learner M02, use target-like morphology in some cases but employ the uninflected verb form in other contexts.

These findings additionally support the claim that the acquisition of target-like verb morphology takes place in a stepwise fashion. Once learners have acquired the verb phrase procedure, they are, in principle, able to perform feature unification operations within the verb phrase, which allows for the exchange of grammatical information between the auxiliary and the lexical verb. In particular, this applies to the value PARTICIPLE = PAST that needs to be exchanged between the verb and the auxiliary. In order for this transfer of grammatical information to take place, the lexical entry for the verb has to be annotated for PARTICIPLE = PAST and the entry for the auxiliary has to be annotated for the constraint equation V-COMP PARTICIPLE = $_c$PAST (see also Section 3.4). In keeping with the claim proposed in the *Multiple Constraints Hypothesis* that the lexicon is annotated gradually in SLA,

I assume that, initially, not all verbs are annotated for this particular information. Furthermore, learners additionally have to acquire the form-function relations involved in the affixation of the verb. This is reflected in the learner data: The majority of learners from stage 4 onwards produces some past participle forms, albeit not in all contexts where this form is required (see Table 7.16).

A further observation relates to the learners' production of auxiliaries and verbal morphology in active sentences: In the speech samples of six learners (P05 [stage 3], M01, M03, M04, M07 [stage 4] and M06 [stage 5]), auxiliaries occur not only in passive sentences but also in actives, as illustrated with the utterances produced by learner M01:

(17)

M01	The woman is clean the table.	active
	The girl is tickle the man.	
	The rabbit is carrying by the woman.	passive
	The carrot is eaten by the woman.	

The same learner applies the past participle form in active sentences in the fish film trial, as in example (18).

(18)

| M01 | The pink fish eaten the white fish. |
| | The orange fish is eaten the white fish. |

The data of learner M06 also contain auxiliaries in both active and passive constructions, as in example (19).

(19)

M06	The girl is clean the table.	active
	The girl is tickle the father.	
	The book is given to the boy.	passive
	The bottle is putten on the table.	
	The rabbit is cuddled by the girl.	

Again, these utterances lend support to the claim that the acquisition of morphosyntactic processing in the production of English passives takes place in a gradual fashion. The application of the suffix '-en' to the verb *put* further implies that the learner has not fully acquired the respective form-function relationship.

Two learners – 'stage 4' learner B03 and 'stage 5' learner B06 – employ different solutions when engaging with the passive task. The speech sample of learner B03

Table 7.17 Sequence of acquisition within morpho-syntactic processing.

Stage	Feature
4	+ auxiliary + verb morphology
3	+ auxiliary − verb morphology
2	− auxiliary − verb morphology

contains five instances of the *get*-passive in the passive task, as in *The father gets pushed by his wife*. Learner B06 produces two instances of 'There's a x' constructions, as in *There's a bottle put on a table from a woman*. However, the speech samples of both learners also exhibit a number of passive constructions with a form of *to be*. Within morpho-syntactic processing, the data reflect the sequence of acquisition shown in Table 7.17.

To sum up, the results of the distributional analysis in terms of morpho-syntactic processing of passive constructions support my hypothesis that, in principle, learners start to acquire feature unification processes within the verb phrase at stage 4. In general, the data reveal that, in the acquisition of morpho-syntactic aspects of the passive, auxiliaries occur first. They appear in the speech samples of two 'stage 3' learners and – with the exception of learner P01 – are employed by all learners from stage 4 onwards. Evidence for feature unification processes is evident from stage 4 onwards. Table 7.16 shows the gradual acquisition of form-function relationships, as target-like verb morphology initially occurs only in limited contexts.

Summary of oral production data passive

The results of the analysis of the oral speech production data for passive constructions obtained in the passive film task are summarized in Table 7.18. The table provides information on the learners' stage of acquisition (columns 1 and 2) as well as on their production of passive constructions (columns 3 and 4). As far as the latter is concerned, the table distinguishes between (1) linear and non-linear argument-function mapping in the passive film (column 3) and (2) morphological marking of the verb, which serves as an indicator for morpho-syntactic processing (column 4). As in Table 7.16, a '+' indicates that a structure was consistently produced by the learner, and a '(+)' indicates that the structure was not produced in all contexts. The figures given in parentheses in the table denote how often a particular feature was applied in a given context. A non-application of the feature is indicated by a '−' in the respective cells. The dotted line in the table indicates the implicational development in the acquisition of non-linear argument-function mapping and morpho-syntactic processing.

On the whole, the results of the distributional analyses of the L2 learners' production data of the passive show that (1) the acquisition of passive constructions takes place implicationally and (2) it follows the hypothesized developmental sequence

Table 7.18 Summary of oral production data of passives: L2 learners Sub-study 2.

Stage	Learner	Production	
		Non-linear argument-function mapping (passive film)	Morpho-syntactic processing verb morphology (passive film)
6	B02	+ (9/9)	+ (8/8)
5	B06	+ (9/9)	(+) (7/8)
	M06	+ (9/9)	(+) (7/8)
	B09	+ (9/9)	(+) (2/8)
4	M03	+ (9/9)	+ (8/8)
	B03	+ (9/9)	+ (8/8)
	B07	+ (9/9)	+ (8/8)
	B01	+ (9/9)	+ (8/8)
	M01	+ (9/9)	(+) (6/8)
	M04	+ (6/9)	(+) (6/8)
	B04	+ (9/9)	(+) (5/8)
	B08	+ (9/9)	(+) (5/8)
	M05	+ (6/9)	(+) (5/8)
	B05	+ (8/9)	(+) (4/8)
	M02	+ (9/9)	(+) (3/8)
	M07	+ (8/9)	(+) (3/8)
	P01	(+) (9/9)	– (0/8)
	P02	(+) (7/9)	– (0/8)
3	P07	+ (9/9)	– (0/8)
	P05	(+) (8/9)	– (0/8)
	P08	(+) (9/9)	– (0/8)
2	P04	(+) (9/9)	– (0/8)
	P03	– (0/9)	– (0/8)
	P06	– (0/9)	– (0/8)

(*linear argument-function mapping* → *non-linear argument-function mapping* → *morpho-syntactic processing*). The finding that, initially, the L2 learners are not capable of performing non-linear argument-function mapping supports the hypotheses concerning the initial constraints of the L2 initial mental grammatical system as spelled out in the *Multiple Constraints Hypothesis*. In particular, this relates to the assumption that the L2 mental lexicon is annotated gradually, which applies to the syntactic features at a-structure level. As discussed in Section 3.6, the syntactic features at a-structure level are a crucial prerequisite for mapping operations that relate the arguments at a-structure level to the grammatical functions at the level of f-structure.

7.2.3 Results comprehension data – passive: Sub-study 2

The results of the analysis of the comprehension data are summarized in Table 7.20. A '+' in a cell indicates that the learner's interpretation of the passive construction with the respective verb was target-like. A '−' in the cell marks those cases where the learner did not interpret the sentence correctly (i.e. by assigning the patient role to the actor in the event). In eight cases, the photo showed the correct interpretation of the sentence but the learner pointed to the wrong actor. In these cases, it is not clear whether the learners understood the researcher's question to point to the Playmobil© figure that carries out the action. Therefore, these instances are labelled with a '(+)' (target-like enactment but unclear agent assignment). Finally, in six cases, the agent of the event could not be unambiguously identified or the scene was not properly enacted. In these instances, the respective cell is marked with a 'u' (for unclear) (see Table 7.19).

Table 7.19 Classifications of interpretations of passives in enactment task: Sub-study 2.

Classifications of interpretations of passive sentences in enactment task

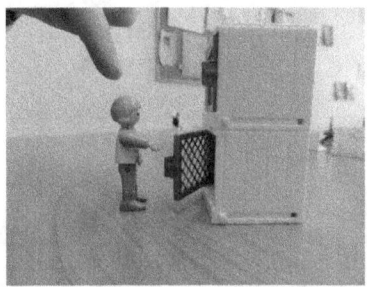

Correct interpretation of the passive sentence *The cage is opened by Lisa* (learner P05) marked as '+' in Table 7.20

Active interpretation of the passive sentence *Tom is chased by the alligator* (learner P02) marked as '−' in Table 7.20

Correct interpretation but wrong agent assignment for the sentence *The horse is ridden by Lisa* (learner P02) marked as '(+)' in Table 7.20

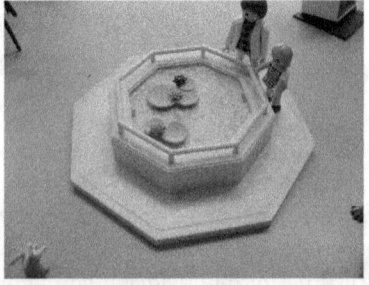

Unclear agent assignment for the sentence *Lisa was taken to the pond by James* (learner M04) marked as 'u' in Table 7.20

When calculating the scalability of Table 7.20, the cells containing a 'u' were excluded from the analysis. These accounted for 2.12 per cent of all data. The coefficient of reproducibility of Table 7.20 is 0.96 and the coefficient of scalability is 0.83. Therefore, the implicational table can be considered to be valid.

As in Sub-study 1, the results presented in Table 7.20 show an implicational development of the acquisition of different passive constructions in L2 comprehension, which suggests that passive structures are acquired gradually in L2 comprehension. The table reveals that the four passives that are comprehended by nearly all twenty-four L2 learners and are therefore claimed to be acquired early are either non-reversible passives as in example (20) or passives with low event probability when interpreted in active voice, as in example (21):[4]

(20) The wheelbarrow is pushed by James.
(21) The horse is ridden by Lisa.

The early acquisition of these structures, which is further supported by the finding that they are comprehended already by learners at stages 2 and 3 of acquisition, can be explained in terms of their prototypicality and, in particular, by their semantic irreversibility. In line with the criteria outlined by Meints (1999a: 71), the four structures constitute prototypical passives: All are transitive constructions with focus on the patient or theme respectively. The verbs denoting the action in the sentences display the features of actionality, punctuality, direct physical contact and visible result. For instance, the sentence *The cage is opened by Lisa* describes a highly punctual action which involves a direct contact between the agent (*Lisa*) and the theme (*the cage*) and leads to a visible result. Most importantly, however, all four passives are semantically irreversible. The plausibility rating displayed in Table 7.21 shows that their active counterpart is considered to be highly implausible. The fact that the semantically irreversible structures are comprehended by nearly all learners in the study regardless of their stage of acquisition supports the claim that semantic information influences the L2 comprehension processes and that initially, L2 parsing is guided by semantic cues.

The structures that occur next in Table 7.20 are passive constructions with three arguments, as in example (22).

(22) James is saved from the tiger by Tom.

The ditransitive passive in example (22) is comprehended by seventeen learners. One learner does not enact the scene properly. The remaining six learners map the first noun phrase onto the agent role and interpret the sentence as James saves Tom from the tiger. This is illustrated in Figure 7.5, which shows the scene enacted by learner P07.[5]

As argued in Section 7.1.2, the parsing of ditransitive passives differs from the parsing of transitive constructions in that L2 learners cannot rely on the processing heuristic N V N and assign the first noun (phrase)/subject to the proto-agent and the second noun (phrase)/object to the proto-patient. In the case of the sentence *James is saved from the tiger by Tom*, the application of the N V N strategy could result in the

Table 7.20 Distributional analysis of comprehension data passives: L2 learners Sub-study 2 (Lenzing 2019: 39).

	1	2	3	4	5	6	7	8	9	10	11	12	13	14	15	16	17	18	19	20	21	22	23	24
	P02	P05	P01	M05	P06	P03	P04	M04	M07	P07	P08	B08	M02	B09	B05	B07	B04	B03	B01	M03	M01	B06	M06	B02
Stage	4	3	4	4	2	2	2	4	4	3	3	4	4	5	4	4	4	4	4	4	4	5	5	6
The giraffe is followed by the zebra.	−	−	+	−	−	−	−	−	−	−	−	−	−	−	+	+	+	+	+	+	+	+	+	u
James is hit by Tom.	−	−	−	−	−	−	−	−	−	−	−	+	+	+	+	+	+	+	+	+	+	+	+	+
The tiger is boxed by the kangaroo.	−	−	−	−	−	−	−	−	−	−	−	−	+	+	+	+	+	+	+	+	+	+	+	+
The calf is kissed by the horse.	−	−	−	+	−	−	(+)	−	−	−	+	+	+	+	+	+	+	+	+	+	+	+	+	+
Tom is chased by the alligator.	−	−	(+)	−	−	−	−	−	−	−	−	−	−	−	+	+	+	+	+	+	+	+	+	+
The rabbit is handed over to James by Lisa.	−	−	−	−	−	+	−	u	−	−	−	−	−	+	−	+	+	+	+	+	+	+	+	+
Lisa is taken to the pond by James.	−	−	−	u	−	−	−	u	+	−	−	+	+	+	+	+	+	+	+	+	+	+	+	+
James is saved from the tiger by Tom.	−	−	−	−	−	−	−	−	+	+	(+)	+	+	+	+	+	+	+	+	+	+	+	+	+
The horse is ridden by Lisa.	(+)	+	+	+	u	+	+	+	+	+	+	+	+	+	+	+	+	+	+	+	+	+	+	+
The horse is showered by Tom.	(+)	+	+	+	(+)	+	+	+	+	+	+	+	+	+	+	+	+	+	+	+	+	+	+	+
The cage is opened by Lisa.	(+)	+	+	+	+	+	+	+	+	+	+	+	+	+	+	+	+	+	+	+	+	+	+	+
The wheelbarrow is pushed by James.	(+)	+	+	+	+	+	+	+	+	+	+	+	+	+	+	+	+	+	+	+	+	+	+	+

Note: u = unclear, (+) = photo shows correct interpretation but learner points to wrong actor.

Table 7.21 Plausibility rating of semantically irreversible passives: Sub-study 2.

Sentence	Mean	SD
James pushes the wheelbarrow	2.04	1.19
The wheelbarrow pushes James	6.18	1.22
Lisa opens the cage	1.25	1.03
The cage opens Lisa	6.64	0.64
Tom showers the horse	2.91	1.74
The horse showers Tom	6.50	1.14
Lisa rides the horse	1.14	0.69
The horse rides Lisa	6.36	1.10

Figure 7.5 Misinterpretation of *James is saved from the tiger by Tom*.

interpretation *James save tiger*. However, the N V N strategy does not account for the processing of the third noun (phrase) *Tom*. The same applies to the remaining two ditransitive constructions *Lisa is taken to the pond by James* and *The rabbit is handed over to James by Lisa* that are both understood by fifteen of the twenty-four learners. In those instances where the L2 learners misinterpret the ditransitive passive forms, they mostly rely on a reversal of argument roles and map the first noun (phrase) onto the agent role and the third noun (phrase) onto the patient/theme role.

As in Sub-study 1, the application of the criteria concerning prototypical passives established by Meints (1999a, b) to ditransitive passives shows that the ditransitive forms in Sub-study 2 also exhibit traits of prototypical passive constructions. Apart from focusing on the patient/theme argument, two of the ditransitive sentences denote highly punctual actions. However, what is perhaps most important in this concern is the fact that in all cases, a direct application of the N V N (N) strategy yields implausible results: *Tom save tiger (from James)*, *Lisa take pond (to James)*, *Rabbit hand over James (to Lisa)* all constitute implausible interpretations of the respective experimental stimulus. Thus, I argue that it is the low event probability in the case of an active interpretation that crucially influences the comprehension process of the ditransitive constructions. This renders an active interpretation of the ditransitives highly unlikely. In line with this, I assume that event plausibility seems to be a major factor in the early occurrence of ditransitive constructions in L2 comprehension.

The comprehension of ditransitive passives is followed by two passives with biased event probability in examples (23) and (24) as well as one construction with neutral event probability (25).

(23) The alligator is chased by Tom. (14 learners)
(24) The tiger is boxed by the kangaroo. (12 learners)
(25) The little calf is kissed by the big horse. (14 learners)

The two passives *The alligator is chased by Tom* and *The tiger is boxed by the kangaroo* encompass some characteristics of prototypical passives, albeit to a lesser degree than the semantically irreversible constructions discussed in this section. Both sentences constitute transitive passives with focus on the patient, and the verbs can be considered to be actional. In the case of *The tiger is boxed by the kangaroo*, the action is furthermore highly punctual and the action includes physical contact as well as a visible result. The most crucial difference to the semantically irreversible constructions comprehended by all learners in the study seems to be related to the probability of the event described in the sentences. The results of the plausibility assessment in Table 7.22 show that both constructions can be considered passives with biased event probability. However, the plausibility effects are not as pronounced as is the case in the semantically irreversible passives.

Symmetrical passives with 'neutral' event probability that appear higher in the implicational hierarchy are seemingly comprehended late in L2 acquisition. The two symmetrical passives in (26) and (27) were understood by eleven and twelve L2 learners respectively.

(26) James is hit by Tom.
(27) The giraffe is followed by the zebra.

Both sentences display neutral event probability as both the active and the passive interpretations are rated as equally (im)plausible (see Table 7.23). In terms of other prototypicality traits, it can be argued that the verb *hit* denotes a more punctual action than the verb *follow*. However, this difference does not seem to have a major impact

Table 7.22 Plausibility rating of biased reversible passives: Sub-Study 2.

Sentence	Mean	SD
Tom chases the alligator	3.63	1.62
The alligator chases Tom	1.93	1.18
The tiger boxes the kangaroo	5.98	2.00
The kangaroo boxes the tiger	4.46	1.73

Table 7.23 Plausibility rating of symmetrical reversible passives: Sub-study 2.

Sentence	Mean	SD
The giraffe follows the zebra	2.54	1.53
The zebra follows the giraffe	2.23	1.36
James hits Tom	1.41	1.09
Tom hits James	1.46	1.00
The little calf kisses the big horse	4.66	1.76
The big horse kisses the little calf	4.45	2.00

on the L2 learners' comprehension process and is probably too subtle to influence the actual parsing of the sentence.

The sentence *The little calf is kissed by the big horse* constitutes somewhat of an exception, as it is comprehended by fourteen learners and in this respect occurs at the same level as the passives with biased event probability. As can be seen from Table 7.23, there is no plausibility bias in interpreting the sentence. Although the verb *kiss* displays some prototypical traits of transitive passives, such as a punctual action which involves direct physical contact, it is not considered to be more prototypical than the verb *hit*. The passive sentence with the latter verb is comprehended by only eleven learners in the study.

I argue that, in all these cases, L2 learners need to rely on syntactic processing to be able to parse the sentence correctly, as they cannot draw on semantic cues. This assumption is supported by the fact that the learners that understand the symmetrical passives in a target-like way are already at higher stages of acquisition (stages 4–6). Overall, the results of the analysis support the proposed gradual development from semantic to syntactic processing.

A further crucial finding is that the implicational acquisition of different types of passives in L2 comprehension correlates with the L2 learners' stages of acquisition according to the PT hierarchy. A Spearman's rank-order correlation was run to assess the relationship between the number of passive constructions comprehended by the learners and their stages of acquisition. The results show a strong positive correlation between the number of comprehended passives and the learners' PT stages, $r_s(24) = 0.62$, $p = 0.001$ (two-tailed).

These results match the ones obtained in Sub-study 1 and provide further evidence for the hypothesis that the processing procedures spelled out in PT also constrain the L2 syntactic parsing process. They are also in line with the assumption that the L2 comprehension process develops gradually from semantic to syntactic processing. This gradual development can be explained by the successive acquisition of processing procedures that are a prerequisite for deep syntactic processing. In keeping with this, the results are in accord with the adaptation of the *Online Cognitive Equilibrium Hypothesis* to SLA proposed in Section 4.3 and the related claim that L2 learners initially rely on the heuristic route in L2 comprehension as they lack the necessary procedures for deep algorithmic processing.

To sum up, the results show (1) an implicational development of the acquisition of different passive constructions in L2 comprehension and (2) a correlation between the number and type of comprehended passive constructions and the learners' PT stages. In my view, a potential explanation for the implicational development of the acquisition of passives in L2 comprehension and the correlation between the passive constructions comprehended by the L2 learners and their stages of acquisition is a gradual development from shallow or semantic processing to syntactic processing.

7.2.4 Relating production and comprehension data: Sub-study 2

In Table 7.24, the results of the complete data analysis are summarized. The table relates the results of the passive comprehension data and the passive production data to the learners' PT stages of acquisition. Again, the table contains only the data obtained in the passive film task, as they exhibit lexical variation regarding the verb. The dotted line in the table shows the implicational development in the L2 acquisition of the two processes.

As can be seen from Table 7.24, there are no cases of production without comprehension in the learner data, but there are a few cases of comprehension without production. This applies to two learners (P03 and P06) and involves non-reversible passive constructions, which are claimed to be processed semantically, and two ditransitive forms (see Table 7.20).

(28) The wheelbarrow is pushed by James. (P03 and P06)
(29) The horse is showered by Tom. (P03 and P06)
(30) The cage is opened by Lisa. (P03 and P06)
(31) James is saved from the tiger by Tom. (P03 and P06)
(32) The rabbit is handed over to James by Lisa. (P03)
(33) The horse is ridden by Lisa. (P03)

A second finding is that there are correlations between the number of comprehended structures and the number of produced structures. This applies to both non-linear argument-function mapping and morpho-syntactic processing. Not all variables were normally distributed, as assessed by a visual inspection of the boxplots and histograms and by Shapiro-Wilk's test ($p = 0.002$ [comprehended structures] and $p < 0.001$

Table 7.24 Overall results: PT stages, comprehension and production of passives: Sub-study 2 (Lenzing 2019: 41).

Stage	Learner	No. of comprehended structures	Production	
			Non-linear argument-function mapping (passive film)	Morpho-syntactic processing (verb morphology)
6	B02	(+) (11/12)	+ (9/9)	+ (8/8)
5	B06	+ (12/12)	+ (9/9)	(+) (7/8)
	M06	+ (12/12)	+ (9/9)	(+) (7/8)
	B09	(+) (10/12)	+ (9/9)	(+) (2/8)
4	M03	+ (12/12)	+ (9/9)	+ (8/8)
	B03	+ (12/12)	+ (9/9)	+ (8/8)
	B07	+ (12/12)	+ (9/9)	+ (8/8)
	B01	+ (12/12)	+ (9/9)	+ (8/8)
	M01	+ (12/12)	+ (9/9)	(+) (6/8)
	M04	(+) (5/12)	(+) (6/9)	(+) (6/8)
	B04	+ (12/12)	+ (9/9)	(+) (5/8)
	B08	(+) (9/12)	+ (9/9)	(+) (5/8)
	M05	(+) (5/12)	(+) (6/9)	(+) (5/8)
	B05	(+) (11/12)	(+) (8/9)	(+) (4/8)
	M02	(+) (8/12)	+ (9/9)	(+) (3/8)
	M07	(+) (7/12)	(+) (8/9)	(+) (3/8)
	P01	(+) (6/12)	+ (9/9)	– (0/8)
	P02	(+) (4/12)	(+) (7/9)	– (0/8)
3	P07	(+) (6/12)	+ (9/9)	– (0/8)
	P05	(+) (4/12)	(+) (8/9)	– (0/8)
	P08	(+) (7/12)	+ (9/9)	– (0/8)
2	P04	(+) (6/12)	+ (9/9)	– (0/8)
	P03	(+) (6/12)	– (0/9)	– (0/8)
	P06	(+) (4/12)	– (0/9)	– (0/8)

[produced structures]). Therefore, a Spearman's rank-order correlation was run to assess the relationship between the number of passive constructions comprehended by the learners and the number of produced structures. The results show a strong positive correlation between the number of comprehended passives and the number of produced passives that exhibit non-linear argument-function mapping, $r_s(24) = 0.64$, $p = 0.01$ (two-tailed) as well as a strong positive correlation between the number of comprehended passives and the number of passives with target-like verbal morphology in production, $r_s(24) = 0.82$, $p < 0.001$ (two-tailed).

The correlations between comprehended structures and produced structures serve as a further indication of a relation between processing in comprehension and production. Although there is not a one-to-one relation between the number of comprehended structures and the number of produced structures in every individual learner, the strong positive correlations between the number of comprehended structures and both the number of produced passive forms with non-linear argument-function mapping and the ones with target-like verbal morphology in production suggest that the two processes do not occur independently of each other. Instead, the results point to a relation between production and comprehension based on the same underlying processing procedures.

The results reveal that the L2 learners acquire non-linear argument-function mapping in production from stage 3 onwards. In comprehension, the data analysis shows an implicational acquisition of different types of passives that reflect a development from semantic to syntactic processing. Finally, the data provide evidence for morpho-syntactic processing in L2 learners in production from stage 4 onwards. What is missing in the data set is clear evidence for morpho-syntactic processing in sentence comprehension. Although the implicational acquisition of passives with different verb types indicates a development from semantic to syntactic processing, the methodology used in Sub-studies 1 and 2 does not allow for firm conclusions as to when exactly (morpho-)syntactic processing of the passive is acquired in sentence comprehension. In order to be able to control for morpho-syntactic cues and to tap into syntactic processing, the sentence-matching reaction-time experiment was implemented in Sub-study 3.

7.3 Sub-Study 3

Like the other two studies, Sub-study 3 is also cross-sectional in design. The learner data were collected at three different schools with thirty-nine learners from four different grades (grade 5, 6, 7 and 8). The learners' age range was between ten and fourteen and they had received four, five and six years of instruction in English respectively. Three learners (SM01, SM06 and S06) were excluded from the analysis, as they did not complete all tasks. Therefore, the data of thirty-six learners were included in the analysis. A detailed overview of the participants is provided in Table 7.25.[6]

The tasks carried out by all thirty-six learners in Sub-study 3 aimed at eliciting (1) oral speech production data to determine the individual learners' stage of acquisition, (2) oral speech production data to investigate the learners' acquisition of the English passive in production, (3) comprehension data to explore the learners' comprehension of English passives and (4) reaction-time data obtained in the sentence-matching experiment to shed light on the learners' morpho-syntactic processing in the comprehension of passives. An overview of the tasks employed in Sub-study 3 is provided in Table 7.26.

Table 7.25 Overview of participants: Sub-study 3.

Participants school 1								
Informants	SM02	SM03	SM04	SM05	SM07	SM08	SM09	
Age	11	11	10	11	11	11	11	
Sex	f	f	f	f	m	f	m	
Grade	5	5	5	5	5	5	6	
Informants	SM10	SM11	SM12	SM13	SM14	SM15	SM16	
Age	11	11	11	11	12	11	11	
Sex	f	f	f	f	f	f	f	
Grade	6	6	6	6	6	6	6	
Participants school 2								
Informants	G01	G02	G03	G04	G05	G06	G07	
Age	11	10	10	11	10	11	11	
Sex	m	m	m	f	f	f	f	
Grade	5	5	5	5	5	5	5	
Informants	G08	G09	G10	G11	G12	G13	G14	G15
Age	10	13	14	14	14	13	14	14
Sex	m	m	f	f	f	m	m	w
Grade	5	8	8	8	8	8	8	8
Participants school 3								
Informants	S01	S02	S03	S04	S05	S07	S08	
Age	14	13	13	13	14	13	14	
Sex	m	f	f	m	m	m	m	
Grade	7	7	7	7	7	7	7	

Table 7.26 Production and comprehension tasks: Sub-study 3.

Type of data	Tasks
Oral speech production I: stages of acquisition	Communicative tasks
Oral speech production II: passive	Fish film Passive film clips 12 target items (passive) 4 distractor items (active)
Comprehension passive I: general	Sentence-picture matching 12 target items (passive) 5 distractor items (active)
Comprehension passive II: morpho-syntactic processing	Sentence-matching reaction-time experiment 12 target items 12 distractor items

All in all, the sessions to elicit the individual learner data lasted approximately 60 minutes. Again, the learners worked on the communicative tasks in pairs, and the passive production and comprehension tasks (film clip, sentence-picture matching task and sentence-matching task) were carried out with a researcher. As in Sub-study 2, the learners' oral speech production data were fully transcribed.

7.3.1 Input session – passive: Sub-study 3

In addition to the data elicitation methodology described in Chapter 6, Sub-study 3 included a further component. A refinement in the methodology implemented in Sub-study 3 addresses the issue that, at the time of data elicitation, not all learners who participated in the study had received formal instruction about the English passive constructions at school. The reason is that the passive is introduced in grades 7 and 8 respectively, depending on the school type. As can be seen from Table 7.28, grade 7 and 8 learners are mostly at stages 4 and 5 of acquisition. However, in order to be able to test the hypotheses concerning the L2 acquisition of the English passive in production and comprehension outlined in this book, it is essential to also include learners at lower stages of acquisition in the study. This implies the inclusion of learners who have not had any formal instruction related to the English passive.

From the theoretical perspective of processability adopted in this book, it does not make a difference whether the learners have received formal instruction related to the structure under investigation or not, as it is hypothesized that learners can only produce/comprehend what they can process. This is captured in the *Teachability Hypothesis* (Pienemann 1984, 1989), which basically 'assumes that the effect of teaching intervention is constrained by the learner's current state of development' (Pienemann 2015: 137). Although the *Teachability Hypothesis* does not constitute a corollary of PT, it can be formalized within the theory and has been supported in a number of empirical studies (see e.g. Baten & Keßler 2019; Pienemann 1998; Roos 2016).

Nevertheless, the question remains as to whether the performance of the L2 learners at grades 7, 8 and 9 in the passive tasks was influenced by the fact that they had been exposed to more input of passive forms in the foreign language classroom than the learners at lower grades. Naturally, this issue cannot be fully clarified in this book. However, I addressed this matter in Sub-study 3 by investigating whether L2 learners who received a short, intensive exposure to passive constructions prior to data elicitation improved their performance on the passive tasks more than controls who did not receive this kind of input.

The learners were divided into two groups, an 'input' group and a 'no input' control group. The 'input' group comprised nineteen learners and the 'control' group consisted of seventeen learners.[7] The 'input' group received a 30-minute input session in English conducted by two researchers from Paderborn University. The aim of the session was to provide (1) input containing a great number of passive forms with different verbs and (2) ample opportunities for the learners to produce passive forms. The input session consisted of two parts. First, the researchers read out a story to the learners, which the learners had to act out with pre-assigned roles. The story, called *Petra and Amy are having a party*, was about a girl's birthday party during which an unexpected event occurs. The plot of the story was unresolved, and it was the learners' task to come up with an ending themselves. The learners were asked to act out and narrate their story ending to the researchers. Afterwards, the learners were asked questions related to the story. These linguistic cues manipulated the global theme or topic in that attention was drawn to the patient/theme argument in order to provide contexts for the production of the passive (see Section 6.3). Question forms included, for instance, *What happened to X?* or *How was X done?*.

The story was specifically designed for the input session. The vocabulary was based on the course book *English G* (Schwarz 2007), as the textbook series was used in all three schools where the data collection took place. The story contained twenty-seven passive forms with twenty-two different types of verbs. The same verbs that were used in the production and in the comprehension passive tasks employed in the data elicitation were included in the story text.

In the second part of the input session, the learners were shown a video clip about a pet that is stolen by a thief and finally saved by a hero. The researchers read out the story to the learners and asked them questions related to the content of the story. Again, the global topic was manipulated and attention was drawn to the patient/theme argument in order to provide cues for the production of passive forms (e.g. *What happened to the pet?*). The video clip was designed for the input session.[8] The story contained fourteen passives with twelve different verbs. Again, the same verbs were included in the story that were used in the passive elicitation tasks.

7.3.2 Results stages of acquisition: Sub-study 3

This section presents the results of the data analysis focusing on the L2 learners' developmental stages. As with the speech samples of the learners in Sub-studies 1 and 2, a distributional analysis of the relevant morpho-syntactic features was conducted. In a next step, the emergence criterion was applied to the data to determine the learners' stages of acquisition.

The distributional analysis of the morpho-syntactic structures produced by the learners in Sub-study 3 is presented in Table 7.27. As in the presentation of the results of Sub-study 2, the figures in the table denote (1) how often a particular morpho-syntactic feature was produced by the individual learners, as indicated by a '+' in the respective cells, and (2) how often a feature was not applied in an obligatory context, as indicated by a '−'. The features that occurred invariantly and are classified as formulaic sequences are presented in parentheses.

In a next step, I applied the emergence criterion to the data to determine the individual learners' stages of acquisition. The results of this analysis are presented in Table 7.28. The table follows the same format as Table 7.14 (Sub-study 2), which summarized the results of the distributional analyses of the morpho-syntactic features produced by the learners that participated in Sub-study 2.

Table 7.27 Distributional analysis of all features: L2 learners Sub-study 3.

Stage	Phenomena	School 1														School 2							
		SM02	SM03	SM04	SM05	SM07	SM08	SM09	SM10	SM11	SM12	SM13	SM14	SM15	SM16	G01	G02	G03	G04	G05	G06	G07	G08
6	Cancel Aux-2nd																						
5	Neg/Aux-2nd-?																						
	Aux-2nd-?					(+1)	+1 (+3)	(+2)	(+2)	(+2)/-1	(+4)/+2	(+2)			+1	(+1) +1	+1	+1	(+1)	(+1)	(+1) +2	(+3) +1	(+2) +1
	V2/INV	+1				+1	–	+1					(+3)	+3	+2								
	3sg -s	+5/-2	+3/-4	+1/-4	+3/-4	-7	+1/-3	+2/-11	+1/-4	-8	-6	-8	+5/-4	+3/-3	-8	+4/-9	+6/-2	+4/-1	+4/-3	+6/-5	+8/-3	-8	+2/-5
4	Copula S(x)				+3 (+9)	(+1)	+1/-2	+6	+7			(+4)/+3	+3		+4			+4	+2		+1		+1
	Wh-copula S(x)	+1		(+3)	+4 (+2)			+3 (+1)	+1				(+2)	(+1)/+2	(+1)/+1	(+5)/+1	+1		+2 (+1)	+2	+1	(+2)	+4
	V-particle																						
3	Verb-First				+1							+1	+1										
	Do-SV(O)-?						–		+4	+2				+1	+1			+1	+2	+9	(+5)/+2	(+6)/+1	
	Aux SV(O)-?				+1								+1	+1									
	Wh-SV(O)-?	+4	+2			+3		+1		+2				+3		+1						+1	+1

Stage	Phenomena	School 1															School 2							
		SM02	SM03	SM04	SM05	SM07	SM08	SM09	SM10	SM11	SM12	SM13	SM14	SM15	SM16	G01	G02	G03	G04	G05	G06	G07	G08
	Adverb-First	+3	+1 (+5)	+1 (+4)	+11 (+4)	+12	+14	+12	+5	+12	+9	+1	+5		+1	+8	+9	+10	+8	+7	+11	+5	
	Poss (Pronoun)		+10	+2	+9/ −7	+5	+5					+8	+3		+2	+4	+3	+2			+2	+2	
	Object (Pronoun)																						
	Plural-s (Det + N agr.)		+2	+1				+1	+1			+1			+1								+2
	Have-Fronting		(+2)	(+3)	(+5)	+3	+3	+1	+2	+4	+6	+1		(+3)	+2	(+4)	(+9)				+1		(+9)
2	S neg V(O)							+2								+3							
	SVO	+3	+15	+13	+4	+3	+1	+15	+11	+4	+3	+12	+13	+8	+14	+49	+15	+7	+7	+11	+4	+8	+15
	SVO-Question	+1														+1							
	-ed												+1										
	-ing				+1		+2		+2	+2			+1	+1 −2	+1 −1	+2						−1	
	Plural-s (Noun)	+1	+1			+2	+2	+6	+2			+1	+3		+2	+7		+4	+2	+4	+6		+2
	Poss-s (Noun)															+2	+1						
1	Words			+4																			

(continues)

		School 2 (continued)							School 3						
Stage	Phenomena	G09	G10	G11	G12	G13	G14	G15	S01	S02	S03	S04	S05	S07	S08
6	Cancel Aux-2nd														
5	Neg/Aux-2nd-?														
	Aux-2nd-?	+2	+3	+3	+1	+1	+1	+8	+1			+4	+1		+1
	V2/INV	+1			+2			(+2)			+2				
	3sg -s	+10	+9	+2 / −2	−9	+4 / −4	+4 / −4	+5		+2 / −6	+3 / −1	+3/ −3	+3	+2	+3 / −6
4	Copula S (x)	(+6) +1	(+6) +3	+6	+6	+5	+9	+2	(+4) +5	(+8) +1	+4	+6	+5	+1	
	Wh-copula S (x)			+3	+2	(+1)	+3	+6	+2	(+1)	+1	+1	+1		(+5)
	V-particle														
3	Verb-First				+2	+2					+4				
	Do-SV(O)-?	+3	+1	+1		+2	+1	+5	+1						
	Aux SV(O)-?													+1	
	Wh-SV(O)-?	+2		+1											
	Adverb-First		+2	+9	+7	+8	+5	+17	+12	+9		+1	+13	+6	+8

		School 2 (continued)							School 3						
Stage	Phenomena	G09	G10	G11	G12	G13	G14	G15	S01	S02	S03	S04	S05	S07	S08
	Poss (Pronoun)	+2		+1	+2			+12	+4	(+8) +1			+2	+8	(+8)
	Object (Pronoun)														
	Plural-s (Det + N agr.)			+1			+2		+2						
	Have-Fronting					+2	+1				+1	(+2)	+1	(+10)	(+8)
2	S neg V(O)														
	SVO	+10	+13	+6	+4	+3	+8	+12		+4	+9	+9	+7	+5	+6
	SVO-Question							+1		+1					
	-ed		+1	+1											
	-ing							+15	+10	+2	+1		+7	+3-4	−1
	Plural-s (Noun)		+3	+5	+4	+1	+4		+2		+3		+7	+4	+3
	Poss-s (Noun)														
1	Words														

Table 7.28 Stages of acquisition: L2 learners Sub-study 3.

Stage	SM02	SM03	SM04	SM05	SM07	SM08	SM09	SM10	SM11	SM12	SM13	SM14	SM15	SM16	G01	G02	G03	G04
6	−	−	−	−	−	−	−	−	−	−	−	−	−	−	−	−	−	−
5	−	−	−	−	−	−	−	−	−	−	−	−	+	(+)	−	−	−	−
4	−	−	−	+	−	−	+	+	−	−	+	+	(+)	+	−	−	+	−
3	+	(+)	−	+	+	+	+	+	+	+	+	+	+	(+)	+	+	+	+
2	+	+	+	+	+	+	+	+	+	+	+	+	+	+	+	+	+	+
1	+	+	+	+	+	+	+	+	+	+	+	+	+	+	+	+	+	+

Stage	G05	G06	G07	G08	G09	G10	G11	G12	G13	G14	G15	S01	S02	S03	S04	S05	S07	S08
6	−	−	−	−	−	−	−	−	−	−	−	−	−	−	−	−	−	−
5	−	(+)	−	−	+	+	+	(+)	−	−	+	−	−	−	+	+	−	−
4	(+)	(+)	−	+	+	+	+	+	+	+	+	−	+	+	+	−	−	−
3	+	+	+	+	+	+	+	+	+	+	+	+	+	(+)	+	+	+	+
2	+	+	+	+	+	+	+	+	+	+	+	+	+	+	+	+	+	+
1	+	+	+	+	+	+	+	+	+	+	+	+	+	+	+	+	+	+

As can be seen from Table 7.28, two learners are at stage 2 of acquisition, fourteen learners have reached stage 3, thirteen learners have acquired features of stage 4 and seven learners are at stage 5. The results also show that five learners produce a limited number of structures from a higher stage. This applies to the learners SM3, SM16, G05, G06 and G12. The data of learner SM3 include a limited number of 'stage 3' structures, learner SM16 uses 'stage 5' structures, the data of G05 display some instances of 'stage 4' structures and learner G06 produces some 'stage 4' and 'stage 5' structures. Finally, learner G12 is presumably about to acquire stage 5, as her data sample contains a limited number of 'stage 5' structures. However, in all cases these features do not occur in sufficient contexts for the structure to be considered as fully acquired. This is indicated by the '+' in parentheses in the respective cells in Table 7.28.

Finally, the data of three learners (SM15, SM16, S04) are to some extent inconclusive with regard to their stage of acquisition due to the overall limited number of defining structures that occur in the data. Learner SM15 produces only a limited number of 'stage 4' structures. In her speech sample, only three 'Wh-Copula S' forms occur, of which one is considered to be formulaic (*What's your name?*). However, at the same time her data contain three instances of 'V2/INV' structures (see example (34)).

(34)

SM15	Who sleep you on the Mars?
	How looks your family?
	What wear you in the Mars?

Naturally, these forms are non-target-like in English. However, in terms of processing, 'V2/INV' structures are located at stage 5 of the PT hierarchy, as the process of feature unification underlying these structures is similar to that of 'Aux-2nd' structures described in Section 3.4 and requires the S-procedure to be in place (see Pienemann 1998: 102ff.).

As the three 'V2/INV' structures produced by learner SM15 occur with sufficient lexical variation, the learner is assumed to have acquired the respective stage. It could be argued at this point that the 'V2/INV' structures produced by learner SM15 constitute cases of transfer from the learner's L1 German. As German is a V2 language, this is indeed a likely scenario. However, the possibility that the 'V2/INV' structures are transferred from the learner's L1 does not affect their categorization in the PT hierarchy. The position on transfer taken in PT is captured in the *Developmentally Moderated Transfer Hypothesis* (DMTH) (see e.g. Pienemann, Lenzing & Keßler 2016), which, in a nutshell, entails that transfer is constrained by the capacity of the L2 language processor. This means that learners can only transfer structures from their L1 when the processor is capable of processing these structures. The DMTH has been empirically supported by a number of studies (see e.g. Haberzettl 2005; Håkansson, Pienemann & Sayehli 2002; Kawaguchi 1999, 2005; Lenzing 2013, 2015a; Pienemann, Keßler & Liebner 2016). In line with these theoretical considerations, it is argued that, although the 'V2/INV' structures produced by learner SM15 might constitute a case of transfer from the learner's L1, these are nevertheless placed at stage 5 of the PT hierarchy. Given that learner SM15 also produced two 'stage 4' structures, it could be argued that no stage gap is present in the learner data. However, the limited number of 'stage 4' structures in the learner's speech sample does not allow a valid claim about whether the structures have been acquired in terms of the emergence criterion.

Similarly, the data sample of learner SM16 contains sufficient instances of the 'stage 4' structure 'Copula S (x)' in order for the structure to be classified as acquired according to the emergence criterion. However, the speech sample exhibits only a limited number of 'stage 3' structures:

(35)

SM16	Have you flowers on the Mars?	Have-Fronting (stage 3)
	Have you pets? On the Mars?	Have-Fronting (stage 3)
	Do you go to school?	Do-Fronting (stage 3)
	On your red house in the sand there are four kids?	Adverb-First poss pronoun plural -s (D+N agr.) (stage 3)

As can be seen from (35), learner SM16 produces different types of syntactic and morphological 'stage 3' structures. However, they do not occur with sufficient variation in the speech sample to be classified as acquired. Finally, the speech sample of learner S04 includes a small number of 'stage 3' structures and a larger number of 'stage 4' and 'stage 5' structures. Again, the data are considered to be inconclusive as far as the acquisition of 'stage 3' structures is concerned. However, as the learner does produce two 'Have-Fronting' structures, it can be argued that there is no stage gap present in the data.

To sum up, it can be seen that the learners in Sub-study 3 are at different levels of acquisition, ranging from stage 2 to stage 5. The data of three learners are to some extent inconclusive, but none of the learners in the study skipped stages.

7.3.3 Results production data – passive: Sub-study 3

As in Sub-study 2, I analysed the learners' speech production data obtained in the passive tasks in terms of (1) underlying argument-function mapping and (2) morpho-syntactic processing. I carried out distributional analyses focusing on the presence/absence of non-linear argument-function mapping and on evidence for morpho-syntactic processing.

Argument-function mapping: Sub-study 3

Table 7.29 depicts the results of the distributional analysis of the L2 learner data in terms of argument-function mapping. The first two columns provide information about the learners and their respective stage of acquisition. The figures given in column 3 denote how often non-linear argument-function mapping occurred in the learner data of the fish film task, and the figures presented in column 4 indicate how often the learners produced structures with non-linear argument-function mapping in the passive film task. A '+' denotes the presence of non-linear argument-function mapping in all contexts, a '+' in parentheses indicates that non-linear argument-function mapping does not occur in all contexts in the data, and a '–' indicates that non-linear argument-function mapping is not present at all in the learner data.

The asterisks in columns 3 and 4 mark those cases where the respective learner relied on non-linear argument-function-mapping in all contexts, including those that require active voice. This is discussed in more detail in this section. The columns in grey denote the learners who received the input session focusing on English passive structures prior to data elicitation (see Section 7.3.1).

The data in Table 7.29 reveal that one of the two learners at stage 2 (SM03) does not produce any instances of non-linear argument-function mapping in either the fish film or the passive film task. Learner SM03 mainly relies on active forms instead, as in *The girl open the bottle*. In these instances, the linear agent-verb-patient order is maintained: The agent is mapped onto the first noun (phrase) and the patient is mapped onto the second noun (phrase). When explicitly asked to start with the fish the arrow points to in the fish film task, learner SM03 relies on her L1 German and inserts the respective L2 lexical items:

Table 7.29 Argument-function mapping in passives: L2 learners Sub-study 3.

Stage	Learner	Non-linear argument-function mapping	
		Fish film	Passive film
5	G15	+ (11/11)	+ (12/12)
	G11	+ (11/11)	+ (12/12)*
	G09	(+) (10/11)	+ (12/12)
	G10	+ (11/11)*	(+) (11/12)
	SM15	(+) (6/11)	(+) (10/12)
	S05	(+) (10/11)	(+) (10/12)
	S04	(+) (8/11)	(+) (8/12)
4	G14	+ (11/11)*	+ (12/12)
	S03	+ (11/11)*	+ (12/12)
	S01	(+) (10/11)	+ (12/12)
	G13	(+) (7/11)	(+) (11/12)
	G03	+ (11/11)	(+) (9/12)
	SM10	(+) (5/11)	(+) (9/12)
	SM09	(+) (6/11)	(+) (8/12)
	G12	(+) (5/11)	(+) (6/12)
	SM16	(+) (8/11)	(+) (6/12)
	G08	(+) (8/11)	+ (6/12)
	SM14	– (0/11)	(+) (9/12)
	SM05	+ (11/11)	(+) (2/12)
	SM13	– (0/11)	(+) (2/12)
3	G04	+ (11/11)	(+) (11/12)
	SM08	(+) (7/11)	(+) (10/12)
	G01	(+) (10/11)	(+) (9/12)
	SM12	– (0/11)	(+) (9/12)
	S07	(+) (9/11)	(+) (8/12)
	SM11	+ (11/11)	(+) (7/12)
	G02	(+) (5/11)	(+) (7/12)
	G06	+ (11/11)	(+) (5/12)
	SM07	(+) (9/11)	(+) (6/12)
	S02	– (0/11)	(+) (2/12)
	S08	– (0/11)	– (0/12)
	SM02	– (0/11)	– (0/12)
	G07	– (0/11)	– (0/12)
	G05	– (0/11)	– (0/12)
2	SM04	(+) (4/11)	(+) (9/12)
	SM03	– (0/11)	– (0/12)

Note. * all items in fish film/passive film in passive voice.

(36)

Researcher	{Fang diesmal mit dem roten Fisch an} (*Begin with the red fish this time*)
SM03	{Ich weiß es nicht, wie ich das sagen soll, wenn (/) weil ich soll ja erst den ersten beschreiben, dass der gefressen wird} (*I don't know how to say it because I'm supposed to describe the one that is being eaten first*)
Researcher	{Mhm Also auf Deutsch weißt du ganz genau was du sagen würdest}. (*In German you would know exactly what to say*)
SM03	The red fish {wird} (*is*) {von} (*from*) the blue fish {gegessen} (*eaten*) {aber das heißt anders} (*but that's different in English*)

Finally, in one case, learner SM03 reverses the order and begins the sentence with the patient in the event:

(37)

SM03	The girl follow a woman. (*The girl is followed by the woman.*)

I argue that the production of this sentence does not indicate the acquisition of non-linear argument-function mapping. Similar to the case of learner P03 in Sub-study 2, learner SM03 is cued to start with the entity the arrow points to and inserts the two arguments in the N V N matrix in the order in which they occur in the passive film task. There are no further cues indicating the acquisition of non-linear argument-function mapping, such as the insertion of an auxiliary or a preposition.

The second 'stage 2' learner (SM04) produces structures with underlying non-linear mapping operations. This applies to four out of eleven structures in the fish film trial and to nine out of twelve structures in the passive film task, as in *The girl see by the woman*. It could be argued that the fact that learner SM04 produces structures that exhibit non-linear argument-function mapping provides counterevidence for my hypothesis that this kind of mapping operation is not acquired before the learners have reached stage 3 of acquisition. Learner SM04 does, in fact, produce a few 'stage 3' structures. However, these are mostly restricted to formulaic 'Have-Fronting' and 'Adverb-First' structures and therefore do not serve as an indication that the learner is at an early point in the acquisition of stage 3.

Unfortunately, the overall number of 'stage 2' learners in Sub-study 3 is limited to two learners. Therefore, the explanatory power of the learner data is limited in this respect. In an ideal world, I would have included more learners at lower stages of acquisition in the study. However, to achieve this aim, I would have had to include more younger learners, as most 'grade 5' learners (the first class at secondary level in Germany) are at a more advanced level of acquisition. My experience with learners at primary school level (see e.g. Lenzing 2013) suggested that such (grade 3 or 4) beginning learners of English would have had severe problems in understanding the passive tasks due to their lack of L2 vocabulary. This would have led to frustration for the learners and a lack of motivation in participating in the data elicitation sessions. Therefore, I decided to restrict the data elicitation to learners from grade 5 onwards.

The results of the distributional analysis displayed in Table 7.29 reveal that – with the exception of learner SM04 – non-linear argument-function mapping appears to be acquired gradually at stage 3. Four 'grade 3' learners (G05, G07, SM02, S08) rely on linear mapping operations and employ different strategies to solve both tasks.

Learner G05 produces different types of solutions to the tasks. In some cases, she simply begins the sentence with the agent in the event and produces sentences in active voice:

(38)

G05	The red fish eats the blue (/) {nein} (*no*) The blue fish eats the red fish. (*The red fish is eaten by the blue fish*).
	The green fish eats the blue fish. (*The blue fish is eaten by the green fish.*)
	The girl (/) (mhm) the mom kissed the girl. (*The girl is kissed by the mother.*)
	The woman carry the rabbit. (*The rabbit is carried by the woman.*)
	The girl hit the ball. (*The ball is hit by the girl.*)

As the first and the third sentences show, she initially attempts to start with the cued entity (the red fish in sentence 1 and the girl in sentence 3) and switches to the agent participant once she notices that her interpretation is not correct.

In the fish film, learner G05 describes the event from the patient's perspective but manages to employ a solution in the active voice. Instead of using the verb *eat*, she uses the expression *X goes in the mouth from Y*:

(39)

G05	The black fish goes in the mouth from the blue fish. (*The black fish is eaten by the blue fish.*)
	The green fish goes in the mouth from the pink fish. (*The green fish is eaten by the pink fish.*)
	The white fish goes in the mouth from the blue fish. (*The white fish is eaten by the blue fish.*)

In some trials of the passive film, she produces a main and a subordinate clause to solve the task, as exemplified in example (40).

(40)

G05	The woman fall down because the kid kick it. *(The woman is kicked by the girl.)*	
	The bottle is on the table because the woman put it on the table. *(The bottle is put on the table by the woman.)*	
	The car drive because the mom push it. *(The car is pushed by the woman.)*	

This strategy enables learner G05 to start with the cued entity and, at the same time, to avoid the use of passive constructions with non-linear argument-function mapping.

Learners G07 and SM02 rely on a *negation-strategy* and in this way produce sentences with linear argument-function mapping:

(41)

G07	The blue fish doesn't eat the green fish. *(The blue fish is eaten by the green fish.)*
	The little girl doesn't follow the big girl. *(The girl is followed by the woman.)*
	The girl doesn't see the woman. *(The girl is seen by the woman.)*
SM02	The red fish don't eat the blue fish. *(The red fish is eaten by the blue fish.)*
	The pink fish don't eat the white fish. *(The pink fish is eaten by the white fish.)*

In other cases, they produce active sentences that do not begin with the cued entity, as illustrated in (42).

(42)

G07	The woman kiss the girl. *(The girl is kissed by the woman.)*
	The girl hit the ball. *(The ball is hit by the girl.)*
SM02	The girl follow the next girl. *(The girl is followed by the woman.)*
	The woman feed the cat. *(The cat is fed by the woman.)*

Learner S08 employs creative solutions to avoid non-linear argument-function mapping. This is exemplified in example (43).

(43)

S08	The orange fish uh swim (/) the orange fish swim from right to left and from the left side came a blue fish, and the blue fish has eaten the orange fish. (*The red fish is eaten by the blue fish.*)
	The purple fish came from the right side to the left side and from the left side came a dark fish and the dark fish has eaten the purple fish.
	The green fish don't eat the pink fish. (*The green fish is eaten by the pink fish.*)
	The pink fish don't eat the white fish. (*The pink fish is eaten by the white fish.*)

Similar to learners G07 and SM02, she uses a *negation-strategy* in some instances. In other cases, she begins the description of the event with the item the arrow points to but employs more than one sentence. In this way, she avoids non-linear argument-function mapping and relies on sentences in active voice instead.

The data displayed in Table 7.29 also show that non-linear argument-function mapping is acquired gradually by the 'stage 3' learners. Similar to the results of Sub-study 2, the structures occurring in the learner data encompass (1) a preposition (target-like or non-target-like) and/or (2) some form of the auxiliary. As in Sub-study 2, the learners do not necessarily produce passive forms in all contexts.

'Stage 3' learner S02, for instance, is presumably about to acquire non-linear argument-function mapping. She produces no passive structures in the fish film task; however, she produces two passive forms in the passive film task.

(44)

S02	*se* (*the*) blue fish eat *se* (*the*) red fish. (*The red fish is eaten by the blue fish.*)
	se (*the*) blue fish swimming to *se* (*the*) green fish and *se* (*the*) green fish eat *se* (*the*) blue fish. (*The blue fish is eaten by the green fish.*)
	The girl follow *se* (*the*) {was heißt Frau} (*what is woman in English*)? (*The woman is followed by the girl.*)
Researcher	woman
S02	woman
	The rabbit is *carrey* (*carry*). (*The rabbit is carried by the woman.*)
	se (*the*) car {was war das Verb nochmal} (*what was the verb again*)?
Researcher	push
S02	push from *se* (*the*) woman. (*The car is pushed by the woman.*)

Learner SM12 (stage 3) produces sentences with non-linear argument-function mapping only in the passive film task. In the fish film, she employs active sentences and relies on a similar strategy as learner G05 to begin the sentence with the fish the arrow points to (see example (45)).

(45)

SM12	The red fish drive in the mouth from the blue fish. (*The red fish is eaten by the blue fish.*)
	The black fish drive in the mouth from the red fish. (*The black fish is eaten by the red fish.*)
	The blue fish drive in the mouth from the green fish. (*The blue fish is eaten by the green fish.*)

In this way, she avoids non-linear mapping operations and still adheres to the task to begin the sentence with the cued entity. In the passive film task, however, the same learner employs the passive form in nine contexts. In the remaining three contexts, learner SM12 produces active sentences with a linear agent-verb-patient order.

The data of the 'stage 4' learners reveal the gradual acquisition of non-linear argument-function mapping: Whereas learner SM13 relies on linear mapping operations in the fish film task and produces merely two passive constructions in the passive film task, learner S03 and learner G14 employ passive constructions in all contexts. Interestingly, both learners use passive forms in all fish film trials, including those that aim at active constructions:

(46)

G14	The orange fish is eaten by the blue fish. (*The red fish is eaten by the blue fish.*)
	The green fish is eaten by the pink fish. (*The green fish is eaten by the pink fish.*)
	The white fish is eaten by the pink fish. (*The pink fish eats the white fish.*)
	The yellow fish is eaten by the black fish. (*The black fish eats the yellow fish.*)

The same applies to 'stage 5' learner G10. A second 'stage 5' learner, G11, produces passive constructions in all passive film trials, as exemplified in example (47).

(47)

G11	The woman is followed by the other woman. (*The girl is followed by the woman.*)
	The book is given to the boy by a girl. (*The book is given to the boy by the girl.*)
	The girl is tickled (/) {nein} (*no*) the man is tickled by the girl. (*The girl tickles the man.*)
	The the room {oder} (*or*) the table is cleaned by a woman. (*The woman cleans the table.*)

The data of the 'stage 5' learners show that they produce passive forms in the majority of contexts. For instance, learners G11 and G15 employ passive forms in all passive contexts. Other learners, such as SM15 and S04, also use a limited number of active constructions.

In addition to the distributional analysis of the passive production data presented in this section, a statistical correlation analysis was carried out to investigate relations between the L2 learners' PT stages and their production of structures with non-linear argument-function mapping. The results of the Spearman's rank-order correlation analysis indicate a significant positive correlation between the learners' stage of acquisition and the number of produced structures with non-linear argument-function mapping, $r_s(36) = 0.545, p = 0.001$.

To sum up, the distributional analysis in terms of non-linear argument-function mapping indicates that – with the exception of learner SM04 – non-linear argument-function mapping is acquired gradually by learners from stage 3 onwards. The correlation analysis reveals a significant correlation between the learners' stage of acquisition and the number of structures with non-linear argument-function mapping. This finding conforms to the results of Sub-study 2. It lends further support to the claim of the *Multiple Constraints Hypothesis* that the L2 learner's mental lexicon is annotated gradually for the syntactic features which enable non-linear mapping operations between arguments and grammatical functions to take place. In keeping with this, it provides evidence for the hypothesis that the acquisition of non-linear argument-function mapping takes place in a gradual fashion by learners from stage 3 onwards.

Morpho-syntactic processing: Sub-study 3

Table 7.30 displays the results of the distributional analysis of the learner data in terms of morpho-syntactic processing. As in Sub-study 2, the analysis is restricted to the data obtained in the passive film task, as the trials exhibit lexical variation with regard to the verb.

As in Table 7.16 in Section 7.2.2, the first two columns in Table 7.30 denote the L2 learners' stages of acquisition. The third column provides information on the number of auxiliaries produced by the individual learners and the fourth column indicates the instances of target-like verb morphology present in the respective learner data. As two trials contain verbs with an unaltered participle form (*put* and *hit*), evidence for the presence of morpho-syntactic processing is only observable in ten out of twelve trial contexts in the passive film. The target-like production of the auxiliary and/or the correct verb morphology is indicated by a '+' in columns three and four respectively. The absence of the feature under investigation is denoted by a '–' in the respective cell. The production of a particular feature in a limited number of contexts is marked by a '+' in parentheses. The asterisk in column 3 (learner G03) indicates that the learner uses the auxiliary *would*, which is further discussed in this section. The learners who had received the additional input session on English passives are highlighted in grey. The dotted line shows the implicational acquisition of auxiliaries and verbal morphology.

The results displayed in Table 7.30 are similar to the ones obtained in Sub-study 2: With the exception of 'stage 2' learner SM04, who produces three instances of an

Table 7.30 Morpho-syntactic processing in passives: L2 learners Sub-study 3.

Stage	Learner	Morpho-syntactic processing	
		Auxiliary	Verb morphology
5	G09	+ (12/12)	+ (10/10)
	G15	+ (12/12)	(+) (9/10)
	G10	(+) (11/12)	(+) (9/10)
	G11	+ (12/12)	(+) (9/10)
	SM15	(+) (10/12)	(+) (7/10)
	S05	(+) (11/11)	(+) (6/10)
	S04	(+) (8/11)	(+) (5/10)
4	G14	+ (12/12)	(+) (8/10)
	S01	+ (12/12)	(+) (7/10)
	G13	(+) (11/12)	(+) (9/10)
	G12	(+) (7/12)	(+) (5/10)
	SM10	(+) (9/12)	(+) (2/10)
	S03	+ (12/12)	– (0/10)
	G03	(+) (9/12)*	– (0/10)
	SM09	(+) (7/12)	– (0/10)
	SM16	(+) (6/12)	– (0/10)
	SM13	– (0/12)	– (0/10)
	G08	– (0/12)	– (0/10)
	SM05	– (0/12)	– (0/10)
	SM14	– (0/12)	– (0/10)
3	SM11	(+) (7/12)	(+) (**2/10**)
	G06	(+) (1/12)	(+) (**2/10**)
	S07	(+) 9/12)	(+) (**1/10**)
	SM08	(+) (6/12)	(+) (**1/10**)
	G04	(+) (11/12)	– (0/10)
	G01	(+) (9/12)	– (0/10)
	G02	(+) (7/12)	– (0/10)
	SM07	(+) (4/12)	– (0/10)
	S02	(+) (1/12)	– (0/10)
	SM12	– (0/12)	– (0/10)
	S08	– (0/12)	– (0/10)
	SM02	– (0/12)	– (0/10)
	G07	– (0/12)	– (0/10)
	G05	– (0/12)	– (0/10)
2	SM04	(+) (**3/12**)	– (0/10)
	SM03	– (0/12)	– (0/10)

Note. * would.

auxiliary in the passive film task (marked in bold), the learners do not begin to produce auxiliaries before stage 3. However, this does not mean that all 'stage 3' and 'stage 4' learners insert an auxiliary in their passive constructions. The data of five 'stage 3' and four 'stage 4' learners do not contain any auxiliary. The latter cases are marked in bold in Table 7.30. This finding confirms the claim concerning the gradual acquisition process of the auxiliaries in passive structures.

As far as full morpho-syntactic processing is concerned, the analysis supports the hypothesis that the production of target-like verb morphology does not begin until the learners have acquired stage 4. The data of four 'stage 3' learners seemingly contradict this assumption: The data of learners SM08, S07, G06 and SM11 contain one or two instances of target-like verb morphology respectively (marked in bold in Table 7.30). However, the more detailed distributional analysis presented in this section reveals that these forms occur arbitrarily in the learner data.

I argued in Section 5.2.2 that the acquisition of feature unification processes within the verb phrase is indicated by the occurrence of target-like verb morphology. In PT, these processes are hypothesized to be acquired at stage 4 of the PT hierarchy. The acquisition of target-like verb morphology also seems to take place in a gradual fashion. Table 7.30 reveals that the data of one 'stage 2' learner (SM03) and five 'stage 3' learners (S08, SM02, SM12, G05 and G07) do not contain any auxiliary and no verb morphology. These learners rely on active constructions in engaging with the passive task. Again, 'stage 2' learner SM04 constitutes an exception in this respect, as she produces passive constructions in nine out of twelve trials of the passive task (see Table 7.29) and also inserts an auxiliary in three of the passive forms, as shown in example (48).

(48)

SM04	The woman (/) the woman kick by the girl.
	The rabbit carry by the woman.
	The cat feed by the woman.
	The car is push by the woman.
	The ball hit (/) is hit by the girl.
	The bottle is put (/) the bottle is (mhm) the bottle is put (uh) over the table by the woman.

The data of four 'stage 4' learners (SM05, SM13, SM14 and G08) also do not contain auxiliaries in passive forms. Learners SM05 and SM13 predominantly rely on active forms when engaging with the passive film task. In some instances, they rely on the *reverse-order* strategy discussed in Section 7.2.2.

Learner SM13 produces two sentences with non-linear argument-function mapping. However, these forms do not contain an auxiliary or verbal morphology. This also applies to the passive forms employed by learner SM14:

(49)

SM14	The kid see by the woman.
	The {Auto} (*car*) push by the (uh) woman.
	The rabbit (uh) carry by the woman.

The learner data in example (49) demonstrate that learner SM14 does not produce auxiliaries or verbal morphology in her passive constructions.

Similar to the data in Sub-study 2, the learner data obtained in Sub-Study 3 reflect the gradual acquisition of auxiliaries in passive forms. Learner SM07, for instance, produces an auxiliary in four trials. In some passive constructions, she inserts the German form *ist* (*is*) instead of the English auxiliary.

(50)

SM07	The woman is (/) the woman is (/) the woman is kick from (/) {von} (*by*) the girl.
	The rabbit is carry {von} (*by*) (uh) woman.
	The cat feed (/) {ist} (*is*) feed {von} (*by*) the woman.
	The bottle {ist} (*is*) put on the table.

Other learners, such as learner SM08, use auxiliaries only in some of the trials. The data of learner SM08 further show that she has not yet acquired subject-verb agreement:

(51)

SM08	The little children are follow from the big children. (*The girl/daughter is followed by the woman/mother.*)
	The woman are kick from the girl.
	The rabbit (uh) carry by the woman.

Learner G03 opts for a creative solution concerning the use of auxiliaries in passive forms. As indicated by the asterisk in Table 7.30, his passive forms contain the construction *would + verb + from* (see example (52)):

(52)

G03	The little woman would follow from the big woman. (*The girl/daughter is followed by the woman/mother.*)
	The wom(/) {nein} (*no*) the book would gives from the woman to the man. (*The book is given to the boy by the girl.*)
	The jug of mineral water would open from the woman (*The bottle is opened by the girl.*)
	The girl (/) (uh) the cat would feed from the woman. (*The cat is fed by the woman/mother.*)

These examples corroborate the claim that auxiliaries are acquired in a stepwise fashion in passive constructions.

The acquisition of verbal morphology also occurs gradually in learners from stage 4 onwards. As mentioned above, the data of four 'stage 3' learners appear to contradict this claim, as these learners produce one or two instances of target-like verbal morphology. However, the distributional analysis of the learner data shows that there is no underlying systematicity in their application of verbal morphology in the passive film task. For instance, the data of learner S07 show substantial variation in his use of verbal morphology in both active and passive constructions. These forms include the morphemes *-ing* and *-ed*, the morpheme *-n* in an active construction, as well as instances of no verbal morphology (see example (53)).

(53)

S07	The little kid is follow**ing** from the (uh) {warte} (*wait*) (uh) (/) from the teacher. (*The girl/daughter is followed by the woman/mother.*)
	The girl is give**n** the boy a book. (*The book is given to the boy by the girl.*)
	The (uh) (/) the water bottle is open**ing** from the girl. (*The bottle is opened by the girl.*)
	The animal was carri**ed** from the teacher. (*The rabbit is carried by the woman/mother.*)
	The cat was **feed** from the woman. (*The cat is fed by the woman/mother.*)

This kind of variation can also be found in the data of learner SM11. She applies the morpheme *-ing* to some verbs and also produces forms that exhibit no verbal morphology. Interestingly, she relies on the *-ing* form in both active and passive constructions in the fish film task, as illustrated in example (54).

(54)

SM11	The pink fish is eat**ing** the white fish. (*The pink fish is eating/eats the white fish.*)
	The pink fish is eat**ing** by the black fish. (*The pink fish is eaten by the black fish.*)
	The little girl is **follow** by the big girl. (*The girl/daughter is followed by the woman/mother.*)
	The car is **push** by the girl. (*The car is pushed by the girl.*)
	The cat is feed**ing** by the woman. (*The cat is fed by the woman/mother.*)
	The girl is kiss**ed** by the woman. (*The girl/daughter is kissed by the woman/mother.*)
	The girl is hear**d** by the woman. (*The girl/daughter is heard by the woman/mother.*)

The data in example (54) show that learner SM11 produces target-like verbal morphology in two cases. However, the detailed distributional analysis also indicates that she does not apply the *-ed* morpheme systematically but alternates between the three options *-ed*, *-ing* and zero-marking.

Table 7.31 Distributional analysis verbal morphology for learner SM11.

Type of suffix	Frequency of occurrence
Ø	2
	(+ 2 unaltered participle forms in the case of *hit* & *put*)
-ing	1
-ed	2

Table 7.31 reveals that learner SM11 produces seven passive forms in the passive film task. As mentioned earlier in this section, two verbs (*hit* and *push*) exhibit an unaltered participle form and are therefore excluded from further analysis. Of the five remaining passive constructions, two sentences contain a verb with zero morphological marking (*follow* and *push*), one verb is marked with the morpheme *-ing* (*feed*) and two verbs occur with the morpheme *-ed* (*kiss* and *hear*). This finding implies that learner SM11 has not yet acquired target-like verbal morphology in passive constructions. Instead, she experiments with different types of morphemes and applies them in a creative way. The data of learners G06 and SM08 also exhibit variability concerning verbal morphology, and the four 'stage 3' learners apply the morpheme *-ed* in merely one or two instances. On the basis of one or two occurrences of a particular structure in a sample, no conclusions can be drawn about its acquisition.

The gradual acquisition of verbal morphology by learners from stage 4 onwards and the related variability in its application is evident in the data of a number of 'stage 4' and 'stage 5' learners. 'Stage 5' learner S05, for instance, produces target-like verbal morphology in six cases. Interestingly, he also employs the *-ed* morpheme in the active distractor sentences as well as in one of the passive trials in which he relies on active instead of passive voice (see example (55)).

(55)

S05	The girl was followed by the woman.	passive context
	The woman was kicked by the girl.	
	The wom(/) (eh) the girl was seen by the woman.	
	The rabbit was carried by the woman	
	The woman cleaned the room. Eh, the table.	active distractors
	The girl tickled the man.	
	(*The*) girl shouted and the woman heared his words. (*The girl is heard by the woman.*)	active instead of passive

The data also reveal that learner S05 overgeneralizes the use of the morpheme *-ed* and applies it to irregular verbs. This shows that (1) he has in principle acquired the feature unification process between the auxiliary and the lexical verb and (2) he has not yet acquired all the relevant form-function relationships involved in the formation of the past participle. This is illustrated in example (56).

(56)

S05	The ball was hitte(/) hit-ted by the girl.
	The cat was f(/) (eh) the cat was feeded by the woman.

The stepwise acquisition of form-function relationships is also reflected in the data of 'stage 4' learner G14, who produces eight instances of target-like verb morphology but also employs instances of interim forms in the case of two irregular verbs, as exemplified in example (57).

(57)

G14	The girl is saw by the woman.
	The bottle is putten down by the woman.
	(*The bottle is put on the table by the woman.*)

Similar to the results obtained in Sub-study 2, the data analysis in Sub-study 3 reveals that some learners employ auxiliaries and/or past participle forms in both active and passive constructions. This is illustrated in example (58) with the utterances of 'stage 4' learner S01.

(58)

S01	The girl is followed by a woman.
	The woman is kicked by a (/) by the girl.
	The girl is tickled the man.
	The woman is put put (/) put the bottle on the table.
	The cat is feeded by the (/) fed by the woman.
	The woman is fed the cat.

The same learner produces the following utterance (59), which nicely exemplifies the stepwise acquisition of form-function relationships.

(59)

S01	The girl is see seeing (/) {nee} (*no*) saw by the woman.

In order to investigate the relation between the L2 learners' stages of acquisition and the number of passive structures with target-like verbal morphology produced by them, a Spearman's rank-order correlation test was carried out. The test revealed a strong positive correlation between the learners' PT stages and the number of structures that exhibit target-like verbal morphology, $r_s(36) = 0.636, p < 0.001$.

All in all, the results of Sub-study 3 for morpho-syntactic processing are consistent with the results obtained in Sub-study 2. With the exception of learner SM04, the analysis shows a gradual development in the acquisition of both the auxiliary (stage 3 onwards) and target-like verbal-morphology in passive constructions (stage 4 onwards). Within morpho-syntactic processing, the data again indicate that the auxiliary in passives is acquired before verbal morphology. Overall, this supports the sequence of acquisition evident in the data of Sub-study 2 (see Table 7.17):

1. −auxiliary, −verbal morphology (stage 2)
2. +auxiliary, −verbal morphology (stage 3 onwards)
3. +auxiliary, +verbal morphology (stage 4 onwards)

A difference in the data set of Sub-study 3 as compared to the one of Sub-study 2 relates to the finding that that four 'stage 4' learners do not produce any auxiliaries (see Table 7.30). However, these learners do not produce any instances of target-like verbal morphology either. As both the acquisition of the auxiliary and target-like use of verbal morphology are assumed to be gradual processes, this finding does not contradict the proposed developmental sequence. The result of the correlation analysis lends further support to the claim that the learners' production of target-like verbal morphology is constrained by PTs processing procedures.

Summary oral production data – passive: Sub-study 3

Table 7.32 summarizes the results of the analysis of the oral production data obtained in the passive film task in Sub-study 3. As in Sub-study 2, the summary is restricted to the data elicited in the passive film, as there is no lexical variation in the fish film data with regard to the verb.

The first two columns in Table 7.32 contain information about the learners and their stage of acquisition. The second two columns provide details of the data analysis in terms of non-linear mapping (column 3) as well as morphological marking on the verb (column 4). As in Table 7.30, a '−' indicates the absence of a particular feature, a '+' denotes its presence and a '+' in parentheses refers to those cases where the structure under investigation was not produced in all contexts. The figures in parentheses show how often a particular feature was produced in a given context by the respective learner. The learners that had received the input session focusing on English passive structures prior to the data elicitation are highlighted in grey. The dotted line in the table indicates the implicational development of non-linear argument-function mapping and morpho-syntactic processing.

The summary of the distributional analysis presented in Table 7.32 shows the implicational nature of the acquisition of the English passive in L2 production. As

Table 7.32 Summary of oral production data of passives: L2 learners Sub-study 3.

Stage	Learner	Production	
		Non-linear argument-function mapping (passive film)	Morpho-syntactic processing verb morphology (passive film)
5	G09	+ (12/12)	+ (10/10)
	G15	+ (12/12)	(+) (9/10)
	G10	(+) (11/12)	(+) (9/10)
	G11	+ (12/12)	(+) (9/10)
	SM15	(+) (10/12)	(+) (7/10)
	S05	(+) (10/12)	(+) (6/10)
	S04	(+) (8/12)	(+) (5/10)
4	G14	+ (12/12)	(+) (8/10)
	S01	+ (12/12)	(+) (7/10)
	G13	(+) (11/12)	(+) (9/10)
	G12	(+) (6/12)	(+) (5/10)
	SM10	(+) (9/12)	(+) (2/10)
	S03	+ (12/12)	− (0/10)
	G03	(+) (9/12)	− (0/10)
	SM09	(+) (8/12)	− (0/10)
	SM16	(+) (6/12)	− (0/10)
	SM13	(+) (2/12)	− (0/10)
	G08	(+) (6/12)	− (0/10)
	SM05	(+) (2/12)	− (0/10)
	SM14	(+) (9/12)	− (0/10)
3	SM11	(+) (7/12)	(+) (**2/10**)
	G06	(+) (5/12)	(+) (**2/10**)
	S07	(+) (8/12)	(+) (**1/10**)
	SM08	(+) (10/12)	(+) (**1/10**)
	G04	(+) (11/12)	− (0/10)
	G01	(+) (9/12)	− (0/10)
	G02	(+) (7/12)	− (0/10)
	SM07	(+) (6/12)	− (0/10)
	S02	(+) (2/12)	− (0/10)
	SM12	(+) (9/12)	− (0/10)
	S08	− (0/12)	− (0/10)
	SM02	− (0/12)	− (0/10)
	G07	− (0/12)	− (0/10)
	G05	− (0/12)	− (0/10)
2	SM04	(+) (**9/12**)	− (0/10)
	SM03	− (0/12)	− (0/10)

in Sub-study 2, the data support the hypothesized developmental sequence (*linear argument-function mapping → non-linear argument-function mapping → morpho-syntactic processing*). With the exception of the data of 'stage 2' learner SM04, whose data are given in bold in Table 7.32, the analysis indicates that learners initially rely on linear argument-function mapping in their speech production. This is then followed by the acquisition of non-linear argument-function mapping, which occurs gradually from stage 3 onwards. In a third step, the learners acquire the feature unification processes as well as the form-function relationships required for target-like morpho-syntactic processing. The analysis reveals that this process also takes place stepwise and is not acquired before stage 4. In the case of the four 'stage 3' learners SM08, S07, G06 and SM11 who produce isolated instances of morphological verb marking, the detailed distributional analysis demonstrates that there is no underlying systematicity in their application of verbal morphology. Furthermore, the occurrence of one or two instances of a particular feature in the speech production data does not allow for any conclusion concerning its acquisition. These cases are marked in bold in Table 7.32.

Results input session – production data passive: Sub-study 3

As mentioned in Section 7.3.1, in Sub-study 3 an input session was included that aimed to investigate whether the performance of the L2 learners participating in the study is influenced by an intensive exposure to passive structures that they received in an additional input session. In order to shed light on this issue, in each grade, the learners were randomly assigned to an 'input' group (19 learners) and a 'control' group (17 learners), and the production data obtained in the passive film task were compared across the two groups.

The data of the two groups were analysed with regard to differences in (1) the number of structures with non-linear argument-function mapping and (2) the number of structures with target-like verb morphology. The data of the structures produced by the 'input' group were not normally distributed, as indicated by both the visual inspection of the boxplots and histograms and by Shapiro-Wilk's test ($p = 0.06$). Therefore, the non-parametric independent-samples Mann-Whitney U test was used to compare the instances of (1) non-linear argument function mapping and (2) target-like verb morphology present in the data of the 'input' and the 'control' group. As far as non-linear argument-function mapping is concerned, the test supports the hypothesis that the distribution of structures exhibiting non-linear argument-function mapping is the same across categories of input: There is no significant difference between the 'input' group (Mean rank = 20.37, $n = 19$) and the 'control' group (Mean rank = 16.41, $n = 17$), $U = 197$, $p = 0.27$. The distribution of morphological marking on the verb also does not differ significantly across the 'input' group (Mean rank = 18.37, $n = 19$) and the 'control' group' (Mean rank = 18.65, $n = 17$), $U = 195$, $p = 0.95$, using an exact sampling distribution for U (Dineen & Blakesley 1973).

The finding that the 'input' group and the 'control' group do not show significant differences in the production of passive constructions suggests that the short, intensive exposure to passive structures received by the 'input' group does not lead to the production of more passive structures in the passive production tasks. In keeping with this, it provides support for the assumption that the fact that learners at lower stages of acquisition do not produce structures exhibiting non-linear argument-function mapping and/or target-like verb morphology is due to processing difficulties rather than to a lack of input. However, as the input session was necessarily limited in time and scope, this conclusion remains tentative and it has to be kept in mind that this issue cannot be fully resolved within the scope of this book. More research is required to further investigate this matter.

7.3.4 Results comprehension data – passive: Sub-study 3

As in Sub-study 1, the comprehension data for passive constructions in Sub-study 3 were elicited with a sentence-picture matching task. The analysis of the comprehension data obtained in the data elicitation session is twofold. In a first step, the data were plotted on an implicational scale to investigate whether it is possible to determine a sequence of acquisition of passive structures. In a second step, a statistical analysis of correlations between the learners' stages of acquisition and the number of comprehended passives was conducted.

The results of the distributional analysis of the L2 learners' comprehension data are presented in Table 7.33. A learner's target-like interpretation of a particular passive structure is marked with a '+' in the respective cell, whereas a '–' in a cell refers to those instances where the learner did not comprehend the respective passive form correctly.

The table shows an implicational sequence in the comprehension of the passive structures by the L2 learners. Table 7.33 yields a coefficient of reproducibility of 0.93 and a coefficient of scalability of 0.82 and is therefore considered to be valid. The implicational sequence in the L2 comprehension of passive structures obtained in Table 7.33 provides further support for the hypothesis that passive structures are acquired gradually in L2 comprehension.

The analysis reveals that the passives that are ranked low in Table 7.33 as they were comprehended by the great majority of learners constitute either non-reversible passives or passives with three arguments. As far as non-reversible passives are concerned, it can be seen that the sentence *The door is opened by the woman* was comprehended by thirty-five out of thirty-six learners. The second non-reversible passive – *The button is pushed by the woman* – is understood by thirty learners. The remaining six learners (G05, G07, SM02, SM05, SM08, SM14) understood the sentence in its active version (*The button pushes the woman*).

The two non-reversible passives exhibit a number of prototypical characteristics: Both structures constitute transitive constructions with the focus on the patient/theme argument. In addition, the actions expressed in both sentences are highly actional and punctual and involve direct physical contact. In the case of the sentence *The door is opened by the woman*, the action denoted by the verb also leads to a visible result. Probably the most important characteristic of the two structures is their semantic irreversibility. The plausibility rating in Table 7.34 shows that the active interpretations of the two passive forms (*The door opens the woman* and *The button pushes the woman*) are perceived to be highly implausible.

Table 7.33 Distributional analysis of comprehension data of passives: Sub-study 3.

Learner	G07	G05	SM 14	SM 03	S02	G02	G03	SM 09	G04	SM 05	SM 10	SM 04	SM 02	SM 08	G06	SM 07	S03	G12
Stage	3	3	4	2	3	3	4	4	3	4	4	2	3	3	3	3	4	4
hear	-	-	-	-	-	-	-	-	-	-	-	-	-	-	-	-	-	+
follow	-	-	-	-	-	-	-	-	-	+	-	-	-	-	-	-	-	+
kick	-	-	-	-	-	-	-	-	-	-	-	-	-	-	-	-	-	-
see	-	-	-	-	-	-	-	-	-	-	-	-	-	-	-	-	+	-
hit	-	-	-	-	-	-	-	-	-	+	-	-	-	-	-	-	-	-
kiss	-	-	-	-	-	-	-	-	-	-	-	-	-	-	-	-	-	+
carry	-	-	-	-	-	-	-	-	-	-	-	+	+	+	+	+	+	+
feed	-	-	-	-	-	-	-	+	+	+	+	+	+	+	+	+	+	+
push	-	-	-	+	+	+	+	+	+	-	+	+	-	-	+	+	+	+
give	-	+	+	-	+	+	+	+	+	+	+	+	-	+	+	+	+	+
put	+	-	+	+	+	+	+	-	+	+	+	-	-	+	+	+	+	+
open	+	+	+	+	+	+	+	+	+	+	+	-	+	+	+	+	+	+

Learner	SM 12	SM 13	SM 11	SM 16	SM 15	S07	G01	G08	G13	S05	S08	S04	G11	S01	G14	G09	G10	G15
Stage	3	4	3	4	5	3	3	4	4	5	3	5	5	4	4	5	5	5
hear	-	+	-	-	+	-	-	-	-	-	+	+	+	+	+	+	+	+
follow	-	-	+	-	-	-	+	+	+	+	+	+	-	+	+	+	+	+
kick	-	-	-	-	-	+	+	+	+	+	+	+	+	+	+	+	+	+
see	-	-	-	+	+	+	+	+	+	+	-	+	+	+	+	+	+	+
hit	+	+	+	+	+	-	-	+	+	+	+	-	+	+	+	+	+	+
kiss	-	+	+	-	+	+	+	+	+	+	+	+	+	+	+	+	+	+
carry	+	-	+	+	+	+	+	+	+	+	+	+	+	+	+	+	+	+
feed	+	-	+	+	+	+	-	+	+	+	+	-	+	+	+	+	+	+
push	+	+	+	+	+	+	+	+	+	+	+	+	+	+	+	+	+	+
give	-	-	+	+	+	+	+	+	+	+	+	+	+	+	+	+	+	+
put	+	+	+	+	+	+	+	+	+	+	+	+	+	+	+	+	+	+
open	+	+	+	+	+	+	+	+	+	+	+	+	+	+	+	+	+	+

Note. See the Appendix for the trial sentences used in Sub-study 3.

Table 7.34 Plausibility rating of non-reversible passives: Sub-Study 3.

Sentence	Mean	SD
The woman opens the door	1.21	0.53
The door opens the woman	6.39	1.07
The woman pushes the button	1.34	0.54
The button pushes the woman	6.23	1.16

In general, the fact that the non-reversible passives are understood by the majority of the learners regardless of their stage of acquisition provides evidence for the assumption that L2 comprehension is guided by semantic cues. Somewhat surprisingly, however, the non-reversible sentence *The button was pushed by the woman* is understood by less learners than the two passives with three arguments. The ditransitive sentences *The plant is put on the table by the man* and *The present is given to the woman by the man* are understood correctly by thirty-two and thirty-one learners respectively. In ditransitive constructions, the N V N processing heuristic cannot be applied in a one-to-one fashion. In the case of the sentence *The present is given to the woman by the man*, the application of the N V N heuristic would yield the semantically and syntactically ill-formed structure *Present give woman*, and it does not account for the thematic role assignment of the entity *the man*.

A potential solution that learners could draw on when relying on linear mapping operations is to assign the beneficiary role to the entity *the man*. This would result in the implausible interpretation *Present give woman to man*. Like in Sub-study 1, this option was not included in the sentence-picture matching task due to its limitation to three pictures per sentence. The five learners that misinterpret the sentence reverse the agent and the beneficiary argument, resulting in the interpretation *The woman gives the man the present*.

The passive *The plant was put on the table by the man* differs from the ditransitive construction discussed above in that two participants in the event are inanimate (*plant* and *table*). A direct mapping of the noun(s) (phrases) at surface structure level to argument roles at a-structure level would result in the highly implausible interpretation *Plant put table to/on man*. Again, this option was not included in the sentence-picture matching task. However, the task contained the equally implausible interpretation *Plant put man on table*. This option is chosen by the four learners that do not comprehend the sentence in a target-like way as exemplified in Figure 7.6 (learner SM04).

Applying the criteria of prototypicality to the ditransitive passives used as experimental stimuli in Sub-study 3, it can be argued that probably the most influential characteristic relates again to their semantic irreversibility: The application of the N V N (N) strategy and the interpretation of the first noun (phrase) in the sentence as the proto-agent yields highly implausible interpretations. In keeping with this, I assume that semantic cues and, in particular, low event probabilities in the case of an active interpretation, are major factors in the early acquisition of ditransitive passives (see also Section 7.2.3).

The two structures that occur next in the implicational table are the biased reversible passives *The cat is fed by the woman* (26 learners) and *The woman is carried by the hero* (24 learners). The comprehension of the latter sentence by the L2 learners in Sub-study 1 was discussed in Section 7.1.2. Its plausibility rating (see Table 7.6 in Section 7.1.2) reveals that the passive interpretation of the sentence is regarded as being more plausible than its active counterpart. However, as pointed out in Section 7.1.2, I assume that factors such as gender stereotypes and stereotypes about typical heroes might play an additional role in the comprehension of the sentence by the young learners.

The passive *The cat is fed by the woman* can also be classified as a biased reversible passive, as indicated by the results of the plausibility rating displayed in Table 7.35. Other prototypicality traits of the passive sentence include the focus on the patient/theme, a punctual action, direct physical contact and a visible result.

The two biased reversible passives are followed by the following three symmetrical reversible passives with both actional and non-actional verbs.

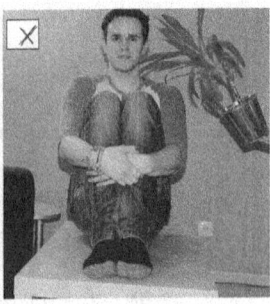

Figure 7.6 Sentence-picture matching learner SM04 (Actor: Sam Cosper).

Table 7.35 Plausibility rating of biased reversible passives: Sub-study 3.

Sentence	Mean	SD
The cat feeds the woman	6.55	0.57
The woman feeds the cat	1.20	0.40

(60) The man is kissed by the woman. (17 learners)
(61) The walker is seen by the bicycle rider. (15 learners)
(62) The boy is kicked by the girl. (13 learners)

The plausibility rating of the sentences displayed in Table 7.9 in Section 7.1.2 shows that the three forms constitute symmetrical reversible passives. Interestingly, the results obtained in the comprehension task in Sub-study 1 yield exactly the same order of acquisition of the three passive forms. As discussed in Section 7.1.2, the main factor that influences the learners' L2 comprehension of these passives seems to be related to their symmetrical reversibility. Other factors associated with prototypicality, such as the degree of actionality expressed by the verb, do not seem to have a major impact in the comprehension of the symmetrical reversible passive forms.

The last two structures in the implicational table are the two symmetrical passives *Santa Clause is followed by the pirate* (14 learners) and *The daughter is heard by the mother* (12 learners). Apart from the fact that the two sentences constitute transitive passives with focus on the patient, the two sentences do not display major characteristics of prototypical passives (see Section 7.1.2). Again, the factor that seems to have a major impact on the L2 comprehension process is the symmetrical reversibility of the two structures. Both interpretations of the two sentences were rated as being equally (un-) likely by the subjects who took part in the plausibility rating. The finding that the two structures are seemingly acquired late as they occur at the top of the implicational hierarchy displayed in Table 7.33 can be explained by the absence of semantic cues in symmetrical reversible passives. In these cases, L2 learners cannot rely on the semantic route in processing but have to make recourse to deep algorithmic processing.

Testing the Integrated Encoding-Decoding Model of SLA 203

This assumption is supported by the fact that the great majority of L2 learners who comprehend the two structures are at higher stages of acquisition (stages 4 and 5).

As in Sub-studies 1 and 2, I investigated whether there is a correlation between the number of passive structures that are comprehended by the L2 learners and the learners' PT stages. Spearman's rho indicates the presence of a strong positive correlation between the L2 learners' PT stages and the number of passive structures comprehended by them, $r_s(36) = 0.614, p < 0.001$ (two-tailed).

This result provides further support for the hypothesis that the processing procedures involved in the L2 speech production process also operate in L2 comprehension. In addition, the correlation between the learners' stages of acquisition and the number of comprehended structures is in line with the claim that there is a gradual development from semantic to syntactic processing in L2 comprehension.

Results input session – comprehension data passive: Sub-study 3

To address the question of whether the learners' comprehension of passives is influenced by an intensive exposure to passive structures in the input, the L2 comprehension data of passives obtained in Sub-study 3 were compared across the 'input' group that received an additional input session prior to data elicitation and the 'control' group that was not exposed to any additional input. As mentioned in Section 7.3.3, the 'input' group encompassed nineteen learners and the 'control' group consisted of seventeen learners. The data violated the normality assumption: Both the visual inspection of the boxplots and histograms and the results of Shapiro-Wilk's test reveal that the number of comprehended structures was not normally distributed for the 'input' group ($p = 0.01$) and only just about normally distributed for the 'control' group ($p = 0.06$). Therefore, the non-parametric independent-samples Mann-Whitney U test was run to determine if there were differences in the number of comprehended structures between the two groups. The number of comprehended structures was not statistically significantly different between the 'input group' (Mean rank = 17.68, $n = 19$) and the 'control group' (Mean rank 19.41, $n = 17$), $U = 195, p = 0.63$, using an exact sampling distribution for U.

This finding lends support to the assumption that the intensive exposure to passive structures in the input session does not lead to significant differences in the comprehension of passive structures in the comprehension task. In keeping with this, the decisive factor in the non-target-like comprehension of passive structures seems to be the lack of necessary L2 processing procedures and not necessarily a lack of input. However, as pointed out in Section 7.3.3, this tentative conclusion has to be viewed within the limitations of the study design. Clearly, more research is needed to develop a full picture of this issue.

7.3.5 Relating production and comprehension data: Sub-study 3

Table 7.36 provides an overview of the comprehension and production data elicited in Sub-study 3. Similar to Table 7.24 presenting the results of Sub-study 2, the L2 learners' comprehension and production data are related to their respective stage of acquisition.

Table 7.36 Overall results: PT stages, comprehension and production of passives: Sub-study 3.

Stage	Learner	No. of comprehended structures	Production	
			Non-linear argument-function mapping (passive film)	Morpho-syntactic processing (passive film)
5	G09	+ (12/12)	+ (12/12)	+ (10/10)
	G15	+ (12/12)	+ (12/12)	(+) (9/10)
	G10	+ (12/12)	(+) (11/12)	(+) (9/10)
	G11	(+) (10/12)	+ (12/12)	(+) (9/10)
	SM15	(+) (10/12)	(+) (10/12)	(+) (7/10)
	S05	(+) (11/12)	(+) (10/12)	(+) (6/10)
	S04	(+) (11/12)	(+) (8/12)	(+) (5/10)
4	G14	+ (12/12)	+ (12/12)	(+) (8/10)
	S01	+ (12/12)	+ (12/12)	(+) (7/10)
	G13	(+) (11/12)	(+) (11/12)	(+) (9/10)
	G12	(+) (9/12)	(+) (6/12)	(+) (5/10)
	SM10	(+) (6/12)	(+) (9/12)	(+) (2/10)
	S03	(+) (7/12)	+ (12/12)	− (0/10)
	G03	(+) (4/12)	(+) (9/12)	− (0/10)
	SM14	(+) (3/12)	(+) (9/12)	− (0/10)
	SM09	(+) (4/12)	(+) (8/12)	− (0/10)
	SM16	(+) (8/12)	(+) (6/12)	− (0/10)
	G08	(+) (11/12)	(+) (6/12)	− (0/10)
	SM13	(+) (6/12)	(+) (2/12)	− (0/10)
	SM05	(+) (5/12)	(+) (2/12)	− (0/10)
3	SM11	(+) (10/12)	(+) (7/12)	(+) **(2/10)**
	G06	(+) (6/12)	(+) (5/12)	(+) **(2/10)**
	S07	(+) (9/12)	(+) (8/12)	(+) **(1/10)**
	SM08	(+) (5/12)	(+) (10/12)	(+) **(1/10)**
	G04	(+) (5/12)	(+) (11/12)	− (0/10)
	G01	(+) (9/12)	(+) (9/12)	− (0/10)
	G02	(+) (4/12)	(+) (7/12)	− (0/10)
	SM07	(+) (6/12)	(+) (6/12)	− (0/10)
	SM12	(+) (6/12)	(+) (9/12)	− (0/10)
	S02	(+) (4/12)	(+) (2/12)	− (0/10)
	S08	(+) (11/12)	− (0/12)	− (0/10)
	SM02	(+) (3/12)	− (0/12)	− (0/10)
	G07	(+) (2/12)	− (0/12)	− (0/10)
	G05	(+) (2/12)	− (0/12)	− (0/10)
2	SM04	(+) (4/12)	(+) **(9/12)**	− (0/10)
	SM03	(+) (3/12)	− (0/12)	− (0/10)

As in Sub-study 2, the results of the L2 learners' passive production presented in Table 7.36 are restricted to data obtained in the passive film task, as the fish film task does not allow for lexical variation concerning the verb. This applies to non-linear argument-function mapping as well as verb morphology.

Table 7.36 reveals that there are no instances of production without comprehension, but there are five cases of comprehension without production. This applies to the 'stage 2' learner SM03 and the 'stage 3' learners G05, G07, SM02 and S08. With the exception of learner S08, their comprehension of passives is restricted to the following structures that occur low in the implicational hierarchy in Table 7.33:

1. *non-reversible passives*
    The door is opened by the woman. (SM02, SM03, G05, G07)
    The button is pushed by the woman. (SM03)
2. *passives with three arguments*
    The plant is put on the table by the man. (SM03, G07)
    The present is given to the woman by the man. (G05)
3. *biased reversible passives*
    The cat is fed by the woman. (SM02)
    The woman is carried by the hero. (SM02)

As argued in Section 7.3.4, in the comprehension of these types of passives, learners can rely on semantic cues and do not need to make recourse to deep algorithmic processing. 'Stage 3' learner S08, however, is an exception in this respect. He comprehends eleven out of twelve passive forms including passives that require syntactic processing. However, he does not produce any structures with non-linear argument-function mapping.

A further analysis of the L2 comprehension and production data elicited in Sub-study 3 focused on relationships between the number of comprehended structures and (1) the number of produced structures with non-linear argument-function mapping and (2) the number of produced structures with target-like verb morphology. Shapiro-Wilk's test indicated that the assumption of normality was violated ($p = 0.005$ for comprehended structures, $p = 0.001$ for structures with non-linear argument-function mapping and $p < 0.001$ for structures with verbal morphology). Therefore, the non-parametric Spearman's rank-order correlation was run to assess the relationship between the comprehension and the production data. There was a strong positive correlation between the number of comprehended structures and the number of structures with non-linear argument-function mapping, $r_s(36) = 0.57, p < 0.001$ (two-tailed), as well as a strong positive correlation between the number of comprehended structures and the number of structures with target-like verbal morphology, $r_s(36) = 0.75, p < 0.001$ (two-tailed).

The correlations between the number of comprehended passives and the number of produced passives are in accordance with the integrated view of L2 processing proposed in this book. As in Sub-study 2, there is no one-to-one relation between the number of comprehended and the number of produced passives in every individual learner. However, the strong positive correlations indicate that the two processes do not occur independently of each other but rely on shared resources. The findings are in line with the assumption that the same underlying processing procedures operate in the two modalities.

To sum up, the results of the data analysis support the proposed developmental sequence of the English passive in L2 acquisition. They are also in line with the key hypotheses of the *Integrated Encoding-Decoding Model of SLA* introduced in Section 4.1. In particular, this applies to the claim that both grammatical encoding and decoding take place in a shared grammatical coder. I argue that the operations taking place in the grammatical coder are based on the processing procedures outlined by Levelt (1989) and spelled out for L2 acquisition in PT. The results of the data analysis are consistent with the assumption that both grammatical encoding and decoding are constrained by processability. In order to further investigate the mechanisms involved in morpho-syntactic processing in L2 comprehension, the sentence-matching reaction-time experiment was implemented as part of the data elicitation in Sub-study 3.

7.3.6 Results of sentence-matching reaction-time experiment: Sub-study 3

As pointed out in Section 6.5, a major methodological challenge in the investigation of L2 comprehension processes is related to the issue of a clear differentiation between shallow, semantic processing and deep, syntactic processing. In my view, the comprehension data obtained with a sentence-picture matching task allow for conclusions concerning two aspects of the comprehension process: (1) semantic factors in processing and acquisition and (2) the acquisition of non-linear argument-function mapping in comprehension and, related to that, the principled capability to map the first noun (phrase)/subject onto the patient/theme argument. However, the data obtained in the sentence-picture matching task do not allow for a clear distinction between semantic and morpho-syntactic processing.

In order to overcome this limitation, I included a sentence-matching reaction-time experiment with auditory stimuli in Sub-study 3 that focuses on different types of ungrammaticalities in passive constructions. In this way, I aimed to tap into morpho-syntactic processing in L2 learners at different stages of acquisition. The rationale behind the sentence-matching technique is as follows: Native speakers of a language are exposed to pairs of matching sentences and are asked to judge whether they are identical or different. Crucially, their responses are faster when the matching sentence pairs are grammatical than when they are ungrammatical. This experimental set-up provides a window on sentence processing operations. The application of the sentence-matching paradigm to L2 acquisition research yields insights into the processing operations taking place in L2 learners. The grammaticality effects observed in native speakers are only expected to occur in L2 learners when they have acquired the necessary processing prerequisites to fully process the respective structure (see Section 6.5.2). Applied to the processing operations involved in the comprehension of passives, I hypothesize that full morpho-syntactic processing of English passive structures in L2 comprehension includes feature unification within the verb phrase to achieve agreement between the auxiliary and the participle. This process requires the verb phrase procedure to be in place, which is acquired at stage 4. In keeping with this,

I argue that learners at different stages of acquisition exhibit different response patterns in the sentence-matching experiment. I hypothesize that the response patterns of learners who are at higher stages of acquisition (stage 4 and above) show grammaticality effects. These effects should not be observable in learners at lower stages of acquisition (stages 2 and 3), as they have not yet acquired the respective processing procedure. In addition to the L2 learners, I included a native speaker control group in the experiment to ensure that the sentence-matching procedure is sensitive in the case of the stimuli used in the experiment.

As outlined in Section 6.3, to be able to make more fine-grained observations about the morpho-syntactic processing of passive constructions, I implemented a number of different conditions in the experiment. On the one hand, I included both non-reversible stimuli (passives with the verb *push* in a non-reversible context) and reversible stimuli (passives with the verb *follow* in a reversible context) in the experiment. In this way, it is possible to investigate whether the syntactic processing of non-reversible passives takes place at the same time or at an earlier stage than the processing of reversible passives. On the other hand, the ungrammatical stimuli were presented in three different conditions to explore the morpho-syntactic processing of passives in more detail. The three conditions are repeated here:

1. Omission of the preposition
   *The orange bike is pushed Ø the old man.
2. Omission of the auxiliary
   *The blue train Ø pushed by Polly and Jack.
3. Omission of the -ed morpheme
   *The little girl is followØ by Emily and Bill.

The following hypotheses underlie the analysis of the reaction-time (RT) data obtained in the experiment:

1. The RT data of the L2 learners who have reached stage 4 or stage 5 of acquisition show grammaticality effects, as these learners have in principle acquired the processing procedure required to perform feature unification within the verb phrase.
2. The RT data of the L2 learners who have not yet acquired stage 4 do not exhibit grammaticality effects.
3. The RT data of the native speaker control group display grammaticality effects.

As far as the different conditions outlined are concerned, I propose the following hypotheses:

1. The grammaticality effects observed in the data of the learners at higher stages of acquisition (4 and 5) are the same for passives with the verb *push* and for passives with the verb *follow*.
2. The three types of omission only yield grammaticality effects in learners at higher stages of acquisition (4 and 5). These effects are probably smaller in the case of

the morphological marking on the verb than in the case of the omission of the preposition and/or the auxiliary, as the morphological marking on the verb does not necessarily have to be processed in comprehension. In order to notice the ungrammaticality of the omission of the preposition, the learners need to have acquired the verb phrase procedure. In the case of the omission of the auxiliary, the sentence could also be processed as a reduced relative clause. In this case, there would be no observable grammaticality effects in native speakers.

In order to test my hypotheses, I divided the learners into the following two groups:

Group 1:
Sixteen learners at stages 2 and 3 (no acquisition of verb phrase procedure, no grammaticality effects expected) (age range 10–13, Mean (M) = 11.25, Standard deviation (SD) = 1.20)

Group 2:
Twenty learners at stages 4 and 5 (acquisition of verb phrase procedure, grammaticality effects expected) (age range 10–14, M = 12.4, SD = 1.50)

In addition to the two learner groups, a native speaker control group was included in the study:

Group 3:
Twenty-three native speakers (grammaticality effects expected) (age range 18–50, M = 29.6, SD = 10.35)

All in all, twenty-seven native speakers participated in the experiment, which was carried out at Paderborn University, Germany and at Flinders University, Adelaide, Australia. Twenty-two females and five males took part in the study. Eight of the native speakers came from the United States, eleven from Australia, seven from England and one from Scotland. Their age range was between eighteen and sixty-five (M = 38.47, SD = 13.59). The data of four native speakers were excluded from the analysis: Two participants had health problems that affected their performance, the data of the other two subjects were excluded due to misunderstandings concerning the task. Therefore, the data of twenty-three native speakers were included in the final analysis.

Analysis and results of reaction-time data: Sub-study 3

The RT data obtained in the sentence-matching experiment were treated in several ways before being analysed statistically. As is standard practice in the analysis of sentence-matching data, only those RT data were included in the analysis that relate to matching sentence pairs (see e.g. Gass 2001; Duffield, Matsuo & Roberts 2007). The RT data of all distractor items (including the non-matching sentence pairs) as well as incorrect responses to matching sentence pairs (i.e. when the participant had pushed the *different* button instead of the *same* button) were removed. The data were then examined for participants' error rates. The criterion to exclude native speaker participants from the analysis was an error rate greater than 15 per cent (see Duffield & White 1999; Verhagen 2009). In determining the subjects' error rate, the non-matching sentence pairs were also taken into account, as they reflect the subjects' overall task performance. No error rate criterion was applied to the learner data, as it is assumed that, in contrast to native speaker errors, learner errors are probably due to phonetic decoding or vocabulary problems and do not necessarily indicate performance errors (see Verhagen 2009).

In a next step, means and standard deviations were calculated for each participant's RT data. All RT data that fell beyond the cut-off value of 2 SD above the group's mean score were excluded from further analysis. It should be noted at this point that, in sentence-matching experiments, a number of different cut-off values have been applied. These range from absolute cut-off points (e.g. 2,000 or 3,000 milliseconds from the onset of the stimulus) to the exclusion of RT data that fall beyond the range of ± 2 SD of an individual's or a group's mean score (for an overview, see e.g. Gass 2001: 426–7). The choice of the cut-off value in this study was guided by the following considerations: In contrast to the majority of sentence-matching experiments that are based on visually presented input in written form, the stimuli in the present experiment are presented aurally. I assume that, when listening to aurally presented stimuli, the decision whether two sentence pairs are identical or not is made very rapidly by the subjects (probably even before the end of the second sentence). Thus I opted against excluding those RT data that fall below 2 SD of a particular mean score.[9] As the experiment consists of only a small number of items in the different conditions, I based the SD value not on the mean scores of the individual participants but on the groups' mean scores (see also Duffield & White 1999).

None of the native speaker data reached the 15 per cent error rate, and therefore no data had to be excluded on this basis. The removal of outliers in the data resulted in an exclusion of 9 per cent of the data in the learner group and 5 per cent of the data in the native speaker group.

The remaining RT data were analysed separately for the three groups. In a first step, the mean RTs and standard deviations for the three groups were calculated for both the grammatical matching and the ungrammatical matching stimuli. These are presented in Table 7.37. According to the mean RT data in Table 7.37, both the learners at higher stages of acquisition (Group 2) and the native speakers (Group 3) are faster in identifying matching grammatical than matching ungrammatical sentence pairs. For the learners at lower stages of acquisition (Group 1), however, there does not seem to be a difference in RT times for the grammatical and the ungrammatical sentences in

Table 7.37 Mean RTs for grammatical and ungrammatical stimuli.

Group	RT mean (grammatical)	SD	RT mean (ungrammatical)	SD
Group 1 learners stages 2 & 3	574 ms	119	564 ms	168
Group 2 learners stages 4 & 5	647 ms	201	769 ms	259
Group 3 native speakers	358 ms	109	409 ms	127

the experiment. When comparing the mean response latencies of Group 1 with the ones of Group 2, it can be seen that (1) the advanced learners' RTs are longer and (2) their standard deviations are higher than those of the beginning learners. The native speaker group, on the other hand, exhibits the shortest RTs and the lowest standard deviations of all three groups.

A potential explanation for these differences is that the beginning learners do not process the sentences syntactically, as they lack the necessary processing prerequisites to syntactically process English passive structures. The advanced learners who have acquired the respective processing prerequisites are, in principle, able to process the sentences syntactically, as indicated by the differences in the mean RTs between grammatical and ungrammatical stimuli. However, they have not yet automatized the respective processing operations and, therefore, their RTs are longer than the ones of the native speakers. The native speakers rely on automatized algorithmic processing, which is reflected in their comparatively short RTs.

For all three groups, separate paired-samples *t*-tests and, in the case of data that violate the normality assumption, Wilcoxon signed rank tests were run on the data for the different conditions. In a first step, I investigated whether the differences in the overall response latencies between the grammatical and the ungrammatical stimuli in the three groups are statistically significant. In a next step, I explored whether there are statistically significant differences in the response latencies for grammatical and ungrammatical items in the different conditions (± preposition, ± auxiliary, ± -*ed* morpheme) as well as for the different verbs (*follow* vs. *push*). As mentioned earlier in this section, the data sample is relatively small, as the items per condition had to be limited to two items in order not to exceed the overall attention span of the learners. Owing to the limited RT data for the different conditions, I did not analyse the data further by means of additional two-way ANOVAs (analysis of variance) to explore the interaction between the different factors, as the analysis would probably not have yielded meaningful results. Instead, I limited the statistical analysis to the presentation of the group mean RTs and the assessment of the data with separate *t*-tests and Wilcoxon signed rank tests respectively. This kind of data analysis has also been applied in other sentence-matching experiments (see Gass 2001). I am aware that the results of the analyses for the different conditions and verb types have to be treated with caution due to the small data set they are based on. However, they might provide first insights into which morpho-syntactic features play a role in L2 processing of passives. Clearly, further research is needed to investigate these issues in more detail.

Results Group 1 (learners stage 2 & 3)

The results of the paired-samples *t*-test for the RT data (grammatical/ungrammatical) of Group 1 indicate that there is no statistically significant difference between the response latencies for the grammatical items and the ones for the ungrammatical items, $t(15) = 0.227, p = 0.823$. The participants' RT data were normally distributed, as assessed by Shapiro-Wilk's test ($p = 0.539$).[10]

The results of the examination of the response latencies in the three different structural conditions are summarized in Table 7.38. The table reveals that the mean RT data for the grammatical and the ungrammatical stimuli in the different conditions are approximately equal. This finding is supported by the results of the statistical tests run on the RT data. In the first condition (preposition present/absent), the RT data were not normally distributed (Shapiro-Wilk's test, $p = 0.019$). Therefore, the non-parametric Wilcoxon signed rank test was used, which shows that the differences between the RTs for the grammatical and the ungrammatical stimuli are not statistically significant, $z = 0.114$, $p = 0.910$ (two-tailed). In the two conditions *auxiliary* and *-ed morpheme*, the assumption of normality was not violated (Shapiro-Wilk's test, $p = 0.981$ [condition *auxiliary*] and $p = 0.565$ [condition *-ed morpheme*]). Two separate *t*-tests were run, which demonstrate that the differences between the RT data for the grammatical and the ungrammatical stimuli in the two conditions are not statistically significant, $t(12) = 0.655$, $p = 0.525$ (two-tailed) for the condition *auxiliary*, and $t(13) = 0.007$, $p = 0.995$ (two-tailed) for the condition *-ed morpheme*.

The same type of analysis was carried out for the mean response latencies for grammatical and ungrammatical stimuli with the two verbs *follow* and *push*. The results are displayed in Table 7.39. The RT data for the stimuli with both verbs were not normally distributed, as assessed by Shapiro Wilk's test ($p = 0.39$ [*follow*] and $p = 0.40$ [*push*]). The Wilcoxon signed rank test determined that, in both conditions, the difference between the mean RTs for grammatical and for ungrammatical stimuli is

Table 7.38 Mean RTs and results *t*-test/Wilcoxon signed rank test for different conditions Group 1 ($\alpha = 0.05$).

Condition	RT mean (grammatical)	SD	RT mean (ungrammatical)	SD	*t*-test/ Wilcoxon signed rank test
Preposition (present/absent)	567 ms	205	571 ms	304	$z = 0.114$, $p = 0.910$
Auxiliary (present/absent)	529 ms	155	527 ms	274	$t(12) = 0.655$, $p = 0.525$
-ed morpheme (present/absent)	588 ms	234	575 ms	281	$t(13) = 0.007$, $p = 0.995$

Table 7.39 Mean RTs and results Wilcoxon signed rank test for different verb types Group 1 ($\alpha = 0.05$).

Verb	RT mean (grammatical)	SD	RT mean (ungrammatical)	SD	Wilcoxon signed rank test
follow	617 ms	188	606 ms	247	$z = -3.450$, $p = 0.730$
push	545 ms	177	508 ms	211	$z = 0.000$, $p = 1.000$

not statistically significant ($z = -3.45$, $p = 0.730$ in the case of *follow* and $z = 0.000$, $p = 1.000$ in the case of *push*, two-tailed).

These findings confirm my initial hypothesis that the RT data of learners at stage 2 and stage 3 of acquisition do not exhibit any grammaticality effects. The lack of statistically significant differences in the response latencies suggests that learners at lower stages of acquisition do not process English passive structures syntactically in L2 comprehension. Instead, they seem to rely on the heuristic route in comprehension, as they have not yet acquired the necessary processing prerequisites that enable them to fully process the structures under investigation.

Results Group 2 (learners stages 4 and 5)

In a first step, the mean RTs of Group 2 for the grammatical and the ungrammatical stimuli were analysed. The data violated the assumption of normality (Shapiro Wilk's test, $p = 0.021$). A Wilcoxon signed rank test determined that the difference between the mean RTs for the grammatical and the ungrammatical stimuli is statistically significant, $z = 2.128$, $p = 0.033$ (two-tailed), $r = 0.47$.

The observed grammaticality effect in the comparison of grammatical and ungrammatical items is in line with my hypothesis that learners from stage 4 onwards respond faster to grammatical than to ungrammatical stimuli. The statistically significant difference in response latencies between the two types of stimuli suggests that the 'stage 4' and 'stage 5' learners in the study process the passive sentences syntactically. The finding supports the assumption that it is the VP procedure that plays a crucial role in the processing of passive constructions, as it enables the learners to carry out feature unification within the verb phrase. Thus, 'stage 4' learners seem to be able to rely on the algorithmic route in the L2 comprehension of English passive constructions.

The results of the analysis of the different structural conditions are summarized in Table 7.40. In the first condition (preposition present/absent), the participants are faster in reacting to grammatical than to ungrammatical stimuli. The difference between the RTs for the two types of stimuli approaches significance, as indicated by the results of the *t*-test, $t(18) = 2.086$, $p = 0.052$ (two-tailed), $d = 1.42$. There is no such difference in the second condition (auxiliary present/absent). The results of the *t*-test show that, in this condition, the difference between the mean RTs is not significant,

Table 7.40 Mean RTs and results *t*-test for different conditions Group 2 ($\alpha = 0.05$).

Condition	RT mean (grammatical)	SD	RT mean (ungrammatical)	SD	*t*-test
Preposition (present/absent)	633 ms	168	797 ms	332	$t(18) = 2.086$, $p = 0.052$
Auxiliary (present/absent)	652 ms	291	663 ms	355	$t(16) = -0.931$, $p = 0.366$
-ed morpheme (present/absent)	628 ms	343	767 ms	387	$t(18) = 1.250$, $p = 0.227$

$t(16) = -0.931$, $p = 0.366$ (two-tailed). The same applies to the third condition (-*ed* morpheme present/absent). The mean RTs suggest that the participants are faster in responding to grammatical than to ungrammatical stimuli. However, the difference is not statistically significant, $t(18) = 1.250$, $p = 0.227$ (two-tailed).

The analysis of the response latencies in the three different conditions shows that the omission of the preposition yields the strongest grammaticality effects, which show a clear tendency to significance. I argue that L2 learners only notice the missing preposition when they fully process the verb phrase. This is illustrated with the sentences in example (63).

(63)
  a) The zebra is followed by the giraffe. (grammatical)
  b) The zebra is followed Ø the giraffe. (ungrammatical)

As pointed out in Chapter 5, there is ample evidence that, at the beginning of the L2 acquisition process, L2 learners process the complex verb construction in passives, for example *is followed*, as one entity and comprehend sentences such as (63a) as active sentences (*The zebra follows the giraffe*). I assume that when L2 learners have not acquired the verb phrase procedure, which enables them to fully process the construction *auxiliary + participle*, the omission of the preposition in cases such as sentence (63b) does not constitute an ungrammaticality in their interlanguage grammar. In these cases, L2 learners rely on the parsing heuristic N V N and do not process the sentence syntactically. It is only when they are able to syntactically process the verb construction that they encounter parsing difficulties when processing sentence (63b), which is evidenced by longer response latencies.

Neither the omission of the auxiliary nor that of the -*ed* morpheme lead to statistically longer response latencies in Group 2. A potential explanation for the missing ungrammaticality effects concerning sentences that do not contain an auxiliary, as in *The zebra Ø followed by the giraffe*, is that advanced learners might process them as reduced relative clauses. If this is the case, the differences in response latencies should also not be statistically significant in native speakers. The finding that there are no grammaticality effects in the case of the omission of the -*ed* morpheme could indicate that the morpheme is redundant in the processing of English passives. Again, this hypothesis would be supported by missing grammaticality effects in the

Table 7.41 Mean RTs and results Wilcoxon signed rank test for different verb types Group 2 ($\alpha = 0.05$).

Verb	RT mean (grammatical)	SD	RT mean (ungrammatical)	SD	Wilcoxon signed rank test
follow	691 ms	284	819 ms	304	$z = 2.427$, $p = 0.015$
push	583 ms	203	729 ms	250	$z = 2.091$ $p = 0.037$

native speaker control group. Overall, it should be kept in mind that the data sample is probably too small to make valid statements concerning the processing in the different conditions. The results can merely serve as a first hint as to which morpho-syntactic features might play a role in processing English passive constructions.

Table 7.41 provides an overview of the results of the analysis of the stimuli with the two verbs *follow* and *push*. The mean RT data suggest that the participants respond faster to grammatical than to ungrammatical sentences regardless of the verb. The results of the Wilcoxon signed rank test show that this difference is statistically significant, $z = 2.427$, $p = 0.015$ (two-tailed), $r = 0.54$ for the verb *follow* and $z = 2.091$, $p = 0.037$ (two-tailed), $r = 0.46$ for the verb *push*. In both cases, the data were not normally distributed (Shapiro-Wilk's test, $p = 0.048$ [*follow*] and $p = 0.012$ [*push*]).

These results imply that, in both cases, the L2 learners in Group 2 rely on the algorithmic route in processing the stimuli. The difference in RTs between the grammatical and the ungrammatical stimuli is significant for sentences with both verbs. This indicates that there is no 'processing advantage' for non-reversible passives (*push*) over reversible passives (*follow*) in conditions where both types of structures are processed syntactically and not semantically. However, due to the small data sample this conclusion has to remain tentative.

Group 3 (native speakers)

As in the analysis of the RT data of Groups 1 and 2, the mean response latencies for the grammatical and the ungrammatical stimuli of the native speaker control group were analysed. A paired samples *t*-test was used to determine whether there is a statistically significant difference between the two mean response latencies. The assumption of normality was not violated (Shapiro Wilk's test, $p = 0.752$). The native speakers were significantly faster in responding to grammatical than to ungrammatical stimuli, $t(22) = 3.628$, $p = 0.001$ (two-tailed), $d = 0.75$. This finding shows that the sentence-matching procedure is sensitive to the stimuli used in the present experiment.

The analysis of the mean RTs for the three different conditions is summarized in Table 7.42. The data were normally distributed (Shapiro Wilk's test, $p = 0.565$). The only condition that yields a grammaticality effect is the omission of the preposition,

Table 7.42 Mean RTs and results *t*-test for different conditions Group 3 ($\alpha = 0.05$).

Condition	RT mean (grammatical)	SD	RT mean (ungrammatical)	SD	*t*-test
Preposition (present/absent)	334 ms	143	439 ms	137	$t(22) = 3.674$, $p = 0.01$
Auxiliary (present/absent)	370 ms	118	395 ms	162	$t(22) = 0.853$, $p = 0.403$
-ed morpheme (present/absent)	368 ms	127	390 ms	176	$t(21) = 0.394$, $p = 0.697$

$t(22) = 3.674$, $p = 0.01$ (two-tailed), $d = 0.76$. Both the condition *auxiliary* and the condition *-ed morpheme* show no statistically significant difference between the grammatical and the ungrammatical items. This is in line with the hypotheses that (1) sentences without auxiliaries might be processed as reduced relative clauses and (2) the *-ed* morpheme is probably redundant in the processing of English passive constructions. Again, the results have to be treated with caution due to the small size of the data sample.

Finally, the response latencies for grammatical and ungrammatical stimuli with the two verbs *follow* and *push* were examined. In both cases, the data did not violate the normality assumption (Shapiro Wilk's test, $p = 0.497$ for the sentences with *follow* and $p = 0.200$ for the ones containing *push*). As can be seen from Table 7.43, the stimuli with the two types of verbs yield grammaticality effects, $t(22) = 2.115$, $p = 0.046$ (two-tailed), $d = 0.44$ (*follow*) and $t(22) = 2.557$, $p = 0.018$, (two-tailed), $d = 0.53$ (*push*). This indicates that the native speakers make recourse to deep algorithmic processing in both types of stimuli. As discussed earlier in this section, the small data sample only allows for tentative conclusions concerning the processing of the experimental items with the two types of verbs.

Results input session: RTs

In order to explore whether the exposure to passive structures in the input session had an effect on the differences in response latencies between grammatical and ungrammatical passive constructions by Group 1 learners (stages 2 and 3) and Group 2 learners (stages 4 and 5), a two-way ANOVA was run (independent variables: input and learner group; dependent variable: RTs). The data of Group 1 were normally distributed (Shapiro-Wilk's test, $p = 0.53$). There were two outliers in the data of Group 2. The two outliers were winsorized (see Wilcox 2012), which led to a normal distribution of all data. There was homogeneity of variances, as assessed by Levene's test for equality of variances, $p = 0.076$. The main effect of learner group on response latencies was statistically significant, $F(1, 36) = 4.43$, $p = 0.043$, with the differences in response latencies being higher in Group 2 ($M = 125.52$, $SD = 196.82$) than in Group 1 ($M = -9.7$, $SD = 170.61$). Partial eta-squared (η^2) was 0.122. The main effect for input was not statistically significant, $F(1, 36) = 0.000$, $p = 0.993$, partial $\eta^2 = 0.000$. The response latencies of the 'input' group (61.30, $SD = 215.79$) were approximately the

Table 7.43 Mean RTs and results *t*-test for different verb types Group 3 ($\alpha = 0.05$).

Verb	RT mean (grammatical)	SD	RT mean (ungrammatical)	SD	t-test
follow	365 ms	136	420 ms	122	$t(22) = 2.115$, $p = 0.046$
push	343 ms	111	407 ms	165	$t(22) = 2.557$, $p = 0.018$

same as the ones of the 'no input' group (70.03, SD = 176.13). There was no interaction between input and learner group, $F(1, 36) = 0.15$, $p = 0.904$, $\eta^2 = 0.000$.

These results reveal that the intensive exposure to English passive structures in the input session had no statistically significant effect on the learners' response latencies in the RT experiment. The findings provide support for the claim that the L2 learners' ability to syntactically process English passive constructions does not primarily depend on the amount of input but rather on the acquisition of the respective processing procedures. However, as the intensive input was limited to one session prior to data elicitation, this conclusion necessarily has to remain a tentative one. Clearly, more research is needed to further investigate this matter.

To put it in a nutshell, the results of the RT experiment support my hypotheses concerning the morpho-syntactic processing of passive structures. As discussed earlier in this section, I assume that grammaticality effects can only be observed in the RT data of those learners who have acquired the necessary processing procedures to syntactically process the respective structures. In the case of the English passive, the learners have to have acquired the verb phrase procedure located at stage 4 of acquisition. Learners at lower stages of acquisition, on the other hand, are expected to show no differences in response latencies, as they have not yet acquired the respective processing prerequisites to process passive forms via the deep algorithmic route. The results of the data analysis are in line with these claims: Whereas the RT data of the advanced learners (stages 4 and 5) display statistically significant grammaticality effects, this is not the case with the learners at stages 2 and 3 of acquisition. This corroborates my assumption that the comprehension of selected passives by learners at lower stages of acquisition is guided by semantic cues and not the result of full morpho-syntactic processing.

The analysis of the RT data for the different conditions (± preposition, ± auxiliary, ± -ed morpheme) indicates that the preposition is most likely a crucial feature in the processing of passive constructions, whereas the -ed morpheme does not seem to play a decisive role in syntactic parsing of aurally presented data. This is also reflected in the data of the native speaker control group. The results for the condition ± auxiliary suggest that the absence of the auxiliary in passive constructions does not lead to statistically significant differences in response latencies in all groups. A potential explanation for this finding is that structures without an auxiliary are interpreted as reduced relative clauses by both advanced learners and native speakers. Clearly, more research is needed to shed light on this issue.

Finally, the results demonstrate that there is no statistically significant difference in RTs for stimuli with the verb *push* in non-reversible constructions and the verb *follow* in reversible passives in all three groups. This suggests that the advanced learners rely on morpho-syntactic processing in the parsing of reversible as well as non-reversible passive constructions.

The analysis investigating the influence of the input session on the RTs of both learner groups shows that the short, intensive input session to passive structures prior to data elicitation does not have a statistically significant effect on the morpho-syntactic processing of passives by the learners in the RT experiment. This lends support to the assumption that the capability to process passive structures syntactically first and foremost depends on the acquisition of the relevant processing procedures.

7.4 Discussion

The results of all three sub-studies provide support for the proposed *Integrated Encoding-Decoding Model* and the adaptation of the *Online Cognitive Equilibrium Hypothesis* to SLA. To recall, the key claims of the model concerning syntactic processing in both modalities are that (1) there is a single syntactic processor underlying grammatical encoding and decoding processes in L2 acquisition, (2) this processor develops stepwise following the predictions of PT and (3) L2 learners draw on the same mental grammatical system in grammatical encoding and decoding. Based on these assumptions, I proposed a developmental sequence of the English passive in L2 acquisition that is assumed to apply to both encoding and decoding. This sequence is outlined in Section 5.2.2 and repeated here:

1. Shallow processing/linear argument-function mapping:
   - the first noun phrase is assigned the role of agent/experiencer
   - syntactic features are missing in the lexicon
2. Non-linear argument-function mapping:
   - the first noun phrase is assigned the role of patient/theme
   - syntactic features become involved in unification processes of argument-function mapping
3. Morpho-syntactic processing:
   - incorporates the c-structure level
   - incorporates both feature unification and form-function relationships

The distributional analyses of the production data obtained in Sub-studies 2 and 3 revealed that the acquisition of passive structures takes place implicationally and they confirmed the proposed sequence of acquisition of the English passive in L2 acquisition.[11] This means that – with the exception of one learner in each study – L2 learners at stage 2 relied on linear mapping operations and produced sentences in active voice. The acquisition of non-linear argument-function mapping was evident in the data of learners from stage 3 onwards whereas evidence for morpho-syntactic processing occurred in the production data of learners from stage 4 onwards. I argue that, in production, the gradual acquisition of non-linear argument-function mapping is in line with the *Multiple Constraints Hypothesis* and its claim that, initially, the L2 learners' mental lexicon is not fully annotated. This applies in particular to the syntactic features at the level of argument structure. As outlined in Section 3.6, the annotation of the L2 mental lexicon for syntactic features is regarded as a prerequisite for non-linear argument-function mapping. In the *Multiple Constraints Hypothesis*, I argue that this annotation constitutes a gradual process, which is part of individual learner variation and cannot be captured in terms of PT's processing procedures. The proposed sequence of acquisition is reflected in the production data of the passive in all three sub-studies and illustrated in Table 7.44.

The analysis of the comprehension data yielded three major results: Firstly, the results of the distributional analyses of the data obtained in the three sub-studies showed an

Table 7.44 Gradual acquisition of processing operations in L2 passives.

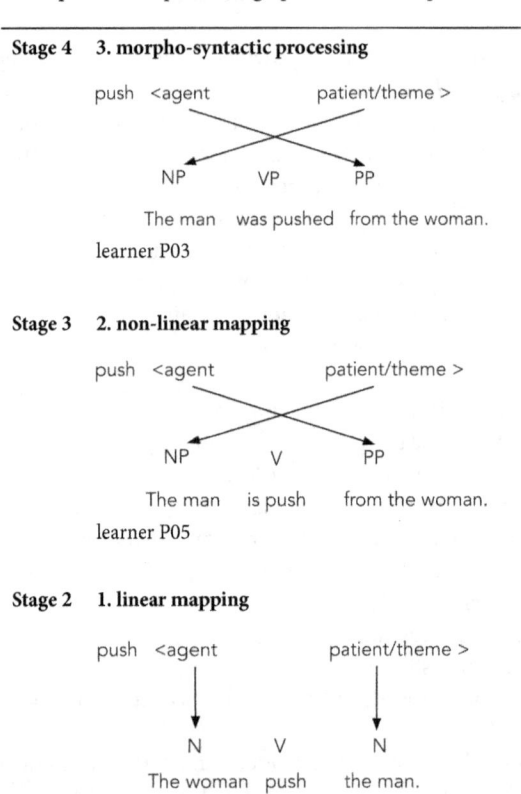

implicational development in the acquisition of different types of passive constructions in L2 comprehension. The implicational sequence of the different passive structures could (at least partly) be explained by the prototypicality of the respective passives. The data indicated that semantically irreversible passives and ditransitive passives were acquired before symmetrical reversible passives. Symmetrical reversible passives are characterized by a lack of semantic cues that could potentially influence the learners' interpretation of the structure. The implicational sequences of different types of passives found in the three sub-studies reflect a development from semantic to syntactic processing in the L2 acquisition process. A second finding concerned the results of statistical correlation tests run on the data, which revealed significant correlations between the number of passive structures comprehended by the learners and their stages of acquisition. These correlations further support the hypothesis of a gradual acquisition development from semantic to syntactic processing in L2 comprehension. Thirdly, the results of the sentence-matching RT experiment implemented in Substudy 3 were in accord with the hypothesized developmental sequence of the English passive in L2 comprehension. The analysis indicated that the L2 learners from stage 4 onwards made recourse to morpho-syntactic processing operations in parsing the trial sentences in the experiment. This was evidenced by statistically significant differences in response latencies between matching grammatical and matching ungrammatical stimuli. As regards the learners at stages 2 and 3, no statistically significant differences in response latencies between matching grammatical and matching ungrammatical sentence pairs were observed, which indicated that they did not rely on morpho-syntactic processing operations in parsing passive constructions.

These results support the hypothesis of a gradual development from semantic to syntactic processing in L2 comprehension. They can be explained by the adaptation of the *Online Cognitive Equilibrium Hypothesis* (Karimi & Ferreira 2016) to SLA (see Section 4.3) and its key claim that, in principle, two routes – the heuristic route and the algorithmic route – operate in parallel in syntactic parsing. As outlined in Section 4.3, I hypothesize that, in addition to the parsing heuristic N V N, semantic aspects such as prototypicality and lexical semantics also play a crucial role in heuristic processing. I further claim that the algorithmic route encompasses PT's processing procedures, which constrain the L2 parsing process. As these procedures are acquired stepwise in the L2 acquisition process, beginning L2 learners are assumed to primarily make recourse to the heuristic route, as they lack the respective processing procedures for deep algorithmic processing. The results of the analysis of the comprehension data corroborate the core assumptions of the model.

When relating the production and the comprehension data obtained in Sub-studies 2 and 3, it could be seen that there were no instances of production without comprehension, but there were several instances of comprehension without production. However, the comprehended structures were mainly restricted to semantically irreversible passives that occurred low in the implicational hierarchy. I argue that, in these cases, learners relied on semantic cues and did not make recourse to deep algorithmic processing. A further finding related to statistically significant correlations between the number of comprehended passives and (1) the number of produced structures with non-linear argument-function mapping and (2) the number of produced structures with target-like verbal morphology. These correlations suggested that there are shared mechanisms underlying both modalities.

To sum up, the results of the analysis of the production and comprehension data were in line with the assumption of the existence of a shared coder in grammatical encoding and decoding that develops stepwise according to the sequence predicted by PT. The results also corroborated the assumptions spelled out in the *Multiple Constraints Hypothesis*, as they indicated a gradual annotation of the L2 mental lexicon for syntactic features. The comprehension data and, in particular, the observed development from semantic to syntactic processing, could be explained by the proposed adaptation of the *Online Equilibrium Hypothesis* to SLA and its core claim that, initially, L2 learners rely on the semantic processing route as their L2 syntactic processor is underdeveloped. In the course of L2 development, the acquisition of the processing procedures required for syntactic operations enables the learners to make recourse to deep algorithmic processing.

A further issue related to the question of whether the fact that the learners at higher stages of acquisition in the study had received previous classroom-based instructions of English passives and thus had been exposed to more input containing passive forms might have influenced the results. I addressed this matter in Sub-study 3 and investigated whether L2 learners who had received a short, intensive input session on passive constructions prior to data elicitation improved their performance on the passive tasks more than controls who had not received additional input. The results revealed that there were no statistically significant differences between the groups in (1) the passive production tasks, (2) the passive comprehension task and (3) the results of the RT experiment. This is in line with the assumption that the ability to process passive structures in both production and comprehension crucially depends on the presence of the respective processing procedures.

Concluding remarks

The aim of this book was to investigate the interface between production and comprehension in L2 acquisition. My main motivation in this endeavour was to explore the possibility that – in contrast to the traditional view that the two processes operate in different modules with two different types of information – production and comprehension are to some extent intertwined and rely on (at least partially) shared resources. In keeping with this, I modelled the grammatical encoding and decoding processes in both modalities and complemented this with a model of the relation between semantic and syntactic processing in SLA.

The model I developed to capture the core processes underlying L2 production and comprehension, the *Integrated Encoding-Decoding Model of SLA*, combines aspects of recent theoretical approaches to production and comprehension processes in human language processing. The integrated view on production and comprehension in SLA was inspired by the work of Kempen (1999, 2000) as well as Kempen and colleagues on the notion of a *shared grammatical workspace* (Kempen, Olsthoorn & Sprenger 2012). The perspective on language production taken in the model is based on some of the key assumptions concerning language generation put forward by Levelt (1989, 1999, 2000) and Levelt, Roelofs and Meyer (1999). As regards comprehension, I adopt core ideas of the *Good-Enough Approach to Language Comprehension* (Christianson et al. 2006; Ferreira & Patson 2007) and its extension, the *Online Cognitive Equilibrium Hypothesis* (Karimi & Ferreira 2016).

The view on L2 acquisition incorporated in the model is the one of PT (Pienemann 1998; Pienemann & Lenzing 2020) and the *Multiple Constraints Hypothesis* (Lenzing 2013). In PT, the processing procedures are claimed to be acquired stepwise in the L2 acquisition process. Applied to the *Integrated Encoding-Decoding Model of SLA*, this means that the development of the L2 coder is governed by the predictions of PT. Thus, the processing procedures constrain the syntactic encoding as well as the decoding process. In line with the claims of the *Multiple Constraints Hypothesis*, it is assumed that the L2 learners draw on the same mental grammatical system in both encoding and decoding and that this system is initially highly constrained at the different levels of linguistic representation spelled out in LFG. A further claim relates to the L2 mental lexicon: This is assumed to be annotated gradually, which also applies to specific syntactic features that are relevant for mapping operations from arguments to grammatical functions and vice versa. The incomplete annotation of the L2 mental lexicon poses further constraints on the grammatical encoding and decoding processes.

The core hypotheses concerning syntactic processing in the *Integrated Encoding-Decoding Model of SLA* are (1) that there is a shared grammatical coder as part of the formulator and (2) that both encoding and decoding processes draw on the same processing procedures. In order to address the relation between semantic and syntactic processing in comprehension, I adapted the *Online Cognitive Equilibrium Hypothesis* to SLA. This adaptation specifies the dynamic relationship between semantic and syntactic processing. Its core claim is that there are two routes in L2 processing, a heuristic route and a deep algorithmic route. I argue that the algorithmic route encompasses the processing procedures required for syntactic operations. Initially, the L2 formulator is underdeveloped and L2 learners are assumed to rely on the semantic route. It is only when they have acquired the respective processing procedures that they can draw on deep algorithmic processing.

The model was tested against empirical data obtained in a study on the L2 acquisition of the English passive by eighty-one learners of English at different stages of acquisition. I chose the English passive as a test case for the empirical study due to the different processes involved in its production and comprehension. First of all, L2 learners need to acquire the operations to process the underlying linguistic non-linearity between arguments and grammatical functions present in passive constructions. In production, non-linear argument-function mapping is required to syntactically realize the patient/theme argument as the first noun phrase. In order to derive the intended meaning in the comprehension of passive constructions, it is also essential to be able to perform non-linear mapping operations. A second aspect involved in the acquisition of passive constructions concerns morpho-syntactic processing. The production of target-like verb morphology serves as an indicator of the acquisition of morpho-syntactic processing in passive constructions. In comprehension, the acquisition of the respective processing procedures enables learners to syntactically parse passive constructions and to derive their meaning in the absence of semantic cues.

On the basis of an analysis of English passives in terms of LFG and PT, I proposed a developmental sequence in the L2 acquisition of English passive constructions. I specified minimal requirements for production and comprehension that I tested in the empirical study. I proposed the following developmental sequence of the varied aspects of passive constructions in L2 acquisition: (1) shallow processing/linear mapping (stage 2); (2) non-linear mapping (gradually, PT stage 3 onwards); (3) morpho-syntactic processing (gradually, PT stage 4 onwards).

The empirical study was cross-sectional in design and consisted of three thematically related sub-studies focusing on different aspects in L2 production and comprehension. The sub-studies encompassed production and comprehension tasks targeting the English passive as well as tasks to elicit speech production data to determine the learners' stages of acquisition. In the comprehension tasks, different types of passives were included in order to shed light on the influence of semantic aspects, such as event probability and prototypicality, on the L2 comprehension process. In the third sub-study, a sentence-matching reaction-time experiment was included to tap into morpho-syntactic processing in comprehension.

All in all, the results of the three sub-studies provided support for the *Integrated Encoding-Decoding Model of SLA* and its complement, the adaptation of the *Online*

Cognitive Equilibrium Hypothesis to SLA. In keeping with this, they corroborated the claims spelled out in PT and the *Multiple Constraints Hypothesis* concerning the stepwise acquisition of processing procedures and the restrictions of the L2 mental grammatical system.

Naturally, the complex issue of potential interfaces between production and comprehension in L2 acquisition cannot be settled within the scope of the research presented here. The theoretical assumptions concerning the operations involved in the two modalities outlined in this book are necessarily limited in several ways. In a similar vein, the empirical evidence of the model is also restricted in a number of aspects.

The limitations of the *Integrated Encoding-Decoding Model* relate to the fact that its main focus is on the syntactic processes involved in L2 production and comprehension. I also addressed the issue of semantic processing in L2 comprehension in that I aimed to integrate some key semantic aspects in my research design. However, these are limited to the notions of lexical semantics, event probability and prototypicality. Other factors that influence the comprehension process, such as frequency of occurrence of particular constructions, prosody and discourse contexts, or non-linguistic factors such as visual contexts or gestures were not taken into account in the proposed model. Also, the different input modes (aurally presented input versus written input) were not explicitly considered in the approach taken in this book.

As far as the limitations of the empirical study are concerned, the study is restricted to the investigation of the English passive by L2 learners of English at different stages of acquisition. Although the English passive seems to be a promising structure to empirically test the core assumptions of the *Integrated Encoding-Decoding Model of SLA* due to the different processes involved in its acquisition, further research is needed to explore the application of the model to other linguistic features and/or different languages. A further limitation of the study relates to the fact that, due to the complex task design, only a few stage 2 learners participated in the study, which limits the explanatory power of the results to a certain extent. To develop a full picture of the processes involved in the L2 acquisition of passives in learners at lower stages, future studies should aim at including a higher number of early L2 learners. Finally, the question of the role of previous input of the structure under investigation has only been touched upon in the present study. Clearly, further research is needed to investigate this issue in more detail.

Notwithstanding these limitations, this book makes a noteworthy contribution to the field of SLA research. This applies in particular to the as yet unresolved questions as to (1) how production and comprehension are related in SLA and (2) how semantic and syntactic processing are related in L2 comprehension. The proposed *Integrated Encoding-Decoding Model* integrates recent psycholinguistic findings supporting an integrated view on syntactic processing and provides a framework for further research on potential interfaces between production and comprehension. I hope that my hypotheses concerning the L2 cognitive architecture of syntactic processing in the two modalities outlined in this work will prove fruitful for further research in this area.

Appendix

Trial sentences Sub-study 3: Sentence-picture matching task (Comprehension)

Symmetrical reversible passives (actional)
The boy is kicked by the girl.
The man is kissed by the woman.
Santa Clause is followed by the pirate.

Distractor item: The thief robs the grandmother.

Symmetrical reversible passives (non-actional)
The walker is seen by the bicycle rider.
The daughter is heard by the mother.

Distractor item: The passenger smells the homeless man.

Biased reversible passives
The cat is fed by the woman.
The woman is carried by the hero.
The ball is hit by the man.

Distractor item: The man pats the dog.

Non-reversible passives
The door is opened by the woman.
The button is pushed by the woman.

Distractor item: The woman washes the T-Shirt.

Passives with three arguments:
The present is given to the woman by the man.
The plant is put on the table by the man.

Distractor item: The monkey puts the baby monkey on the table.

Notes

Chapter 1

1. A main difference between the two approaches relates to the way the information flow between the different components in the speech production system is conceptualized. Whereas modular models generally assume that information flows in only one direction, spreading-activation models propose that information can spread in both directions, that is, forward and backward.
2. In a later version (Levelt 1999), Levelt refers to Kempen's *Performance Grammar* (Kempen 1999) (see Section 2.2).
3. Levelt does not view production and comprehension as mirror images of each other, in the sense that exactly the same processes occur in a reverse order. He argues that '[t]he aims of the two systems are deeply different: attaining completeness is a core target of production; ambiguity is hardly ever a problem. Attaining uniqueness in the face of massive ambiguity is a core target of speech perception; completeness of parsing should definitely be avoided – it would make the system explode' (Levelt 2001: 242).
4. Other approaches that assume that the parser is initially restricted in terms of available information include, for example, the proposals by Abney (1989), Crocker (1995) and Pritchett (1992).
5. For further studies supporting the idea that the processor relies on heuristics in parallel to a full syntactic analysis, see van Herten, Kolk & Chwilla (2005) and Kolk et al. (2003).
6. Karimi and Ferreira (2016) do not specify how exactly deep syntactic parsing takes place, that is, they do not integrate a theory of grammar into their model. I argue that their account is, in principle, compatible with the core tenets of LFG, the grammatical framework underlying the *Integrated Encoding-Decoding Model of SLA*.

Chapter 2

1. In his later version of the *Blueprint for a Speaker*, Levelt (1999: 98, 117) also refers to 'a slimmed-down version' of Kempen's *Performance Grammar* in his conceptualization of syntactic composition.
2. Although the example sentences are in English, the experiments were carried out in Dutch.
3. In addition to the paraphrasing task, a so-called *proofreading task* was included in the research design, which served as a control task. In this task, both hypotheses yield the same predictions.

Chapter 3

1. Examples (2)–(4) are adapted from Lenzing (2016: 5) and Bresnan (2001: 307).
2. Once L2 learners have acquired the procedure that is necessary to be able to process a particular feature, such as the '3sg -s', they are, *in principle*, able to produce this feature. However, this does not mean that learners apply this feature in all obligatory contexts straightaway and that they use this form in a target-like way.
3. In LFG, constraint equations demand the presence of a specific value and ensure that this value occurs in the respective f-structure (see Falk 2001: 78).
4. Note that rule (R3) only specifies the position of the auxiliary. It does not account for its morphological form and does not ensure subject-verb agreement (see Pienemann 1998: 174).
5. In the current version of the PT hierarchy applied to L2 English, the structure 'yes/no inversion' is labelled 'Copula S (x)' (see Table 3.4).
6. In contrast to the lexical morpheme 'plural -s (noun)' which occurs at stage 2 of the PT hierarchy, the feature 'plural -s (DET + N agr.)' is located at stage 3. In this case, the value for the diacritic feature 'number' has to be unified between the determiner and the noun. According to PT, this type of feature unification within the NP requires the acquisition of the phrasal procedure (see Lenzing 2013: 179).
7. In this book, the discussion of acquisition is limited to the acquisition of developmental morpho-syntactic features. However, I am well aware that the term 'acquisition' is not restricted to the learner's acquisition of morpho-syntax but also includes other aspects of the L2 learner's communicative repertoire.
8. For an approach to unambiguously identify formulaic sequences in learners' speech samples, see Lenzing (2013) and the discussion in Section 7.2.1.
9. For a more detailed discussion on issues related to the notions of emergence and acquisition, see Nicholas, Lenzing and Roos (2019).
10. It should be noted here that different criteria have been proposed in the literature. Guttman (1944: 150), for instance, argued that scales of 85 per cent or better would be 'efficient approximations to perfect scales'. Rickford (2002: 157) maintains that 'the statistical acceptable rate for scalability or the Index of Reproducibility is 90 percent, not the 85 percent figure that has been accepted in a number of linguistic studies'. He additionally points out that 'an IR of .93 approximates the .05 level of significance'.
11. The term pseudo-passive is used in the study to refer to passives with non-target-like morphology.
12. Tag questions were included in the *Predictive Framework* (Pienemann & Johnston 1987), which was based on different theoretical assumptions than PT.
13. As in subject-verb agreement with lexical verbs, the structure 'copula agreement', as in *The alligators are green*, requires interphrasal information exchange in PT. However, it has been observed that learners are able to process this type of agreement earlier than assumed by Buyl and Housen, that is, at stage 4 (see Lenzing 2008).

Chapter 4

1. The term prototype can be understood in different ways. For instance, it can be used in the sense of a *prototype-as-exemplar* to refer to 'specific instances of a category' (Taylor 2003: 64). According to the *prototype-as-subcategory* approach, a

particular entity exemplifies the prototype. In the *prototype-as-abstraction* approach, the prototype is more abstract. It refers to the conceptual centre of a specific category which is not necessarily related to a specific instance or subcategory (Taylor 2003: 64).
2 The *Lexical Preference Principle* states that, when processing a lexical item, learners will focus on meaning instead of grammatical form 'when both encode the same semantic ("real world") information' (VanPatten 2020: 108). The *Preference for Nonredundancy Principle* maintains that learners are more likely to process grammatical markers that are non-redundant in terms of meaning before they process 'redundant meaningful markers' (VanPatten 2020: 109).

Chapter 5

1 The term *pseudo-passive* is used in a different sense by Quirk et al. (1985) than by Keatinge and Keßler (2009), who used the term to refer to interim forms of the passive in L2 acquisition (see Section 3.8).
2 The notion of initial default linear mapping in comprehension is compatible with VanPatten's *First Noun Principle* and the related claim that L2 learners initially interpret the first noun in the sentence as the agent/subject (VanPatten 1996: 34).

Chapter 6

1 For an overview of definitions of the term *task*, see Ellis (2003).
2 It could be argued at this point that the habitual action task constitutes a semi-communicative task: Although there is an information gap present, the exchange of information among the participants is not necessarily central to the outcome of the task.
3 Lexical-conceptual factors, such as animacy and accessibility, also have an effect on the choice of active versus passive voice (e.g. Bock & Warren 1985; MacDonald, Bock & Kelly 1993).
4 The procedural skill hypothesis entails that 'procedural routines, once automated, are similar in native speakers and non-native speakers' and that SLA can be viewed as 'the acquisition of procedural skills' (Pienemann 1998: 215).
5 Different approaches to modelling the reading process and the interface between spoken and written language production and comprehension have been proposed in the literature (for a brief introduction, see e.g. Hulme & Snowling 2014).
6 In SLA studies, the target-filler ratio is not employed in a uniform manner: Whereas Bley-Vroman and Masterson (1989) also use a 1:1 ratio of target-filler items, the ratio in Duffield and White's (1999) study is 2.5:1. Gass (2001) applies a 2:1 target-filler ratio, Slabakova (1997) a 2:1.5 and Verhagen (2009) a 1:1.5 ratio. In some studies, the number of distractor items is not mentioned explicitly (e.g. Duffield et al. 1998; Eubank 1993).
7 Timing issues play a crucial role in sentence-matching experiments. However, as observed by Gass (2001: 424), experimental setups differ with respect to the delay between the presentation of the two sentences of a pair on the computer screen.

I based the delay time on the study by Verhagen (2009, 2011) and a personal communication with Verhagen. In addition, I tested different delay times in a pilot study with five L2 learners of English as well as a number of native speakers in order to make sure that an appropriate break occurred between the sentences.

Chapter 7

1. In North Rhine-Westphalia (NRW), the state where the data elicitation took place, English was introduced at primary school level at grade 3 in 2003/4 and at grade 1 (2nd term) in 2008/9. This is why the 'grade 5' learners had received four years of instruction and the 'grade 7' learners also had four years of instruction in English at the time of data collection.
2. In line with the hypotheses spelled out in PT, I assume that, initially, the L2 learners process NPs as nouns. It is only when they have acquired the phrasal procedure that they are able to fully process NPs. In a similar vein, I argue that the L2 learners are only able to process the initial NP as subject and the second NP as object when they have acquired the mapping operations between arguments and grammatical functions.
3. The L2 learners that participated in the study are at different levels of acquisition, which includes beginners as well as more advanced learners. As far as the latter are concerned, it was not always possible to obtain information on all the textbooks that they had worked with in their previous English classes. Therefore, I decided to classify only a limited number of structures as formulae that are commonly introduced at primary school level as evidenced by two major primary school textbooks used in NRW, *Playway* (Gerngross & Puchta 2008a, b) and *Ginger* (Hollbrügge & Kraaz 2008). These two books are used in many schools in the area the data collection took place (see also Lenzing 2008).
4. Apart from one unclear case – the sentence *The horse was ridden by Lisa* is not enacted properly by learner P06 – all learners interpret the four semantically irreversible passives in a target-like way. In six cases, the learners point to the wrong actor, which is marked with a (+) in Table 7.20.
5. The small Playmobil© figure is named *Tom* and the large figure is called *James*.
6. The columns given in grey denote those learners that received an input session on English passive structures prior to the data elicitation (see Section 7.3.1 for details).
7. As pointed out in Section 7.3, the data of three learners had to be excluded from the analysis. Therefore, the distribution of the learners across the two groups is not even.
8. The film clip was designed by A. Aust, L. Michaelis and J. Zimmermann as part of a seminar project.
9. The same criterion was applied by Duffield, Matsuo & Roberts (2007) in a sentence-matching experiment using stimuli presented in written form.
10. To evaluate the assumptions of normality of the participants' RT data, I additionally carried out visual inspection of the histograms and boxplots for all groups and conditions.
11. As pointed out in Section 7.1, the production data of the passive obtained in Sub-study 1 were not included in the analysis.

References

Abney, S. P. (1989), 'A computational model of human parsing', *Journal of Psycholinguistic Research*, 18: 129–44.
Aitchison, J. (2012), *Words in the mind: An introduction to the mental lexicon*, Malden, MA: Blackwell.
Akers, G. (1981), *Phonological variation in the Jamaican continuum*, Ann Arbor, MI: Karoma.
Altmann, G. T. M. and M. J. Steedman (1988), 'Interaction with context during human sentence processing', *Cognition*, 30: 191–238.
Altmann, G. T. M., K. Y. van Nice, A. Garnham and J. A. Henstra (1998), 'Late closure in context', *Journal of Memory and Language*, 38: 459–84.
Altmann, L. J. P. and S. Kemper (2006), 'Effects of age, animacy and activation order on sentence production', *Language and Cognitive Processes*, 21 (1–3): 322–54.
Andersen, R. W. (1978), 'An implicational model for second language research', *Language Learning*, 28: 221–82.
Awad, M., J. E. Warren, S. K. Scott, F. E. Turkheimer and R. J. S. Wise (2007), 'A common system for the comprehension and production of narrative speech', *Journal of Neuroscience*, 27: 11455–64.
Badecker, W., M. Miozzo and R. Zanuttini (1995), 'The two-stage model of lexical retrieval: Evidence from a case of anomia with selective preservation of grammatical gender', *Cognition*, 57: 193–216.
Bailey, C.-J. N. (1973a), 'The patterning of linguistic variation', in R. Bailey and J. Robinson (eds), *Varieties of present-day English*, 156–87, New York: Macmillan.
Bailey, C.-J. N. (1973b), *Variation and linguistic theory*, Arlington, VA: Center for Applied Linguistics.
Barton, S. B. and A. J. Sanford (1993), 'A case study of anomaly detection: Shallow semantic processing and cohesion establishment', *Memory and Cognition*, 21: 477–87.
Basso, A., A. R. Lecours, S. Moraschini and M. Vanier (1985), 'Anatomoclinical correlations of the aphasias as defined through computerized tomography: Exceptions', *Brain and Language*, 26: 201–29.
Baten, K. (2013), *The acquisition of the German case system by foreign language learners*, Amsterdam: John Benjamins.
Baten, K. and J.-U. Keßler (2019), 'Research timeline. The role of instruction: Teachability and processability', in R. Arntzen, G. Håkansson, A. Hjelde and J.-U. Keßler (eds), *Teachability and learnability across languages*, 9–26, Amsterdam: John Benjamins.
Baten, K. and S. Verbeke (2015), 'The acquisition of the ergative case in Hindi as a foreign language', in K. Baten, M. Van Herreweghe, A. Buyl and K. Lochtmann (eds), *Theory development in Processability Theory*, 71–104, Amsterdam: John Benjamins.
Bates, E. and A. Devescovi (1989), 'Crosslinguistic studies of sentence production', in B. MacWhinney and E. Bates (eds), *The cross-linguistic study of sentence processing*, 225–53, New York: Cambridge University Press.

Bates, E., I. Bretherton and L. Snyder (1988), *From first words to grammar*, Cambridge: Cambridge University Press.

Bates, E., P. Dale and D. Thal (1995), 'Individual differences and their implications for theories of language development', in P. Fletcher and B. MacWhinney (eds), *Handbook of child language*, 96–151, Oxford: Basil Blackwell.

Bates, E., B. MacWhinney, C. Caselli, A. Devescovi, F. Natale and V. Venza (1984), 'A cross-linguistic study of the development of sentence interpretation strategies', *Child Development*, 55 (2): 341–54.

Bayley, R. (1999), 'The primacy of aspect hypothesis revisited: Evidence from language shift', *Southwest Journal of Sociolinguistics*, 18 (2): 1–22.

Beck, M.-L. (1998), 'L2 acquisition and obligatory head movement: English-speaking learners of German and the local impairment hypothesis', *Studies in Second Language Acquisition*, 20: 311–48.

Benedict, H. (1979), 'Early lexical development: Comprehension and production', *Journal of Child Language*, 6: 183–200.

Bever, T. G. (1970), 'The cognitive basis for linguistic structures', in J. R. Hayes (ed.), *Cognition and the development of language*, 279–362, New York: Wiley.

Bickerton, D. (1971), 'Inherent variability and variable rules', *Foundations of Language*, 7 (4): 457–92.

Bickerton, D. (1973), 'The nature of a creole continuum', *Language*, 49 (3): 640–69.

Binkofski, F., K. Amunts, K. M. Stephan, S. Posse, T. Schormann, H. J. Freund, K. Zilles and R. J. Seitz (2000), 'Broca's region subserves imagery of motion: A combined cytoarchitectonic and fMRI study', *Human Brain Mapping*, 11 (4): 273–85.

Bley-Vroman, R. and D. Masterson (1989), 'Reaction time as a supplement to grammaticality judgments in the investigation of second language learners' competence', *University of Hawaii Working Papers in ESL*, 8: 207–45.

Bloom, L. (1974), 'Talking, understanding, and thinking', in R. L. Schiefelbusch and L. L. Lloyd (eds), *Language perspectives: Acquisition, retardation and intervention*, 285–311, Baltimore, MD: University Park Press.

Blumstein, S. E. (1995), 'The neurobiology of the sound structure of language', in M. S. Gazzaniga (ed.), *The cognitive neurosciences*, 915–30, Cambridge, MA: MIT Press.

Bock, J. K. (1986), 'Syntactic persistence in language production', *Cognitive Psychology*, 18: 355–87.

Bock, J. K. (1987), 'Coordinating words and syntax in speech plans', in A. Ellis (ed.), *Progress in the psychology of language*, 337–90, London: Lawrence Erlbaum Associates.

Bock, J. K. and J. C. Cutting (1992), 'Regulating mental energy: Performance units in language production', *Journal of Memory and Language*, 31: 99–127.

Bock, J. K. and Z. M. Griffin (2000), 'The persistence of structural priming: Transient activation or implicit learning?' *Journal of Experimental Psychology: General*, 129: 177–92.

Bock, J. K. and W. J. M. Levelt (1994), 'Language production: Grammatical encoding', in M. A. Gernsbacher (ed.), *Handbook of psycholinguistics*, 945–84, London: Academic Press.

Bock, J. K. and C. A. Miller (1991), 'Broken agreement', *Cognitive Psychology*, 23 (1): 45–93.

Bock, J. K. and R. K. Warren (1985), 'Conceptual accessibility and syntactic structure in sentence formulation', *Cognition*, 21 (1): 47–67.

Bock, J. K., H. Loebell and R. Morey (1992), 'From conceptual roles to structural relations: Bridging the syntactic cleft', *Psychological Review*, 99 (1): 150–71.
Bock, J. K., G. S. Dell, F. Chang and K. H. Onishi (2007), 'Persistent structural priming from language comprehension to language production', *Cognition*, 104 (3): 437–58.
Branigan, H. P. (1995), 'Language processing and the mental representation of syntactic structure', PhD thesis, University of Edinburgh.
Branigan, H. P., M. J. Pickering and A. A Cleland (2000), 'Syntactic co-ordination in dialogue', *Cognition*, 75 (2): B13–B25.
Bresnan, J. (2001), *Lexical-functional syntax*, Malden, MA: Blackwell.
Bresnan, J., ed. (1982), *The mental representation of grammatical relations*, Cambridge, MA: MIT Press.
Bresnan, J. and J. M. Kanerva (1989), 'Locative inversion in Chicheŵa: A case study of factorization in grammar', *Linguistic Inquiry*, 20 (1): 1–50.
Bresnan, J. and R. M. Kaplan (1982), 'Introduction: Grammars as mental representations of language', in J. Bresnan (ed.), *The mental representation of grammatical relations*, xvii–lii, Cambridge, MA: MIT Press.
Brown, R. (1973), *A first language: The early stages*, Cambridge, MA: Harvard University Press.
Buyl, A. (2015), 'Studying receptive grammar acquisition within a PT framework', in K. Baten, A. Buyl, K. Lochtman and M. Van Herreweghe (eds), *Theoretical and methodological developments in Processability Theory*, 139–68, Amsterdam: John Benjamins.
Buyl, A. (2019), 'Is morphosyntactic decoding governed by Processability Theory?', in A. Lenzing, H. Nicholas and J. Roos (eds), *Widening contexts for Processability Theory: Theories and issues*, 73–101, Amsterdam: John Benjamins.
Buyl, A. and A. Housen (2013), 'Testing the applicability of PT to receptive grammar knowledge in early immersion education: Theoretical considerations, methodological challenges and some empirical results', in A. Flyman Mattson and C. Norrby (eds), *Language acquisition and use in multilingual contexts*, 13–27, Lund: Lund University Press.
Buyl, A. and A. Housen (2015), 'Developmental stages in receptive grammar acquisition: A Processability Theory account', *Second Language Research*, 31 (4): 523–50.
Carter, R. and M. McCarthy (1999), 'The English get-passive in spoken discourse: Description and implications for an interpersonal grammar', *English Language and Linguistics*, 3 (1): 41–58.
Chambers, S. and K. Forster (1975), 'Evidence for lexical access in a simultaneous matching task', *Memory and Cognition*, 3: 549–59.
Chan, A., E. Lieven and M. Tomasello (2009), 'Children's understanding of the agent-patient relations in the transitive construction: Cross-linguistic comparisons between Cantonese, German, and English', *Cognitive Linguistics*, 20: 267–300.
Chan, A., K. Meints, E. Lieven and M. Tomasello (2010), 'Young children's comprehension of English SVO word order revisited: Testing the same children in act-out and intermodal preferential looking tasks', *Cognitive Development*, 25: 30–45.
Chang, F. (2002), 'Symbolically speaking: A connectionist model of sentence production', *Cognitive Science*, 26 (5): 609–51.
Chapman, R. S. and L. L. Kohn (1978), 'Comprehension strategies in two- and three-year-olds: Animate agents or probable events?', *Journal of Speech and Hearing Research*, 21: 746–61.

Chapman, R. S. and J. F. Miller (1975), 'Word order in early two and three word utterances: Does production precede comprehension?', *Journal of Speech, Language, and Hearing Research*, 18: 355–71.
Christianson, K., S. G. Luke and F. Ferreira (2010), 'Effects of plausibility on structural priming', *Journal of Experimental Psychology: Learning, Memory, and Cognition*, 36: 538–44.
Christianson, K., A. Hollingworth, J. F. Halliwell and F. Ferreira (2001), 'Thematic roles assigned along the garden path linger', *Cognitive Psychology*, 42: 368–407.
Christianson, K., C. C. Williams, R. T. Zacks and F. Ferreira (2006), 'Younger and older adults' "good enough" interpretations of garden path sentences', *Discourse Processes*, 42: 205–38.
Clahsen, H. (1980), 'Psycholinguistic aspects of L2 acquisition', in S.W. Felix (ed.), *Second language development: Trends and issues*, 57–79, Tübingen: Narr.
Clahsen, H. and C. Felser (2006), 'Grammatical processing in language learners', *Applied Psycholinguistics*, 27: 3–42.
Clahsen, H. and C. Felser (2018), 'Some notes on the Shallow Structure Hypothesis', *Studies in Second Language Acquisition*, 40(3), 693–706.
Clahsen, H. and U. Hong (1995), 'Agreement and null subjects in German L2 development: New evidence from reaction-time experiments', *Second Language Research*, 11: 57–87.
Clark, E. V. (1980), 'Here's the top: Nonlinguistic strategies in the acquisition of orientational terms', *Child Development*, 51: 329–38.
Clark, E. V. (1993), *The lexicon in acquisition*, Cambridge: Cambridge University Press.
Clark, E. V. and B. F. Hecht (1983), 'Comprehension, production, and language acquisition', *Annual Review of Psychology*, 34: 325–49.
Clark, H. H. (1996), *Using language*, Cambridge: Cambridge University Press.
Clark, H. H. and B. C. Malt (1984), 'Psychological constraints on language: A commentary on Bresnan and Kaplan and on Givon', in W. Kintsch, J. R. Miller and P. G. Polson (eds), *Methods and tactics in cognitive science*, 191–214, Hillsdale, NJ: Lawrence Erlbaum Associates.
Cleland, A. A. and M. J. Pickering (2003), 'The use of lexical and syntactic information in language production: Evidence from the priming of noun-phrase structure', *Journal of Memory and Language*, 49: 214–30.
Clifton, C., L. Frazier and C. Connine (1984), 'Lexical expectations in sentence comprehension', *Journal of Verbal Learning and Verbal Behavior*, 23 (6): 696–708.
Clifton, C., S. Speer and S. P. Abney (1991), 'Parsing arguments: Phrase structure and argument structure as determinants of initial parsing decisions', *Journal of Memory and Language*, 30 (2): 251–71.
Clifton, C., M. J. Traxler, R. Williams, M. Mohammed, R. K. Morris and K. Rayner (2003), 'The use of thematic role information in parsing: Syntactic processing autonomy revisited', *Journal of Memory and Language*, 49: 317–34.
Cook, A. E. (2014), 'Processing anomalous anaphors', *Memory and Cognition*, 42 (7): 1171–85.
Corrigan, R. (1986), 'The internal structure of English transitive sentences', *Cognition*, 14: 420–31.
Crain, S. and J. Fodor (1987), 'Sentence matching and overgeneration', *Cognition*, 26: 123–69.
Crain, S. and M. Steedman (1985), 'On not being led up the garden path: The use of context by the psychological syntax processor', in D. R. Dowty, L. Karttunen and

A. M. Zwicky (eds), *Natural language parsing*, 320–58, Cambridge: Cambridge University Press.
Crocker, M. W. (1995), *Computational psycholinguistics: An interdisciplinary approach to the study of language*, Dordrecht: Kluwer.
Crystal, D., P. Fletcher and M. Garman (1976), *The grammatical analysis of language disability*, London: Arnold.
Dalrymple, M. (2001), *Syntax and semantics: Lexical functional grammar*, Vol. 34, San Diego: Academic Press.
De Bot, K. (1992), 'A bilingual production model: Levelt's "Speaking" model adapted', *Applied Linguistics*, 13 (1): 1–24.
DeCamp, D. (1971), 'Toward a generative analysis of a post-creole speech continuum', in D. Hymes (ed.), *Pidginization and creolization of languages*, 349–70, New York: Cambridge University Press.
Dell, G. S. (1986), 'A spreading-activation theory of retrieval in sentence production', *Psychological Review*, 93: 283–321.
Dell, G. S. and P. G. O'Seaghda (1991), 'Mediated and convergent lexical priming in language production: A comment on Levelt et al.', *Psychological Review*, 98: 604–14.
Dell, G. S., F. Chang and Z. M. Griffin (1999), 'Connectionist models of language production: Lexical access and grammatical encoding', *Cognitive Science*, 23: 517–42.
Di Biase, B. (2008), 'Focus-on-form and development in L2 learning', in J.-U. Keßler (ed.), *Processability approaches to second language development and second language learning*, 197–219, Newcastle upon Tyne: Cambridge Scholars Publishing.
Di Biase, B. and S. Kawaguchi (2002), 'Exploring the typological plausibility of Processability Theory: Language development in Italian second language and Japanese second language', *Second Language Research*, 18: 272–300.
Dineen, L. C. and B. C. Blakesley (1973), 'Algorithm AS 62: Generator for the sampling distribution of the Mann-Whitney U statistic', *Applied Statistics*, 22: 269–73.
Dittmar, N. (1980), 'Ordering adult learners according to language abilities', in S. Felix (ed.), *Second language development*, 205–31, Tübingen: Narr.
Duffield, N. and L. White (1999), 'Assessing L2 knowledge of Spanish clitic placement: Convergent methodologies', *Second Language Research*, 15: 133–60.
Duffield, N., A. Matsuo and L. Roberts (2007). 'Acceptable ungrammaticality in sentence matching', *Second Language Research*, 23 (2): 155–77.
Duffield, N., P. Prévost and L. White (1997), 'A psycholinguistic investigation of clitic placement in second language acquisition', in E. Hughes, M. Hughes and A. Greenhill (eds), *Proceedings of the 21st Boston University conference on language development*, 148–59, Somerville, MA: Cascadilla Press.
Duffield, N., S. Montrul, J. Bruhn de Garavito and L. White (1998). 'Determining L2 knowledge of Spanish clitics on-line and off-line', in A. Greenhill, M. Hughes, H. Littlefield and H. Walsh (eds), *Proceedings of the 22nd Boston University conference on language development*, 177–88, Somerville, MA: Cascadilla Press.
Dulay, H. and M. K. Burt (1974), 'Natural sequences in child second language acquisition', *Language Learning*, 24 (1): 37–53.
Dunn-Rankin, P. (1983), *Scaling methods*, Hillsdale, NJ: Lawrence Erlbaum Associates.
Dyson, B. (2010), 'Learner language analytic methods and pedagogical implications', *Australian Review of Applied Linguistics*, 33 (3): 30.1–30.21.
Edwards, A. (1948), 'On Guttman's scale analysis', *Educational and Psychological Measurement*, 8: 313–18.

Eisele, J. and B. Lust (1996), 'Knowledge about pronouns: A developmental study using a truth-value judgement task', *Child Development*, 67 (6): 3086–100.
Ellis, N. C. (2012), 'Frequency-based accounts of SLA', in S. Gass and A. Mackey (eds), *Handbook of second language acquisition*, 193–210, London: Routledge and Taylor & Francis.
Ellis, R. (1994), *The study of second language acquisition*, Oxford: Oxford University Press.
Ellis, R. (2003), *Task-based language learning and teaching*, Oxford: Oxford University Press.
Ellis, R. (2005), 'Measuring implicit and explicit knowledge of a second language: A psychometric study', *Studies in Second Language Acquisition*, 27: 141–72.
Ellis, R. (2008), 'Investigating grammatical difficulty in second language learning: Implications for second language acquisition research and language testing', *International Journal of Applied Linguistics*, 18: 4–22.
Ellis, R. and S. Loewen (2007), 'Confirming the operational definitions of explicit and implicit knowledge in Ellis (2005)', *Studies in Second Language Acquisition*, 29 (1): 119–126.
Erickson, T. A. and M. E. Mattson (1981), 'From words to meaning: A semantic illusion', *Journal of Verbal Learning and Verbal Behavior*, 20 (5): 540–51.
Eubank, L. (1993), 'Sentence matching and processing in L2 development', *Second Language Research*, 9: 253–80.
Falk, Y. (2001), *Lexical-functional grammar: An introduction to parallel constraint-based syntax*, Stanford: CSLI Publications.
Ferreira, F. (2003), 'The misinterpretation of noncanonical sentences', *Cognitive Psychology*, 47: 164–203.
Ferreira, F. and C. Clifton Jr. (1986), 'The independence of syntactic processing', *Journal of Memory and Language*, 25: 348–68.
Ferreira, F., K. G. D. Bailey and V. Ferraro (2002), 'Good enough representations in language comprehension', *Current Directions in Psychological Science*, 11: 11–15.
Ferreira, F., K. Christianson and A. Hollingworth (2001), 'Misinterpretations of garden-path sentences: Implications for models of sentence processing and reanalysis', *Journal of Psycholinguistic Research*, 30 (1): 3–20.
Ferreira, F. and N. D. Patson (2007), 'The "good enough" approach to language comprehension', *Language and Linguistics Compass*, 1: 71–83.
Ferreira, F., P. E. Engelhardt and M. W. Jones (2009), 'Good enough language processing: A satisficing approach', in N. Taatgen, H. Rijn, J. Nerbonne and L. Schomaker (eds), *Proceedings of the 31st Annual Conference of the Cognitive Science Society*, 413–18, Austin, TX: Cognitive Science Society.
Ferreira, V. S. and L. R. Slevc (2007), 'Grammatical encoding', in M. G. Gaskell (ed.), *The Oxford handbook of psycholinguistics*, 453–69, Oxford: Oxford University Press.
Ferreira, V. S., A. Morgan and L. R. Slevc (2018), 'Grammatical encoding', in S. Rueschemeyer and M. G. Gaskell (eds), *The Oxford handbook of psycholinguistics*, 2nd edn, 432–57, Oxford: Oxford University Press.
Ferreira, F. and J. Stacey (2000), 'The misinterpretation of passive sentences', unpublished manuscript.
Flores d'Arcais, G. B. (1975), 'Some perceptual determinants of sentence construction', in G. B. Flores D'Arcais (ed.), *Studies in perception*, 344–75, Milan: Martello-Giunti.
Flynn, S. and B. C. Lust (1980), 'Acquisition of relative clauses: Developmental changes in their heads', *Cornell Working Papers in Linguistics*, 1: 33–45.

Foley, C.A., Z. Núñez Del Prado, I. Barbier and B. C. Lust (1997), 'Operator-variable binding in the initial state: An argument from English VP ellipsis', *Cornell Working Papers in Linguistics*, 15: 1–19.

Ford, M. (1982), 'Sentence planning units: Implications for the speaker's representation of meaningful relations underlying sentences', in J. Bresnan (ed.), *The mental representation of grammatical relations*, 797–827, Cambridge, MA: MIT Press.

Ford, M. and V. M. Holmes (1978), 'Planning units and syntax in sentence production', *Cognition*, 6: 35–53.

Forster, K. (1979), 'Levels of processing and the structure of the language processor', in W. E. Cooper and E. Walker (eds), *Sentence processing: Psycholinguistic studies presented to Merrill Garrett*, 27–85, Hillsdale, NJ: Lawrence Erlbaum Associates.

Frazier, L. (1987), 'Sentence processing: A tutorial review', in M. Coltheart (ed.), *Attention and performance*, 559–86, Hillsdale, NJ: Lawrence Erlbaum Associates.

Frazier, L. (1990), 'Exploring the architecture of the language system', in G. Altmann (ed.), *Cognitive models of speech processing: Psycholinguistic and computational perspectives*, 409–33, Cambridge, MA: MIT Press.

Frazier, L. and C. Clifton Jr. (1996), *Construal*, Cambridge, MA: MIT Press.

Frazier, L. and K. Rayner (1982), 'Making and correcting errors during sentence comprehension: Eye movements in the analysis of structurally ambiguous sentences', *Cognitive Psychology*, 14: 178–210.

Freedman, S. and K. Forster (1985), 'The psychological status of overgenerated sentences', *Cognition*, 19: 101–31.

Freegard, G. (2012), *Response pads: The design, development and results of a bespoke response box, and subsequent testing, for comparison purposes, of various devices used for reaction time measurements in psychological experiments*', University of Swansea. Available online: http://psy.swan.ac.uk/staff/freegard/Response%20Box%20Report.pdf (accessed 16 September 2017).

Friederici, A. D. (1998), 'The neurobiology of language comprehension', in A. D. Friederici (ed.), *Language comprehension: A biological perspective*, 263–301, Berlin: Springer.

Friederici, A. D. (2002), 'Towards a neural basis of auditory sentence processing', *Trends in Cognitive Sciences*, 1 (6): 78–84.

Friedman, N. and R. Novogrodsky (2004), 'The acquisition of relative clause comprehension in Hebrew: A study of SLI and normal development', *Journal of Child Language*, 31 (3): 661–81.

Gambi, C. and M. Pickering (2017), 'Models linking production and comprehension', in E. M. Fernández and H. Smith Cairns (eds), *The handbook of psycholinguistics*, 7: 157–82, Malden, MA: Wiley-Blackwell.

Garrett, M. F. (1976), 'Syntactic processes in sentence production', in R. Wales and E. Walker (eds), *New approaches to language mechanisms*, 231–56, Amsterdam: North Holland.

Garrett, M. F. (1980), 'Levels of processing in language production', in B. Butterworth (ed.), *Language production, Vol. 1: Speech and talk*, 170–220, London: Academic Press.

Garrett, M. F. (1982), 'Production of speech: Observations from normal and pathological language use', in A. W. Ellis (ed.), *Normality and pathology in cognitive functions*, 19–76, London: Academic Press.

Garrett, M. F. (1988), 'Processes in language production', in F. J. Newmeyer (ed.), *Linguistics: The Cambridge survey, Vol. 3: Language, psychological and biological aspects*, 69–96, Cambridge: Cambridge University Press.

Garrett, M. F. (2000), 'Remarks on the architecture of language processing systems', in Y. Grodzinsky and L. Shapiro (eds), *Language and the brain: Representation and processing*, 31–69, San Diego: Academic Press.

Gass, S. (2001), 'Sentence matching: A re-examination', *Second Language Research*, 17 (4): 421–41.

Gazzaniga, M., R. B. Ivry and G. R. Mangun (2002), *Cognitive neuroscience: The biology of the mind*, New York: W.W. Norton.

Georgiades, M. S. and J. P. Harris (1997), 'Biasing effects in ambiguous figures: Removal or fixation of critical features can affect perception', *Visual Cognition*, 4: 383–408.

Gerngross, G. and H. Puchta (2008a), *Playway 3 rainbow edition: Teacher's book*, Innsbruck: Helbling.

Gerngross, G. and H. Puchta (2008b), *Playway 4 rainbow edition: Teacher's book*, Innsbruck: Helbling.

Gertner, Y., C. Fisher and J. Eisengart (2006), 'Learning words and rules: Abstract knowledge of word order in early sentence comprehension', *Psychological Science*, 17: 684–91.

Gibson, E. and N. J. Pearlmutter (1994), 'A corpus-based analysis of psycholinguistic constraints on prepositional-phrase attachment', in C. Clifton, L. Frazier and K. Rayner (eds), *Perspectives on sentence processing*, 181–98, Hillsdale, NJ: Lawrence Erlbaum Associates.

Gilquin, G. (2006), 'The place of prototypicality in corpus linguistics: Causation in the hot seat', in S. T. Gries and A. Stefanowitsch (eds), *Corpora in cognitive linguistics: Corpus-based approaches to syntax and lexis*, 159–92, Berlin: de Gruyter.

Givón, T. (1986), 'Prototypes: Between Plato and Wittgenstein', in C. Craig (ed.), *Noun classes and categorization*, 77–102, Amsterdam: John Benjamins.

Glahn, E., G. Håkansson, B. Hammarberg, A. Holmen, A. Hvenekilde and K. Lund (2001), 'Processability in Scandinavian second language acquisition', *Studies in Second Language Acquisition*, 23 (3): 389–416.

Glaser, W. R. and F.-J. Düngelhoff (1984), 'The time course of picture-word interference', *Journal of Experimental Psychology: Human Perception and Performance*, 10: 640–54.

Gleitman, L. R., D. January, R. Nappa and J. C. Trueswell (2007), 'On the give and take between event apprehension and utterance formulation', *Journal of Memory and Language*, 57 (4): 544–69.

Goldrick, M. (2007), 'Connectionist principles in theories of speech production', in M. G. Gaskell (ed.), *The Oxford handbook of psycholinguistics*, 515–30, Oxford: Oxford University Press.

Goodenough, W. H. (1944), 'A technique for scale analysis', *Educational and Psychological Measurement*, 4: 179–90.

Goodluck, H. (1996), 'The act-out task', in D. McDaniel, C. McKee and H. Smith Cairns (eds), *Methods for assessing children's syntax*, 147–62, Cambridge, MA: MIT Press.

Gordon, P. C., R. Hendrick and M. Johnson (2001), 'Memory interference during language processing', *Journal of Experimental Psychology: Learning, Memory, and Cognition*, 27: 1411–23.

Gordon, P. C., R. Hendrick and M. Johnson (2004), 'Effects of noun phrase type on sentence complexity', *Journal of Memory and Language*, 51: 97–114.

Griffin, Z. M. and V. S. Ferreira (2006), 'Properties of spoken language production', in M. J. Traxler and M. A. Gernsbacher (eds), *Handbook of psycholinguistics*, 2nd edn, 21–59, Amsterdam: Academic Press.

Grosjean, F. (2013), 'Speech production', in F. Grosjean and P. Li (2013), *The psycholinguistics of bilingualism*, 50–69, Malden, MA: Wiley-Blackwell.

Grüter, T. (2005), 'Comprehension and production of French object clitics by child second language learners and children with specific language impairment', *Applied Psycholinguistics*, 26: 363–91.

Guest, G. (2000), 'Using Guttman scaling to rank wealth: Integrating quantitative and qualitative data', *Field Methods*, 12 (4): 346–57.

Guttman, L. A. (1944), 'A basis for scaling qualitative data', *American Sociological Review*, 91: 139–50.

Haberzettl, S. (2005), *Der Erwerb der Verbstellung in der Zweitsprache Deutsch durch Kinder mit typologisch verschiedenen Muttersprachen. Eine Auseinandersetzung mit Theorien zum Syntaxerwerb anhand von vier Fallstudien*, Tübingen: Niemeyer.

Hagoort, P. (2005), 'On Broca, brain, and binding: A new framework', *Trends in Cognitive Sciences*, 9 (9): 416–23.

Hagoort, P. (2006), 'On Broca, brain and binding', in Y. Grodzinsky and K. Amunts (eds), *Broca's region*, 240–51, Oxford: Oxford University Press.

Håkansson, G., M. Pienemann and S. Sayehli (2002), 'Transfer and typological proximity in the context of second language processing', *Second Language Research*, 18 (3): 250–73.

Hakuta, K. (1982), 'Interaction between particles and word order in the comprehension of simple sentences in Japanese children', *Developmental Psychology*, 18: 62–76.

Han, Y. and R. Ellis (1998), 'Implicit knowledge, explicit knowledge and general language proficiency', *Language Teaching Research*, 2: 1–23.

Hatch, E. and H. Farhady (1982), *Research design and statistics for applied linguistics*, Rowley: Newbury House.

Hatch, E. and A. Lazaraton (1991), *The research manual: Design and statistics for applied linguistics*, Rowley: Newbury House.

Hatcher, A. G. (1949), 'To get/be invited', *Modern Language Notes*, 64 (7): 433–46.

Hendriks, P. (2014), *Asymmetries between language production and comprehension*, Dordrecht: Springer.

Hill, F. (1998), 'Acquisition of the passive', *Kansas Working Papers in Linguistics*, 23 (2): 63–70.

Hollbrügge, B. and U. Kraaz (2008), *Ginger 1*, Berlin: Cornelsen.

Holmes, V. M. (1988), 'Hesitations and sentence planning', *Language and Cognitive Processes*, 3: 323–61.

Hopper, P. J. and S. A. Thompson (1980), 'Transitivity in grammar and discourse', *Language*, 56: 251–97.

Huang, J. and E. Hatch (1978), 'A Chinese child's acquisition of English', in E. Hatch (ed.), *Second language acquisition: A book of readings*, 118–31, Rowley: Newbury House Publishers.

Huddleston, R. (1984), *Introduction to the grammar of English*, Cambridge: Cambridge University Press.

Hulme, C. and M. J. Snowling (2014), 'The interface between spoken and written language disorders', *Philosophical Transactions of the Royal Society B*, 369 (1634): 1–8.

Ibbotson, P. and M. Tomasello (2009), 'Prototype constructions in early language acquisition', *Language and Cognition*, 1: 59–85.

Imbo, I., A. Szmalec and A. Vandierendonck (2009), 'The role of structure in age-related increases in visuo-spatial working memory span', *Psychologica Belgica*, 49 (4): 275–91.

Itani-Adams, Y. (2007), 'Lexical and grammatical development in Japanese-English bilingual first language acquisition', in F. Mansouri (ed.), *Second language acquisition research: Theory-construction and testing*, 173–98, Cambridge: Cambridge Scholars Press.

Jackendoff, R. (1972), *Semantic interpretation in generative grammar*, Cambridge, MA: MIT Press.

Jaeger, T. F. (2010), 'Redundancy and reduction: Speakers manage syntactic information density', *Cognitive Psychology*, 61: 23–62.

Jegerski, J. (2014), 'Self-paced reading', in J. Jegerski and B. VanPatten (eds), *Research methods in second language psycholinguistics*, 20–49, New York: Routledge.

Jiang, N. (2012), *Conducting reaction time research in second language acquisition*, New York: Routledge.

Johnson-Laird, P. N. (1968), 'The choice of the passive voice in a communicative task', *British Journal of Psychology*, 59 (1): 7–15.

Johnstone, R. (2000), 'Context-sensitive assessment of modern languages in primary (elementary) and early secondary education: Scotland and the European experience', *Language Testing*, 17 (2): 123–43.

Just, M. A. and P. A. Carpenter (1980), 'A theory of reading: From eye fixations to comprehension', *Psychological Review*, 87: 329–54.

Just, M. A. and P. A. Carpenter (1992), 'A capacity theory of comprehension: Individual differences in working memory', *Psychological Review*, 99: 122–49.

Kaplan, R. M. and J. Bresnan (1982), 'Lexical-functional grammar: A formal system for grammatical representation', in J. Bresnan (ed.), *The mental representation of grammatical relations*, 173–281, Cambridge, MA: MIT Press.

Karimi, H. and F. Ferreira (2016), 'Good-enough linguistic representations and online cognitive equilibrium in language processing', *Quarterly Journal of Experimental Psychology*, 69 (5): 1013–40.

Katz, J. J. and J. A. Fodor (1963), 'The structure of a semantic theory', *Language*, 39 (2): 170–210.

Kawaguchi, S. (1999), 'The acquisition of syntax and nominal ellipsis in JSL discourse', in P. Robinson (ed.), *Representation and process: Proceedings of the Third Pacific Second Language Research Forum*, 1: 85–93, Tokyo: Pacific Second Language Research Forum.

Kawaguchi, S. (2005), 'Argument structure and syntactic development in Japanese as a second language', in M. Pienemann (ed.), *Cross-linguistic aspects of Processability Theory*, 253–98, Amsterdam: John Benjamins.

Kawaguchi, S. (2016), 'Question constructions, argument mapping, and vocabulary development in English L2 by Japanese speakers: A cross-sectional study', in J.-U. Keßler, A. Lenzing and M. Liebner (eds), *Developing, modelling and assessing second languages*, 35–64, Amsterdam: John Benjamins.

Kawaguchi, S. and B. Di Biase (2012), 'Acquiring procedural skills in L2: Processability theory and skill acquisition', *Studies in Language Sciences*, 11: 68–95.

Keatinge, D. and J.-U. Keßler (2009), 'The acquisition of the passive voice in L2-English: Perception and production', in J.-U. Keßler and D. Keatinge (eds), *Research in second language acquisition: Empirical evidence across languages*, 69–94, Newcastle upon Tyne: Cambridge Scholars Publishing.

Keenan, E. L. (1987), *Universal grammar: 15 Essays*, London: Croom Helm.

Kempen, G. (1996), 'Computational models of syntactic processing in human language comprehension', in T. Dijkstra and K. De Smedt (eds), *Computational psycholinguistics:*

Symbolic and subsymbolic models of language processing, 192–220, London: Taylor & Francis.
Kempen, G. (1999), *Human grammatical coding*, Unpublished manuscript.
Kempen, G. (2000), 'Could grammatical encoding and grammatical decoding be subserved by the same processing module?', *Behavioral and Brain Sciences*, 23: 38–9.
Kempen, G. (2014), 'Prolegomena to a neurocomputational architecture for human grammatical encoding and decoding', *Neuroinformatics*, 12: 111–42.
Kempen, G. and E. Hoenkamp (1987), 'An incremental procedural grammar for sentence formulation', *Cognitive Science*, 11 (2): 201–58.
Kempen, G., N. Olsthoorn and S. Sprenger (2012), 'Grammatical workspace sharing during language production and language comprehension: Evidence from grammatical multitasking', *Language and Cognitive Processes*, 27: 345–80.
Kennison, S. M. (2001), 'Limitations on the use of verb information during sentence comprehension', *Psychonomic Bulletin & Review*, 8: 132–8.
Kersten, K., A. Rohde, C. Schelletter and A. K. Steinlen, eds (2010), *Bilingual preschools, Vol 1: Learning and development*, Trier: Wissenschaftliger Verlag Trier.
Keßler, J.-U. (2006), *Englischerwerb im Anfangsunterricht diagnostizieren. Linguistische Profilanalysen und der Übergang von der Primar- in die Sekundarstufe I*, Giessener Beiträge zur Fremdsprachendidaktik, Tübingen: Narr.
Keßler, J.-U. and M. Pienemann (2011), 'Research methodology: How we know about developmental schedules', in M. Pienemann and J.-U. Keßler (eds), *Studying Processability Theory: An introductory textbook*, 83–96, Amsterdam: John Benjamins.
Kibort, A. (2004), 'Passive and passive-like constructions in English and Polish', PhD thesis, University of Cambridge.
Kibort, A. (2005), 'The ins and outs of the participle-adjective conversion rule', in M. Butt and T. Holloway King (eds), *Proceedings of the LFG05 conference, University of Bergen*, 205–25, Stanford, CA: CSLI Publications.
Kim, A. and L. Osterhout (2005), 'The independence of combinatory semantic processing: Evidence from event-related potentials', *Journal of Memory and Language*, 52: 205–25.
Kim, M. (2008), 'A cognitive approach to the acquisition of passives in Korean', *Berkeley Linguistics Society*, 34 (1): 199–207.
Kimball, J. (1973), 'Seven principles of surface structure parsing in natural language', *Cognition*, 2: 15–47.
Klin, C. M., A. E. Guzman, K. M. Weingartner and A. S. Ralano (2006), 'When anaphor resolution fails: Partial encoding of anaphoric inferences', *Journal of Memory and Language*, 54: 131–43.
Kolk, H. H. J. (1998), 'Disorders of syntax in aphasia', in B. Stemmer and H. A. Whitaker (eds), *Handbook of neurolinguistics*, 249–60, San Diego, CA: Academic Press.
Kolk, H. H. J. and A. D. Friederici (1985), 'Strategy and impairment in sentence understanding by Broca's and Wernicke's aphasics', *Cortex*, 21: 47–67.
Kolk, H. H. J., D. J. Chwilla, M. van Herten and P. J. W. Oor (2003), 'Structure and limited capacity in verbal working memory: A study with event-related potentials', *Brain and Language*, 85: 1–36.
Kormos, J. (2006), *Speech production and second language acquisition*, Mahwah, NJ: Lawrence Erlbaum Associates.
Kroeger, P. R. (2004), *Analyzing syntax: A lexical-functional approach*, Cambridge: Cambridge University Press.
Kuperberg, G. R. (2007), 'Neural mechanisms of language comprehension: Challenges to syntax', *Brain Research*, 18 (1146): 23–49.

Labov, W. (1973), 'The boundaries of words and their meanings', in C.-J. Bailey and R. W. Schuy (eds), *New ways of analysing variation in English*, 340–73, Washington, DC: Georgetown University Press.

Lakoff, G. (1987), *Women, fire, and dangerous things: What categories reveal about the mind*, Chicago: University of Chicago Press.

Lameli, A. (2004), 'Hierarchies of dialect features in a diachronic view: Implicational scaling of real time data', in B.-L. Gunnarsson, L. Bergström, G. Eklund, S. Fridell and L. H. Hansen (eds), *Language variation in Europe: Papers from the second international conference on language variation in Europe (ICLaVE 2), Uppsala-University, Sweden, June 12–14: 2003*, 253–66, Uppsala: Uppsala University Press.

Langacker, R. W. (1987), *Foundations of cognitive grammar, Vol. 2: Descriptive application*, Stanford, CA: Stanford University Press.

Larsen-Freeman, D. and M. Long (1991), *An introduction to second language acquisition research*, London: Longman.

Lempert, H. (1978), 'Extrasyntactic factors affecting passive sentence comprehension by young children', *Child Development*, 49 (3): 694–9.

Lempert, H. (1990), 'Acquisition of passives: The role of patient animacy, salience, and lexical accessibility', *Journal of Child Language*, 17 (3): 677–96.

Lenzing, A. (2008), 'Teachability and learnability: An analysis of primary school textbooks', in J.-U. Keßler (ed.), *Processability Approaches to second language development and second language learning*, 221–41, Newcastle upon Tyne: Cambridge Scholars Publishing.

Lenzing, A. (2013), *The development of the grammatical system in early second language acquisition: The Multiple Constraints Hypothesis*, Amsterdam: John Benjamins.

Lenzing, A. (2015a), 'Constraints on processing: L1 transfer and the L2 initial mental grammatical system', in K. Baten, M. Van Herreweghe, A. Buyl and K. Lochtmann (eds), *Theory development in Processability Theory*, 113–38, Amsterdam: John Benjamins.

Lenzing, A. (2015b), 'Exploring regularities and dynamic systems in L2 development', *Language Learning*, 65 (1): 89–122.

Lenzing, A. (2016), 'The development of argument structure in the grammatical system of early L2 learners', in J.-U. Keßler, A. Lenzing and M. Liebner (eds), *Developing, modelling and assessing second languages*, 3–34, Amsterdam: John Benjamins.

Lenzing, A. (2019), 'Towards an integrated model of grammatical encoding and decoding in SLA', in A. Lenzing, H. Nicholas and J. Roos (eds), *Widening contexts for Processability Theory: Theories and issues*, 13–48, Amsterdam: John Benjamins.

Lenzing, A. and M. Pienemann (2015), 'Exploring the interface between morphosyntax and discourse/pragmatics/semantics', in K. Baten, M. Van Herreweghe, A. Buyl and K. Lochtmann (eds), *Theory development in Processability Theory*, 105–12, Amsterdam: John Benjamins.

Lenzing, A., H. Nicholas and J. Roos (eds) (2019), *Widening contexts for Processability Theory: Theories and issues*, Amsterdam: John Benjamins.

Levelt, W. J. M. (1989), *Speaking: From intention to articulation*, Cambridge, MA: MIT Press.

Levelt, W. J. M. (1999), 'Producing spoken language: A blueprint of the speaker', in P. Hagoort and C. M. Brown (eds), *The neurocognition of language*, 94–122, Oxford: Oxford University Press.

Levelt, W. J. M. (2000), 'Psychology of language', in K. Pawlik and M. K. Rosenzweig, (eds), *International handbook of psychology*, 151–67, London: SAGE Publications.

Levelt, W. J. M. (2001), 'Relations between speech production and speech perception: Some behavioral and neurological observations', in E. Dupoux (ed.), *Language, brain and cognitive development: Essays in honour of Jacques Mehler*, 241–56, Cambridge, MA: MIT Press.

Levelt, W. J. M., A. Roelofs and A. S. Meyer (1999), 'A theory of lexical access in speech production', *Behavioral and Brain Sciences*, 22: 1–75.

Levine, W. H., A. E. Guzman and C. M. Klin (2000), 'When anaphor resolution fails', *Journal of Memory and Language*, 43: 594–617.

Long, M. H. and C. J. Sato (1984), 'Methodological issues in interlanguage studies: An interactionist perspective', in A. Davies, C. Criper and A. P. R. Howatt (eds), *Interlanguage*, 253–80, Edinburgh: Edinburgh University Press.

Love, T., M. Walenski and D. Swinney (2009), 'Slowed speech input has a differential impact on on-line and off-line processing in children's comprehension of pronouns', *Journal of Psycholinguistic Research*, 38 (3): 285–304.

Luka, B. J. and H. Choi (2012), 'Dynamic grammar in adults: Incidental learning of natural syntactic structures extends over 48 h', *Journal of Memory and Language*, 66: 345–60.

Lust, B. and M. Blume (2016), *Research methods in language acquisition: Principles, procedures, and practices*, Berlin: De Gruyter Mouton.

MacDonald, J. L., J. K. Bock and M. H. Kelly (1993), 'Word and world order: Semantic, phonological, and metrical determinants of serial position', *Cognitive Psychology*, 25: 188–230.

MacDonald, M. C. and M. H. Christiansen (2002), 'Reassessing working memory: Comment on Just and Carpenter (1992) and Waters and Caplan (1996)', *Psychological Review*, 109: 35–54.

MacDonald, M. C. and Y. Hsiao (2018), 'Sentence comprehension', in S. Rueschemeyer and M. G. Gaskell (eds), *The Oxford handbook of psycholinguistics*, 2nd edn, 171–91, Oxford: Oxford University Press.

MacDonald, M. C. and M. S. Seidenberg (2006), 'Constraint satisfaction accounts of lexical and sentence comprehension', in M. J. Traxler and M. A. Gernsbacher (eds), *Handbook of psycholinguistics*, 2nd edn, 581–612, San Diego: Academic Press.

MacDonald, M. C., N. J. Pearlmutter and M. S. Seidenberg (1994), 'The lexical nature of syntactic ambiguity resolution', *Psychological Review*, 101: 676–703.

Mackey, A., M. Pienemann and I. Thornton (1991), 'Rapid Profile: A second language screening procedure', *Language and Language Education: Working Papers of the National Languages Institute of Australia*, 1: 61–82.

Maess, B., S. Koelsch, T. C. Gunter and A. D. Friederici (2001), 'Musical syntax is processed in the area of Broca: An MEG study', *Nature Neuroscience*, 4: 540–5.

Maratsos, M. P. (1974), 'Children who get worse at understanding the passive: A replication of Bever', *Journal of Psycholinguistic Research*, 3 (1): 65–74.

Maratsos, M. P., D. Fox, J. Becker and M. Chalkley (1985), 'Semantic restrictions on children's passives', *Cognition*, 19: 167–91.

Marchman, V. A., E. Bates, A. Burkardt and A. B. Good (1991), 'Functional constraints of the acquisition of the passive: Toward a model of the competence to perform', *First Language*, 11 (31): 65–92.

McClelland, J. L. (1998), 'Connectionist models and Bayesian inference', in M. Oaksford and N. Chater (eds), *Rational models of cognition*, 21–52, New York: Oxford University Press.

McIver, J. P. and E. G. Carmines (1981), *Unidimensional scaling*, Beverly Hills, CA: SAGE Publications.

McRae, K., M. J. Spivey-Knowlton and M. K. Tanenhaus (1998), 'Modeling the influence of thematic fit (and other constraints) in on-line sentence comprehension', *Journal of Memory and Language*, 38: 283–312.

Medojevic, L. (2014), 'The effect of the first year of schooling on bilingual language development: A study of second and third generation Serbian-Australian 5-year-old bilingual children from a processability perspective', PhD thesis, University of Western Sydney.

Meints, K. (1999a), 'Prototypes and the acquisition of the English passive', in B. Kokinov (ed.), *Perspectives on cognitive science*, 4: 67–77, Sofia: NBU Press.

Meints, K. (1999b), *Typizitätseffekte im Erwerb des englischen Passivs: Eine empirische Untersuchung*, Wiesbaden: DUV.

Meisel, J., H. Clahsen and M. Pienemann (1981), 'On determining developmental sequences in natural second language acquisition', *Studies in Second Language Acquisition*, 3 (2): 109–35.

Menenti, L., S. M. Gierhan, K. Segaert and P. Hagoort (2011), 'Shared language: Overlap and segregation of the neuronal infrastructure for speaking and listening revealed by functional MRI', *Psychological Science*, 22 (9): 1173–82.

Menzel, H. (1953), 'A new coefficient for scalogram analysis', *Public Opinion Quarterly*, 17: 268–80.

Mervis, C. B. and E. Rosch (1981), 'Categorization of natural objects', *Annual Review of Psychology*, 32: 89–115.

Meyer, A., F. Huettig and W. Levelt (2016), 'Same, different, or closely related: What is the relationship between language production and comprehension?', *Journal of Memory and Language*, 89: 1–7.

Miller, G.A. (1962), 'Some psychological studies of grammar', *American Psychologist*, 17 (11): 748–62.

Mitchell, D.C. (1994), 'Sentence Parsing', in M. A. Gernsbacher (ed.), *Handbook of psycholinguistics*, 375–409, San Diego, CA: Academic Press.

Mitchell, D.C. and V. M. Holmes (1985), 'The role of specific information about the verb in parsing sentences with local structural ambiguity', *Journal of Memory and Language*, 24: 542–59.

Naghdipour, B. (2015), 'The impact of L1 reading directionality mode on L2 reading fluency', *Journal of AsiaTEFL*, 12 (1): 53–77.

Nagy, N., C. Moisset and G. Sankoff (1996), 'On the acquisition of variable phonology in L2', *University of Pennsylvania Working Papers in Linguistics*, 3 (1): 111–26.

Nicholas, H., A. Lenzing and J. Roos (2016), 'Old wine in new bottles? Mastering re-emerged concepts'. Paper presented at the *16th International Symposium of Processability Approaches to Language Acquisition (PALA)*, Chuo University, Tokyo, Japan.

Nicholas, H., A. Lenzing and J. Roos (2019), 'How does PT's view of acquisition relate to the challenge of widening perspectives on SLA?', in A. Lenzing, H. Nicholas and J. Roos (eds), *Widening contexts for Processability Theory: Theories and issues*, 391–8, Amsterdam: John Benjamins.

Nicol, J. L., K. I. Forster and C. Veres (1997), 'Subject-verb agreement processes in comprehension', *Journal of Memory and Language*, 36 (4): 569–87.

Nozari, N., G. S. Dell and M. F. Schwartz (2011), 'Is comprehension necessary for error detection? A conflict-based account of monitoring in speech production', *Cognitive Psychology*, 63 (1): 1–33.
Nunan, D. (1989), *Designing tasks for the communicative classroom*, Cambridge: Cambridge University Press.
O'Grady, W. (1997), *Syntactic development*, Chicago: University of Chicago Press.
Ortega, L. (2009), *Understanding second language acquisition*, London: Hodder Arnold.
Pallotti, G. (2007), 'An operational definition of the emergence criterion', *Applied Linguistics*, 28 (3): 361–82.
Piaget, J. (1952), *The origins of intelligence*, New York: International University Press.
Piaget, J. (1977), *The development of thought: Equilibration of cognitive structures*, New York: Viking.
Piaget, J. (1985), *The equilibrium of cognitive structures*, Chicago: University of Chicago Press.
Pica, T., R. Kanagy and J. Falodun (1993), 'Choosing and using communicative tasks for second language instruction', in G. Crookes and S. M. Gass (eds), *Tasks and language learning: Integrating theory and practice*, 9–34, Clevedon: Multilingual Matters.
Pickering, M. J. (1999), 'Language comprehension', in S. Garrod and M. Pickering (eds), *Language processing*, 123–53, Hove: Psychology Press.
Pickering, M. J. and H. P. Branigan (1999), 'Syntactic priming in language production', *Trends in Cognitive Sciences*, 3 (4): 136–41.
Pickering, M. J., J. F. McLean and H. P. Branigan (2013), 'Persistent structural priming and frequency effects during comprehension', *Journal of Experimental Psychology: Learning, Memory, and Cognition*, 39: 890–7.
Pickering, M. J. and S. Garrod (2004), 'Toward a mechanistic psychology of dialogue', *Behavioral and Brain Sciences*, 27 (2): 169–90.
Pickering, M. J. and S. Garrod (2007), 'Do people use language production to make predictions during comprehension?', *Trends in Cognitive Sciences*, 11 (3): 105–10.
Pickering, M. J. and S. Garrod (2013), 'An integrated theory of language production and comprehension', *Behavioural and Brain Sciences*, 36 (4): 329–47.
Pickering, M. J. and M. J. Traxler (1998), 'Plausibility and recovery from garden paths: An eye-tracking study', *Journal of Experimental Psychology: Learning, Memory, and Cognition*, 24 (4): 940–61.
Pickering, M. and R. P. G. van Gompel (2006), 'Syntactic parsing', in M. J. Traxler and M. A. Gernsbacher (eds), *Handbook of psycholinguistics*, 2nd edn, 455–503, London: Academic Press.
Pickering, M. J., M. J. Traxler and M. W. Crocker (2000), 'Ambiguity resolution in sentence processing. Evidence against frequency-based accounts', *Journal of Memory and Language*, 43: 447–75.
Pickering, M. J., H. P. Branigan and J. F. McLean (2002), 'Constituent structure is formulated in one stage', *Journal of Memory and Language*, 46 (3): 586–605.
Pienemann, M. (1981), *Der Zweitspracherwerb ausländischer Arbeiterkinder*, Bonn: Bouvier.
Pienemann, M. (1984), 'Psychological constraints on the teachability of languages', *Studies in Second Language Acquisition*, 6 (2): 186–214.
Pienemann, M. (1989), 'Is language teachable? Psycholinguistic experiments and hypotheses', *Applied Linguistics*, 10 (1): 52–78.
Pienemann, M. (1990), *LARC research projects 1990*, Sydney: NLIA/LARC.

Pienemann, M. (1992), 'Assessing second language acquisition through Rapid Profile', unpublished manuscript.

Pienemann, M. (1998), *Language processing and second language development: Processability Theory*, Amsterdam: John Benjamins.

Pienemann, M. (2005), 'An introduction to Processability Theory', in M. Pienemann (ed.), *Cross-linguistic aspects of Processability Theory*, 1–60, Amsterdam: John Benjamins.

Pienemann, M. (2008), 'A brief introduction to Processability Theory', in J.-U. Keßler (ed.), *Processability approaches to second language development and second language learning*, 9–29, Newcastle upon Tyne: Cambridge Scholars Publishing.

Pienemann, M. (2015), 'An outline of Processability Theory and its relationship to other approaches to SLA', *Language Learning*, 65: 123–51.

Pienemann, M. (n.d.), *Rapid Profile*. Unpublished manuscript.

Pienemann, M., J.-U. Keßler and M. Liebner (2006), 'Englischerwerb in der Grundschule: Untersuchungsergebnisse im Überblick', in M. Pienemann, J.-U. Keßler and E. Roos (eds), *Englischerwerb in der Grundschule: Ein Studien- und Arbeitsbuch*, 67–88, Paderborn: Schöningh/UTB.

Pienemann, M. and M. Johnston (1987), 'Factors influencing the development of language proficiency', in D. Nunan (ed.), *Applying second language acquisition research*, 45–142, Adelaide: National Curriculum Resource Centre: AMEP.

Pienemann, M., A. Lenzing and J.-U. Keßler (2016), 'Developmentally moderated transfer in second language development', in J.-U. Keßler, A. Lenzing and M. Liebner (eds), *Developing, modelling and assessing second languages*, 79–98, Amsterdam: John Benjamins.

Pienemann, M. and A. Lenzing (2020), 'Processability Theory', in B. VanPatten, G. Keating and S. Wulff (eds), *Theories in second language acquisition: An introduction*, 3rd edn, 162–91, New York: Routledge.

Pienemann, M. and A. Mackey (1993), 'An empirical study of children's ESL development and Rapid Profile', in P. McKay (ed.), *ESL development: Language and literacy in schools*, 2: 115–259, Canberra: Commonwealth of Australia and National Languages and Literacy Institute of Australia.

Pienemann, M., B. Di Biase and S. Kawaguchi (2005), 'Extending Processability Theory', in M. Pienemann (ed.), *Cross-linguistic aspects of Processability Theory*, 199–251, Amsterdam: John Benjamins.

Pinker, S. (1982), 'A theory of the acquisition of lexical-interpretive grammars', in J. Bresnan (ed.), *The mental representation of grammatical relations*, 655–726, Cambridge, MA: MIT Press.

Pinker, S. (1984), *Language learnability and language development*, Cambridge, MA: Harvard University Press.

Pinker, S. (1989), *Learnability and cognition: The acquisition of argument structure*, Cambridge, MA: MIT Press.

Pinker, S., D. S. Lebaux and L. A. Frost (1987), 'Productivity and constraints in the acquisition of the passive', *Cognition*, 26 (3): 195–267.

Poesio, M., P. Sturt, R. Artstein and R. Filik (2006), 'Underspecification and anaphora: Theoretical issues and preliminary evidence', *Discourse Processes*, 42: 157–75.

Pritchett, B. L. (1992), *Grammatical competence and parsing performance*, Chicago: University of Chicago Press.

Quirk, R., S. Greenbaum, G. Leech and J. Svartvik (1985), *A comprehensive grammar of the English language*, London: Longman.

Radden, G. (2008), 'The cognitive approach to language', in J. Andor, B. Hollósy, T. Laczkó and P. Pelyvás (eds), *When grammar minds language and literature: Festschrift for Prof. Béla Korponay on the occasion of his 80th birthday*, 387–412, Debrecen: Institute of English and American Studies.

Ravem, R. (1968), 'Language acquisition in a second language environment', *International Review of Applied Linguistics*, 6: 165–85.

Rayner, K. and L. Frazier (1987), 'Parsing temporarily ambiguous complements', *Quarterly Journal of Experimental Psychology*, 39: 657–73.

Rayner, K., M. Carlson and L. Frazier (1983), 'The interaction of syntax and semantics during sentence processing: Eye movements in the analysis of semantically biased sentences', *Journal of Verbal Learning and Verbal Behavior*, 22: 358–74.

Rickford, J. R. (1979), 'Variation in a creole continuum: Quantitative and implicational approaches', PhD thesis, University of Pennsylvania.

Rickford, J. R. (1991), 'Variation theory: Implicational scaling and critical age limits in models of linguistic variation, acquisition and change', in T. Huebner and C. A. Fergueson (eds), *Crosscurrents in second language acquisition and linguistic theories*, 225–46, Amsterdam: John Benjamins.

Rickford, J. R. (2002), 'Implicational scales', in J. K. Chambers, P. Trudgill and N. Schilling-Estes (eds), *The handbook of language variation and change*, 142–67, Oxford: Blackwell.

Roberts, L. (2012), 'Psycholinguistic techniques and resources in second language acquisition research', *Second Language Research*, 28 (1): 113–27.

Roelofs, A. (1992a), 'Lemma retrieval in speaking: A theory, computer simulations, and empirical data,' PhD thesis, NICI Technical Report 92-08, University of Nijmegen, Nijmegen.

Roelofs, A. (1992b), 'A spreading-activation theory of lemma retrieval in speaking', *Cognition*, 42: 107–42.

Roelofs, A. (1993), 'Testing a non-decompositional theory of lemma retrieval in speaking: Retrieval of verbs', *Cognition*, 47: 59–87.

Roelofs, A. (1997), 'The weaver model of word-form encoding in speech production', *Cognition*, 64: 249–84.

Roos, J. (2007), *Spracherwerb und Sprachproduktion: Lernziele und Lernergebnisse im Englischunterricht der Grundschule*, Tübingen: Gunter Narr.

Roos, J. (2016), 'Acquisition as a gradual process: Second language development in the EFL classroom', in J.-U. Keßler, A. Lenzing and M. Liebner (eds), *Developing, modelling and assessing second languages*, 121–34, Amsterdam: John Benjamins.

Rosch, E. (1973), 'On the internal structure of perceptual and semantic categories', in T. E. Moore (ed.), *Cognitive development and the acquisition of language*, 111–44, New York: Academic Press.

Rosch, E. (1975a), 'Cognitive reference points', *Cognitive Psychology*, 7: 532–47.

Rosch, E. (1975b), 'Cognitive representations of semantic categories', *Journal of Experimental Psychology: General*, 104 (3): 192–233.

Rosch, E. (1975c), 'Universals and cultural specifics in human categorization', in R. W. Brislin, S. Bochner and W. J. Lonner (eds), *Cross-cultural perspectives on learning*, 177–206, New York: Wiley.

Rosch, E. (1978), 'Principles of categorization', in E. Rosch and B. B. Lloyd (eds), *Cognition and categorization*, Hillsdale, NJ: Lawrence Erlbaum Associates.

Rosch, E. (1988), 'Coherences and categorization: A historical view', in F. S. Kessel (ed.), *The development of language and language researchers: Essays in honor of Roger Brown*, 373–92, Hillsdale, NJ: Lawrence Erlbaum Associates.

Rosch, E. and C. B. Mervis (1975), 'Family resemblances: Studies in the internal structures of categories', *Cognitive Psychology*, 7: 573–605.

Rosch, E., C. Simpson and S. R. Miller (1976), 'Structural bases of typicality effects', *Journal of Experimental Psychology: Human Perception and Performance*, 2: 491–502.

Ruder, K. F. and A. Finch (1987), 'Toward a cognitive-based model of language production', in H. W. Dechert and M. Raupach (eds), *Psycholinguistic models of production*, 109–38, Westport, CT: Ablex.

Rudin, C. (1985), *Aspects of Bulgarian syntax: Complementizers and WH constructions*, Columbus, OH: Slavica.

Salvucci, D. D. and N. A. Taatgen (2008), 'Threaded cognition: An integrated theory of concurrent multitasking', *Psychological Review*, 115: 101–30.

Sanford, A. and P. Sturd (2002), 'Depth of processing in language comprehension: Not noticing the evidence', *Trends in Cognitive Sciences*, 6 (9): 382–6.

Sankoff, G. (1973), 'Above and beyond phonology in variable rules', in C.-J. Bailey and R. W. Schuy (eds), *New ways of analysing variation in English*, 44–61, Washington, DC: Georgetown University Press.

Sayehli, S. (2013), *Developmental perspectives on transfer in third language acquisition*, Travaux de l'Institute de Linguistique de Lund, 51.

Schubotz, R. I. and D. Y. von Cramon (2001), 'Interval and ordinal properties of sequences are associated with distinct premotor areas', *Cerebral Cortex*, 11 (3): 210–22.

Schwarz, H., ed. (2007), *English G 21 Band A 1*, Berlin: Cornelsen.

Segaert, K., L. Menenti, K. Weber, K. Petersson and P. Hagoort (2012), 'Shared syntax in language production and language comprehension: An fMRI study', *Cerebral Cortex*, 22: 1662–70.

Slabakova, R. (1997), 'Some aspect-related constructions in English: A sentence-matching investigation', in A. Sorace, C. Heycock and R. Shillcock (eds), *Proceedings of the GALA 97 conference on language acquisition*, 450–5, Edinburgh: Human Communication Research Centre.

Slobin, D. (1966), 'Grammatical transformations and sentence comprehension in child and adulthood', *Journal of Verbal Language and Verbal Behaviour*, 13: 219–27.

Slobin, D. (1968), 'Recall of full and truncated passive sentences in connected discourse', *Journal of Verbal Learning and Verbal Behaviour*, 7: 876–81.

Somashekar, S., B. C. Lust, J. Gair, T. K. Bhatia, V. Sharma and J. Khare (1997), 'Principles of pronominal interpretation in Hindi "jab" clauses: Experimental test of children's comprehension', in S. Somashekar, K. Yamakoshi, M. Blume and C. A. Foley (eds), *Papers on language acquisition: Cornell University working papers in linguistics*, 65–87, Ithaca, NY: CLC.

Spenader, J., E.-J. Smits and P. Hendriks (2009), 'Coherent discourse solves the pronoun interpretation problem', *Journal of Child Language*, 36: 23–52.

Spinner, P. (2011), 'Second language assessment and morpho-syntactic development', *Studies in Second Language Acquisition*, 33: 529–61.

Spinner, P. (2013), 'Language production and reception: A Processability Theory study', *Language Learning*, 63 (4): 704–39.

Spinner, P. and S. Jung (2018), 'Production and comprehension in processability theory: A self-paced reading study', *Studies in Second Language Acquisition*, 40: 295–318.

Spinner, P. and S. Jung (2019), 'Productive and receptive processes in PT', in A. Lenzing, H. Nicholas and J. Roos (eds), *Widening contexts for Processability Theory: Theories and issues*, 49–71, Amsterdam: John Benjamins.

Sridhar, S. N. (1988), *Cognition and sentence production: A cross-linguistic study*, New York: Springer.

Sridhar, S. N. (1989), 'Cognitive structures in language production: A crosslinguistic study', in B. MacWhinney and E. Bates (eds), *The crosslinguistic study of sentence processing*, 209–24, New York: Cambridge University Press.

Stephens, G. J., L. J. Silbert and U. Hasson (2010), 'Speaker-listener neural coupling underlies successful communication', *Proceedings of the National Academy of Sciences of the United States of America*, 107 (32): 14425–30.

Stolz, T., S. Lestrade and C. Stolz (2014), *The crosslinguistics of zero-marking of spatial relations*, Berlin: De Gruyter.

Strohner, H. and K. E. Nelson (1974), 'The young child's development of sentence comprehension: Influence of event probability, non-verbal context, syntactic form, and strategies', *Child Development*, 45 (3): 567–76.

Stromswold, K. (2006), *Why children understand and misunderstand sentences: An eye-tracking study of passive sentences*, New Brunswick, NJ: Rutgers University Center for Cognitive Science Technical Report TR-85.

Sudhalter, V. and M. D. S. Braine (1985), 'How does comprehension of passives develop? A comparison of actional and experiential verbs', *Journal of Child Language*, 12 (2): 455–70.

Svartvik, R. (1966), *On voice in the English verb*, The Hague: Mouton.

Swets, B., T. Desmet, C. Clifton and F. Ferreira (2008), 'Underspecification of syntactic ambiguities: Evidence from self-paced reading', *Memory and Cognition*, 36: 201–16.

Tabor, W. and M. K. Tanenhaus (1999), 'Dynamical models of sentence processing', *Cognitive Science*, 23: 491–515.

Taylor, J. R. (2003), *Linguistic categorization*, 3rd edn, Oxford: Oxford University Press.

Thal, D. J. and M. Flores (2001), 'Development of sentence interpretation strategies by typically developing and late-talking toddlers', *Journal of Child Language*, 28 (1): 173–93.

Thornton, R. and M. C. MacDonald (2003), 'Plausibility and grammatical agreement', *Journal of Memory and Language*, 48: 740–59.

Tomlin, R. S. (1995), 'Focal attention, voice, and word order: An experimental, cross-linguistic study', in P. Downing and M. Noonan (eds), *Word order in discourse*, 517–54, Amsterdam: John Benjamins.

Tomlin, R. S. (1997), 'Mapping conceptual representations into linguistic representations: The role of attention in grammar', in J. Nuyts and E. Pederson (eds), *Language and conceptualization*, 162–89, Cambridge: Cambridge University Press.

Tooley, K. M. and J. K. Bock (2014), 'On the parity of structural persistence in language production and comprehension', *Cognition*, 132 (2): 101–36.

Traxler, M. J. (2012), *Introduction to psycholinguistics: Understanding language science*, Malden, MA: Wiley-Blackwell.

Traxler, M. J., M. J. Pickering and C. Clifton (1998), 'Adjunct attachment is not a form of lexical ambiguity resolution', *Journal of Memory and Language*, 39 (4): 558–92.

Trofimovich, P., E. Gatbonton and N. Segalowitz (2007), 'A dynamic look at L2 phonological learning: Seeking processing explanations for implicational phenomena', *Studies in Second Language Acquisition*, 29 (3): 407–48.

Trudgill, P. (1986), *Dialects in contact*, Oxford: Blackwell.

Trueswell, J. C. (1996), 'The role of lexical frequency in syntactic ambiguity resolution', *Journal of Memory and Language*, 35: 566–85.

Trueswell, J. C., M. K. Tanenhaus and S. Garnsey (1994), 'Semantic influences on parsing: Use of thematic role information in syntactic ambiguity resolution', *Journal of Memory and Language*, 33: 285–318.

Turner, E. A. and R. Rommetveit (1967), 'Experimental manipulation of the production of active and passive voice in children', *Language and Speech*, 10 (3): 169–80.

Ullman, M. T., R. Pancheva, T. Love, E. Yee, D. Swinney and G. Hickok (2005), 'Neural correlates of lexicon and grammar: Evidence from the production, reading, and judgment of inflection in aphasia', *Brain and Language*, 93: 185–38.

Vainikka, A. and M. Young-Scholten (1994), 'Direct access to X'-theory: Evidence from Korean and Turkish adults learning German', in T. Hoekstra and B. D. Schwartz (eds), *Language acquisition studies in generative grammar: Papers in honor of Kenneth Wexler from the 1991 GLOW workshops*, 265–316, Amsterdam: John Benjamins.

Van Gompel, R. P. G. and M. J. Pickering (2007), 'Syntactic parsing', in G. Gaskell (ed.), *The Oxford handbook of psycholinguistics*, 289–307, Oxford: Oxford University Press.

Van Herten, M., H. H. Kolk and D. J. Chwilla (2005), 'An ERP study of P600 effects elicited by semantic anomalies', *Cognitive Brain Research*, 22: 241–55.

Van Gompel, R. P. G., M. J. Pickering and M. J. Traxler (2000), 'Syntactic ambiguity resolution is not a form of lexical ambiguity resolution', in A. Kennedy, D. Heller, J. Pynte and R. Raddach (eds), *Reading as a perceptual process*, 621–48, Amsterdam: Elsevier.

Van Gompel, R. P. G., M. J. Pickering and M. J. Traxler (2001), 'Reanalysis in sentence processing: Evidence against current constraint-based and two-stage models', *Journal of Memory and Language*, 45: 225–58.

Van Gompel, R. P. G., M. J. Pickering, J. Pearson and S. P. Liversedge (2005), 'Evidence against competition during syntactic ambiguity resolution', *Journal of Memory and Language*, 52: 284–307.

Van Gompel, R. P. G., M. J. Pickering, J. Pearson and G. Jacob (2006), 'The activation of inappropriate analyses in garden-path sentences: Evidence from structural priming', *Journal of Memory and Language*, 55: 335–62.

VanPatten, B. (1984), 'Morphemes and processing strategies', in F. Eckman, L. Bell and D. Nelson (eds), *Universals of second language acquisition*, 88–98, Cambridge: Newbury House.

VanPatten, B. (1996), *Input processing and grammar instruction: Theory and research*, Norwood, NJ: Ablex.

VanPatten, B. (2020), 'Input processing in adult L2 acquisition', in B. VanPatten, G. Keating and S. Wulff (eds), *Theories in second language acquisition: An introduction*, 3rd edn, 105–27, New York: Routledge.

Vecera, S. P., A. V. Flevaris and J. C. Filapek (2004), 'Exogenous spatial attention influences figure-ground assignment', *Psychological Science*, 15: 20–26.

Verhagen, J. (2009), 'Finiteness in Dutch as a second language', PhD thesis, Vrije Universiteit, Amsterdam and Max Planck Institute for Psycholinguistics.

Verhagen, J. (2011), 'Verb placement in second language acquisition: Experimental evidence for the different behaviour of auxiliary and lexical verbs', *Applied Psycholinguistics*, 32: 821–58.

Vigliocco, G., T. Antonini and M. F. Garrett (1997), 'Grammatical gender is on the tip of Italian tongues', *Psychological Science*, 8: 314–17.

Vosse, T. and G. Kempen (2000), 'Syntactic structure assembly in human parsing: A computational model based on competitive inhibition and a lexicalist grammar', *Cognition*, 75: 105–43.

Vosse, T. and G. Kempen (2009), 'In defense of competition during syntactic ambiguity resolution', *Journal of Psycholinguistic Research*, 38 (1): 1–9.

Wadsworth, B. J. (1989), *Piaget's theory of cognitive and affective development*, 4th edn, New York: Longman.

Wang, K. (2009), 'Acquiring the passive voice: Online production of the English passive construction by Mandarin speakers', in J.-U. Keßler and D. Keatinge (eds), *Research in second language acquisition: Empirical evidence across languages*, 95–119, Newcastle upon Tyne: Cambridge Scholars Publishing.

Wang, K. (2011), *The fish was eaten: The acquisition of the English passive construction by Chinese learners of ESL*, Riga: LAP Lambert Academic Publishing.

Watermeyer, M. (2010), 'Ausagieren von Sätzen versus Satz-Bild-Zuordnung: Vergleich zweier Methoden zur Untersuchung des Sprachverständnisses anhand von semantisch reversiblen Sätzen mit Objektvoranstellung bei drei- und fünfjährigen Kindern', Dipl. thesis, University of Potsdam.

Watermeyer, M. and C. Kauschke (2013), 'Ausagieren oder Satz-Bild-Zuordnung? Zwei Methoden zur Untersuchung des Grammatikverständnisses im Vergleich', *LOGOS*, 21 (4): 264–78.

Wierzbicka, A. (1985), *Lexicography and conceptual analysis*, Ann Arbor, MI: Karoma.

Wilcox, R. (2012), *Introduction to robust estimation and hypothesis testing*, 3rd edn, Waltham, MA: Elsevier.

Willmes, K. and P. Poeck (1993), 'To what extent can aphasic syndromes be localized?', *Brain*, 116: 1527–40.

Wilson, S. M., A. P. Saygin, M. I. Sereno and M. Iacoboni (2004), 'Listening to speech activates motor areas involved in speech production', *Nature Neuroscience*, 7 (7): 701–2.

Wittgenstein, L. (1953), *Philosophical investigations*. New York: Macmillan.

Wode, H. (1976), 'Developmental sequences in naturalistic L2 acquisition', The Ontario Institute for Studies in Education, *Working Papers on Bilingualism*, no. 11: 1–13.

Zhang, Y. (2004), 'Processing constraints, categorical analysis, and the second language acquisition of the Chinese adjective suffix –de (ADJ)', *Language Learning*, 54 (3): 437–68.

Index of subjects

accessibility 11, 17, 227 n.3
accuracy 27, 73–5, 81–4, 86
acquisition criterion/criteria 81, 84–5, 87, 138
acquisition process 1–3, 65, 67, 69, 74, 76, 91, 97, 103, 105, 109, 117, 120, 146, 191, 213, 218–19, 221
actional passive(s) 100, 120
active (voice) 24, 43–4, 66, 100–1, 105, 107, 121–4, 137, 139, 141, 143, 146, 153, 155–6, 161, 164–5, 168, 173, 182, 185–9, 191, 193–5, 199, 201, 213, 217, 227
active form(s) 100, 105, 107, 120–1, 153, 182, 191
active interpretation 120–1, 139, 143, 164, 168, 199, 201
adjunct (ADJ) 61–2, 65, 108
adverb-first (ADV) 60, 62, 64, 66, 81, 148, 152, 177–8, 181, 184
affixation 112–14, 161
agent 13, 24–5, 53, 55, 62, 67, 69, 93, 97, 99–104, 106–10, 114, 122–5, 135, 139, 141, 143, 152, 155, 164–5, 167, 182, 185, 188, 201, 217, 227 n.2 (Chapter 5)
algorithmic route 26–7, 97–8, 145, 212, 214, 216, 219, 222
analysis of correlation (*see* correlation analysis)
analysis of variance(s) (ANOVA) 210, 215
animacy 96, 227 n.3
animate 93, 99, 102–3, 120
aphasia 1, 31–2
argument(s) 52–6, 67, 69–70, 92, 101, 106–11, 120–6, 127, 128, 130, 142–3, 155–6, 163, 165, 167–8, 175, 184, 189, 199–201, 205–6, 221–2, 224, 228 n.2
argument structure (a-structure) 15–16, 50, 52–5, 67–71, 92, 101, 106–11, 130, 163, 201, 217
articulator 9

assumption of normality (*see* normality assumption)
asymmetry(s) 1, 32–3
attachment preferences 27–8
attention 10, 86, 118, 122–5, 175, 210
attributes 50–1, 94–6
auditory stimuli 131, 206
automaticity 10
autonomous 9, 10, 48–9
autonomously (*see* autonomous)
Aux 2nd 81

biased reversible passive(s) 120–1, 125–8, 139, 141, 143, 145, 169, 201–2, 205, 224
Broca's area 31–2

Cancel inversion 60, 65
canonical 60–1, 67–8, 103, 152
category procedure 58–60
chance performance 84, 127, 138
chunk(s) 74–5, 133, 147
coder (*see* syntactic coder)
coefficient of reproducibility 77–8, 84, 86, 139, 165, 199
coefficient of scalability (CS) 77–8, 86, 139, 165, 199
communicative task(s) (*see* tasks)
conceptual message 10–11, 13, 15–17, 35, 91
conceptualizer 9–11, 16, 91–2
connectionist 7–8
constituent(s) 7, 13, 15–17, 23, 50–2, 55–6, 59–61, 64, 66–7, 70, 110
constituent structure (c-structure) 7, 13, 15–16, 50–2, 55, 61, 65–70, 92, 110–11, 114, 135, 217
constraint(s) 4, 21–2, 47, 50, 57, 59, 69, 71, 80, 91–93, 98, 100, 107, 153, 163
constraint-based model(s) 20–1, 35
constraint equation(s) 62–5, 112, 160, 226 n.3

control group 82, 86, 174, 198, 203, 207–8, 214, 216
correlation(s) 144, 169–72, 189, 196, 199, 203, 205, 218–19
correlation analysis 139, 144, 169, 171, 189, 196, 205
cross-sectional 3, 75–7, 84, 117, 136, 145, 172, 222
cut-off point(s) 73, 86, 139, 209
cata collection 117, 119, 136, 141, 145, 175, 228 n.1, 3

data elicitation 5, 87, 119, 128, 145, 174–5, 182, 185, 196, 199, 203, 206, 216, 220, 228 n.1, 6
decoding 1–3, 18, 29–32, 34–40, 42, 44–5, 89–92, 114–15, 132, 135, 144, 206, 209, 217, 219, 221–2
dedicated-workspaces 38–40
deep processing 26
deep syntactic algorithm (*see* syntactic algorithm)
demoted 109
demotional 108
determiner (DET) 17, 55, 60, 73, 149, 177, 179, 226 n.6
developmental path 47
developmental problem 47
developmental stage(s) 68, 73–5, 115, 117, 119, 136, 138, 145–6, 175
Developmentally Moderated Transfer Hypothesis (DMTH) 181
direct mapping 34, 61, 69, 71, 92, 98, 110, 130, 143–5, 201
directional difference(s) 2, 34, 45, 91–2, 131
discourse-pragmatic 4, 68
disequilibrium 25, 97
distractor item(s) 85, 126–7, 137, 143, 146, 173, 208, 224, 227 n.6
distributional analysis/analyses 4, 71–2, 75, 81–2, 140, 144, 146–8, 150–3, 157, 162, 166, 175–6, 182, 185, 189, 191, 193–4, 196, 198–200, 217
ditransitive 121, 143, 168, 170, 201
ditransitive construction(s) 120, 142–3, 167–8, 201
ditransitive passive(s) 121, 142–4, 165, 167–8, 201, 218

dual-processor 29–31, 33
dual-processor architecture 4, 18, 30–1, 33, 89, 91
dual route 25, 92, 97, 136

ELIAS Grammar Test 84–5, 126
emergence 70, 74–5, 81, 84, 138–9
emergence criterion 4, 71, 73–5, 84, 146–7, 150–2, 175, 181, 226 n.9
enactment task(s) 118, 126–8, 145–6, 164
encoding 1–3, 7–9, 11–13, 15–18, 29–32, 34–40, 42, 44–5, 48, 89–92, 96, 106, 114–15, 131, 135, 144, 206, 217, 219, 221–2
English as a second language (ESL) 80–3, 85
equilibrium 25–8, 97
error minimization 79
error rate(s) 208–9
event probability/probabilities 2, 4, 90, 92–4, 96, 101–3, 105, 115, 120, 136, 139, 141, 165, 168–9, 201, 222–3
event-related potential (ERP) 22, 25
expectancy violations 39–40

feature unification 17, 37, 55–7, 60–1, 64, 66, 71, 73, 91, 105, 109–11, 114–15, 130, 135, 159–60, 162, 181, 191, 195, 198, 206–7, 212, 217, 226 n.6
filler items 121, 133, 227 n.6
fish film 80, 118, 123–5, 146, 153–8, 160–1, 173, 182–5, 187–8, 193, 196, 205
fMRI adaptation 43–4
focal attention (*see* attention)
form-function relationship(s) 112, 114–15, 135, 161–2, 195, 198, 217
formulae 59–60, 66, 147, 228 n.3
formulaic pattern(s) 147, 151, 153
formulaic sequence(s) 72, 74–5, 146–7, 175, 226 n.8
formulator(s) 9, 11, 34–5, 57, 91–2, 108, 110–11, 222
frequency effects 21, 27
functional magnetic resonance imaging (fMRI) 42, 44
functional processing 11, 13, 15–16, 35
functional structure (f-structure) 50–1, 54–5, 67–71, 92, 101, 107, 109–11, 130, 163, 226 n.3

Garden-Path Model 19–22
German 3, 80, 113, 136, 155, 159, 181–2, 192
global control 122–3, 125
Good-Enough approach 3–4, 7, 22, 24–5, 221
Goodenough Edwards 79
grammatical coder 29, 40, 91–2, 206
grammatical decoding (*see* decoding)
grammatical encoding (*see* encoding)
grammatical function(s) 13, 15–17, 21, 50, 54–6, 67, 69–70, 92, 101, 105–11, 130, 163, 189, 221–2, 228 n.2
grammatical information 49, 54–5, 58–61, 64, 66, 82, 160
grammatical memory store 48–9, 91
grammatical system 3–4, 69–71, 89, 91, 98, 130, 135, 145, 163, 217, 221, 223
grammaticality effect(s) 131, 206–8, 212–16
grammaticality judgement task (GJT) 81, 86, 129, 131
group mean scores 82–3

heuristic processing 25–6, 97, 145, 219
heuristic route 26–8, 97–8, 143, 145, 170, 212, 219, 222
hierarchy of processability (*see* processability hierarchy)
human language processing (*see* morpho-syntactic processing)

idiosyncratic forms (*see* idiosyncratic utterances)
idiosyncratic utterances 147, 159
implausible 20, 24, 120–2, 139, 142–3, 156, 165, 168, 199, 201
implicational 76–9, 81–4, 86, 138–9, 143, 152, 159, 162, 165, 168–70, 172, 189, 196, 202, 205, 218–19
implicational scale(s) 76–9, 83–4, 86, 139, 199
implicational scaling 4, 71, 76–9, 81, 84–5, 139
implicational sequence(s) 144, 199, 218
implicational table 77–8, 82, 86, 139, 142, 165, 201–2
inanimate 93, 103, 120, 201
Incremental Procedural Grammar 11, 16, 37

incremental processing 10, 16, 19, 34–5, 37, 49
information gap 119, 227 n.2 (Chapter 6)
initial state 66, 69–71, 89
input group 174
input session 174–5, 182, 189, 196, 198–9, 203, 215–16, 220, 228 n.6
instruction(s) 17, 124–5, 134, 136, 145, 172, 174, 220, 228 n.1
Integrated Encoding–Decoding Model 1–5, 7–8, 11, 16, 18–19, 28, 37, 45, 49–50, 87, 89–91, 93–4, 96–9, 135, 206, 217, 221–3, 225 n.6
interactive models 19–20, 22
interface(s) 1–2, 4, 29, 81, 87, 131, 221, 223, 227 n.5
interim output 26–7, 97–8
interlanguage 58, 67–9, 71–2, 74–7, 118–19, 138, 160, 213
interphrasal morphemes 59–60
interpretation 11, 19, 24, 27, 73, 78, 98, 101–2, 127, 139, 141–3, 164, 166–8, 185, 199, 201, 218–19

L1 acquisition 73, 94, 101–4, 120–1, 124, 128, 143
language generation 7–8, 10, 18, 57–8, 108, 221
language processor 3, 19–20, 22, 29, 31, 34, 36, 47–9, 57, 59, 69, 80, 89–90, 93, 114, 135–6, 153, 181, 217, 225 n.5
lemma(s)/lemmata 10, 13–18, 30, 34, 37, 58–60
lemma access 13, 60, 147
Levelt's model of sentence generation 4, 18
lexemes 34, 91–2
lexical access 8
lexical entry/entries 49, 54–5, 60, 63–4, 69, 107–8, 112–13, 160
Lexical-Functional Grammar (LFG) 3–4, 11, 15, 17, 37, 48–50, 51–7, 61–2, 65–7, 69–71, 87, 90–1, 105, 107–8, 114, 221–2, 225 n.6, 226 n.3
lexical frame(s) 35–6
lexical item(s) 13–14, 34, 36, 58–9, 75, 110, 182, 227 n.2 (Chapter 4)
lexical mapping 110

Lexical Mapping Theory (LMT) 54, 67, 105, 107–8
Lexical Mapping Hypothesis 67–8
lexical morpheme(s) 59–60, 226 n.6
lexical network(s) 13–16
lexical processes 70–1, 92, 147
lexical selection 13, 15
lexical variation 74, 124, 152, 158, 170, 181, 189, 196, 205
lexical verb(s) 63–4, 75, 160, 195, 226 n.13
lexicon 7–8, 10–11, 13, 30, 36–7, 54, 58–9, 63–4, 70, 74–5, 91–3, 108–10, 112, 114, 130, 135, 147, 160, 163, 189, 217, 219, 221
linear argument–function mapping 101, 114, 135, 153, 163, 186, 198, 217
linear mapping 66–7, 107, 110, 142, 185, 188, 201, 217–18, 222, 227 n.2 (Chapter 2)
linearization 11, 37, 49
linearization problem 11, 49, 66
linguistic profile(s) 5, 71–2, 118
linguistic representation(s) 1–3, 8, 21, 23–8, 33, 36, 43, 50–1, 55–7, 66–71, 82, 86, 90–1, 95, 98, 115, 122, 127, 130–2, 221
logical problem 47

main clause 20, 23, 27, 38
Mann Whitney U test 198, 203
many-to-one relationship(s) 112–13
mapping operation(s) (*see also* mapping principles) 34, 50, 54–5, 57, 66–8, 69, 71, 91–2, 98, 101, 107, 114, 128, 135, 145, 156, 163, 184–5, 188–9, 201, 217, 221–2, 228 n.2
mapping principle(s) (*see also* mapping operations) 50, 55, 57, 66, 68
matching grammatical (*see* matching grammatical sentence pairs)
matching grammatical condition (*see* matching grammatical sentence pairs)
matching grammatical sentence pairs 129, 132–4, 209
matching sentence pairs 129, 206, 208
matching ungrammatical condition (*see* matching ungrammatical sentence pairs)

matching ungrammatical sentence pairs 129, 132, 209, 219
mean(s) 82–3, 121–2, 141, 144, 167, 169, 198, 200, 202–3, 208–15
mental grammatical system (*see* grammatical system)
mental lexicon (*see* lexicon)
minimal requirements 3, 5, 114–15, 222
modular 7–8, 19–20
modular model(s) 19, 22, 225 n.1 (Chapter 1)
modularity 8
module(s) 1, 18–19, 29, 35, 221
morpheme(s) 14, 60, 71–5, 113, 119, 132, 152, 193–5, 207, 210–16, 226 n.6
morpho-lexical operation(s) 106, 109–10
morpho-syntactic processing 1–5, 25, 29, 32, 34–5, 42, 44, 89–90, 92–4, 96–8, 106, 114–15, 118, 128, 131–2, 135–6, 144, 152–3, 157–9, 161–3, 169–73, 182, 189–91, 196–8, 203, 205–7, 216–19, 221–3
morphological processing 112, 204
morphological variation 73, 75, 150–2, 160
morphology 51, 60, 75, 85, 205, 219, 222, 226 n.11
Multiple Constraints Hypothesis 3–4, 8, 18, 45, 47, 69–71, 89–92, 110, 112, 130, 160, 163, 189, 217, 219, 221, 223

N V N strategy 97, 142, 165, 167
native speaker(s) 38, 43–4, 81–2, 84, 86, 94, 97–8, 121, 123, 129–30, 133, 206–10, 213–16, 227 n.4, 228 n.7 (Chapter 6)
negation-strategy 186–7
neural circuits 32
neuroimaging 3–4, 42
neuronal substrate 42, 44
non-actional passives 120
non-linear argument–function mapping 110, 114–15, 135, 152–7, 159, 162–3, 170–2, 182–9, 191, 196, 198–9, 205, 217, 219, 222
non-linear mapping 68, 107, 110–11, 128, 188–9, 196, 218, 222
non-linearity 56, 67, 101, 110, 222
non-matching sentence pairs 208

non-reversible passive(s) 102, 105, 115, 120–1, 125–6, 128, 132, 141–2, 165, 170, 199–200, 205, 207, 214, 216, 224
non-target-like 72–3, 75, 147, 153, 181, 187, 203, 226 n.11
normality assumption 203, 205, 210–12, 214–15
noun phrase(s) (NP) 13, 17, 20, 23, 27, 36, 38, 54–5, 60–2, 65, 67, 73, 101–2, 111, 114, 135, 143, 165, 217, 222, 226 n.6, 228 n.2
null hypothesis 75, 147, 150

object (OBJ) 15, 20, 23–4, 27, 50, 54, 61–3, 65–7, 81, 106–8, 142, 149, 165, 177, 179, 228 n.2
obligatory context(s) 71–2, 122, 147, 152, 175, 226 n.2
oblique(s) (OBL) 54, 67, 101–2, 106, 108, 110–12
one-to-many relationship(s) 112–13
Online Cognitive Equilibrium Hypothesis 3–5, 7, 19, 23, 25–7, 89–90, 93, 97, 115, 136, 144–5, 170, 217, 219, 221–3
open slot 147
oral speech production (*see* speech production)

paraphrase 38
paraphrasing 38–40, 225 n.3 (Chapter 2)
parser 19–24, 26, 34–5, 37, 40, 92, 97, 225 n.4
parsing 19–22, 26, 29, 31–2, 34–5, 37, 91–2, 96–8, 115, 136, 142–3, 145, 165, 169–70, 213, 216, 219, 225 n.3 (Chapter 1) & n.6
parsing heuristic(s) 20, 24, 27, 97, 213, 219
participle 19, 63–4, 99–101, 111–15, 158, 160–1, 189, 194–5, 206, 213
passive construction(s) (*see also* passive) 3–5, 67–8, 87, 96, 98–105, 108, 110–12, 115, 117, 120–5, 127, 132, 135–6, 139, 144–5, 152, 157, 159–62, 164–5, 168–71, 174, 186, 188, 191–6, 198–9, 206–7, 212, 214–16, 218–20, 222
passive film 146, 153–4, 156–8, 160, 162–3, 170–1, 173, 182–4, 186–9, 191, 193–4, 196–8, 204–5
passivization 100, 105–11, 154

past participle (*see* participle)
patient/theme 13, 20, 53, 67, 101–2, 106, 109–10, 114, 122–3, 128, 135, 139, 141, 167–8, 175, 199, 201, 206, 217, 222
Performance Grammar 36–7, 225 n.2 (Chapter 1) & n.1 (Chapter 2)
perspective-taking 9, 122–3
phonological encoding 7, 11, 13, 31
phrasal morphemes 59–60
phrasal procedure 58–60, 62, 110–11, 226 n.6, 228 n.2
physical contact 103, 139, 141, 143, 165, 168–9, 199, 201
plausibility 20, 23–5, 34, 97, 121–2, 124, 139, 141, 143–4, 165, 167–9, 199–202
plural-s 149, 177, 179
positional processing 11, 13, 15–16, 37, 57
possessive pronoun(s) 81, 151
prepositional phrase(s) (PP(s)) 17, 101, 111
preverbal message(s) 9–11, 91–2
primary school 73, 147, 151, 185, 228 n.1, 228 n.3
priming 35–6, 41–2, 44
principle of natural order 11
procedural skill hypothesis 130, 227 n.4
processability 48, 61, 65, 67–8, 80, 91, 98, 131, 145, 174, 206
processability hierarchy 48, 57–60, 65, 68
Processability Theory (PT) 3–5, 8, 11, 16–17, 37, 45, 47–9, 55, 57–62, 65–72, 75, 79–87, 89–92, 105, 107–8, 110–11, 114, 117–19, 124, 135–6, 138–9, 144, 152–3, 159, 169–71, 174, 181, 189, 191, 196, 203–4, 206, 217, 219, 221–3, 226 n.5, 226 n.6, 226 n.12, 226 n.13, 228 n.2
processing capacity/capacities 33, 47
processing component(s) 9–10, 48–9, 57, 91
processing heuristic(s) 25–6, 142, 165, 201
processing operations (*see* processing procedures)
processing prerequisites 3, 81, 147, 206, 210, 212, 216
processing procedure(s) 3–4, 48, 57–9, 74, 81, 91–2, 97–8, 105, 110, 112–13, 115, 129–32, 136, 138, 145, 170, 172, 196, 203, 206–7, 210, 216–23
processing route(s) 22, 26, 28, 97, 219
processor (*see* language processor)

proposition(s) 11, 49, 122
proto-agent 24, 142, 165, 201
proto-theme 24
prototypical 95–6, 103–4, 120, 139, 141–3, 165, 168–9, 199, 202
prototypical traits 169
prototypicality 2, 4, 92–4, 96–7, 101–3, 120, 139, 143, 145, 165, 201–2, 218–19, 222–3
psychological plausibility 28, 36, 50, 56
punctual action(s) 103, 139, 143, 165, 168–9, 201

Rapid Profile 137–8
reaction time(s) (RT(s)) 40, 83–5, 96, 129, 131–2, 172, 207–16, 218, 220, 228 n.10
reaction-time experiment(s) 5, 15, 83, 118, 128, 172–3, 206, 216, 218, 220, 222
reanalysis 20–4, 35
reduced relative clause(s) 19–20, 208, 213, 215–16
reflexive pronoun(s) 39–40
repair 31, 39–40
representation (*see* linguistic representation)
response latencies 39, 129–30, 210–16, 219
response pattern(s) 78–9, 131, 207
retrieval 7, 9, 34, 48
reverse-order strategy 155–6, 191
reversibility 96, 102–3, 105, 120, 124, 139, 143, 202
reversible passive(s) 102, 105, 120–1, 125–6, 127, 143–4, 169, 201–2, 207, 214, 216, 218, 224

salience (*see* saliency)
saliency 96, 122–3, 125
scalability 77–8, 139, 165, 226 n.10
second language acquisition (SLA) 1–5, 7–8, 11, 16, 29, 37, 45, 47, 57, 66, 73–6, 78–9, 82, 89–91, 93–4, 97–8, 130, 160, 221, 223, 227 n.4
self-monitoring 18, 30–1
self-paced reading 82–3, 85
semantic aspects 1–5, 50, 89–90, 92, 96–7, 99, 115, 128, 145, 219, 222–3

semantic cues 21, 82, 92–3, 102, 120, 136, 143, 165, 169, 200–2, 205, 216, 218–19, 222
semantic factor(s) 2, 20, 89–90, 92, 94, 98, 101–2, 104–5, 115, 120, 125, 206
semantic irreversibility 139, 165, 199, 201
semantic processing 3, 25, 90, 92, 105, 115, 136, 144–5, 170, 206, 219, 223
semantic role(s) (*see* thematic role(s))
semantic route 3, 92, 202, 222
semantically ill-formed 156
sentence completion task 80
sentence-matching 5, 118, 128–31, 133, 172–4, 206–10, 214, 218, 222, 227 n.7
sentence-picture matching 43, 84, 118, 126–8, 136–8, 141–2, 145, 173–4, 199, 201–2, 206, 224
sentence procedure (S-procedure) 17, 58–61, 65, 67, 181
sentence processing 1, 19–23, 25, 28, 33, 36, 94, 97, 125, 129–31, 136, 206
shallow processing 23, 26, 82, 90, 94, 97–8, 114, 135–6, 217, 222
Shapiro Wilk's test 170, 198, 203, 205, 210–12, 214–15
shared grammatical coder 3, 92, 206, 222
shared grammatical workspace 3–4, 33, 37–8, 89, 91, 98, 221
shared mechanisms 219
single-processor 31, 36
single-processor architecture 4, 30–3, 37, 45, 89, 91
Spearman's rank order correlation (*see* correlation analysis)
speech comprehension system 9, 18, 91
speech production 4–5, 7–8, 18, 31, 35–6, 42, 48, 58, 71, 80–1, 83–4, 92, 117–19, 122–3, 131–2, 136–8, 145–6, 152–3, 162, 172–4, 182, 198, 203, 222, 225 n.1 (Chapter 1)
stage(s) of acquisition 3, 5, 59, 61, 63, 80, 82–3, 105, 111, 114, 117–18, 123, 125, 136–8, 144–7, 151–3, 158, 162, 165, 169–70, 172–5, 180, 182, 184, 189, 196, 199–200, 203, 206–7, 209, 212, 216, 218, 220, 222–3
standard deviation(s) 121–2, 208–10
statistical analysis 139, 199, 210
structural persistence 41–2

subject (SUBJ) 15, 17, 20, 23–4, 27, 38, 39–40, 43, 49–50, 54–5, 61–3, 65, 67–8, 71, 75, 100–2, 106–8, 110–13, 122, 124, 129, 142, 153–4, 165, 206, 227 n.2 (Chapter 5), 228 n.2
subject-verb agreement 36, 49, 61, 75, 129, 160, 192, 226 n.4, n.13
subordinate clause(s) 20, 23, 59–60, 65, 186
subordinate clause procedure 58, 60
surface form 10, 69, 71, 91–2, 110
surface structure(s) 9–11, 17, 49, 66, 92, 142, 201
SVO 60–2, 66, 84, 149, 152, 177, 179
symmetrical reversibility 143, 202
symmetrical reversible 128, 132
symmetrical reversible passive(s) 120, 125–6, 127, 143–4, 169, 201–2, 218, 224
syntactic algorithms 24–6, 136
syntactic building blocks 37
syntactic category 13, 17, 54, 58–60, 70, 110
syntactic coder 4, 37, 135, 206, 219, 221
syntactic feature(s) 54, 55, 68–70, 72, 92, 109–10, 114, 135, 163, 189, 217, 219, 221
syntactic processing (*see* morpho-syntactic processing)
syntactic route 3, 136
syntax 13, 15, 18, 20, 32, 34, 36–7, 42, 50, 54, 56–7, 60–1, 74, 93, 96, 105

target items 132, 137, 146, 173
target language 58, 71–2, 74, 82, 118
target-like 64, 72, 75, 80, 108, 111–12, 139, 141, 153, 157–60, 162, 164, 169, 171–2, 187, 189, 191, 193–6, 198–9, 201, 205, 219, 222, 226 n.2, 228 n.4
tasks 1, 5, 30, 35, 38, 40–4, 80–2, 85–6, 96, 105, 117–20, 122–3, 126–31, 133, 136–7, 145–6, 153, 172–5, 182, 185, 198, 220, 222

Teachability Hypothesis 174
temporarily ambiguous sentence(s) 19–21, 23, 27, 35–6
textbook(s) 73, 147, 150–1, 175, 228 n.3
thematic role assignment(s) 24, 201
thematic role(s) 15, 53–4, 69, 105–7
3sg-s 61, 66, 71–2, 75, 81, 84, 98, 119, 148, 152, 159–60, 176, 178, 226 n.2
trajectories 48, 65, 68–9, 71
transfer 47, 54–5, 59, 160, 181
transitive passive(s) 168–9, 202
trial sentences 101, 121, 126, 200, 219, 224
t-test(s) 210–12, 214–15
two-stage model(s) 19, 22
typological plausibility 56–7

unanalyzed unit 147
ungrammatical stimuli 40, 85, 132, 207, 209–15, 219
ungrammaticality effects 129, 213
Universal Grammar (UG) 69, 130
Unrestricted Race Model 22

V2/INV 148, 176, 178, 180–1
value(s) 13, 17, 39, 50–1, 55, 63, 78, 81–2, 106, 160, 209, 226 n.3, n.6
verb(al) morphology 112, 154, 158–63, 171–2, 189–99, 205, 219, 222
verb phrase (VP(s)) 13, 17, 59, 100, 110–11, 113–15, 159–60, 162, 191, 206–8, 212–13, 216
visible result 103–4, 139, 143, 165, 168, 199, 201

WEAVER++ 13
Wernicke's area(s) 31
Wh-words 62, 64
Wilcoxon signed rank test(s) 210–14
word order 17, 30, 48, 57–62, 67, 124–5, 127, 152
working memory 21, 27, 49
world knowledge 24, 93

www.ingramcontent.com/pod-product-compliance
Lightning Source LLC
Chambersburg PA
CBHW072133290426
44111CB00012B/1870